IMAGINATIVE MINDS

PROCEEDINGS OF THE BRITISH ACADEMY · 147

IMAGINATIVE MINDS

Edited by
ILONA ROTH

Published for THE BRITISH ACADEMY
by OXFORD UNIVERSITY PRESS

Oxford University Press, Great Clarendon Street, Oxford OX2 6DP

Oxford New York

Auckland Cape Town Dar es Salaam Hong Kong Karachi
Kuala Lumpur Madrid Melbourne Mexico City Nairobi
New Delhi Shanghai Taipei Toronto

With offices in
Argentina Austria Brazil Chile Czech Republic France Greece
Guatemala Hungary Italy Japan Poland Portugal Singapore
South Korea Switzerland Thailand Turkey Ukraine Vietnam

Published in the United States
by Oxford University Press Inc., New York

British Library Cataloguing in Publication Data
Data available

Library of Congress Cataloging in Publication Data
Data available

Typeset by
J&L Composition, Filey, North Yorkshire
Printed in Great Britain
on acid-free paper by
Antony Rowe Limited
Chippenham, Wiltshire

ISBN 978–0–19–726419–5
ISSN 0068–1202

Contents

Part IV Imagination, Cognition, and Creative Thinking

Part V Cognitive Architecture of the Imagination

Part VI Atypical Imagination and Brain Mechanisms

List of Illustrations and Tables

Notes on Contributors

*Speaker at 'Imaginative Minds' symposium, British Academy, 2004.

Susan Blackmore* is a psychologist and writer whose research on consciousness, memes, and anomalous experiences has been published in over 60 academic papers, as well as book chapters, reviews, and popular articles. She has a regular blog in the *Guardian*, and often appears on radio and television. Her book *The Meme Machine* (1999) has been translated into 12 other languages and more recent books include a textbook *Consciousness: An Introduction* (2003) and *Conversations on Consciousness* (2005).

Pascal Boyer* is Henry Luce Professor of Individual and Collective Memory at Washington University in St Louis. He studied philosophy and anthropology at the Universities of Paris and Cambridge. His research projects are in three main areas: the neuro-cognitive systems which have evolved in humans to support the acquisition of cultural knowledge, concepts, and norms; the role of standard cognitive architecture in furnishing the recurrent properties of religious concepts and norms in different cultures; the nature of individual and cultural memory processes, considered within an interdisciplinary framework. He is author of *Religion Explained* (2001, Heinemann).

Stephanie M. Carlson is Associate Professor in the Institute of Child Development at the University of Minnesota, where she directs research on young children's executive function, pretend play, and social cognition. Her research is funded by the National Institute of Child Health and Human Development (NICHD). She serves as Consulting Editor of *Developmental Psychology* and on the Board of Directors of the Jean Piaget Society.

Nicholas Cook* is Professorial Research Fellow in Music at Royal Holloway, University of London, where he directs the AHRC Research Centre for the History and Analysis of Recorded Music (CHARM). He is the author of articles and books on a wide variety of musicological and theoretical subjects, and his *Music: A Very Short Introduction* has been translated into 11 languages. His latest book is a study of the music theorist Heinrich Schenker in the cultural context of *fin-de-siècle* Vienna. Former editor of *Journal of the Royal Musical Association* and chair of the 2001 RAE Music panel, he was elected a Fellow of the British Academy in the same year.

Ian Cross* teaches at the University of Cambridge where he is Director of the Centre for Music & Science and a Fellow of Wolfson College. He has published widely in the field of music cognition, including two co-edited Academic Press books *Musical Structure and Cognition* (1985) and *Representing Musical Structure* (1991), which helped to set the research agenda in the field. His principal research focus is on music as a biocultural phenomenon, involving collaboration with psychologists, anthropologists, archaeologists, and neuroscientists.

Gregory Currie* is Professor of Philosophy and Dean of Arts, University of Nottingham. Before joining the Nottingham department he was Professor of Philosophy and Head of the School of Arts at Flinders University of South Australia. He is a Fellow of the Australian Academy of Humanities and a Past President of the Australasian Association of Philosophy. His most recent book is *Arts and Minds* (2005, Oxford University Press) and his current project is on irony and point of view in the arts. He is also author, with Ian Ravenscroft, of *Recreative Minds: Imagination in Philosophy and Psychology* (2002, Oxford University Press), and an editor of *Mind and Language*.

John G. Geake is Professor of Education at the Westminster Institute of Education, Oxford Brookes University where he leads the Institute's research in gifted education. He is also a Research Collaborator with the Centre for Functional Magnetic Resonance Imaging of the Brain, University of Oxford, where he conducts fMRI research into the neural correlates of analogical thinking as a basis for high creative intelligence.

Paul L. Harris* is a developmental psychologist with interests in the development of cognition, emotion, and imagination. After studying psychology at Sussex and Oxford, he taught at the University of Lancaster, the Free University of Amsterdam and the London School of Economics. In 1980, he moved to Oxford where he was Professor of Developmental Psychology and Fellow of St John's College. In 2001, he migrated to Harvard where he holds the Victor S. Thomas Professorship of Education. He is a Fellow of the British Academy and of the Norwegian Academy of Science and Letters. For 2006–2007, he received a Guggenheim award. His latest book *The Work of the Imagination* appeared in 2000 (Blackwell).

Melissa Koenig is Assistant Professor in Cognitive Development at the Institute of Child Development at the University of Minnesota. Her primary interests lie at the interface of language development and social cognition. Recent publications include 'The role of social cognition in early trust' with

Paul Harris in *Trends in Cognitive Sciences* and 'Word learning' with Amanda Woodward in the *Oxford Handbook of Psycholinguistics*.

Morten L. Kringelbach is Senior Research Fellow at the Department of Physiology, Anatomy and Genetics, University of Oxford and Extraordinary JRF at The Queen's College. His main research interests are in understanding the functional neuroanatomy of human conscious and unconscious processing, and in particular those aspects related to pleasure, desire, emotion, learning, reward, and hedonic processing.

Steven Mithen* is Head of the School of Human and Environmental Sciences, and Professor of Early Prehistory at the University of Reading. His research interests span from the origin of *Homo c.* 2 million years ago to the invention and spread of agriculture up to 5000 BC. His projects fall into three areas: Late Pleistocene and Early Holocene hunter-gatherers and early farmers, the evolution of the human mind and computational archaeology. He has directed fieldwork in Western Scotland and is currently co-directing excavations in Wadi Faynan, Southern Jordan. His books include *The Prehistory of the Human Mind* (1996) and *After the Ice* (2003). He has edited volumes on *Human Creativity* (1998) and *Hunter-Gatherer Landscape Archaeology* (2001). His most recent book is *The Singing Neanderthals: The Origins of Music, Language, Mind and Body*. He is a Fellow of the British Academy.

Daniel Nettle* is Professor in Psychology at Newcastle University. His interests include personality, creativity, and evolutionary psychology. He is author of *Strong Imagination: Madness, Creativity and Human Nature*; *Happiness: The Science Behind Your Smile*; and *Personality: What Makes You the Way You Are* (all published by Oxford University Press).

David G. Pearson is a lecturer in cognitive psychology at the University of Aberdeen in Scotland. His research covers theoretical and applied aspects of visuo-spatial cognition, including mental imagery and memory for visual and spatial information. He currently serves on the Research Board of the British Psychological Society, and the Academy of Learned Societies for the Social Sciences. He teaches a range of courses at Aberdeen, including Consciousness, Mental Imagery and Creative Thinking, and Human Memory.

Ilona Roth* is Senior Lecturer in Psychology, in the Department of Life Sciences at the Open University. She studied P.P.P. at Oxford, and completed a D.Phil. in experimental psychology. Her psychology texts, including, as editor, *Introduction to Psychology* (1990) and as co author with V. Bruce, *Perception and Representation* (1995), television programmes, and audio-visual materials have been studied by many thousand Open University students, and extensively used in the wider academic domain. Recent publications include 'Imagination' in the *Oxford Companion to the Mind* (2004). Her current research on poetry by autistic individuals forms part of a broader project on imagination and self-awareness, and their manifestations in neuropsychiatric conditions, notably autism spectrum disorders and dementia.

Alison B. Shawber is a doctoral candidate at the University of Oregon. Her research areas include the development of children's imagination, pretend play, and the neural correlates of mental imagery.

Thomas Suddendorf is Associate Professor in the School of Psychology, University of Queensland. His research interests include the cognitive abilities of primates and young children, and the evolution of the human mind. Of particular interest to him are representational capacities such as those related to understanding of self, time, and mind. His most recent publications include 'The evolution of foresight' with Michael Corballis (*Behavioral and Brain Sciences*, 2007), 'Do chimpanzees (*Pan troglodytes*) and two-year-old children (*Homo sapiens*) understand double invisible displacement?' with Emma Collier-Baker (*Journal of Comparative Psychology*, 2006), 'Self-recognition beyond the face' with Virginia Slaughter and Mark Nielsen (*Child Development*, 2006), and 'Foresight and evolution of the human mind' (*Science*, 2006). He recently received the Frank A. Beach Award of the American Psychological Association.

Marjorie Taylor is Professor of Psychology at the University of Oregon. Her research interests include imagination and pretend play, imaginary companions, development of the fantasy–reality distinction, cross-cultural differences in fantasy behaviour, consciousness, and creativity. She is author of *Imaginary Companions and the Children Who Create Them* (1999, Oxford University Press). She is currently working on a book about the relationships that develop between adult fiction writers and the characters in their novels.

Mark Turner* is Institute Professor and Professor and Chair of Cognitive Science at Case Western Reserve University. His most recent book publication is an edited volume, *The Artful Mind: Cognitive Science and the Riddle of Human Creativity* (Oxford University Press). His other books and articles include *Cognitive Dimensions of Social Science: The Way We Think about Politics, Economics, Law, and Society* (Oxford), *The Literary Mind: The Origins of Thought and Language* (Oxford), *Reading Minds: The Study of English in the Age of Cognitive Science* (Princeton), and *Death is the Mother of Beauty* (Chicago). He has been a Fellow of the Institute for Advanced

Study, the John Simon Guggenheim Memorial Foundation, the Center for Advanced Study in the Behavioral Sciences, the National Humanities Center, and the National Endowment for the Humanities. He is external research professor at the Krasnow Institute for Advanced Study in Cognitive Neuroscience and distinguished fellow at the New England Institute for Cognitive Science and Evolutionary Psychology. In 1996, the Académie française awarded him the Prix du Rayonnement de la langue et de la littérature françaises.

Andrew Whiten* is Professor of Evolutionary and Developmental Psychology, and Wardlaw Professor of Psychology at the University of St Andrews. Recent research has focused on social learning, traditions, and culture in both human and non-human primates. Recent publications have included 'The second inheritance system of chimpanzees and humans' (*Nature*, 2005), 'Conformity to cultural norms of tool use in chimpanzees' (*Nature*, 2005), 'Faithful replication of foraging techniques along cultural transmission chains by chimpanzees and children' (*PNAS* 2006), and 'The evolution of animal "cultures" and social intelligence' (*Phil. Trans. Roy. Soc. B* 2007). He is a Fellow of the Royal Society of Edinburgh and a Fellow of the British Academy.

Foreword

There are few problems in science that are perhaps quite so tantalizing, and so difficult, as the workings of the human mind. Over centuries, understanding our thoughts has attracted interest from many fields, ranging from philosophy, to neuroscience, to psychology, to computer science, to archaeology, and to anthropology. That variety of approach has inevitably led to an extraordinary diversity of ideas and models. Very often this has meant focusing on a particular 'trick' of the mind which underlies its evolution, operation, power, and success. Classically, this was the rational mind, our ability to reason our way through any problem. Many have focused on language, and on the way it provides flexibility of thought, and extraordinary combinatorial faculties. Archaeologists and anthropologists have paid particular attention to symbolic thought, often as an extension to language, for the way in which it allows detachment from the here and now, and opens up the possibilities for creating a world of the mind as important as the material one. In recent years we have seen the mind as a computer, with algorithms for everything; the mind as a series of modules like a Swiss Army knife, each one specialized to carry out its particular function, and, of course, the mind as a social diary, playing out the intricacies of our complex social lives. Music, emotion, technology, planning, all have been recognized as playing a part.

At first sight it might seem that, in bringing together the papers of this book to focus on imagination, Ilona Roth is simply providing yet another 'trick'. For language, or sociality, or reason, read imagination. It is certainly almost impossible to think of the human mind without the imagination—indeed, it is an act of imagination just to pose the question. Imagination pervades our thinking very deeply. Perhaps, though, imagination is more than just another trick.

Both across the spectrum of thinking about the human mind and across the characteristics of the human mind itself, very different aspects are emphasized. For some it might be the ability to construct narratives; for others it might be Machiavellian strategic thinking and planning; for yet others it might be making complex technologies from hand axes to computers; and so on across the whole range of skills, even poetry and falling in love. Different people also seem to have quite different cognitive strengths and weaknesses across this spectrum. For each of these abilities, though, it can be argued that it is the capacity to imagine that makes them so potent. Early storytellers must have used their imagination to construct their narratives. Proto-politicians in the Palaeolithic must have used their imagination to plot and scheme their way to the top of the probably literally greasy pole. The artists of the Dordogne needed to imagine in their heads the shapes and shadows of the bison they painted deep in dark caves. And from the first tools to be chipped out of rocks, to the extraordinary complexities of modern material culture, there must have been a cognitive model of technology. Prior to any action, whether it is technological, political, or aesthetic, there must be an 'imaginative' mental state. So in studying evolution, the concept of the imagination has the power to be more neutral about the actual cognitive abilities that produce actions or thoughts. This provides it with greater unifying power in looking for what makes the human mind both unique and effective.

However, while we can grasp this quite simply, and probably all agree, somewhat unimaginatively, that this must be the case, we are still left with a major problem. Unwrapping the word or 'concept 'imagination' is far from straightforward. It can mean something as simple as a basic 'what-if' thought about an item of food, through to the extraordinary imagination that must have underlain the thoughts of both Shakespeare and Newton. While it is a universal of the human mind, it also varies from individual to individual and from mode of thought to mode of thought. So while on the one hand we have in the concept of the imagination the possibility of finding something that unifies the various creativities of the human mind, on the other we also have a very poor understanding of exactly what it means—let alone the role it may have played in evolution.

It is that hard problem that Ilona Roth has asked the contributors to this volume to address. Appropriately enough, the papers cover an enormous range, from chimpanzees coping with various challenges, to the pattern of human cognitive evolution, to abilities such as music and art, and from the limited capacities of autistic children to the flights of creativity of the imaginative genius. We are still a long way from a workable, let alone unified, theory of how the imagination operates, but these papers represent a major step towards a better understanding of how the human mind evolved and what are its most special characteristics.

Robert Foley
Leverhulme Professor of Human Evolution,
University of Cambridge and Fellow of the British Academy

Acknowledgements

This collection of essays grew from a two-day inter-disciplinary symposium on 'Imaginative Minds' organized with the support and funding of The British Academy, and held at their premises on 30 April to 1 May 2004. Professors Ruth Finnegan and Uta Frith were kind enough to sponsor my original proposal for the meeting. Angela Pusey and Joanne Blore helped me in organizing the meeting while Abigail Cooke coordinated the website. Many of the current chapters are by symposium speakers (names asterisked in the list of biographical entries), their contributions complemented by a small number of chapters commissioned subsequently. Other symposium speakers were Professor Karin Barber, Professor Ian Robertson, and Dr John Harrison. Chairs were Professor Uta Frith, Dr Daniel Nettle, Dr Richard Stevens, and Dr Ilona Roth. Discussants were Professor Margaret Boden, Professor Robert Foley, and Professor Dan Sperber. My warm thanks are due to all who made the original meeting such a success, and all who have travelled with me on the journey to produce this volume. Besides the authors, this latter group includes Ros Woodward, who has edited the material, and Amritpal Bangard, Janet English, and James Rivington of the British Academy publications department. Finally, I give special thanks to my late father, Martin Roth F.R.S., F.Med.Sci., whose powers of imagination, in his medical and scientific work, his musicianship, and his appreciation of the arts have always been a source of inspiration to me.

I.R.

Introduction

Imaginative Minds:
Concepts, Controversies, and Themes

ILONA ROTH

'The Imagination is one of the highest prerogatives of man. By this faculty he unites former images and ideas, independently of the will, and thus creates brilliant and novel results.' Charles Darwin (reprinted 1995)

'Imagination is more important than knowledge. Knowledge is limited. Imagination circles the world.' Attributed to Albert Einstein (quoted in Calaprice 2005)

THE PRE-EMINENT ROLE OF IMAGINATION in human thought is one that both Darwin and Einstein clearly recognized. Their enthusiasm for the concept is echoed in many contemporary academic fields, and also in everyday social attitudes. In a world in which scientific ideas and technological processes, and even routine daily activities, are subject to rapid and frequent innovation and change, the supreme flexibility and inventiveness of mind we associate with imagination have become highly prized. Teachers and parents are encouraged to promote imagination in children, and in adult life a high premium is placed on activities, whether in business, science, the visual and performing arts, or other branches of life, that show imagination or creativity. Yet despite what seems the obvious relevance of imagination to psychology and the cognitive sciences, and of these disciplines to exploring the imagination, many researchers in these fields have been reluctant to engage directly with the concept. This volume takes up the challenge of filling this theoretical and empirical lacuna. It brings together explanatory perspectives from both within and beyond the cognitive sciences, with the goal of enhancing the salience of imagination as a construct, or cluster of constructs, relevant to understanding human mind and behaviour.

Since the potential scope of the topic is vast, it is necessary to sample selectively within the total field, while providing scope for the discourse and debate across disciplinary boundaries which is a key objective of this project.

The focus of the book is the imaginative operations of the human mind: why and in what ways are humans (and arguably some other primates) imaginative? What are the consequences for their behaviour and their cultural worlds? These questions are considered in terms of the evolutionary origins of imagination, its expression in children, the cognitive processes and brain mechanisms involved, and the cultural 'products' that both emanate from and serve to sustain imaginative thought. The volume places a substantial emphasis upon scientific approaches, notably those of psychology, neuroscience, and evolutionary studies, but also embraces perspectives from philosophy and the humanities. In practice there are no clear-cut distinctions here: many of the approaches represented cross the 'arts–science' divide in the true spirit of interdisciplinary integration appropriate to a construct that is both central to the arts and humanities and a fundamental property of human cognition.

The remainder of this introduction sets arguments for a contemporary exploration of 'imaginative minds' into historical and theoretical context, and outlines the themes and issues that structure this volume.

DEFINING IMAGINATION

We use the word 'imagination' frequently and take it for granted that we know what we mean. Yet the word has multiple definitions in the *Oxford English Dictionary* (1989) including the formation of mental images, usually assumed to be visual, but also, by implication, auditory, tactile, and so on; states of mind such as daydreaming, characterized by fantasy and the spontaneous flow of thought from one idea to another; the mental activity of considering or planning possible (or impossible) courses of action—often known as counterfactual or 'what if?' thinking; creative imagination—the power of framing highly novel or original ideas and cultural products. Literary and philosophical definitions cover a similar spectrum of meanings, one significant addition being figurative or metaphorical thinking, in which one concept or entity is thought of or treated as another—what might be called 'as if' thinking.

The various meanings may seem somewhat unrelated. However, they have in common a reference to the human mind's capacity to elaborate concepts, images, and ideas that do not correspond to current or past reality, and that may never be actualized. In this sense, imagination appears fundamental to the mental apparatus that differentiates humans, in degree if not in kind, from other species. It is this that enables humans to operate flexibly and effectively in highly complex social groupings, to contemplate intricate plans for possible (and impossible) future action, and to envisage the consequences without enacting them. It is this that enables humans to conceive of works of art, literature, poetry, and music, to appreciate these cultural 'products', and also to make discoveries and innovations in scientific and technological fields. Without such creative imagination, human society would be quite unrecognizable and very dull.

A possible objection to such a wide-ranging concept of imagination is that the territory so delineated becomes indistinguishable from thought in general: after all, what is human thought if it is not abstract, hypothetical, flexible, and creative? While a full answer to this objection is beyond the scope of this introduction, two important points can be made here. Firstly, even without hard and fast criteria for distinguishing imagination from thought in general, the former construct encapsulates the most quintessential and special characteristics of cognition, and these merit special and separate consideration. Secondly, the thinking style of some individuals on the autism spectrum gives us a glimpse of what thought is like when stripped of much of its imaginative quality. This apparent dissociation between imaginative thought and other forms of cognition argues that a meaningful distinction can be made.

HISTORICAL BACKGROUND TO
A SCIENCE OF THE IMAGINATION

The generally low salience of imagination within contemporary psychology and the fragmentary treatment of major constituents such as imagery, counterfactual thinking, and creativity owe much to a turbulent past. In his historical overview of the imagination, Thomas (1999a,b) shows how different meanings have evolved, coalesced, and split from one another in keeping with changing philosophical and epistemological world views. This complex background has undoubtedly coloured the shades of meaning associated with current notions, and the conceptual issues that dominated early thinking find echoes in contemporary concerns that this volume will highlight.

First of these is what kind of 'mental faculty' is the imagination, and what work does it do? As Thomas outlines, even Aristotle's early conception incorporated components with distinct but interacting roles, prefiguring contemporary interest in the mind's 'functional architecture'—its sub-systems and how they are orchestrated. Aristotle proposed *phantasia* (of which *imaginatio* is the Latin translation) and *koine aesthesis*, which translates as the *sensus communis,* as parts of a wider faculty having the role of combining experiences into so-called *phantasmata*, meaning coherent mental representations. Just as *sensus communis* refers not to 'common sense' but to the binding of outputs from sensory systems into coherent percepts, so the connotations of fantasy evoked by the words *phantasia* and *phantasmata* are somewhat misleading. For Aristotle, *phantasmata* arose either as veridical representations of the 'here and now' based on sensory inputs, or as the remembered products of previous experiences. In short, while Aristotle's conception was prescient in some ways, it offered little scope for the fantasy and counterfactual thinking that are inherent in the modern concept of the imagination.

In mediaeval philosophies, ideas about the components and functions of the imagination were further embellished by speculation about possible anatomical substrates. Moreover, separating imagination both conceptually and anatomically from the *sensus communis* freed it from dealing only with present or past reality, allowing slightly more scope for fanciful ideation, within its role of consolidating and transforming mental images for storage in memory. A couple of hundred years on, however, Descartes reunited imagination and *sensus communis,* locating them on the surface of the tiny pineal gland as collecting point for perceptual, memory, and 'imaginary' images. Importantly, the functions so assembled were not part of Descartes' concept of the rational, but incorporeal mind, but rather the point of inter-face with it. Here then the Cartesian dualist view of the mind finds expres-sion alongside the notion, central to modern neuropsychological thinking, that parts of the brain may play distinctive roles in mental operations— including imagination.

Within the empiricist and mechanistic philosophies that characterized the flowering of science in the 17th century, the notion of *sensus communis* dis-appeared, and the concept of imagination expanded to take the overall role of associating contiguous sense impressions. Hume (1739/1740) described the imagination as enduring traces of our transient perceptual experiences, which deliver our belief in continuous objects existing in the external world, and our grouping of objects into conceptual kinds represented by words. These image-based functions for the imagination once again represent a partial sub-set of current meanings. But Hume's sceptical empiricism also introduced a negative 'valence' which has overshadowed the concept's subsequent develop-ment. For Hume the imagination was ubiquitous, but also the product of an unfortunate 'psychological habit' of believing in a world whose existence can-not be rationally established. That creative works of art and literature (let alone scientific discoveries) might emanate from this same fictive mental uni-verse left the thinkers of the day unimpressed. Asked for his view of poetry, Newton dismissed it as 'a kind of ingenious nonsense' (see Abrams 1953).

It is in reaction to this intellectual environment that first Kant and then the writers of the 19th century Romantic movement reformulated imagin-ation in an overtly positive way, challenging its status as a passively negligent or decadent thought form. From the 'super-ordinate, almost mystical role' of the imagination in Kant's philosophy (O'Connor and Aardema 2005) to the Romantics' rehabilitation of ancient associations with originality, passion, and fantasy, the concept was reframed. Within Romanticism the role of imagination in perception became that of an active force that enables humans to mentally construct reality. Beyond this, as Thomas (1999a) describes, links with cognitive theory and epistemology were loosened in favour of tighter links to aesthetics. Thus the concept acquired positive new associations with creativity and dreaming.

Of course the Romantic movement embraces subtle variations which can only be hinted at here. For instance, celebration of the non-rational nature of imaginative thought is strongly associated with the Romantics, hence William Blake's comment to Sir Joshua Reynolds, 'What has reason to do with the Art of Painting? . . . one power alone makes a poet; Imagination, the Divine Vision' (see Wittkower 1973, p. 306). Yet Wordsworth (1850/1971) identified imagination with 'Reason in her most exalted mood'. Similarly, while fantasy is both extolled within Romantic ideology and explored within its canon, there are dissenting voices. Thus Byron writes of literature: 'But I hate things all fiction. . . there should always be some foundation of fact for the most airy fabric—and pure invention is but the talent of a liar' (see Marchand 1982, p. 335).

Notwithstanding such qualifications, the central role of imagination in the Romantic philosophy of mind did little to recommend it to subsequent critics of the movement. With the growth of 19th century science, the connotations of unfettered and dreamy thinking meant that imagination came, once again, to be viewed as primitive, antithetical to science and to other activities requiring 'organised thought' (Daston 1998). This recurring negativity served to undermine the status of imagination as a useful attribute of mind, or as one worthy of scientific investigation. Consequently, apart from the works of Jean-Paul Sartre, it virtually disappeared from both philosophy and mainstream psychology in the early twentieth century (O'Connor and Aardema 2005).

Behaviourism and Psychoanalysis

During the heyday of Behaviourist (stimulus–response) psychology in the early decades of the twentieth century, the repudiation of imagination as a psychological construct was reinforced within a wider project to relegate complex attributes of mind to theoretical obscurity. At its most extreme, the behaviourist view was that phenomena such as consciousness and imagination were meaningless because they comprise unobservable (i.e. mental) events, which do not lend themselves to objective measurement. J. B. Watson famously denied that he experienced mental images (see Pearson in Chapter 9), let alone acknowledged more recondite phenomena of the imagination. Yet some of the same attributes that had contributed to the demise of imagination—as a primitive, associative, and non-rational form of thought—resonated strongly with psychoanalytical models of mind, originating in Freud's own work in the late nineteenth and early twentieth centuries. Freud and his disciples embraced imagination, equating it with fantasy, dreaming, and pathology—forms of 'primary process' thinking guided by the Pleasure principle, as distinct from 'secondary process' thinking guided by the Reality principle (Freud 1911/1961). The psychoanalytic movement thus deserves credit for keeping some psychological interest in imagination going during the dark days of behaviourism, though ironically their theoretical take on this concept has also helped to keep it beyond the pale of mainstream experimental psychology.

FROM 20TH TO 21ST CENTURY: CHALLENGES FOR A SCIENCE OF THE IMAGINATION

With the decline of behaviourism in the 1970s, and the rise of cognitive approaches, which treat the workings of the human mind as their central focus, topics such as the psychology of consciousness have been substantially rehabilitated into the mainstream of psychology. By contrast, the psychology of imagination has remained somewhat at the margins until just recently. This low salience is reflected in the infrequent appearance of imagination as an index term, let alone a topic, in dictionaries and textbooks. An entry on imagination in the 2nd edition of the *Oxford Companion to the Mind* was written by the present author partly to address this lack (Roth 2004).

Several theoretical tensions have worked together to impede the development of imagination as a coherent field within psychology and the cognitive sciences. These interwoven issues are set out here as reference points to bear in mind when reading the chapters in this volume.

Rational or Irrational Thought?

This distinction, framed here by Ulric Neisser (1967) as a general explanatory challenge for cognitive psychology, strongly echoes the early philosophical debates about the nature of imagination:

> Historically, psychology has long recognised the existence of two different forms of mental organisation. The distinction has been given many names: 'rational' vs. 'intuitive', 'constrained' vs. 'creative', 'logical' vs. 'pre logical',

'realistic' vs. 'autistic',[1] 'secondary process' vs. 'primary process'. To list them together casually may be misleading . . . Nevertheless, a common thread runs through all the dichotomies. Some thinking and remembering is deliberate, efficient, and obviously goal-directed; it is usually experienced as self-directed as well. Other mental activity is rich, chaotic and inefficient; it tends to be experienced as involuntary, it just 'happens'. It often seems to be motivated, but not in the same way as directed thought; it seems not so much directed towards a goal as associated with an emotion. (Neisser 1967, p. 297)

Neisser went on to argue that these dichotomies could be reduced, via a computational analogy, to the difference between sequential and parallel mental processing. In the former, items of information are dealt with one at a time, the outcome of each stage influencing the next one. In the latter, many items are processed simultaneously, the outcomes being potentially richer, but less predictable. Neisser argued that each of these human processing modes could be scientifically explored using appropriate methods. But he was optimistic in supposing that cognitive psychology would resolve the conceptual and epistemological difficulties so neatly. The mental processes distinguished by Neisser appear as mutually exclusive categories: as *either* rational *or* intuitive, constrained *or* creative forms of thought, and the belief that one set of these phenomena lies beyond the legitimate subject matter of scientific psychology has not disappeared. Forms of thinking that are 'deliberate, efficient and goal-directed' are typically considered not only more rational, but also much more accessible by the methods of science than those that are 'rich, chaotic and inefficient', and this has served to circumscribe the field in which cognitive scientists have operated.

Yet imagination is *par excellence* the conceptual cluster that straddles the divide represented by Neisser's distinctions. It embraces forms of thought that can be both rational and intuitive, both logical and prelogical, though not necessarily at the same time. For instance, Martindale (1999) is one of several researchers who suggest that both 'convergent' or logical and 'divergent' or creative thinking are involved in such activities as scientific discovery and the solving of logical problems. The initial phase, which may be experienced as the focused mental work, is dominated by logical, reality-oriented reasoning. Following this there is typically an incubation period, in which the person may experience a lack of progress or 'block'. Finally there is an illumination or solution, often when the individual's mind has not been focused on the problem for a while. Martindale proposes that both incubation and

---

[1] Autistic is used here not in its current sense, but as the psychiatrist Bleuler (1951) used it to represent free-associative, wishful thinking characteristic of dreaming, day-dreaming, and children's play.

illumination phases are characterized by the free-associative, 'primary-process' thinking, which has traditionally been viewed as playing no role in the scientific process.

The challenge, then, is to approach the imagination within a framework sufficiently broad in its theoretical scope and eclectic in its methodological perspectives to transcend this conceptual and empirical divide. In this volume, we encounter imagination both in its seemingly less rational guise, as the source of inspiration for fiction, poetry, and music, and in its more reality-oriented role of solving everyday problems and predicting the behaviour of others.

Imagery and Imagination

As has been shown, the idea that mental imagery is an integral component of imaginative thinking has long antecedents. From Aristotle onwards the functions of imagination have been closely linked to perception, and to the notion of perceptual experience which persists in the absence of sensory input. According to this view, when we imagine, we do so, at least in part, by bringing mental images to mind. However, philosophical analyses that emerged after the early twentieth century moratorium on the imagination, notably by Ryle (1949) and White (1990), have challenged its connection with imagery (O'Connor and Aardema 2005). According to these accounts imagination should be considered as a form of pretending (Ryle) or counterfactual thinking (White) mediated by 'propositional' thought processes. Such language-like, non-pictorial cognition is, on the face of it, distinct from mental imagery, considered as 'seeing pictures in the mind's eye', or equivalent in the 'mind's ear'. Equally, as Thomas (1999b) notes, imagination of the creative kind cannot be reduced to just the 'separation and recombination of parts of pictorial images', the model that seems most consistent with an account of imagery as pictorial mental representation.

Yet it would be perverse to introduce a survey of the imagination by foreclosing on the relationship between imagery and imagination. It is generally acknowledged that imagery need not be reduced to the naive form of 'picture theory' critiqued by Ryle, and with this insight new possibilities emerge. Currie and Ravenscroft (2002) argue that imagery plays a role in what they call 'recreative' imagination—the capacity to imagine something from a different perspective or viewpoint. And there is both anecdotal and systematic evidence that imagery is involved in some forms of creative imagination. In short, the inclusion of imagery in an account of the imagination can be readily justified.

Distinct, Linked, or Unified Phenomena?

Faced with such an apparently complex and Janus-faced construct as the imagination, it is not surprising that cognitive psychologists have tended either to ignore it altogether, or to approach it in a fragmentary way. Thus several *aspects* of the imagination have been developed as separate fields of psychological enquiry, notably:

- mental imagery;
- developmental phenomena—especially pretence, defined as the childhood activity of imbuing events, objects, or entities with imaginary properties; fantastical beliefs, for instance in fairies, magic, and imaginary companions;
- theory of mind—the capacity to conceive of the thoughts and feelings of others, considered as social imagination in some accounts;
- counterfactual thinking—imagining 'what might have been' or 'what if . . .';
- creativity.

Undoubtedly each of these fields has gathered considerable momentum during the cognitive era, but separate theoretical development has reinforced the notion that the imaginative processes under consideration are essentially distinct, or even that a particular approach encompasses the full extent of the concept. Thus Thomas (1999b) notes that cognitive imagery theories are sometimes presented as if they covered all that there is to know about imagination.

In this context, work emphasizing the links between imaginative phenomena is to be welcomed. Leslie (1987; Leslie and Roth 1993) pioneered an influential theory linking pretence and theory of mind as aspects of the capacity to suspend disbelief in order to conjure with hypothetical possibilities, whether imagining that a stick is a gun, or imagining what someone else might be thinking. Work by Suddendorf and Fletcher-Flinn (1997), Hobson (2002), and others has highlighted relationships between children's capacity for theory of mind and their ability to think creatively. Much of this work is informed by the characteristic pattern of deficits in Autism Spectrum Disorders (ASD). These include difficulties in a range of imaginative skills, perhaps indicating a common substrate for these capacities (see Craig 1997 and Roth in Chapter 13). Research by Finke and colleagues (1992) and others (see Robertson 2002) provides evidence that promoting people's capacity for mental imagery enhances certain aspects of creativity, though Boden (2004) questions this relationship. Further important contributions are Thomas's (1999b) proposals for a theoretical synthesis of imagery and imagination, and Byrne's (2006) work on the relationship between counter-factual ('what if?') imagination and creativity.

The extent to which such empirical and theoretical links call for a unified treatment of the imagination is a matter of debate. For instance, Currie and Ravenscroft (2002) draw a clear distinction between creative imagination, as the capacity to 'do things in a new way', and recreative imagination as the capacity to 'put ourselves in the place of another, or in the place of our own future, past or counterfactual self'. They argue, with Tomasello (2000), that while creativity qua inventiveness may play a role in some forms of human recreative imagination, the former is a less sophisticated skill also seen in some non-human primates, while the latter involves the complex and exclusively human skill of perspective taking.

This volume makes new contributions to both the integration and differentiation of forms of imagination. For instance, Mithen (Chapter 1) proposes the evolution of a cumulative sequence of imaginative capacities culminating in the exceptional creative imagination of modern humans. Whiten and Suddendorf (Chapter 2) echo Currie and Ravenscroft in considering inventiveness, at least, a cognitively less demanding form of imagining, though especially well developed in great apes. They differ in emphasizing the scope for elements of recreative-like imagination in the cognitive repertoire of these primates.

Cultural Expressions of the Imagination

The debate about how far forms of imaginative thinking can be explained in terms of common operating principles must be informed, above all, by their strikingly diverse cultural manifestations. Hence this volume considers different areas of human life that evoke imaginative behaviour, and highlights both commonalities and differences among the processes involved. Among the cultural domains considered here are music, visual art, fiction, poetry, religion, and supernatural beliefs.

To explain such diverse activities in terms of a similar set of imaginative processes is certainly a challenge. Chapters 10–12 by Turner, Boyer, and Nettle offer different perspectives on the question of common or distinct operating principles.

Individual Minds and Imaginative Contexts

A psychological focus on imaginative minds encourages us to consider the processes of individual cognition. Moreover, individuals are said to differ in imaginative capacities, notably for imagery (Cornoldi and Vecchi 2003) and creativity (Simonton 2002). Recent accounts of creativity temper the exceptionality implied by such differences by emphasizing the 'everyday' creativity that all individuals display in tasks such as cooking, gardening, and nurturing children (Boden 2004), and by stressing the creative potential of people working in groups (Paulus and Nijstad 2003).

To understand imagination in all its forms, we need to range yet further from individual minds to acknowledge the sociocultural contexts in which they are situated. For imagination is not just a unidirectional process in which minds, whether individually or collectively, generate imaginative thoughts and outputs. Beyond these mental operations, culture furnishes the material for imagination, notably, but by no means exclusively in 'high-end' forms such as works of literature and art, music, dance, and drama, all of which depend for their meanings on the imaginative engagement that they evoke in individual minds. A story, for instance, has no impact if it does not trigger an imaginative response in which the reader enters the world that it sets out to create. And its impact will be even greater if it evokes a similar response in different minds. To this extent imaginative minds are in continuous interplay with culture, both augmenting and shaping its materials, and being sustained and altered by them. There are strong arguments, then, for combining the theories and methods of psychology and cognitive science with wider cross-disciplinary perspectives that address this interface.

CROSS-DISCIPLINARY PERSPECTIVES

While imagination has received fragmentary treatment in psychology, striking insights are emerging from approaches that have reconfigured traditional disciplinary boundaries. For instance, the field of cognitive archaeology uses studies of artefacts and archaeological remains from early prehistory to draw inferences about the evolving imaginative capacities of the minds which created them (see Mithen 1996 and Chapter 1). Cognitive anthropology combines the theories and methods of experimental psychology with those of anthropology and evolutionary theory, to study the interplay of cultural phenomena with universal modes of imaginative thought (see Boyer 2001 and Chapter 11). Other fruitful fusions include literary studies with cognitive science (Fauconnier and Turner 2002 and Turner in Chapter 10) and musicology with evolutionary theory (Cross 2003 and Chapter 7).

The application of philosophical analysis to psychological phenomena has, of course, a long history. But the current rapprochement of philosophy and psychology, in the approach known as philosophy of mind, is especially strong, and also particularly fruitful for the study of imagination (see for instance Currie and Ravenscroft 2002 and Currie in Chapter 8).

Finally, rapid developments in the field of cognitive neuroscience, including the use of techniques such as fMRI (functional magnetic resonance imaging) to monitor the activity of the brain during thought processes, potentially offer powerful insights into the brain and neural substrates of the imaginative mind. This approach is represented by Geake and Kringelbach in Chapter 14.

This brief overview has sought to demonstrate that the study of imaginative minds is a field with a promising future, which stands to benefit, appropriately, from the creative confluence of different theoretical and methodological perspectives. We now turn to a discussion of the six sub-themes that structure the chapters in this volume, and the issues and debates that underpin the discussion throughout.

THEMES

Evolution of the Imagination

The book opens with a focus on how, when, and why the modern human capacity for imagination evolved. Drawing upon evidence from the archaeological and fossil record, Mithen argues that the imaginative capacities of our chimpanzee-like hominid common ancestor 4.5 million years ago were limited to the everyday planning and decision-making necessary to hunt or fashion stone tools. Presenting creative imagination as the 'jewel in the crown' of the imaginative capacities of modern humans, he constructs a seven stage model showing how the limited imaginative repertoire of our common ancestor might have evolved, through cumulative and perhaps overlapping steps, into the elaborate panoply of modern human imaginative skills. He sees 'cognitive fluidity'—the capacity to transpose ideas between different cognitive domains—as fundamental for this. With cognitive fluidity laws that apply in one domain of 'folk' knowledge, such as our intuitive understanding of biology or physics, can be broken in another. Thus a child engaged in a pretend fight readily treats an ordinary twig as a sword; an adult may believe in life after death, or that supernatural beings can travel through solid objects.

Also working within the explanatory framework of biological evolution, but using the methods of comparative psychology, Whiten and Suddendorf consider common ancestors of humans and great apes as far back as 14 million years, and come to somewhat different conclusions from Mithen concerning their likely imaginative repertoire. Drawing upon a range of experimental and observational studies of contemporary chimpanzees and other apes, they infer that the common ancestors which these species resemble would have been both inventive and capable of secondary representation—that is, operating with multiple non-veridical representations as is necessary for pretence, mirror self-recognition, and 'mind-reading' the intentions of others. Much of the difference between Mithen's and Whiten's positions arises less from conflicting empirical evidence than from a slightly different conception of the orchestration of human imaginative capacities. Mithen sees creative imagination as the most complex and sophisticated cognitive skill, for which mind-reading is one of the evolutionary building blocks. Whiten argues that inventiveness, a significant, though not the only, component of human creativity, is less cognitively complex than the suite of skills subsumed by secondary representation.

Finally in this section, Blackmore considers imagination within a framework presented as radically different from the biological evolutionary approaches exemplified by Mithen and Whiten and Suddendorf. She challenges the view that genes for imaginative cognition would have been selected because they confer an adaptive and reproductive advantage on individuals who possess them, with an alternative mechanism based on memes—cultural replicators that serve to ensure the spread and prevalence of certain innovatory ideas and practices within and across cultures. Nonetheless, there is a sense in which this 'memetic' approach, built upon an idea of Richard Dawkins (1993), is advanced as complementary to, rather than contradictory of, the biological model.

Development of Imagination in Children

In this section the focus shifts from the development of imagination across evolutionary history to development within the childhood years. Two chapters focus on different ways in which imagination both colours the mental world of the child and lays the foundations for adult cognition, social interaction, and cultural learning. Both chapters are cast within the developmental psychology paradigm and are extensively informed by findings from experimental and observational studies of young children.

Taylor and her colleagues consider a striking and perplexing form of counterfactual or 'what if?' imagining, in their fascinating account of children's interactions with imaginary others. Far from being invariably compliant and well behaved, a significant proportion of these childhood 'friends' are disobedient or badly behaved. The capacity not only to conjure such non-real companions, but to furnish them with traits beyond the child's own control, is impressive indeed. Further, the psychological outcomes for children who have imaginary companions are almost all positive, underlining the importance of this form of counterfactual imagination in cognitive and emotional development and social adjustment.

Harris and Koenig broaden the focus from thinking about non-real beings, considering also how children deal with entities and events which, though real, have not been directly observed by them. They point out that the role of imagination extends to just such situations. Faced with a claim such as 'the Earth is round' the child draws upon imagination to form a working model that incorporates this view. However, his or her acceptance of such imagined entities is critically modulated by evaluation of the testimony that generated the claim: children do not accept unreliable testimony on trust. In this sense, they are cautious disciples in their readiness to assimilate potentially fantastical concepts into their store of real-world knowledge.

Mind into Culture: Perspectives on Musical Imagination

From a consideration of the ways in which imagination scaffolds the child's individual and social development, the emphasis shifts to one of the most universal cultural manifestations of the human imagination—music. Though not everyone has the imaginative capacity to compose music, musical imagination is universal in the sense that everyone, except those rare individuals with amusia, has the capacity to engage with music through performing and/or listening. Cook outlines how 'improvisatory imagination' infuses both the process of composition and the creative act involved in performing and listening. Moreover, he argues, the interpretation of music, even something as complete as a Mozart score, is a social act, in which the interpretive responses of individuals must be coordinated and interwoven to achieve a creative result.

This integration of individual and social elements in musical imagination is a continuing thread in the chapter by Cross, which has a special focus on music outside the Western tradition. In this arena, the roles of composer, performer, and listener, and the boundaries between music and dance, are frequently much less clear-cut than in classical Western music. Consequently, he argues, scientific approaches that analyse the ways in which music has its impact on the human auditory system, and musicological approaches that emphasize the ways in which music is embedded in social and cultural traditions, must be closely integrated if we are to fully understand what music means.

Imagination, Cognition, and Creative Thinking

From the interplay between mind and culture, the focus shifts to some of the mental operations which underpin imaginative thought. Currie's chapter emphasizes once again that imagination is not the exclusive preserve of exceptionally creative individuals such as composers or writers, but is equally at work in the mind of the beholder. He considers the forms of imagination that enable a reader to engage with a narrative, arguing that this must be understood not only in terms of the imaginative content of the reader's thoughts about the story, but also the stance or point of view which the reader adopts, this being subtly or implicitly prescribed by the narrative itself.

While Currie sees the mental images that the reader may conjure while reading a story as incidental to the processes at the heart of narrative engagement, mental imagery is the central focus of Pearson's chapter. There are many celebrated anecdotal accounts of the role of visual imagery in the creative thinking of scientists, composers, writers, and others. Pearson shows how the methods and models of cognitive psychology have provided a more robust foundation for some of these claims, elucidating the factors that may enhance or undermine the creative quality of image-based thinking. He concludes by addressing the controversial question of the phenomenal status of mental imagery and just what causal role it might play in creativity.

Echoing Mithen's emphasis on cognitive flexibility as a key evolutionary foundation for modern human imagination, Pearson's analysis centres on the notion of creative mental synthesis—the process of manipulating different sources of information and combining them to generate entirely new ideas or insights. Turner argues that an analogous process—the capacity for conceptual integration or 'blending'—lies at the core of all imaginative cognition. Blending enables humans to draw simultaneously upon different conceptual frameworks, articulating their elements within novel frameworks from which powerful new ideas emerge. Turner illustrates how pervasive characteristics of human cognition, including attributing mental states to both humans and other animals, understanding fiction and pictorial representations, can be interpreted as sophisticated forms of blending.

Cognitive Architecture of the Imagination

The chapters by Boyer and Nettle continue the theme of operating principles for the imagination and consider how such processes might be organized and instantiated within the cognitive system. Both chapters draw upon the notion of domain-specificity (Cosmides and Tooby 1994), according to which the mind consists of a set of modular cognitive mechanisms, each specialized to deal with a different class of knowledge about the world. Their conclusions regarding the application of this principle to the imagination are subtly different.

Boyer argues that the bases for 'high-end' imaginative activities, in which category he includes engaging with fiction, religious belief, and ritual, are to be found in more everyday 'productive' imagining rooted in counterfactual or 'what if?' type inference processes. Though such tacit everyday inferences are a generic property of cognition, their character is specialized and specific to different domains of knowledge. For instance our inferences about the behaviour of intentional agents such as humans are different from those about inanimate objects. If we strike another human being, we might expect them to cry out, show signs of pain, and perhaps to retaliate. If we strike a vase, our expectations are different—for instance that the vase will shatter or spill water on the floor. Boyer argues that imaginative premises, for instance about the activities of gods and ancestors, may arise from fairly minor violations of the default set of expectations for the relevant domain. Since imaginative premises in stories, religions, and other fields often concern the same culturally universal themes, he suggests that these premises are pre-selected by a process that favours their survival and replication over other potential premises with less memorability and cognitive relevance.

Nettle's chapter shifts the focus again from the kind of imaginative ideas that many individuals share, to the more exceptional imagination of highly creative individuals. It has long been thought that creative artists have temperamental and cognitive attributes similar to those of people with mental disorders. Thus Redfield Jamison (1993) explored the likely incidence of bipolar disorder in the families of famous writers such as Tennyson. Nettle presents important new data on the raised incidence of schizotypy in artists and poets. He extrapolates from this connection to a model of the imagination that marries domain-specificity with a form of interdomain cross-talk. There is a generic operating principle here akin to Mithen's notion of cognitive fluidity but, like Boyer, Nettle repudiates the notion of a general 'faculty' of the imagination.

Atypical Imagination and Brain Mechanisms

Nettle's chapter demonstrates that much can be learned about the imagination from atypical cases. This theme continues here with Roth's exploration of imagination on the autism spectrum. People with ASD are usually assumed to have impaired capacity for many of the forms of imagination discussed in this volume. Yet some individuals have talent in fields usually associated with creativity, notably visual art, music, and poetry. Roth considers the dimensions and implications of this profile of deficits and skills, and describes the insights from her own work on autistic spectrum poets.

The complex picture of continuities and discontinuities among forms of imagination that emerges from both this and earlier chapters call for a mapping of the relevant cognitive processes onto brain mechanisms. While studies of these mechanisms are at an early stage, Geake and Kringelbach offer a valuable survey of what is known. They range widely across different phenomena, and shed light on the way common operating principles nonetheless recruit many different brain areas and networks in support of the exquisite complexity of the imaginative mind.

Note. My thanks to Elizabeth Archibald, Lesel Dawson, and Mirka Horova for their helpful comments.

In this book 'hominid' denotes ancestral relatives of humans since the divergence from the chimpanzee lineage. The term 'hominin' is gradually superseding this usage.

References

Abrams, M. H. 1953: *The Mirror and the Lamp: Romantic Theory and the Critical Tradition*. Oxford: Oxford University Press.

Bleuler, E. 1951: Autistic thinking. In Rapaport, D., *Organisation and Pathology of Thought*. New York: Columbia Press, 199–437. (Orig. publ. 1912 as Das autistiche, *Denken Jahrbuch für Psychoanalytysche und Psychopathologische Forschungen*.)

Boden, M. A. 2004: *The Creative Mind: Myths and Mechanisms* (2nd edn). London and New York: Routledge.

Boyer, P. 2001: *Religion Explained*. London: Heinemann.

Byrne, R. 2006: *The Rational Imagination: How People Create Alternatives to Reality*. Cambridge, MA: MIT Press.

Calaprice, A. (ed.) 2005: *The New Quotable Einstein*. Princeton, NJ: Princeton University Press.

Cornoldi, C. and Vecchi, T. 2003: *Visuo-spatial Working Memory and Individual Differences* (Essays in Cognitive Psychology). Hove: Psychology Press.

Cosmides, L. and Tooby, J. 1994: Origins of domain specificity: The evolution of functional organisation. In Hirchfeld, L. A. and Gelman, S. A. (eds), *Mapping the Mind*. Cambridge: Cambridge University Press.

Craig, J. 1997: Imagination and creativity in autism and Asperger's Syndrome, Unpublished PhD Thesis, University of Cambridge.

Cross, I. 2003: Music and evolution: causes and consequences. *Contemporary Music Review*, 22(3), 79–89.

Currie, G. and Ravenscroft, I. 2002: *Recreative Minds*. Oxford: Clarendon Press.

Darwin, C. reprinted 1995: *The Descent of Man and Selection in Relation to Sex*, 2nd edn). London: The Folio Society.

Daston, L. 1998: Fear and loathing of the imagination in science. *Daedalus*, 127, 73–95.

Dawkins, R. 1993: Viruses of the mind. In Dahlbohm, B. (ed.) *Dennett and His Critics: Demystifying Mind*. Oxford: Blackwell.

Fauconnier, G. and Turner, M. 2002: *The Way We Think: Conceptual Blending and the Mind's Hidden Complexities*. New York: Basic Books.

Finke, R. A., Ward, T. B. and Smith, S. M. (eds) 1992: *Creative Cognition: Theory, Research and Application*. Cambridge, MA: MIT Press.

Freud, S. 1911/1961: Formulations of the two principles of mental functioning. In J. Strachey (ed. and trans.), *The Standard Edition of the Complete Psychological Works of Sigmund Freud*, Vol. 12. London: Hogarth Press.

Hobson, P. 2002: *The Cradle of Thought*. London: Macmillan.

Hume, D. 1739/1740: *A Treatise of Human Nature*, edn of L. A. Selby-Bigge, 1888. Oxford: Oxford University Press.

Leslie, A. 1987: Pretense and representation: the origins of 'theory of mind'. *Psychological Review*, 94, 412–426.

Leslie, A. and Roth, D. 1993: What autism teaches us about metarepresentation. In Baron-Cohen, S., Tager-Flusberg, H., and Cohen, D. (eds), *Understanding Other Minds: Perspectives from Autism*. Oxford: Oxford University Press.

Marchand, L. A. (ed.) 1982: *Lord Byron: Selected Letters and Journals*. London: John Murray.

Martindale, C. 1999: Biological bases of creativity. In Sternberg, R. J. (ed.), *Handbook of Creativity*. Cambridge: Cambridge University Press.

Mithen, S. 1996: *A Prehistory of the Mind*. London: Thames and Hudson.

Neisser, U. 1967: *Cognitive Psychology*. New York: Appleton-Century-Crofts.

O'Connor, K. P. and Aardema, F. 2005: The imagination: cognitive, pre-cognitive, and meta-cognitive aspects. *Consciousness and Cognition*, 14, 233–256.

Oxford English Dictionary 1989: prepared by Simpson, J. A. and Weiner, E. S. C. Oxford: Clarendon Press.

Paulus, P. B. and Nijstad, B. A. (eds) 2003: *Group Creativity: Innovation through Collaboration*. Oxford: Oxford University Press.

Redfield Jamison, K. 1993: *Touched with Fire: Manic-depressive Illness and the Artistic Temperament*. New York: Simon and Schuster Free Press Paperbacks.

Robertson, I. 2002: *The Mind's Eye*. London: Bantam.

Roth, I. 2004: Imagination. In Gregory, R. L. (ed.), *The Oxford Companion to the Mind*, 2nd Edn. Oxford: Oxford University Press.

Ryle, G. 1949: *The Concept of Mind*. London: Hutchinson.

Simonton, D. K. 2002: Creativity. In Snyder, C. R. and Lopez, S. J., *Handbook of Positive Psychology*. Oxford: Oxford University Press.

Suddendorf, T. and Fletcher-Flinn, C. M. 1997: Theory of mind and the origins of divergent thinking. *Journal of Creative Behaviour*, 31, 59–69.

Thomas, N. J. T. 1999a: Imagination. In Eliasmith, C. (ed.), *Dictionary of Philosophy of Mind* [WWW document] URL http://www.artsci.wustl.edu./philos/MindDict/imagination.htm

Thomas, N. J. T. 1999b: Are theories of imagery theories of imagination? An active perception approach to conscious mental content. *Cognitive Science*, 23(2), 207–245.

Tomasello, M. 2000: *The Cultural Origins of Human Cognition*. Cambridge, MA: Harvard University Press.

White, A. R. 1990: *The Language of Imagination*. Oxford: Blackwell.

Wittkower, R. 1973: Genius: Individualism in art and artists. In Wiener, P. P. (ed.), *Dictionary of the History of Ideas*, vol. 2. New York: Charles Scribner's Sons, 297–312.

Wordsworth, W. 1850/1971: *The Prelude*. Edn of J. C. Maxwell. Harmondsworth: Penguin.

Part I

EVOLUTION OF THE IMAGINATION

1

Seven Steps in the Evolution of the Human Imagination

STEVEN MITHEN

Abstract. The archaeological and fossil record suggests that our hominid ancestors and relatives possessed imaginative abilities that were used in day-to-day living, such as when thinking about hunting and gathering or making stone tools. But there is no evidence that they possessed a creative imagination, the type we usually associate with activities such as art and science. This was most likely restricted to *Homo sapiens*, which appear in the fossil record at *c.*200,000 years ago. I argue that the creative imagination of *H. sapiens* was the product of a long evolutionary history within which seven key developments in biological and cultural evolution can be identified: the evolution of theory of mind capacities, a distinctively human life history and domain-specific intelligences, the origin of music, language, and cognitive fluidity, the extension of mind by material culture, and the appearance of sedentary farming communities.

INTRODUCTION

MODERN HUMANS ARE THE PRODUCT OF at least six million years of evolution since the divergence of our lineage from that which led to the chimpanzee. It is normally assumed that the common ancestor was similar to the chimpanzee because of the ape-like brain size and post-cranial characteristics of the earliest hominid species, which date to 4.5 million years ago. If the common ancestor also had a mind like the chimpanzee, we must conclude that its imaginative powers were limited. How limited depends on how one defines the imagination and interprets the behaviour of chimpanzees today.

Proceedings of the British Academy **147**, 3–29. © The British Academy 2007.

One aspect of the human imagination is that which we use every day, perhaps every waking moment of every day, as we go about our business of working and living. We constantly have to make decisions and often do so by imagining future scenarios from the choices we have available—which type of sandwich to have for lunch, whether to travel by car or train, who to sit next to at a dinner party. Such decisions involve both foresight and the contemplation of alternatives. It is conceivable that chimpanzees, and perhaps a wide variety of other animals, have an imagination of this type as it appears to be synonymous with consciousness, which some ethologists and philosophers claim is found among many species (Dawkins 1993). So when a chimpanzee manufactures a stick for extracting termites, it may be engaged in foresight—imagining the process of poking the stick into a hole, extracting it, and then licking off the termites—and it may also be contemplating alternative choices, with regard to either what size of stick to use or whether to eat termites or fruit. It may, however, entirely lack both foresight and ability to select between options—we simply do not know, and perhaps we can never know. We can, however, be confident that chimpanzees lack another aspect of the modern human imagination, that which we can refer to as the creative imagination.

Precisely how the 'creative imagination' should be defined is a subject of considerable debate, as explained by Ilona Roth in her Introduction. The definition I will adopt for this chapter is the ability to combine different types of knowledge and ways of thinking to create novel ideas and insights. This is the imagination we invoke when attempting to explain how Shakespeare was able to write his plays or Darwin discovered the principles of natural selection. Although none of us may aspire to, let alone attain, such achievements, we all have the potential for a creative imagination and may employ this to write poetry, to paint pictures, and to undertake science.

While a creative imagination is unique to modern humans in the world today, the extent to which a creative imagination of this type was found in other now extinct species of the *Homo* genus remains unclear. The Neanderthals, for instance, had brains as large, and in some cases larger, than modern humans and survived for more than 250,000 years during the Middle and Later Pleistocene in Europe, a period of considerable environmental change and stress (Stringer and Gamble 1993; Gamble 1999). They made complex stone artefacts, engaged in big game hunting, and undertook some activities that required black pigment (D'Errico and Soressi 2002). All of these required the 'day-to-day' type imagination, such as for planning hunts and selecting nodules of stone for tool making. Whether they also possessed a creative imagination is more contentious as there is no unambiguous evidence for this in the material record, although some artefacts remain subject to debate (e.g. the Berekhat Ram 'figurine', see D'Errico and Nowell 2000).

The likely use of black pigment provides us with the greatest dilemma as this could be for utilitarian or symbolic purposes—my own preference is for the former (Mithen 2005).

The apparent absence of Neanderthal rock art and other signs of a creative imagination might reflect the absence of the necessary social and economic conditions for this to have become manifest rather than the absence of the requisite cognitive abilities in this species. Alternatively, the relevant evidence may simply have not survived or not yet been discovered. I think it more likely, however, that Neanderthals lacked the cognitive capacity for a creative imagination. More generally, it appears from the archaeological evidence that the creative imagination is restricted to the single member of the *Homo* genus that has survived today, *Homo sapiens*, and that the survival and pre-eminent success of our species can be partly explained by the possession of that imagination (Mithen 1996, 2001). In this regard, *Homo sapiens*'s ability to think more creatively about making tools, exploiting the landscape, constructing social relationships, and even about supernatural worlds of gods and ice age spirits enabled them to out-compete the Neanderthals and all other members of the *Homo* genus for resources. This creative imagination also enabled them not only to survive but also to flourish through the harshest periods of environmental change during the late Pleistocene.

Although restricted to modern humans, the creative imagination cannot have simply sprung from nothing with the origin of *Homo sapiens* at *c.*200,000 years ago. It is the product of a long evolutionary history, involving both biological and cultural change that began soon after the divergence of the two lineages that led to modern humans and the African apes. I believe we can identify seven critical steps in that process (Figure 1.1). I will describe these in chronological order and with some indication of the dates at which they most likely emerged. This is, however, a simplification: each of the steps should be thought of as a gradual evolutionary process rather than a discrete event, although a process that often provided the necessary foundation for the next step towards the modern creative imagination.

STEP 1: A THEORY OF MIND, 6.0–1.8 MILLION YEARS AGO

Having a 'theory of mind' is normally understood as possessing the ability to know that other individuals have beliefs and thoughts that are different from one's own. It is, however, a complex and rather ill-defined phenomenon, or rather one open to multiple interpretations (Carruthers and Smith 1996). There are likely to be at least two elements which are logically separable: (1) the ability to know that other people have beliefs and thoughts (i.e. that they have minds) and (2) that these beliefs and thoughts are different from one's

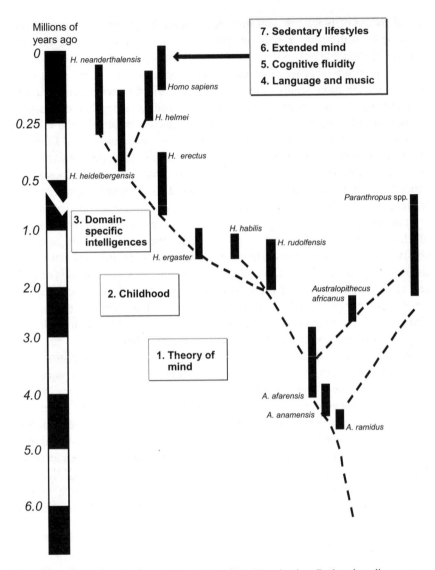

Figure 1.1. Seven steps in the evolution of the human imagination. Rather than discrete steps, these should be envisaged as evolutionary processes occurring over long periods of time, especially with regard to theory of mind and the evolution of childhood.

own. In principle, one could know that other people have beliefs and thoughts, but assume that these thoughts are the same as one's own, i.e. lack the ability to take the perspective of another.

Since the late twentieth century, there has been a considerable amount of research on theory of mind in the fields of developmental psychology, ethology and palaeoanthropology (e.g. Byrne and Whiten 1988, 1992; Whiten 1991; Povinelli 1993, 1999; Baron-Cohen *et al.* 1999). Although widely recognized as being a critical cognitive ability for modern humans, considerable disagreement continues as to what constitutes a theory of mind, hence the title of Carruthers and Smith's 1996 book *Theories of Theories of Mind.* Similarly, the evolutionary history of theory of mind capacity and how this relates to the evolution of language remains unclear (Dunbar 1998; Mithen 1999).

Despite some strong claims, it has proved surprisingly difficult to establish whether chimpanzees have a theory of mind (Whiten and Suddendorf in Chapter 2). The tests undertaken on human infants and children rely to a large extent on the children telling the experimenter what they think. Because chimpanzees are unable to communicate with humans in a sufficiently detailed and unambiguous fashion, trying to establish what they know about another chimpanzee's mind is inevitably fraught with methodological problems. Increasingly complex experimental designs have been formulated without any widespread agreement. My own view is that chimpanzees have a limited, if any, understanding of other minds. As such, the fully fledged theory of mind capacity seen in humans must have evolved after the split with the common human–chimpanzee ancestor at around six million years ago.

One useful manner in which to characterize varying theory of mind capacities within and across species is by using the terminology of 'orders of intentionality' as introduced by the philosopher Daniel Dennett (1996). By having a belief, one has a 'single order of intentionality'. If I were to have a belief about your belief, I would have a second order of intentionality. If I were then to have a belief about what you believe a third party believes, I would have a third order of intentionality. And so on. In this respect chimpanzees would be designated as having one, or at very most two, orders of intentionality, while modern humans routinely engage in thoughts that require four and sometimes even five orders of intentionality. Dunbar (2004) has argued that one can track the evolution of increasingly greater levels of intentionality through the fossil record by estimating brain size; this relies on his 'social brain' hypothesis—that the enlargement of the brain during human evolution has been a consequence of selection for ever more complex social skills.

A major problem with Dunbar's (2004) social brain hypothesis is that it requires Neanderthals and other large-brained non-modern *Homo* to have the same order of intentionality as *Homo sapiens*, even though their patterns of behaviour and thought appear quite different from the archaeological evidence they have left behind.

Although Dunbar's arguments are unlikely to be correct for the latter stages of human evolution, they appear to have great veracity for the earlier

stages—for the appearance of the first members of *Homo* with brains significantly larger than the *c.*450 cm³of modern chimpanzees. *Homo habilis* and
Homo rudolfensis had brain sizes that exceeded 500 cm³ and 700 cm³ respectively, while some specimens of *Homo ergaster* at 1.75 million years ago (mya)
had brain capacities that exceeded 850 cm³ (Johanson and Edgar 1996),
although other specimens remained below 700 cm³ (Gabunia *et al.* 2000). In
light of a correlation between group size and brain size among modern non-
human primates, Dunbar argues that these earlier species were living in larger
groups than modern-day chimpanzees and that this would have created selective pressures for theory of mind capacities and enhanced communication
(Dunbar 1996, 2004; Aiello and Dunbar 1993). With more individuals to
potentially compete and cooperate with, those who could anticipate the
behaviour of other individuals by 'imagining' what they were thinking would
have gained a reproductive advantage.

    The need to live in relatively large groups can be explained by the environ-
mental changes of the early Pleistocene, most notably the increasing open-
ness of the landscapes and the increased role of hunting and scavenging
(Aiello and Wheeler 1995). Nevertheless, it is not easy to identify a clear
cause and effect as there would have been feedbacks between brain size,
diet, technology, and social interaction as illustrated in Figure 1.2. That the
evolution of a theory of mind—perhaps up to three orders of intentionality—was a central feature of this nexus of interactions during the early
Pleistocene is a persuasive argument. This would have provided the first step
in the evolution of the imaginative capacities of the modern human mind.

STEP 2: THE EVOLUTION OF HUMAN LIFE HISTORY, 2.0–0.1 MILLION YEARS AGO

Human life history contrasts with that of modern apes in several key respects
(Bogin 1999, 2003). First, there is the phenomenon of 'secondary altriciality'.
This refers to the combination of a long gestation and the period of relative
infant helplessness after birth during which brain size continues a foetal rate
of growth for another year. Second, there is the developmental phase that we
call 'childhood', which lies between weaning and the capacity to feed and
protect oneself. Third is the adolescent growth spurt, and fourth the extensive
post-menopausal lifespans that are uniquely found in the human species. For
chimpanzees and gorillas, death follows soon after the loss of reproductive
capacity.

    Each of these life-history phases can be argued to contribute to the fully
evolved and developed human imagination. Infancy and childhood are periods when brain growth occurs within cultural settings that will influence the

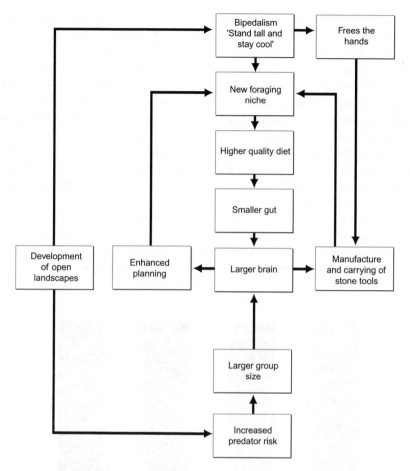

Figure 1.2. Feedbacks between dietary change, brain size, tool making, and bipedalism during the Early Pleistocene, based on arguments in Aiello (1996) and Aiello and Wheeler (1995).

type of neural networks that are formed; adolescence is a period of adult capabilities but usually without adult responsibilities; the elderly play a key role in the transmission of information to younger generations and are able to draw on long-term experience when formulating ideas.

The evolution of modern human life-history patterns has become a key topic within evolutionary anthropology during the past decade, but remains little understood (Thompson *et al.* 2003) (Figure 1.3). Bogin (1999) has suggested that childhood first appears with the earliest *Homo*, and adolescence only with *H. sapiens*, while O'Connell *et al.* (1999; Hawkes *et al.* 1997) have argued that post-menopausal lifespans evolved with *H. erectus*. Although the specific details remain to be established, it is clear that changing life-history patterns were partly a consequence of the evolutionary conflicts

arising from bipedalism, large body, and large brain size (Key and Aiello
1999). To be effective, bipedalism requires a narrow pelvis, which then
inhibits the birthing of large-brained infants. To resolve this, humans have
evolved to give birth to infants whose skulls literally become temporally
deformed during birth, and who then continue their foetal rates of growth.
The necessary outcomes are relatively helpless infants that require considerable investment from nursing mothers. The probable reason why post-
menopausal lifespans may have been selected is that those infants and
nursing mothers who gained support from their grandmothers/mothers had
increased chance of survival, while the grandmothers would have been
enhancing the survival of their own genes into the next generation
(O'Connell *et al.* 1999).

   If the evolution of large brains and bipedalism are indeed related to the
appearance of a human-like life-history pattern, then the key species of
concern is *H. ergaster*, appearing in the fossil record at *c.*1.8 million years
ago. The KNM-WT 15000 fossil, otherwise known as the Nariokotome boy

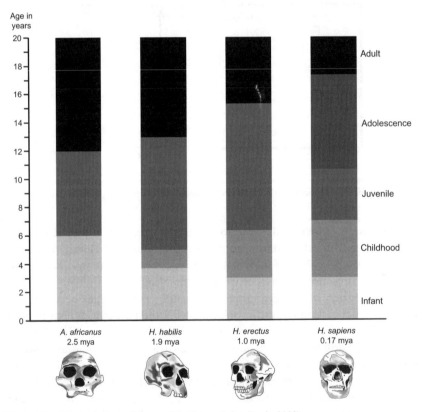

Figure 1.3.   The evolution of human life history (after Bogin 2003).

(Walker and Leakey 1993), is the best-preserved specimen. Ageing this specimen has been difficult with estimates ranging between 11 and 15 years old, but it evidently had a modern human stature and bipedal gait. This specimen had a cranial capacity of 880 cm^3, estimated to have reached 909 cm^3 as an adult—twice as large as that of a chimpanzee but only equivalent to a modern human child. As such, *H. ergaster* appears to be a species without any useful living primate analogy, and with a life history that was most probably intermediary between modern humans and modern apes (Krovitz *et al.* 2003).

Quite when the fully modern human life history evolved remains unclear. Recent studies of the growth lines on Neanderthal teeth indicate that Neanderthal children may have grown up significantly quicker than those of modern humans (Rozzi and Bermudez de Castro 2004) and hence it may have been only in the *H. sapiens* lineage after the split from the Neanderthals that the fully modern human life-history pattern evolved with an extended period of childhood. This may well have a causal relationship to what appears to be the unique presence of symbolic thought and language in *H. sapiens* and the overall greater capacity for imagination in our species when compared with all of our hominid ancestors and relatives.

Several hominid species existed after 1.6 million years ago, all characterized by modern stature, bipedalism, and relatively large brains. These include *H. ergaster*, *H. erectus*, *H. heidelbergensis*, *H. neanderthalensis*, and, more controversially, *H. antecessor* and *H. helmei*. While these exhibit significant differences in their cranial and post-cranial morphology and may have had different technological traditions, and linguistic and cognitive capacities, I believe they are sufficiently similar to be referred to by the collective term 'Early Humans'. Hence in the following text I will use this term for the bipedal, large-brained hominids of the Middle and late Pleistocene, with the exclusion of *H. sapiens*.

STEP 3: DOMAIN-SPECIFIC INTELLIGENCES, 2.0–0.25 MILLION YEARS AGO

Human creative imagination is often characterized as the ability to combine different types of knowledge and ways of thinking to create novel ideas and insights. This is closely related to Boden's (2004) ideas regarding the exploration and transformation of conceptual spaces and provides the basis for the term 'blending' as used by Turner (1996, and Chapter 10), as well as my own notion of cognitive fluidity (Mithen 1996). It can only happen, of course, if human minds have ideas and ways of thinking to combine in the first place. In this regard, a key step in the evolution of the human imagination was the appearance of cognitive domains or mental modules dedicated to specific types of thought and behaviour that provided the 'raw material' for imaginative thoughts.

We have already considered one of these—the theory of mind. Understanding that other people have minds and that these minds may contain beliefs and desires different from one's own is likely to rely on specialized neural networks that have evolved/developed for this specific purpose and that can be usefully referred to as a mental module. This module appears to be inhibited from working in those individuals who suffer from autism as they typically have an impaired ability to empathize with other individuals (Baron-Cohen 2003; Roth in Chapter 13). Similarly, language, music, and mathematics appear to rely on distinct mental modules as each of these capacities can be lost while leaving other mental capacities unaffected (Pinker 1997; Butterworth 1999; Peretz and Coltheart 2003; Mithen 2005). Some evolutionary psychologists argue that the whole of the human mind is constituted by mental modules that originally evolved to 'solve problems' that our ancestors faced in Pleistocene and earlier environments (Cosmides and Tooby 1994). In contrast, some development psychologists argue that mental modularity is principally a product of brain maturation in cultural contexts (Karmiloff-Smith 1992).

The fossil and archaeological records appear to support the evolutionary psychologists' position that distinct ways of thinking and stores of knowledge evolved in human ancestors to address problems they faced in their social and natural environments (Mithen 1996; Figure 1.4)—although how these are moulded by the developmental context remains unclear. By 1.4 mya two key events in human evolution had occurred. First, hominids had dispersed out of Africa. Precisely when, why, and how this was achieved remains unclear (Straus and Bar-Yosef 2001; Mithen and Reed 2002). Crucial evidence comes from the site of Dmanisi in Georgia, where *H. ergaster* was present by 1.7 mya. *H. ergaster/H. erectus* fossils have been claimed in Java by 1.8 mya.

The most startling of recent discoveries has been the discovery of a dwarfed species of *Homo* in the Indonesian island of Flores, designated as *Homo floresiensis* (Brown *et al.* 2004). The known species date to the late Pleistocene but stone artefacts from the island have been dated to 0.8 million years (Morwood *et al.* 1998) and suggest colonization by *H. erectus*. Isolation of this species on a small island in the absence of predators may have then led to a reduction in its size, a process that has been frequently recorded for mammals such as elephants and deer.

The evidence from Flores Island raises two key issues regarding creativity. First, does the 0.8 million year old arrival of *H. erectus* on that island (if that is indeed what happened) indicate more advanced levels of technology and

Figure 1.4. Domain-specific intelligences of the Early Human mind (after Mithen 1996).

planning, such as to build sea-going rafts, than have previously been attrib-uted to this species? I suspect not, as the necessary isolation of *H. erectus* on Flores to result in the dwarfing process suggests a lack of regular movement between the islands. I suspect they arrived on Flores by some form of eco-logical accident rather than through deliberate purpose. The second issue raised by Flores is more profound: the brain size of *H. floresiensis* was less than 400 cm^3—less than that of a modern-day chimpanzee. And yet this species appears to have manufactured stone artefacts and engaged in what amounts to big game hunting. What we do not understand, of course, is what happens to the structure and organization of brains during an evolutionary process of size reduction as would have occurred during the evolutionary transition from *H. erectus*.

With regard to Europe, a *Homo* presence has been claimed in southern Spain at 1.8 mya, but the most persuasive early date is 0.8 mya at Atapuerca in northern Spain. By 500,000 years ago, *Homo heidelbergensis*— a descendant of *H. ergaster*— was established in northern Europe and engaged in big game hunting. Throughout this period of the Middle Pleistocene there were substantial degrees of climatic and environmental change at all time scales ranging from millennium to seasonal, requiring hominids to constantly adjust their behavioural strategies (Gamble 1999). In light of such factors, I have previously argued that early humans must have possessed equivalent levels of zoological and botanical knowledge to that found among historically documented hunter-gatherers (Mithen 1996). I have referred to this as a 'natural history intelligence' and argued that this is the basis for intuitive biology as found in modern human infants and the universal principles of ethnobiological classification that are found among modern humans (Atran 1990; Berlin 1992).

The cognitive processes required for making complex stone artefacts are as different from those required for interaction with the social world as those required for interaction with the natural world. By complex stone artefacts I refer to those that involve platform preparation, forward planning, mental rotation, and a general understanding of fracture dynamics. None of these is necessarily required for the manufacture of Oldowan flakes, choppers, and scrapers. They are essential, however, for the production of handaxes and cleavers that appear in the African archaeological record from 1.4 mya, and become a pervasive element of the Middle Pleistocene archaeological record throughout the Old World. Further levels of technical knowledge and skill are evident after 250,000 years ago when tools using the Levallois technique are present (see Van Peer 1992). This technique was particularly mastered by the Neanderthals in Europe and Western Asia and is as sophisticated as any methods used to produce stone artefacts by modern humans. The use of the Levallois technique or bifacial knapping methods most likely required a bundle of mental modules, some of which had specifically evolved for manipulating physical objects and some of which may have been part of a general intellectual capability. This so-called 'technical intelligence' (Mithen 1996) arguably provides the intuitive physics found in modern human infants today (Spelke 1991).

With the evolution of specialized mental modules for interaction with the social, natural, and physical worlds, Early Humans had acquired what I have called a 'domain-specific' mentality. That is, they possessed cognitive processes as complex and diverse as found within modern humans but these were restricted to specific domains of activity. Hence theory of mind and the other cognitive processes involved in social interaction, which I have referred to as forming a 'social intelligence', could not be used for thinking about animals or material objects, just as those for making stone tools could not be used for interacting with other people. It is only this type of mentality, I believe, that can explain both the sophisticated types of Early Human behaviour that are evident from the archaeological record, and the cultural conservatism that existed throughout the Middle and much of the later Pleistocene (Mithen 1996).

With regard to the imagination, the domain-specific mentality of Early Humans would have allowed imaginative thoughts within but not across cognitive domains. So *H. heidelbergensis* or *H. neanderthalensis* could have imagined the future behaviour of animals when planning their hunting activity, or imagined what would happen to a nodule of stone when struck with a hammerstone or piece of antler. But they were severely constrained at imagining how to design new stone artefacts to improve their hunting activity as that would have required simultaneously drawing on cognitive processes within their natural history and technical intelligences. Consequently we find the production of a small number of general-purpose hunting implements rather than a wide range of specialized artefacts as produced by modern humans, whether in prehistory or recent times. Nevertheless, those intelligences and the cognitive modules they contained ultimately provided the 'raw materials' for the creative explosion that happened with the origin of modern humans in Africa after 200,000 years ago. A necessary ingredient for that was the evolution of fully modern language.

STEP 4: THE ORIGIN OF LANGUAGE AND MUSIC, 250,000–100,000 YEARS AGO

There has been a remarkable surge of interest in the evolution of language, and more recently music since 1995. Particularly influential have been ideas regarding the significance of gesture (Hewes 1973; Corballis 2002) and 'gossip' (Dunbar 1996), while Bickerton (e.g. 1995, 2003) has promoted the idea of a proto-language constituted by words but lacking grammatical rules. The volume by Christiansen and Kirby (2003) demonstrates the diversity of opinions and approaches that now exist regarding language origins, and the absence of a consensus for when and why this occurred. Similarly, there are diverse views regarding the origin of music (Wallin *et al.* 2000), and its relationship, if any, with the origin of language (Brown 2000).

One of the core reasons for the continuing disagreements about the origin of language is that the fossil and archaeological records appear to tell quite different stories. The fossil record indicates that by the time of

H. neanderthalensis (0.25 mya), and probably even *H. heidelbergensis* (0.5 mya) a vocal tract effectively indistinguishable from our own had evolved (Arensburg *et al.* 1989; Clegg 2001); moreover, owing to the complexity of hominid behaviour prior to 0.5 mya, it is difficult to explain the enlargement of the brain after that date if this was not to provide additional neural circuitry for complex vocal communication. On the other hand, the absence of symbolic artefacts in the archaeological records of pre-modern humans, the limited indications of site structure, and the extreme levels of cultural conservatism, appear to be clear signs that behaviour had not been mediated by language (Mithen 1996, 2005).

There is, therefore, a paradox regarding the origin of language: the fossil evidence suggests that it was relatively early so that *H. heidelbergensis* and *H. neanderthensis* as well as *H. sapiens* would have been language-using species, while the archaeological record suggests that language was restricted to *H. sapiens* alone. This paradox can be resolved by recognizing that the communication systems of Early Humans were considerably more complex than has previously been appreciated—quite different from the vocalizations of present-day non-human primates—but were nevertheless fundamentally different from modern human language.

My own research argues that the Early Human communication system had five key characteristics—see Mithen (2005) for a detailed discussion of the following arguments. First, I follow Wray (1998, 2000) in believing that the utterances were holistic rather than compositional. Modern human language is compositional in the sense that utterances are constituted by words, each with their own individual meanings, which are combined with others by grammatical rules to create additional, emergent, meanings. Wray has argued that proto-language was quite different: each utterance had a single meaning and was not formed out of sub-units that could be combined in alternative ways. This is a quite different form of proto-language from that proposed by Bickerton and is one that is far more compatible with the archaeological record. As Wray (1998, 2000) noted, a holistic proto-language would predict the type of cultural conservatism that appears to be characteristic of the Early Humans.

The second feature of the Early Human communication system is that it was predominantly manipulative rather than referential in nature. By this I mean that it acted to manipulate the behaviour of others rather than to change their knowledge of the world. Third, it is likely to have been multimodal, in the sense that gesture, facial expression, and body language in general played a key role in the communication system. Although these continue to play an important role in modern human language (Beattie 2003), I suspect that this is substantially diminished from that found among Early Humans.

Early Human communication is also likely to have been musical in character, making significant use of variation in pitch, melody, and rhythm to influence the meaning of the holistic utterance. This music-like feature of Early Human communication would have been present in both Early Humans' vocal utterances and their body movements, the latter facilitated by the evolution of bipedalism, which considerably enhanced the expressive use of the human body. The fifth and final character of Early Human communication would have been mimesis, as argued by Donald (1991). The imitation of animals, specific people, events, and so forth, by both gesture and the voice, is likely to have been essential to the holistic utterances of Early Humans, and is a further feature that continues within language today, especially with regard to gesture.

In light of its likely characteristics of being holistic, manipulative, multi-modal, musical, and mimetic, I have referred to Early Human communication system by the acronym of Hmmmmm (Mithen 2005). This appears to have provided Early Humans with a sufficiently complex and sophisticated system to be compatible with their evolved vocal tracts and large brains, but one that lacked the two key features of modern human language—words and grammatical rules.

Hmmmmm provided the evolutionary precursor of both language and music (Figure 1.5). Wray (2000) has used the term 'segmentation' for the evolutionary process by which people began to place specific meanings on syllables or phonemes that had been parts of holistic utterances, while Kirby (2000, 2002) has shown how a compositional language can evolve out of a holistic communication system if the latter has to pass through a cultural learning bottleneck. Such processes most likely transformed the Early Human communication systems of the immediate ancestor of *H. sapiens* in Africa, sometimes referred to as *H. helmei* (Foley and Lahr 1997; McBreaty and Brooks 2000), or perhaps of the earliest *H. sapiens* themselves, soon after modern humans evolved at around 200,000 years ago (White *et al.* 2003; Ingman *et al.* 2000). The dating of the most recent mutation of the *FOXP2* gene (Enard *et al.* 2002), one that is known to be related to grammar (Lai *et al.* 2001; Bishop 2002), to this time period provides additional and quite independent support that this date marks the appearance of language.

This date would have also been the origin of music, which can be conceived as the remnants of Hmmmmm once its language-like elements had been removed into the newly evolved language systems (Mithen 2005). The remainder was a complementary communication system that specialized in expressing emotions and facilitating group bonding, roles that are still achieved by music today.

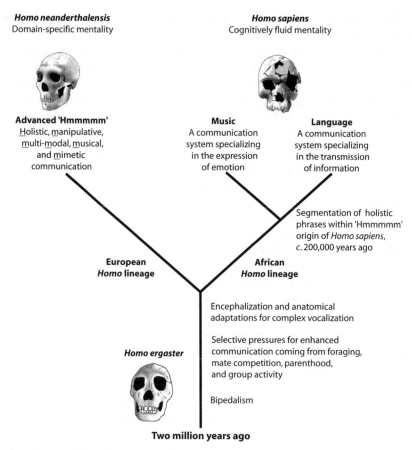

Homo neanderthalensis
Domain-specific mentality

Homo sapiens
Cognitively fluid mentality

Advanced 'Hmmmmm'
Holistic, manipulative, multi-modal, musical, and mimetic communication

Music
A communication system specializing in the expression of emotion

Language
A communication system specializing in the transmission of information

Segmentation of holistic phrases within 'Hmmmmm' origin of *Homo sapiens*, *c.* 200,000 years ago

European *Homo* **lineage**

African *Homo* **lineage**

Encephalization and anatomical adaptations for complex vocalization

Homo ergaster

Selective pressures for enhanced communication coming from foraging, mate competition, parenthood, and group activity

Bipedalism

Two million years ago

'Hmmmm': "A prelinguistic 'musical' mode of thought and action", John Blacking (1973)

Figure 1.5. The evolution of Hmmmmm, music, and language (after Mithen 2005).

STEP 5: COGNITIVE FLUIDITY, 250,000–100,000 YEARS AGO

Language enables a far more efficient exchange of information and ideas between individuals than could have been achieved by Hmmmmm. Clarke (1997) has characterized language as enabling the development of a distributed cognition which creates ideas that could never have been entirely conceived within a single human mind alone. This is not, however, the only or perhaps even the most significant impact of language on the human capacity for imagination. As I argued in *The Prehistory of the Mind* (Mithen 1996), language would have 'delivered' cognitive fluidity to the human mind in terms of enabling ways of thinking and stores of knowledge to be shared between cognitive domains, that created new types of thoughts and cultural behaviour

(Figure 1.6). Carruthers (2002) supports such claims. He argues that the 'imagined sentences' we create in our minds allow the outputs from one intelligence/domain/module to be combined with those of another and thereby creates new types of conscious thoughts (Figure 1.7).

It is with language, therefore, that the 'raw material' of the human imagination—those cognitive domains I described above—could be exploited to enable types of ideas that were quite beyond the mentality of Hmmmmm-using Early Humans. Here I am specifically thinking of ideas such as imaginary entities that are part-human and part-animal, which require the combination of natural history and social knowledge (Boyer 1994; Mithen 1996). Such entities play an important role in the first representational images known to human kind, are frequently found in prehistoric rock art traditions, and are pervasive in the religious systems of hunter-gatherer communities.

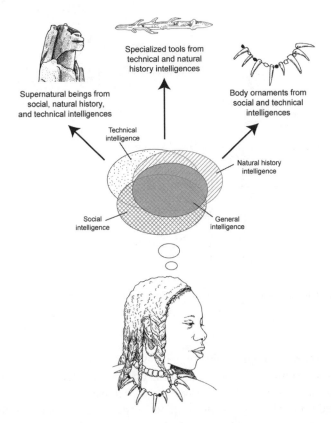

Figure 1.6. Cognitive fluidity—by integrating stores of knowledge and ways of thinking from previously isolated intelligences, humans were able to generate new types of thoughts resulting in new types of cultural behaviour (after Mithen 1996).

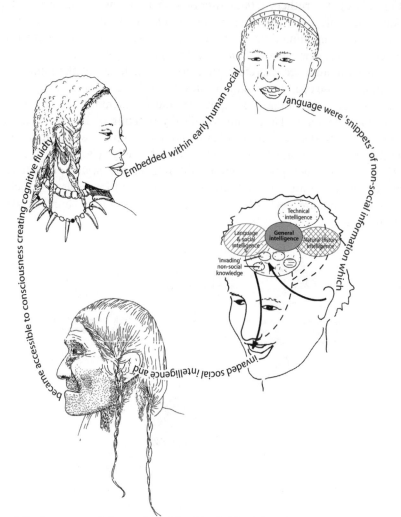

Figure 1.7.   Language and the creation of cognitive fluidity (after Mithen 1996).

Other types of cognitively fluid ideas would have had more practical value. By combining aspects of natural history and technical intelligence, modern humans were able to design more effective hunting weapons, those specialized for exploiting specific animals in specific circumstances. Similarly, by combining social and technical intelligences, modern humans were able to use material objects to mediate their social interactions, the earliest evidence of which are the shell beads found at Blombos Cave dating to c.70,000 BP (Henshilwood *et al*. 2004), the site which also has the earliest traces of symbolic designs (Henshilwood *et al*. 2002). More generally, cognitive fluidity provided the possibility for metaphorical and symbolic thought; it enabled the development of art, religion, and science.

STEP 6: THE EXTENDED MIND,
250,000 YEARS AGO TO THE PRESENT

The types of thoughts made possible by cognitive fluidity lacked a solid evolutionary basis within the mind, since the powers of human memory are limited. They could be effectively maintained, manipulated, and transmitted only by down-loading such thoughts into material culture, initially paintings and sculpture and then, 5000 years ago, writing. Such material extensions of thought are critical to the human imagination and should be conceived as part of the human mind itself.

Ideas about religious beings are the most striking example. These require the combination of different types of knowledge (Boyer 1994; Mithen 1996); sometimes that of people and animals to create ideas about supernatural beings, as reflected, for instance, in the ice age carving of the 'man-lion' from Hohlenstein-Stadel; sometimes those of people and material objects for animistic ideas, such as statues of the Virgin Mary that shed tears. Explaining such ideas to other people when they lack any material representation is difficult because there is no natural basis for such ideas within the mind. If I were to describe to you a man I knew who was married but kept having love affairs with other women, you could readily imagine the type of person he is, and accurately 'guess' a lot more about his character. You can do this because ideas about relationships and emotions are deeply embedded in the human mind as part of our evolved social intelligence. If, however, I describe to you a man I know who can move through walls, has infinite knowledge, and does not need to eat, you could not make additional inferences about the character of that man and would have difficulty in passing such 'knowledge' on to a third party, just as I would have difficulty in maintaining the idea of that 'man' within my own mind. To overcome the limitations of the human mind in this regard, I can down-load that thought into either a representational or a symbolic image to act as a 'cognitive anchor' (Mithen 1998; Figure 1.8).

Day (2004) draws on such arguments and those put forward by Clarke (1997, 2003), Dennett (1996), and Hutchins (1995) to conclude that:

Material culture as
a cognitive anchor for
'unnatural ideas'

Cognitively fluid minds
with 'unnatural ideas'
(e.g. about supernatural beings)

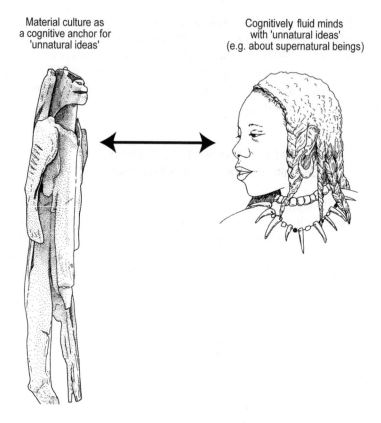

Figure 1.8. The extended mind, illustrated with the 'man-lion' figure from Hohlenstein-Stadel, *c.*30,000 BP.

> The broad spectrum of rituals, relics, scriptures, statues and buildings typically associated with religious traditions are no longer seen as mere ethnographic icing on the computational cake. Rather than thin cultural 'wrap arounds' that dress up real cognitive processes going on underneath, they begin to look like central components of the relevant machinery of religious thought . . . Without these elaborate layers of cognitive technology the gods would be, to one degree or another, unthinkable. (Day 2004, pp. 116–117)

This is one aspect of what is more generally referred to as the extended mind (Clarke and Chalmers 1998), and includes the use of material culture as a means to overcome the limits of human memory (notebooks, diaries, North-American Indian calendar sticks) and computational thought (calculators and computers). The material culture extensions to the mind are the cognitive equivalent of how clothes, architecture, and technology extend human physical and physiological abilities.

Using material culture in this way is a consequence of cognitive fluidity, and enabled a fundamental increase in human imaginative powers. It reached its apotheosis with writing as this enabled ideas to be off-loaded and then transmitted in quite explicit form across the generations so that our own imaginations can still be enhanced today by the thoughts of, say, Homer, Shakespeare and Darwin.

STEP 7: SEDENTARY FARMING LIFESTYLES, 11,600 YEARS AGO TO THE PRESENT

The right conditions for the invention of writing emerged with sedentary and farming lifestyles. These created the social and economic need for this form of communication, which originally appeared as a means of record keeping. Farming was necessary to provide an economic surplus to support the specialists who learnt to read and write, and who manufactured the crafts for exchange. Sedentary lifestyles provided a massive expansion of the extended mind by enabling the construction of monumental architecture and the accumulation of material possessions. Sedentism and farming do not always go hand-in-hand (see Mithen 2003 for a review). The archaeological record provides evidence for sedentary hunter-gatherers, such as the Jomon of Japan (Habu 2004) and the Early Natufian of Western Asia (Bar-Yosef 1998); similarly the cultivation of crops and animals in Mesoamerica and the Andes appears to have occurred within mobile lifestyles (Smith 1995), while pastoralists are by definition non-sedentary farmers. While developments in the prehistoric sedentary hunter-gatherer and mobile-farmer communities were impressive, it was the combination of sedentism with farming that had the most striking cultural impacts—the rise of 'civilization'.

This is most dramatically illustrated in south-west Asia. The earliest settled farming communities arose in the Early Holocene within the western and central parts of the Fertile Crescent, represented by the Pre-Pottery Neolithic B villages and towns, such as Jericho and 'Ain Ghazal in the Jordan Valley and Çayönü in South-East Turkey (Bar-Yosef and Meadow 1995; Mithen 2003). These were present by 10,000 years ago and had witnessed remarkable cultural growth by 8500 years ago as evident from the artworks and architecture at sites such as Çatalhöyük in Anatolia (Mellaart 1967) and 'Ain Ghazal (Schmandt-Besserat 1998) in the Jordan Valley. Although not sustained in the Jordan Valley because of environmental degradation, this development of towns and trading formed the cultural precursor to the first civilizations of Mesopotamia, where writing originated.

The development of such sedentary and farming lifestyles increased the imaginative potential of modern human minds. This was partly due to the

specialists, supported by economic surplus, who could initially devote themselves to craft skills and eventually to poetry, mathematics, music, and science;
it was also partly due to the manner in which minds were further extended,
initially by monumental architecture and artworks, then by writing, and
today by such devices as film and the Internet.

CONCLUSION

Another palaeoanthropologist might have included additional or alternative
steps to the modern human imagination to the seven that I have proposed.
It was traditionally argued, for instance, that the first Oldowan stone tools
marked a cognitive Rubicon in human evolution. The knowledge we have
today regarding the diversity of tool use by chimpanzees questions the
extent to which the Oldowan marks such as a threshold, and indicates that
a distinctive *Homo* technology only begins with the Acheulian.

As bipedalism has implications for the evolution of language, social
organization, subsistence, and technology (Aiello 1996), this might legit-
imately be included as a critical step in its own right rather than merely playing
a supporting role in the evolution of the imagination. Similarly, one might
wish to emphasize reflexive consciousness rather than cognitive fluidity, or
writing itself rather than the more general notion of an extended mind.

Two points need emphasis before I conclude. First, although I have
characterized the evolution of the imagination as consisting of seven steps, I
do not mean to imply that this was a progressive process in the sense of a
gradual improvement of the human condition. The extent and complexity of
human imagination certainly have increased, but these have had deleterious
as well as beneficial effects for humankind. The modern human imagination
has created not only the great works of literature, art, and science, but also
the holocaust and global terrorism. Second, in the evolutionary scenario I
have proposed, 'imagination' itself is rarely, if ever, subject to selection. Its
evolutionary history is principally as a by-product of other developments:
modern human life history evolved under conditions of changing body and
brain size but fortuitously created conditions in which brains matured under
cultural influences and provided children with 'time to play'; language was
most likely selected to enhance the communication of information but fortuitously led to the creation of new ideas by enabling cognitive fluidity. The
modern human creative imagination was largely an accident of evolutionary
history.

In conclusion, I would stress that the human imagination is the product
of an evolutionary process that did not cease with the appearance of
anatomically modern humans or language. Its evolution is ongoing today,

not necessarily in the biological sense but in the continued invention of new types of material culture that augment and extend the powers of the human mind—in Andy Clarke's (2003) terms we are now 'natural born cyborgs'. Whether there are limits to the human imagination, and whether we have reached these limits is quite unknown. But it is telling, I believe, that just a few decades ago palaeoanthropologists could not have possibly imagined the wealth of data that we now have about the origins of modern humans and complex society, especially with regard to the contribution that genetics now makes to the study of the human past. Nor that they should be able to have such a fruitful exchange of ideas with psychologists, philosophers, musicologists, and linguists on the nature of the human imagination as occurred at the conference from which this volume has derived.

Note. I am most grateful to Ilona Roth for organizing the Imaginative Minds conference, for inviting me to participate and for providing comments on a draft of this contribution.

References

Aiello, L. C. 1996: Terrestriality, bipedalism and the origin of language. In Runciman, W. G., Maynard-Smith, J. and Dunbar, R. I. M. (eds), *Evolution of Social Behaviour Patterns in Primates and Man.* Oxford: Oxford University Press, 269–290.

Aiello, L. C. and Dunbar, R. I. M. 1993: Neocortex size, group size, and the evolution of language. *Current Anthropology,* 34, 184–193.

Aiello, L. C. and Wheeler, P. 1995: The expensive-tissue hypothesis. *Current Anthropology,* 36, 199–220.

Atran, S. 1990: *Cognitive Foundations of Natural History: Towards an Anthropology of Science.* Cambridge: Cambridge University Press.

Arensburg, B., Schepartz, L. A., Tillier, A. M., Vandermeersch, B. and Rak, Y. 1989: A reappraisal of the anatomical basis for speech in Middle Palaeolithic hominids. *American Journal of Physical Anthropology,* 83, 137–156.

Bar-Yosef, O. 1998: The Natufian culture in the Levant, threshold to the origins of agriculture. *Evolutionary Anthropology,* 6, 159–177.

Bar-Yosef, O. and Meadow, R. H. 1995: The origins of agriculture in the Near East. In Price, T. D. and Gebauer, A. B. (eds), *Last Hunters–First Farmers: New Perspectives on the Transition to Agriculture.* Santa Fe, New Mexico: School of American Research Press, 39–94.

Baron-Cohen, S. 2003: *The Essential Difference.* London: Allen Lane.

Baron-Cohen, S., Tager-Flusberg, H. and Cohen, D. J. (eds) 1999: *Understanding Other Minds: Perspectives from Developmental Cognitive Neuroscience.* Oxford: Oxford University Press.

Beattie, G. 2003: *Visible Thought: The New Language of Body Language.* London: Routledge.

Berlin, B. 1992: *Ethnobiological Classification: Principles of Categorization of Plants and Animals in Traditional Societies*. Princeton, NJ: Princeton University Press.

Bickerton, D. 1995: *Language and Human Behaviour*. Seattle: University of Washington Press.

Bickerton, D. 2003: Symbol and structure: A comprehensive framework for language evolution. In Christiansen, M. H. and Kirby, S. (eds), *Language Evolution*. Oxford: Oxford University Press, 77–93.

Bishop, D. V. M. 2002: Putting language genes in perspective. *Trends in Genetics*, 18, 57–59.

Blacking, J. 1973: *How Musical is Man?* Seattle: University of Washington Press.

Boden, M. 2004: *The Creative Mind: Myths and Mechanisms*, 2nd edn. London and New York: Routledge.

Bogin, B. 1999: *Patterns of Human Growth* (2nd edn). Cambridge: Cambridge University Press.

Bogin, B. 2003: The human pattern of growth and development. In Thompson, J. L., Krovitz, G. E. and Nelson, A. J. (eds), *Patterns of Growth and Development in the Genus* Homo. Cambridge: Cambridge University Press, 14–44.

Boyer, P. 1994: *The Naturalness of Religious Ideas: A Cognitive Theory of Religion*. Berkeley: University of California Press.

Brown, P., Sutikna, T., Morwood, M. J., Soejono, R. P., Jatmiko, Wayhu Saptomo, E. and Rokus Awe Due 2004: A new small-bodied hominin from the Late Pleistocene of Flores, Indonesia. *Nature* 431, 1055–1061.

Brown, S. 2000: The 'musilanguage' model of human evolution. In Wallin, N. L., Merker, B. and Brown, S. (eds), *The Origins of Music*. Cambridge, MA: Massachusetts Institute of Technology, 271–300.

Butterworth, B. 1999: *The Mathematical Brain*. London: Macmillan.

Byrne, R. W. and Whiten, A. (eds) 1988: *Machiavellian Intelligence: Social Expertise and the Evolution of Intellect in Monkeys, Apes and Humans*. Oxford: Clarendon Press.

Byrne, R. W. and Whiten, A. 1992: Cognitive evolution in primates: evidence from tactical deception. *Man (N.S.)*, 27, 609–627.

Carruthers, P. 2002: The cognitive functions of language. *Brain and Behavioral Sciences*, 25, 657–726.

Carruthers, P. and Smith, P. (eds) 1996: *Theories of Theories of Mind*. Cambridge: Cambridge University Press.

Christiansen, M. and Kirby, S. (eds) 2003: *Language Evolution*. Oxford: Oxford University Press.

Clarke, A. 1997: *Being There: Putting Brain, Body and World Together Again*. Cambridge, MA: MIT Press.

Clarke, A. 2003: *Natural Born Cyborgs: Minds, Technologies, and the Future of Human Intelligence*. Oxford: Oxford University Press.

Clarke, A. and Chalmers 1998: The extended mind. *Analysis*, 58, 7–19.

Clegg, M. 2001: The Comparative Anatomy and Evolution of the Human Vocal Tract. Unpublished Thesis, University of London.

Corballis, M. 2002: *From Hand to Mouth: The Origins of Language*. Princeton, NJ: Princeton, University Press.

Cosmides, L. and Tooby, J. 1994: Origins of domain specificity: the evolution of functional organization. In Hirschfeld, L. A. and Gelman, S. A. (eds), *Mapping the Mind*. Cambridge: Cambridge University Press, 85–116.

Dawkins, M. S. 1993: *Through Our Eyes Only?: The Search for Animal Consciousness*. Oxford: Freeman.

Day, M. 2004: Religion, off-line cognition and the extended mind. *Journal of Cognition and Culture*, 4, 101–121.

Dennett, D. 1996: *Kinds of Minds: Towards an Understanding of Consciousness*. New York: Basic Books.

Donald, M. 1991: *Origins of the Modern Mind*. Cambridge, MA: Harvard University Press.

Dunbar, R. 1996: *Grooming, Gossip and Language*. London: Faber and Faber.

Dunbar, R. I. M. 1998: Theory of mind and the evolution of language. In Hurford, J. R., Studdert-Kennedy, M. and Knight, C. (eds), *Approaches to the Evolution of Language*. Cambridge: Cambridge University Press, 92–110.

Dunbar, R. 2004: *The Human Story*. London: Faber and Faber.

Enard, W., Przeworski, M., Fisher, S. E., Lai, C. S., Wiebe, V., Kitano, T., Monaco, A. P. and Paabo, S. 2002: Molecular evolution of *FOXP2*, a gene involved in speech and language. *Nature*, 418, 869–872.

D'Errico, F. and Nowell, A. 2000: A new look at the Berekhat Ram figurine: Implications for the origin of symbolism. *Cambridge Archaeological Journal*, 10, 123–167.

D'Errico, F. and Sorressi, M. 2002: Systematic use of pigment by Pech de l'Aze Neanderthals: Implications for the origin of behavioural modernity. Palaeoanthropology Society Meeting Abstracts, 19–20 March, Denver, Co. *Journal of Human Evolution*, 42 (3), A13.

Foley, R. and Lahr, M. M. 1997: Mode 3 technologies and the evolution of modern humans. *Cambridge Archaeological Journal*, 7, 3–36.

Gabunia, L. Vekua, A., Lordkipanidze, D., Swisher, C. C. III., Ferring, R., Justus, A., Niordadze, M., Tvalchrelidze, M., Antón, S. C., Bosinski, G., Joris, O., de Lumley, M.-A., Majsuardze, G. and Mouskhelishvlli, A. 2000: Earliest hominid cranial remains from Dmanisi, Republic of Georgia: taxonomy, geological setting and age. *Science*, 288, 1019–1025.

Gamble, C. 1999: *The Palaeolithic Societies of Europe*. Cambridge: Cambridge University Press.

Habu, J. 2004: *Ancient Jomon of Japan*. Cambridge: Cambridge University Press.

Hawkes, K., O'Connell, J. F. and Blurton-Jones, N. G. 1997: Hadza women's time allocation, offspring provisioning, and the evolution of long post-menopausal life-spans. *Current Anthropology*, 38, 551–578.

Henshilwood, C. S., d'Errico, F., Yates, R., Jacobs, Z., Tribolo, C., Duller, G. A. T., Mercier, N., Sealy, J. C., Valladas, H., Watts, I. and Wintle, A. G. 2002: Emergence of modern human behavior: Middle Stone Age engravings from South Africa. *Science*, 295, 1278–1280.

Henshilwood, C., d'Errico, F., Vanhaeren, M., van Niekerk, K. and Jacobs, Z. 2004: Middle stone age shell beads from South Africa. *Science*, 304, 404.

Hewes, G. 1973: Primate communication and the gestural origin of language. *Current Anthropology*, 14, 5–24.

Hutchins, E. 1995: *Cognition in the Wild*. Cambridge, MA: MIT Press.

Ingman, M., Kaessmann, H., Paabo, S. and Gyllensten, U. 2000: Mitochondrial genome variation and the origin of modern humans. *Nature*, 408, 708–713.

Johanson, F. D. and Edgar, B. 1996: *From Lucy to Language*. London: Weidenfeld and Nicolson.

Karmiloff-Smith, A. 1992: *Beyond Modularity: A Developmental Perspective on Cognitive Science*. Cambridge, MA: MIT Press.

Key, C. A. and Aiello, L. C. 1999: The evolution of social organization. In Dunbar, R., Knight, C. and Power, C. (eds), *The Evolution of Culture*. Edinburgh: Edinburgh University Press, 15–33.

Kirby, S. 2000: Syntax without natural selection: How compositionality emerges from vocabulary in a population of learners. In Knight, C., Studdert-Kennedy, M. and Hurford, J. R. (eds), *The Evolutionary Emergence of Language: Social Function and the Origins of Linguistic Form*. Cambridge: Cambridge University Press, 303–323.

Kirby, S. 2002: Learning, bottlenecks and the evolution of recursive syntax. In Briscoe, E. (ed.), *Linguistic Evolution through Language Acquisition: Formal and Computational Model*. Cambridge: Cambridge University Press, 173–204.

Krovitz, G. E., Thompson, J. L. and Nelson, A. J. 2003: Hominid growth and development from australopithecines to Middle Pleistocene Homo. In Thompson, J. L., Krovitz, G. E. and Nelson, A. J. (eds), *Patterns of Growth and Development in the Genus* Homo. Cambridge: Cambridge University Press, 271–292.

Lai, C. S. L., Fisher, S. E., Hurst, J. A., Vargha-Khadem, F. and Monaco, A. P. 2001: A forkhead-domain gene is mutated in a severe speech and language disorder. *Nature*, 413, 519–523.

McBreaty, S. and Brooks, A. 2000: The revolution that wasn't: A new interpretation of the origin of modern human behavior. *Journal of Human Evolution*, 39, 453–563.

Mellaart, J. 1967: *Çatal Hüyök: A Neolithic Town in Turkey in Anatolia*. London: Thames and Hudson.

Mithen, S. J. 1996: *The Prehistory of the Mind: A Search for the Origin of Art, Science and Religion*. London: Thames and Hudson.

Mithen, S. J. 1998: The supernatural beings of prehistory and the external storage of religious ideas. In Renfrew, C. and Scarre, C. (eds), *Cognition and Material Culture: The Archaeology of Symbolic Storage*. Cambridge: McDonald Institute of Archaeological Research, 97–106.

Mithen, S. J. 1999: Palaeoanthropological perspectives on the theory of mind. In Baron-Cohen, S., Flusberg, H. T. and Cohen, D. (eds), *Understanding Other Minds: Perspectives from Autism and Cognitive Neuroscience*. Oxford: Oxford University Press, 494–508.

Mithen, S. J. 2001: The evolution of the imagination: An archaeological perspective. *SubStance*, 30, 28–54.

Mithen, S. J. 2003: *After the Ice: A Global Human History, 20,000–15,000 BC*. London: Weidenfeld and Nicolson.

Mithen, S. J. 2005: *The Singing Neanderthal: The Origins of Music, Language, Mind and Body*. London: Weidenfeld and Nicolson.

Mithen, S. J. and Reed, M. 2002: Stepping out: A computer simulation of hominid dispersal from Africa. *Journal of Human Evolution*, 43, 433–462.

Morwood, M. J., O'Sullivan, P. B., Aziz, F. and Raza, A. 1998: Fission-track ages of stone tools and fossils on the east Indonesian island of Flores. *Nature*, 392, 173–176.

O'Connell, J. F., Hawkes, K. and Blurton-Jones, N. G. 1999: Grandmothering and the evolution of *Homo erectus*. *Journal of Human Evolution*, 36, 461–485.

Peretz, I. and Coltheart, M. 2003: Modularity of music processing. *Nature Neuroscience*, 6, 688–691.

Pinker, S. 1997: *How the Mind Works*. New York: Norton.

Povinelli, D. J. 1993: Reconstructing the evolution of the mind. *American Psychologist*, 48, 493–509.

Povinelli, D. J. 1999: *Folk Physics for Apes*. Oxford: Oxford University Press.

Rozzi, R. and Bermudez de Castro, J. M. 2004: Surprisingly rapid growth rate in the Neanderthals. *Nature*, 428, 936–939.

Schmandt-Besserat, D. 1998: 'Ain Ghazal 'monumental' figures. *Bulletin of the American Schools of Oriental Research*, 310, 1–17.

Smith, B. D. 1995: *The Emergence of Agriculture*. New York: Scientific American Library.

Spelke, L. 1991: Physical knowledge in infancy: Reflections on Piaget's theory. In Carey, S. and Gelman, R. (eds), *Epigenesis of Mind: Studies in Biology and Culture*. Hillsdale, NJ: Erlbaum, 133–169.

Stringer, C. B. and Gamble, C. 1993: *In Search of the Neanderthals*. London: Thames and Hudson.

Straus, L. and Bar-Yosef, O. 2001: Out of Africa in the Pleistocene. *Quaternaria International* 75.

Thompson, J. L., Krovitz, G. E. and Nelson, A. J. (eds) 2003: *Patterns of Growth and Development in the Genus* Homo. Cambridge: Cambridge University Press.

Turner, M. 1996. *The Literary Mind*: New York: Oxford University Press.

Van Peer, P. 1992: *The Levallois Reduction Strategy*. Madison, WI: Prehistory Press.

Walker, A. and Leakey, R. 1993: *The Nariokotome* Homo erectus *Skeleton*. Berlin: Springer Verlag.

Wallin, N. L., Merker, B. and Brown, S. (eds) 2000: *The Origins of Music*. Cambridge, MA: Massachusetts Institute of Technology.

White, T. D., Asfaw, D., DeGusta, D., Tilbert, H., Richard, G. D., Suwa, G., Howell, F. C. 2003: Pleistocene *Homo sapiens* from the Middle Awash, Ethiopia. *Nature*, 423, 742–747.

Whiten, A. (ed.) 1991: *Natural Theories of Mind: Evaluation, Development and Simulation of Everyday Mindreading*. Oxford: Blackwell.

Wray, A. 1998: Protolanguage as a holistic system for social interaction. *Language and Communication*, 18, 47–67.

Wray, A. 2000: Holistic utterances in protolanguage: the link from primates to humans. In Knight, C., Studdert-Kennedy, M. and Hurford, J. R. (eds), *The Evolutionary Emergence of Language: Social Function and the Origins of Linguistic Form*. Cambridge: Cambridge University Press, 285–302.

2

Great Ape Cognition and the Evolutionary Roots of Human Imagination

ANDREW WHITEN AND THOMAS SUDDENDORF

Abstract. We describe the evidence in great ape behaviour for two aspects, or 'levels', of imagination. The first is inventiveness: the capacity to generate novelty and diversity of behavioural responses to any given environmental circumstance. We report serendipitous evidence of such inventiveness arising in the course of our experimental studies of problem solving in chimpanzees. A review of related, systematic comparisons in the literature supports the conclusion that the great apes—chimpanzee, gorilla, and orang-utan—are particularly imaginative in this sense, in comparison with other primates.

The second sense of imagination refers to operating mentally in a 'pretend' world. This goes beyond inventiveness, for pretence involves holding in mind distinctions between the hypothetical and the real. There is intriguing but limited evidence for this aspect of imagination in great apes. We suggest it is a manifestation of a more general capacity for secondary representation, which may underwrite a cluster of cognitive abilities in great apes, including means–end reasoning, tracking invisible displacements of objects, and reading simple mental states, for which there is more robust, experimental evidence than exists for pretence per se.

Because these cognitive phenomena appear common to all the great apes, we infer that they characterized our common ancestor approximately 14 million years ago. Together, they would have formed a vital springboard for the later evolution of more far-reaching imaginative powers in human descendants.

Proceedings of the British Academy **147**, 31–59. © The British Academy 2007.

INTRODUCTION: STUDYING THE EVOLUTION OF IMAGINATION

THE IMAGINATIVE POWERS OF HUMANS clearly exceed those of other species: the products are all around us, some even speeding into deep space. Yet these powers did not spring from nowhere. Like so many of our most sophisticated mental attributes, their complexity suggests they did not arise *de novo*. Instead, they evolved on the shoulders of the distinctive psychology of our pre-human ancestors. This chapter attempts to delineate key characteristics of those critical ancestral foundations.

There are several different methodological routes to understanding how our imagination (or any other psychological phenomenon) has been shaped by its evolutionary past. One utilizes the archaeological record of our ancestors' past activities, as in the work of Mithen (1996, and Chapter 1). Such studies rely on the preservation of artefacts made by ancestral hominids, starting with stone tools around 2.6 million years ago, and they become more informative as the record becomes progressively richer. But to understand the significance of what went before, we must turn to different evidence, the subject of the present chapter.

We know from the combined genetic and fossil evidence that the ancestors of present-day humans and chimpanzees were African apes living about 5–6 million years ago (Waddell and Penny 1996; Wildman *et al.* 2003). The same evidence indicates that if we travelled yet further back in time we would meet, still in Africa, the ancestor that these species shared with the gorilla, and yet further back, the common ancestor of all the great apes, including the orang-utan (Figure 2.1). The lucky preservation of several descendent genera means that we can apply systematic methods to inferring aspects of the psychology of the ancestors (e.g. Byrne 1995; Suddendorf 2004). At the core of such comparative approaches lies the identification of common psychological characteristics, shared by all descendants of the particular ancestral stage of interest: for example, we might compare all the great apes, or perhaps only chimpanzees and humans, depending on precisely which ancestral node in the family tree we wish to cast our inferences back to, from about 14 up to 5 million years ago (see the two nodes circled in Figure 2.1).

This comparative approach thus complements the archaeological analyses in its time frame. Both approaches rely on empirical evidence from which inferences about the past are drawn, but the data used are quite different, each with its own benefits and drawbacks. The archaeological data are inherently historical—preserved remains of the past—but these provide only very indirect sources of information about such psychological characteristics as imagination. The primate evidence becomes 'historical' only through application of the comparative method, yet the data can speak much more directly about behaviour and psychology, because they are drawn from currently living animals, that we can study by close observation and experiment.

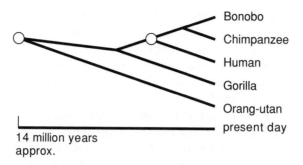

Figure 2.1. Based on the latest genetic analyses (Wildman *et al.* 2003), the lines that led to humans and to chimpanzees split 5.1 million years ago, the line that led to gorillas split 6.3 million years ago and orang-utans diverged 13.8 million years ago. The scale shown here would need to approximately double to accommodate the common ancestor of these great apes and old-world monkeys like the macaques and langurs represented in Figures 2.4 and 2.5. Old World monkeys split off from the line that led to modern great apes some 25.3 million years ago. The two nodes circled are referred to on page 32.

Note that this application of the comparative method is in principle applicable to progressively more ancient ancestors shared with yet broader groups. We could, for example, extend analyses to the ancestral mammal, or ancestral vertebrate state. We focus here on the 'ape window' in evolutionary time, in part because its recency gives it special relevance to humans, and in part because mounting evidence suggests that some particularly distinctive psychological phenomena relevant to the topic of imagination evolved within this window.

DISTINGUISHING TWO MAJOR ASPECTS OF IMAGINATION

Like many psychological terms used in both everyday life and cognitive science, 'imagination' is a somewhat flexible term that can refer to several loosely related phenomena. These need to be discriminated once our purpose is a more serious scientific scrutiny. In doing this comparatively, we find ourselves with a largely blank sheet, insofar as 'imagination' is not listed in the most comprehensive recent review of primate cognition (Tomasello and Call 1997). We suggest that for an evolutionary analysis, a useful distinction can be made between two senses of 'imagination' that, reassuringly, map respectively to the first two, versus the last, of the three everyday definitions of imagination recorded in *The Concise Oxford English Dictionary* (1. 'mental faculty forming images of external objects not present to the senses'; 2. 'fancy'; 3. 'creative faculty of the mind'), as well as to Roth's dissection of imagination in the Introduction to this volume.

The first and second of these definitions refer to imagining something that is not a currently perceived state of the world (the OED elaborates on 'fancy' as the 'faculty of calling up things not present'). The act of *pretending* is perhaps the clearest case of this, and indeed the two concepts may be used almost as synonyms, as when we describe a toddler's play extending to an 'imaginary' or 'pretend' world. Pretence, along with certain other phenomena we hypothesize to share its advanced cognitive substrate, is one of the two main senses of imagination we pick out for comparative analysis.

The other sense corresponds to the OED's third definition, which refers to what we will label *inventiveness*. We say an imaginative person is somebody with a highly inventive or generative mind, and this aspect of imagination is one we shall also examine comparatively. Related terms and concepts include creativity, innovation (Reader and Laland 2003), and response breadth (Sterelny 2003).

Although both pretence and inventiveness are relevant to the study of imagination, we suggest they are not of equal psychological status. Rather, invention is the broader phenomenon, with pretence a more rarefied subcategory. The emergence of pretend play in children, for example, is accompanied by a capacity to create mental worlds inhabited by a multitude of non-real beings, objects, properties, and narratives. The pretend aspect of imagination thus appears to invoke the inventive aspect to a greater or lesser extent. By contrast, inventiveness can exist without the specific capacity to pretend. Machine intelligence provides an illustration. Computational machines, from a simple random-number generator to those that compose poetry or music, can display various levels of structured inventiveness, and we can reasonably describe as more imaginative those that can compose the more elaborate poetic or musical repertoires: however, to achieve this they do not need a capacity for pretence. The same appears true for animal behaviour.

THE NATURE OF PRETENCE VERSUS INVENTIVENESS

The distinctions we are drawing, between imagination of pretend worlds versus imagination as inventiveness, need spelling out in a little more depth before we turn to the comparative, empirical data available. First, what are the minimum requirements, cognitively, of the act of pretence?

In a ground-breaking analysis, Leslie (1987) took the case of a child pretending that a banana is a telephone as an example. Leslie pointed out that the traditional formulation in the writings of Piaget and other developmental psychologists—that the child is mentally representing the banana as a telephone—cannot be the whole story. The primary function of perception and cognition, Leslie noted, is to represent reality as faithfully as possible, facilitating adaptive programmes of action. Simply representing the banana as a telephone would corrupt and confuse this basic function.

What is required instead is to hold on to the primary representation of the banana as banana, while in addition generating a second representation of it as telephone, which is specifically marked as 'pretend' and thus 'decoupled' or 'quarantined' (in Leslie's terms) from the constraints involved in primary, faithful representations of reality. Leslie described these pretend representations as *second-order representations*, on account of the way in which they appeared to be derived from primary representations. He noted that this formulation shows striking parallels with the processes labelled 'theory of mind', in which a primary mental state in one person is re-represented by a second, 'mindreading' individual, thus creating a second-order mental state (e.g. John *thinks* Jill *likes* him; or more closely paralleling the topic at hand, John *pretends* Jill *likes* him). Accordingly, Leslie hypothesized that the developmental origins of theory of mind, and its underlying capacity for second-order representation (also termed 'metarepresentation' by Leslie) may lie in the pretend play typically emerging in a child's second year.

Shortly later, Perner (1991) elaborated on these themes, developing a theoretical analysis from which we have drawn the framework for our appraisal of the data on great ape cognition. Perner proposed three stages in children's cognitive development. The first, limited to *primary representations*, functions to represent reality as faithfully as possible and characterizes infancy, whereas by the third phase, emerging around 4–5 years of age, the child becomes capable of what is for Perner now true *metarepresentation*, understanding the nature of representation sufficiently well to attribute mental states as complex as false beliefs to others (and indeed to oneself). In between, typically starting with the emergence of pretence midway through the second year, the child becomes capable of what Perner called *secondary representation*.

This intermediate period, and its cognitive achievements, were also of course the focal points of Leslie's analysis sketched above. However, Perner's formulation was subtly but importantly different from Leslie's. Perner argued that children at this stage become capable of operating with *multiple psychological models*, rather than the single primary model of reality that characterized their earlier mental life: this is how they can now class an object simultaneously as not only a (real) banana, but as a (pretend) telephone. But Perner argued it was incorrect to think that the pretend representation really (re-) represents the primary one, as implied by the term 'second-order' representation. Referring instead to *secondary representations,* he argued these are merely 'parasitic' on primary representations that exist in parallel. Moreover, Perner argued that the term 'metarepresentation' should be reserved for the much later emerging capacity to understand the nature of mental representation (and, thus, mis-representation).

The distinctions between the Perner and Leslie theories may seem abstruse or even nitpicking, yet they are important for our thinking about the development of imagination as manifested in young children, which in turn provides a framework for investigating imagination in other species. A feature of Perner's analysis we need to highlight is that the 'multiple models' hypothesis opens the way to explain not just pretence, but a suite of cognitive developments that emerge in the second year of children's lives. These, as Perner (1991) suggested, include domains as diverse as tracking hidden dis-placement of objects, means–end reasoning, mirror self-recognition, and understanding of simple mental states. To the extent these all rest on a capa-city for secondary representation, we have a much broader base of phenom-ena to examine in our investigations of imagination in great apes, reviewed later in this chapter. We suggest the evidence indicates that the great apes are distinctive among primates in the achievements they show across this broad panoply of psychological capacities.

So let us now turn to *inventiveness*, which we can define as the power to generate behavioural innovations. 'Creativity', 'generativity', 'innovation', and 'productivity' represent allied concepts, but these terms often carry other special meanings in the behavioural and cognitive sciences which leads us to avoid using them in this context.

Human beings are extraordinarily inventive. Through use of recursive cognitive processes, humans display an open-endedness in language (Chomsky 1988), thought (Corballis 2002), and action (combining objects and then using the combinations as objects in further manipulation, for example: Greenfield 1991) that may go a long way towards explaining our special status on this planet (e.g. Corballis 2003). Other species may not exhibit such a capacity for open-ended recursion, but they appear to vary significantly on a more basic dimension of inventiveness. Comparative psy-chologists' attempts to explicitly study this have mainly involved offering different species a range of objects to interact with and recording the range and diversity of responses made. How many innovations can the species *generate*? What innovations do they have the 'imagination' to produce? We shall review the results in relation to findings from some of our own recent research. Here, the point we emphasize is that this dimension of imagination seems logically independent of any capacity for pretence, or secondary repre-sentation in general. One species may exhibit a greater range of actions than does another when faced with the same set of target objects, without any signs of pretence (although it surely remains true that with pretence, an even greater range of actions—using a stick as a 'horse', or 'gun', for example—become possible). Inventiveness at some level, then, can be expected to be more widely apparent in the animal kingdom than secondary representation, just as we observe inventiveness in infants during the primary representation stage. Indeed, trial-and-error learning, which has been shown in all vertebrates studied and many invertebrates such as insects, would appear to rest on a certain degree of inventiveness to create the new directions for the 'trial' element of trial-and-error learning to take place. Nevertheless, relatively little research has explicitly attempted to scrutinize exactly what is occurring when an animal 'does something new'. We look at this in the next section.

INVENTIVENESS

A Case Study

We will illustrate the generativity in great ape behaviour we are alluding to through a set of serendipitous findings that arose in a study conducted by AW, with primary aims other than studying inventiveness. The objective of the study was to establish what form(s) of social learning occur in young chimpanzees faced with a new foraging task. A 'two-action' method was applied, in which some participants saw a model open an 'artificial fruit' (Figure 2.2) using one technique, while those in an alternative condition saw a different technique being used (Whiten 1998; Whiten et al. 1996). This permits a quantitative assessment of whether the young chimpanzees copied aspects of the particular alternative technique they had witnessed.

Figure 2.2. An artificial fruit being manipulated by a young chimpanzee. Constructed to study observational learning of food processing skills, such devices are designed to be analogues of natural foods, which require a series of 'shelling' manipulations to remove defences. The chimpanzee is grasping one of two bolts described in the text.

Subjects and Materials

The chimpanzees were wildborn youngsters, orphaned through such causes as the bushmeat trade, and living in a sanctuary in Guinea, West Africa. They were divided into two age groups, 3–5 and 5–7 years of age, half in each group being allocated to one of the two experimental conditions, with four individuals in each. At this age, such youngsters can be handled safely and relatively easily introduced into the required experimental configurations.

The artificial 'fruit' used is shown in Figure 2.2. It was designed to simulate the kinds of natural problems posed by protected foods such as hardshelled fruits, which may require a sequence of pulling, poking, tearing, and twisting actions to open them. The artificial fruit had a crucial additional feature: each 'defence' could be removed in one of two quite different ways. Given each subject saw only one of these modelled, imitative matching could subsequently be measured very effectively.

Procedure

The social learning experiment and its results will be reported fully elsewhere. For present purposes, it is sufficient to appreciate only certain essential components. Each chimpanzee was brought by a human caretaker to a cubicle screened from participants in the alternative condition, and watched repeated demonstrations by another familiar human, of how to open the fruit to gain the food reward inside. Participants in one condition saw the bolts pulled and twisted out, the pin turned before removal, and the handle turned to release the lid and allow the food to be removed. Those in the alternative condition saw the bolts poked out using an index finger, the pin twisted before removal, and the handle pulled up to release the lid. On each of five days, following their observations of the model, each participant was then allowed to tackle the fruit themselves.

Précis of Social Learning Results

Counts of participants' actions coded by researchers blind to what each chimpanzee had seen showed an extremely strong and statistically significant social learning effect for the older group. The effect of particular relevance to the analysis of inventiveness below is that those youngsters who had witnessed bolts being pulled and twisted out replicated these movements successfully and economically, rarely or never poking the bolts, whereas those that had watched poking performed massive numbers of pokes. In the first trial the average number of pokes for the four chimpanzees who had seen poking was 175; for the other group it was only 0.3. The record, 367 pokes, was achieved by a chimpanzee who had originally witnessed a poking model, during its fifth trial.

Each bolt requires only one strong poke to dislodge it, so why these inordinately high counts? The answer, evident in the videotaped behaviour, is that these youngsters typically poked the bolt, but did not push it right through. They would then poke it back, with the same effect. They continued to poke it back and forth until eventually, apparently by some lucky circumstance, it moved far enough to exit. For this reason the chimpanzees in the poke condition took around 20 times as long to open the fruit as their peers in the pull-and-twist condition, which appeared to come more naturally to these young chimpanzees. In some cases the 'poke' subjects worked determinedly for over 10 minutes, itself a testimony to the power of socially mediated learning. At any point these youngsters must have been capable of pulling out the bolts instead, as did their peers in the other group, but to do so did not occur to them.

Inventiveness

As we watched these extraordinary performances again and again, we began to notice an interesting phenomenon that had not been part of the planned analysis. As the older chimpanzees in the poke group failed to poke out the bolts, so they began to invent variations on this basic approach. Accordingly, we reviewed the totality of their efforts and drew up a catalogue of all the different ways they attempted to deal with the problem they had hit.

Figure 2.3 represents the combined output of the four chimpanzees concerned, classified hierarchically. This shows how a principal form of variation arises from whether one hand, or both, or some other body part, or a tool, is applied to the task; further variation then occurs at the level of the digits used, how each is used, and various symmetric or asymmetric combinatorial use of hands, digits, or objects. All together, these chimpanzees generated 38 different ways to approach the task of poking through the uncooperative bolts. On the basis of their peers' behaviour, they could have simply pulled the bolts out at any point: yet the variations they generated, as illustrated in Figure 2.3, were all on the 'theme' of poking-through, which they had watched a model successfully execute.

Discussion of Case Study Findings

Our central conclusion is that these data, delineating the invention of alternative actions in what became a problem-solving episode, demonstrate imagination—in the sense that these young chimpanzees were able to envisage a considerable diversity of different approaches. One kind of objection to this conclusion is that the term 'envisage', which we intend to imply some degree

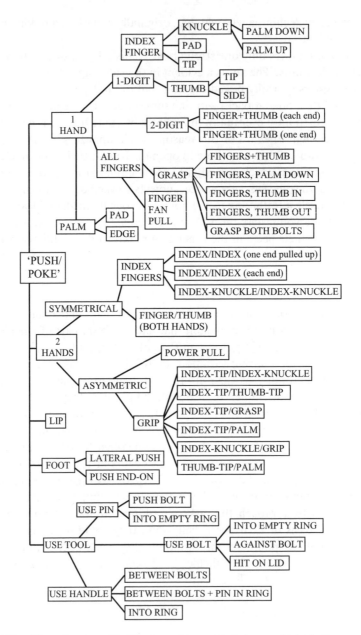

Figure 2.3. Alternative ways of poking or pushing out bolts in an artificial fruit, generated by four juvenile chimpanzees after witnessing demonstrations of this technique that employed only a single index finger. These varieties of technique were produced in the course of lengthy, frustrated efforts to dislodge the bolts.

of intentionality in the inventiveness observed, is unwarranted: are these chimpanzees not simply 'doing everything their bodies can do', having hit a certain problem? There are two answers to this objection, one focused on why the chimpanzees do not do more, and the other on why they do not do less. The first of these answers recognizes that participants did not simply generate outputs of the chimpanzee action repertoire at random: if they had, they would have pulled the bolts out. Instead, their efforts were directed to generating possibilities within their behavioural potentials that could complete the particular job of poking-through that they had seen demonstrated as a successful solution to the task at hand (as opposed to pulling through, done so easily in the other group). Some of these actions resembled ones they must have done before in other contexts, such as poking things with various varieties of digit configuration. But others were as novel as utilizing different components of the fruit they had already removed (pin, handle, a bolt) to push any remaining bolt. These actions seem more consistent with directed application of invention to the job of *poking* than with any merely 'random' trial and error.

Turning to why they produced as many variants as they did, we must emphasize that all these things the chimpanzees tried do need to be actively generated. What we mean by this can be appreciated if chimpanzees are compared with other quite different primates, such as monkeys, a variety of which have also taken part in our experiments with similar artificial fruits (scaled down appropriately for body size: Caldwell and Whiten 2004). In the case of marmosets, we were unable, despite sustained and varied efforts, even to have a model learn to dismantle a miniature version of the fruit shown in Figure 2.2 (Caldwell and Whiten 2004). In the case of baboons (yet unpublished), most participants could complete the task and showed some evidence of social learning, but their repertoire was markedly smaller than that shown in Figure 2.3. This, it must be acknowledged, cannot yet offer the systematic quantitative comparison needed here, because the problem faced was not explicitly replicated (in a real sense, the chimpanzees created their own problem by not poking the bolts right out, and a comparable situation for the baboons could not be assumed). However, we cannot ignore the fact that the baboons never tried to use task components as tools, a finding that parallels the observation that in the wild, baboons at Gombe watch potential models—chimpanzees—using tools to fish for termites, without ever attempting it themselves. Baboons are manipulative monkeys with hands much more like humans (including more similar thumb to finger ratios) than are those of great apes. It thus may be that the monkey/great ape difference is rather that the baboons *cannot imagine* doing all that the young chimpanzees can.

Accordingly our working hypothesis is that the fortuitous findings about inventiveness in these studies are telling us something very interesting about the behavioural manifestation of one dimension of imagination in chimpanzees, which appears to map well to its counterpart in humans.

Comparative Tests of Response Diversity

These fortuitous results emphasize the potential for more direct comparisons of the imaginative response of different species when confronted with essentially the same challenge. In the case of humans, individual differences in people's imaginative powers have been examined through a variety of formal 'creativity' tests, including some which focus on response diversity. For example, a series of standard objects (such as a cup) is presented, and the subject is asked to think of as many uses they can think of for each (Ward 1968). Human children begin to show some such capacity very early on in their pre-school years, but interestingly they improve significantly once they can pass false-belief tasks (Suddendorf and Fletcher-Flinn 1997, 1999). Passing false-belief tasks indicates the transition to metarepresentations in Perner's (1991) theory and also implies a capacity for recursion (i.e. beliefs about beliefs; see Corballis 2003). Children with autism, who fail such false-belief tasks, also do poorly on similar measures of creativity (Scott and Baron-Cohen 1996). However, even young children and children with autism show some aspects of creativity by generating multiple uses for target objects (see also Roth on autistic creativity in Chapter 13). So too do animals. Comparative psychologists have attempted to measure this by offering standard objects to a range of animals and comparing their behavioural, rather than verbal, responses.

One of the most cited classic studies of this kind was by Glickman and Sroges (1966), who presented sets of wooden blocks, dowels, chains, and rubber tubing to over 100 species of mammals and reptiles living in zoos. However, these authors recorded only the global categories of tactile and visual exploration, thus identifying differences perhaps more aptly described as curiosity than invention. They discovered that two groups, made up of 49 species of primates and 23 species of carnivores respectively, showed curiosity scores not significantly different from each other, but more than twice as high as the rodents and other mammalian taxa tested. Focusing on the great apes tested, and converting the data presented to the percentage of observation time spent in exploration, we find an average of 59% for the five great apes (chimpanzees and gorillas) tested, as against 29% for the other primates. Such curiosity might partly explain correlated differences in the truer measures of inventiveness we next examine, but we should note the converse hypothesis: that the great apes spend longer in exploration because they can imagine more things to do with the manipulanda.

This was more directly assessed in a striking yet now relatively neglected study by Parker (1974a,b) that logged the diversity of actions directed at the same manipulandum by orang-utans, gorillas, chimpanzees, and several species of monkey. The manipulandum was a knotted rope with one end secured outside the cage. Analysis of the action profiles applied to this was extremely detailed, differentiating body parts used (111 categories), actions performed (173 categories including pressing, throwing, rubbing, wadding, twisting, wrapping, and draping; for example, 11 different ways of 'wrapping' were recorded), and aspect of manipulandum contacted (8 categories). Parker compared several measures of diversity of response, of which two appear the most elaborate and instructive. One is the number of ways in which different body parts were combined with different actions. There were dramatic differences on this measure, shown as 'COMB', the third column of the four illustrated in Figure 2.4. Statistical tests showed that the scores for each of the great ape species were consistently greater than those for each of the other primates.

Parker also computed a more complex index of diversity that acknowledged that, for any two species showing the same number of combinations measured as above, the species for which predicting 'what the animal will do next' is more difficult shows the most diversity (and in relation to our own

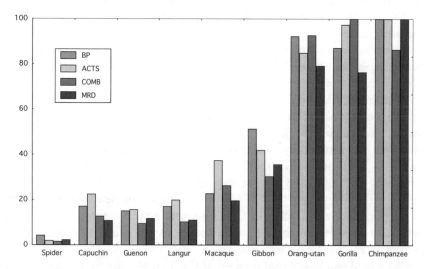

Figure 2.4. Four measures of 'creativity' in different primates' manipulations of a standard rope manipulandum (after data in Parker 1974a, Tables 3 and 4). Data have been recalculated as a percentage of the maximal score by any primate (the chimpanzee in most cases, the gorilla in one) to allow expression of all four measures on a single scale. BP = number of body parts applied, maximally 35; ACTS = number of different actions applied, maximally 40; COMB = product of BP × ACTS, MRD – 'manipulation response diversity' (see text for further explanation). Subjects included New World monkeys (spider monkey and capuchin), Old World monkeys (guenon, langur, macaque), a lesser ape (gibbon), and three great apes.

framework, perhaps the most imagination). This would be the species whose scores were more equally distributed over the actions used, as opposed to a species that focused mainly on just a few. Accordingly, exploiting Shannon and Weaver's (1964) index of uncertainty, Parker computed an index of manipulation response diversity that corrected for differences in frequencies of the actions used. The results of this more sophisticated approach are shown as 'MRD', the final column of the four illustrated in Figure 2.4. We find the same dramatic great ape/monkey differences as revealed by the 'raw combinations' analysis summarized above, although now it is the chimpanzee that turns in the highest score, rather than the gorilla. Torigoe (1985) extended Parker's approach in a study encompassing 74 primate species. Unfortunately, the data for individual species were not differentiated in a form that would allow direct comparison with Parker's results shown in Figure 2.4, but Torigoe's conclusion was similar; that the great apes were responsible for the greatest diversity of action/body-part/substrate combinations.

Great Ape Inventiveness

The data from the 'artificial fruit' case study and the systematic species comparisons outlined above are consistent with each other and complementary, for the case study represents a micro-analysis of the kind of action-diversity logged in the comparative studies. The two approaches also complement each other in a more fundamental way. In the comparative studies, the context can be described as essentially playful, rather than functional: a manipulable object is simply provided, eliciting a diversity of manipulative reactions. This provided replicable comparisons of response diversity between great apes and other species, but tells us nothing about the functional context in which this aspect of imaginative inventiveness has provided functional outcomes favoured by evolutionary selection pressures. In the artificial fruit experiments, by contrast, the chimpanzees were pursuing clear goals of opening a 'fruit' and obtaining food (consistent with this, exploration reduced markedly once food was obtained). In this context, the payoff of persistent generation of a diversity of approaches in tackling a specific problem was apparent in eventual success in copying the approach (apparently a difficult one, for these chimpanzees) that had been witnessed.

We would emphasize that because of the limited space available here, the focus of the analyses above has been the relatively narrow one of object-directed actions. Even here, we have not been able to discuss relevant work on behaviour in the wild, exemplified by Russon's (2003) analyses of innovation and creativity in orang-utans. It is also important to acknowledge that similar phenomena are likely in other domains, such as social life. Indeed, the

'Machiavellian intelligence' hypothesis is that the social world of anthropoid primates is inherently complex and the principal force selecting for greater intelligence (Byrne and Whiten 1988; Whiten and Byrne 1997). The social flux at the heart of this appears inherently likely to favour some kind of moment-to-moment creativity, getting an individual one step ahead in the social gaming at stake. Deception and countering deception represent an obvious arena (Whiten and Byrne 1988b; Byrne 2003). However, our grasp of exactly what is happening in such apparently tortuous social manoeuvring remains tentative, and does not yet afford the kinds of controlled comparative studies possible in the technical domain that we have therefore preferred to focus on above.

PRETENCE AND SECONDARY REPRESENTATION

Secondary Representation in Great Apes?

The concept of secondary representation was described earlier on page 35, together with its alignment with more advanced connotations of 'imagination' than implied by the raw inventiveness discussed above. As we noted, Perner (1991) proposed that secondary representation may explain not only 'imagining things' in pretence, but a range of cognitive achievements that typify a child's second year. These include representing hidden displacements of objects, means–end reasoning, interpreting external representations, mirror self-recognition, understanding emotions, and beginning to recognize mental phenomena such as intending and seeing.

Independently, Whiten (1996, 2000) and Suddendorf (1998, 1999) suggested that a capacity for secondary representation can make sense of a somewhat parallel set of psychological achievements in the great apes, for which evidence has accumulated in recent years. The convergence in our initially separate, yet matching, conjectures on this encouraged us to collaborate on a fuller, comprehensive survey of the available evidence for these correlations, spanning both children's cognitive development, and comparative psychology (Suddendorf and Whiten, 2001, 2003; see also Suddendorf 2004).

As we anticipated, we found that comparable studies had typically not been done in equal measure across the great ape species, let alone other primates. Most often, studies have been completed with chimpanzees but not the other great apes, although in some cases it is the chimpanzee for whom good comparable data remain lacking. Similarly, evidence is more patchy for some of the cognitive realms listed above than others, and the same is true for the confidence one can have in the conclusions that can be drawn. Indeed only for one realm, self-recognition in mirrors, could we say there was 'undisputed evidence' for the ability. Nevertheless, we concluded that overall, the data available fit the predicted pattern of concurrent achievements in the great apes, whereas evidence in other animals is absent or weak.

Pretence in Great Apes?

As we have suggested, pretence is the realm of secondary representation that constitutes the fullest expression of the power of imagination as we think of it in the human case. Accordingly, we consider it first in outlining the evidence for the various realms of secondary representation. Encouragingly, there is evidence to consider for each great ape species (Table 2.1). However, to some extent because of its very nature, the evidence is difficult to interpret in this realm, in comparison with some others.

For example, there are multiple records of young great apes that have been raised in close association with humans, playing with dolls or toy animals 'as if' the doll or toy were the real thing: for example, they may bathe the doll, or make the toy animal 'bite' themselves or others (e.g. Savage-Rumbaugh 1986; Matevia *et al.* 2002). Reviewing such studies, Call and Tomasello (1996) concluded that all great ape species have been recorded performing such activities. The question is, are they truly *pretending*? Tomasello and Call (1997) suggest a plausible counter-explanation is that these great apes are merely mimicking human behaviour, dipping the doll in a bath per-

Table 2.1.   Putative examples of pretence in great apes in the research literature.

Author	Genus	Type of evidence
Hayes (1951)	Chimpanzee	Imaginary pull-toy.
Patterson and Linden (1981)	Gorilla	Using sign language, describes rubber tube as 'elephant stink' and 'nose'.
Tanner (1985)	Gorilla	Treating shell as cigarette, then earring.
de Waal (1986)	Chimpanzee	Group share excited attention to non-existent object.
Savage-Rumbaugh (1986)	Chimpanzee	Empty jar and spoon treated as if full. Acting as if bitten by doll.
Savage-Rumbaugh and McDonald (1988)	Bonobo, chimpanzee	Hiding and revealing non-existent objects.
Whiten & Byrne (1988b); Byrne and Whiten (1990)	Chimpanzee, gorilla	Tactical deceptions: temporarily acting as if not aware of attractive hidden objects.
Jensvold and Fouts (1993)	Chimpanzee	Using sign language for tickling and other actions with dolls.
Wrangham & Peterson (1996)	Chimpanzee	Treating a log as an infant (in the wild).
Russon (2002)	Orang-utan	Elaborate deceptive episodes.
Matevia *et al.* (2002)	Gorilla	Treating dolls as if suckling, describing them drinking, animating their limbs.

haps, while a keen researcher looks on and adds the gloss 'you're giving him a bath!' One counter to such scepticism is to point out that other animals, including monkeys, who experience the same intimate relations with humans do not appear to perform such acts (Bolwig 1959; Bertrand 1969, 1976; Hopf 1970). Repeatedly putting a toy such as an alligator into the correct configuration for it to 'bite', for example, seems readily meaningful to great apes in a way it has not been recorded as doing in home-reared monkeys.

Leslie (1987) suggested what could count as stronger observational evidence. If a child is truly operating in a 'pretend mode' in which the significance of actions is systematically decoupled from reality, then logical implications of events quarantined within the pretend world should be followed through. Thus, if a truly empty cup containing pretend juice is inverted and the child proceeds to 'mop up' the implied spillage, this implies the child is operating in a pretend world, dependent on secondary representation.

Putative records of great ape pretence rarely involve this level of complexity; indeed, to our knowledge no author publishing putative cases of great ape pretence has so far embraced Leslie's idea and attempted systematically to discern such evidence in relation to the material they are dealing with. One of the best candidate cases remains Hayes' (1951) observations of the young chimpanzee Viki, described as repeatedly pulling along a pretend pull toy, as she did real ones. In these cases there was nothing there. On two separate occasions, a week apart, Viki acted as if getting the cord tangled around a plumbing knob. On one occasion 'placing both fists one above the other in line with the knob, she strained backward as in a tug of war. Eventually there was a little jerk and off she went again, trailing what to my mind could only be an imaginary pull toy'. This appears to be the kind of evidence Leslie asked for, although one must always wonder how much the great ape is 're-enacting' actions it performed previously, rather than inventing a more novel scenario. Whiten and Byrne (1991), Whiten (1996, 2000), and Suddendorf and Whiten (2001) describe other such cases scattered in the literature.

If the dolls and toy animals referred to above are props for true pretence, evidence of these same kinds of logical connotation being appreciated deserve the greatest attention. When the gorilla Koko, trained in sign language, was given an ape doll she hugged it and signed 'DRINK'. Perhaps because Koko is known sometimes to put such dolls to her nipple and sign 'DRINK', her caretaker asked (through voice and sign), 'Where does the baby drink?' Instead of putting the doll to her nipple, Koko responded by taking the doll's thumb to its mouth (forming what the researcher logged as the sign 'DRINK'), then the doll's index finger to its mouth (forming what the researcher logged as the sign for 'MOUTH'). She thus appeared to follow through a pretence-logic, that if this stuffed object is an ape, like other apes Koko knows, it could be made to 'reply' to the researcher's query. But this episode, one of many similar ones described by Matevia *et al.* (2002), also well illustrates the difficulties of interpretation of this material. Was Koko providing the strong evidence of pretence suggested by Leslie? Probably if similar actions were seen in a child, we would be content to say yes. But was she really signing, or just indicating the doll's mouth, happening to be holding its hand in hers? Was this a yet more elaborate mimicking of the kind Tomasello and Call (1997) suggested, of something she had seen her signing caretakers do with dolls (as, in fact, the researcher responded by doing, in the episode described).

Our judgement is that the corpus of putative pretend actions of great apes, although often weak when scrutinized individually, viewed as a whole does suggest an ability that appears rather different from anything seen in other primates and is sometimes consistent with the kind of pretence that signals secondary representation. That said, we must acknowledge that such behaviour is rare compared with the ubiquitous pretend play of young children; only two chapters of a recent whole volume devoted to the topic offered new data for great apes (Matevia *et al.* 2002; Russon 2002).

Other Competences Dependent on Secondary Representation

Fortunately, the evidence for certain other cognitive realms thought to call on secondary representations is clearer than it is for pretence. This is often because experimental tests have been applied, an approach less suited to the inherently spontaneous nature of pretence. Of the seven other realms reviewed by Suddendorf and Whiten (2001), the evidence on great ape cognition is most clear for five of them. Here we discuss these five in turn, examining the case for associating each with the concept of 'imagination'.

Tracking Invisible Displacements

In classic tests that Piaget (1954) developed in work with young children, an opaque container (which may be a hand) enclosing an object passes behind or within another (e.g. a blanket) and when it emerges is shown to be empty. In the middle of their second year human infants become able to respond appropriately, searching for the object where logically it must have remained. To do this, they need to go beyond the primary representations of what they have seen, to imagine the invisible past trajectory of the target object. In Suddendorf's (1999) terms, the infant evidences a 'collating mind' that can link a mental model of the current situation (primary representation: 'box empty') with a mental model of the past situation (secondary representation: 'object in box under blanket').

Experimental tests of this ability need to be careful to exclude the learn-ing of habitual search rules during repeated testing, a concern neglected by several early studies (Natale and Antinucci 1989). When additional tests con-trolling for such strategies were implemented, great apes have still tracked invisible displacements (gorilla, Natale *et al.* 1986; orang-utans, de Blois *et al.* 1998; Call 2001; and chimpanzees, Call 2001; Collier-Baker *et al.* 2006), while monkeys have not (e.g. de Blois and Novak 1994). Domestic dogs are the only other mammalian species to reportedly pass this test (Gagnon and Doré 1992), but a closer look reveals the use of simple search rules (Collier-Baker *et al.* 2004). Of the many mammalian species tested, only great apes have convincingly shown a capacity for tracking invisible displacement.

Means–End Reasoning

Mentally constructing a series of actions to solve a novel problem and attain a future goal also becomes apparent in a child's second year. This capacity, by its very nature, requires the ability to go beyond primary representations of the problem, imagining the hypothetical world within which newly created means will attain the ends desired.

Köhler's (1917) analyses of insight learning in chimpanzees' tool-making are frequently cited as textbook examples of this, but we should note that what Köhler emphasized was the great ape's insight that they had constructed a tool suitable to achieve a solution, rather than any clear 'foresight' (Tomasello and Call 1997). The actions looked more like trial-and-error (even if highly inventive). Better illustrations of secondary representation come from other studies. A chimpanzee studied by Döhl (1966, 1968, 1969) was presented with an array of ten locked boxes, the key to each box lying in another box and visible through a clear top. One box contained food. The chimpanzee was able to survey the array and then successfully choose the cor-rect series of boxes and the keys contained in them, to gain the food. In effect, this is a complex maze, solution to which required the great ape to imagine the alternative pathways and begin with the one that will work. Kawai and Matsuzawa (2000) report success in a chimpanzee's performance on a task physically very different (using a touch screen to identify a rising set of ordi-nal numbers), yet apparently requiring the same underlying capacity for sec-ondary representation. They concluded that the chimpanzee must have 'planned her actions before making her first choice' (Kawai and Matsuzawa 2000, p. 39).

Using External Representations

A symbol, say a picture, is an object in its own right as well as a representa-tion of something else. Research with search tasks, where a picture or scale model informs about the location of a target in a room, suggested that children begin to use such external representations for their searches only from about age 30 months onwards (e.g. DeLoache 1987). Given their performance on other indicators, we predicted that even younger children should have the basic representational resources to pass this task (Suddendorf and Whiten 2001). Since the representation and the real room are physically separate, to succeed the child must be able to imagine one while viewing the other, and collate the two representations. Using a procedure that avoids perseveration errors, Suddendorf (2003) recently demonstrated that indeed even 24-month-olds can use a photograph or video to find an object hidden in a represented room. This brings the time of emergence of this skill into the same period as the other indicators of early secondary representation we discuss (Suddendorf and Whiten, 2001).

Using this search task paradigm, chimpanzees have also been shown to have the representational means to use scale models to find hidden targets (Kuhlmeier *et al.* 1999; Kuhlmeier and Boysen 2001). Poss and Rochat (2003) provided further evidence that chimpanzees and one orang-utan could successfully use video to guide their search.

Mirror Self-recognition

Of all the abilities discussed here, recognizing oneself in a mirror is the most clearly documented. Relying on both spontaneous self-exploration and removal of experimentally placed marks on the face, evidence has been gained repeatedly for chimpanzees and orang-utans; and less commonly in gorillas (Swartz *et al.* 1999, for a review). Far from all pass the mark tests: in Swartz *et al.*'s review, 43% of chimpanzees, 50% of orang-utans and just 31% of gorillas. Nevertheless there is a stark contrast between these findings and the way in which other primates respond to their mirror image.

As with the 2-year-old child, a great ape's self-recognition requires simultaneous recognition of the reflected self, and the self that is the object of primary perception. On first thought, this may be difficult to link to imagination, insofar as the reflection is not an imaginary being—indeed that it is *really oneself*, rather than somebody else, is exactly what most other animals do not recognize. However, it may be equally true that the problem for these other animals is that they are unable to imagine that the image is other than the stranger that primary perception presents it as.

Recognizing Simple States of Mind

Although children do not achieve a fully representational theory of mind until after the age of 4, already by 2 years they recognize the difference between basic states of mind that include emotions, seeing, and intentions

(Perner 1991; Suddendorf and Whiten 2003 for a review). This requires secondary representation of those states, differentiated from the self's state of mind: for example, someone may be able to see something one cannot, or the other way round.

Collating the latter two representations—I see X but you cannot—is potentially useful in various functional contexts, from helping an ignorant companion to deceiving them. A large corpus of episodes of 'tactical deception' assembled by Whiten and Byrne (1988a) constituted one of the first resources used to probe non-human primates' recognition of states of mind in the course of their natural social interactions. Whiten and Byrne (1988b) concluded that for chimpanzees at least, the evidence pointed towards abilities to recognize both intent and visual attention. Having assembled an expanded database (Byrne and Whiten 1990), Byrne and Whiten (1992) extended this inference to the great apes more generally.

More recent experimental studies, so far conducted only with chimpanzees, have generated several results consistent with these conclusions, although there is also a substantial corpus of negative findings (see Suddendorf and Whiten 2003, for discussion). For example, experiments involving chimpanzees interacting with humans indicated very limited appreciation of 'seeing' (Povinelli and Eddy 1996). However, experiments based on competition for food between chimpanzees that had differential visual access to it were interpreted as showing that chimpanzees do recognize seeing (Hare *et al.* 2000), and even the implications of past seeing, that could equate to differentiating the states of knowledge versus ignorance (Hare *et al.* 2001). Other studies have produced evidence for an appreciation of the distinction between intent versus accident among both chimpanzees and orang-utans (Call and Tomasello 1998).

The reason these competencies are taken to require secondary representation has been explained above. This can be related directly to the concept of imagination in that, much as in pretence, the mindreader has to imagine a hypothetical state of mind in another being that may be quite different from their own, current, primary state.

GENERAL DISCUSSION

Dissecting Imagination

We have distinguished two different aspects of imagination that can be fruitfully addressed with available data on great ape cognition. The first, invention, is in some guise widespread in animal behaviour, else how could behaviour evolve? Under the heading of 'innovation', related phenomena in a wide variety of vertebrate species have recently been documented (Reader and Laland 2003). Nevertheless, we noted evidence that anthropoid primates are particularly curious and creative, and that within the primates, great apes stand out in their inventive propensity.

These are thus essentially differences of degree. However when we turn to imagination in the sense of pretence and other manifestations of secondary representation, we appear to shift to distinctions that are more appropriately thought of as qualitative: the hypothesis is that great apes, alone among primates, achieve secondary representation, with consequences across a number of different cognitive domains, several surveyed above.

The co-occurrence of the qualitative with the 'merely' quantitative distinctiveness of the great apes may, however, have multiplicative significance. In short, a being that is capable of secondary representations and also highly inventive, may achieve particularly striking and beneficial behavioural outputs. In relation to means–end reasoning, for example, they could become persistent and inventive solvers of a wide array of problems. In Machiavellian social competition, they could become formidably unpredictable psychological adversaries. Plainly, such descriptions are apt characterizations of the extremes to which human evolution has taken these effects, but in lesser ways they appear evident in the great apes, and therefore, we infer, were being shaped in the ancient cognitive ancestry we share with them. From this perspective human imagination seems not so much a mysterious, totally new phenomenon in nature, but rather as an elaboration on foundations we can now begin to discern.

There is another way in which the two forms of imagination we distinguished might interact. Given that secondary representation allows the generation of hypothetical situations, a being that achieves this might become more effective in the diversity of behavioural outputs possible. Testing this conjecture requires another group evidencing secondary representation, phylogenetically different from great apes, and it is so far unclear that such exists (Suddendorf and Whiten 2001 survey the patchy data): the best current candidates appear to be cetaceans.

Why Do the Great Apes Express the Imagination They Do?

Understanding imagination in the great apes may help us understand why we humans have the powers we have, but we can in turn ask why great apes have the special manifestations of imagination we have sketched above. As Tinbergen (1963) taught us, there are several different kinds of answer to any such question: functional, phylogenetic, developmental, and causal. Byrne (1997), Dunbar (2003), and Barrett *et al.* (2003) offer quite different func-

tional hypotheses, which in turn emphasize either technical or social consequences. Here we have insufficient space to arbitrate on these, focusing
instead on one likely aspect of causation for which a set of well-researched
data can be called on.

If we ask what mechanisms underlie great apes' imaginative capabilities,
then it seems a major factor may lie in the large size of their brains. This, of
course, is only the beginnings of an answer, for one has still to specify how a
large brain achieves what it does. But the basic point about brain size has
been raised often in the past, typically in relation to 'intelligence' rather than
imagination. Passingham (1982), for example, offered a careful comparative
dissection of the significance of large brain size in the great apes and discussed
its correlation with various measures of cognitive sophistication.

Passingham's approach recognized, as one must, that inter-specific brain
size differences are to some extent predictable from body size, and so he
focused on relative measures, such as Jerison's (1973) encephalization quotient (EQ), that assesses the size of the brain relative to that predicted for the
'average mammal' on the basis of brain/body regression analyses. This, however, neglects that a certain proportional excess of brain size will reflect a
larger *absolute* amount of neural tissue in larger individuals, and for higher
cognitive processes, it may be the resulting absolute 'computational power'
that matters. Jerison himself attempted to compute a measure of such 'excess
neurons', but using a somewhat convoluted reliance on reconstructed archaic
mammalian brain volumes. Here we offer a more straightforward and transparent alternative. In Figure 2.5, for each of those species shown in Figure
2.4, we have taken Jerison's (1973, Table 16.3) EQ and used it to compute the
absolute mass of brain tissue that represents an excess over that predicted for
an average mammal of the same body size. As their name betokens, the great
apes are distinctively larger in body size than other primates, and Figure 2.5
illustrates the correlated benefits they enjoy in absolute neural resources,
beyond that typically 'required' of a mammal of their size. The scale of these
resources could be a critical factor in generating the cognitive phenomena
reviewed in this paper. If so, the interesting question remains of whether such
phenomena would arise naturally through extending existing brain construction processes to absolutely greater neural masses, or whether mutations were
involved that gave these processes a qualitatively new twist. At the level of
individual neurons there are suggestions that a qualitative difference evolved
in the form of large 'spindle-cell' neurons, found in great apes, but apparently
not in monkeys (Nimchinsky *et al.*, 1999).

To conclude by turning the argument round the other way, it would be
surprising if the neural resources of great apes illustrated in Figure 2.5 did
not have cognitive correlates and in this chapter we have explored what some
of these may be. The index computed for Figure 2.5 also illustrates, however,

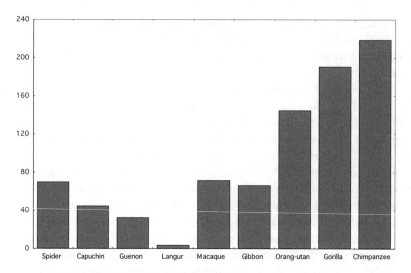

Figure 2.5. An index of excess, absolute neural resource mass. Bars represents the brain mass (grams) of each species shown in Figure 2.4, as an excess over that of an average mammal of the same body weight, as computed from the encephalization quotient (EQ) calculated by Jerison (1973, Table 16.3). See text for further explanation.

how far beyond that of our closest relatives we might expect human imagination to extend, for the corresponding human figure is in excess of 1.1 kg— approximately five times the neural mass at the disposal of the chimpanzee.

Note. AW was supported by a Leverhulme Major Research Fellowship and TS by an Australian Research Council Discovery grant (DP0557424) during the writing of this paper.

References

Barrett, L., Henzi, P. and Dunbar, R. 2003: Primate cognition: from 'what now?' to 'what if?' *Trends in Cognitive Science*, 7, 494–497.

Bertrand, M. 1969: *The Behavioural Repertoire of the Stumptail Macaque*. Basel: Karger.

Bertrand, M. 1976: Acquisition by a pigtail macaque of behaviour patterns beyond the natural repertoire of the species. *Zeitschrift für Tierpsychologie*, 42, 139–169.

de Blois, S. T. and Novak, M. A. 1994: Object permanence in rhesus monkeys (*Macaca mulatta*). *Journal of Comparative Psychology*, 108, 318–327.

de Blois, S. T., Novak, M. A. and Bond, M. 1998: Object permanence in orangutans (*Pongo pygmaeus*) and squirrel monkeys (*Saimiri sciureus*). *Journal of Comparative Psychology*, 112, 137–152.

Bolwig, N. 1959: A study of the behaviour of the chacma baboon, *Papio ursinus*. *Behaviour*, 14, 136–163.

Byrne, R. W. 1995: *The Thinking Ape*. Oxford: Oxford University Press.

Byrne, R. W. 1997: The Technical Intelligence hypothesis: An additional evolutionary stimulus to intelligence? In Whiten, A. and Byrne, R. W. (eds), *Machiavellian Intelligence II: Extensions and Evaluations.* Cambridge: Cambridge University Press, 289–311.

Byrne, R. W. 2003: Novelty in deceit. In Reader, S. M. and Laland, K. N. (eds), *Animal Innovation.* Oxford: Oxford University Press, 237–259.

Byrne, R. W. and Whiten, A. 1988: *Machiavellian Intelligence: Social Expertise and the Evolution of Intellect in Monkeys, Apes and Humans.* Oxford: Oxford University Press.

Byrne, R. W. and Whiten, A. 1990: Tactical deception in primates: the 1990 database. *Primate Report*, 27, 1–101.

Byrne, R. W. and Whiten, A. 1992: Cognitive evolution in primates: evidence from tactical deception. *Man*, 27, 609–627.

Caldwell, C. A. and Whiten, A. 2004: Testing for social learning and imitation in common marmosets, *Callithrix jacchus*, using an 'artificial fruit'. *Animal Cognition*, 7, 77–85.

Call, J. 2001: Object permanence in orangutans (*Pongo pygmaeus*), chimpanzees (*Pan troglodytes*), and children (*Homo sapiens*). *Journal of Comparative Psychology*, 115, 159–171.

Call, J. and Tomasello, M. 1996: The effect of humans on the cognitive development of apes. In Russon, A. E., Bard, K. A. and Parker, S. T. (eds), *Reaching into Thought.* Cambridge: Cambridge University Press, 371–403.

Call, J. and Tomasello, M. 1998: Distinguishing intentional from accidental actions in orangutans (*Pongo pygmaeus*), chimpanzees (*Pan troglodytes*) and human children (*Homo sapiens*). *Journal of Comparative Psychology*, 112, 192–206.

Chomsky, N. 1988: *Language and Problems of Knowledge: The Managua Lectures.* Cambridge, MA: MIT Press.

Collier-Baker, E., Davis, J. and Suddendorf, T. 2004: Do dogs (*Canis familiaris*) understand invisible displacement? *Journal of Comparative Psychology*, 118, 421–423.

Collier-Baker, E., Davis, J., Nielsen, M. and Suddendorf, T. 2006: Do chimpanzees (*Pan troglodytes*) understand single invisible displacement? *Animal Cognition*, 9, 55–61.

Corballis, M. C. 2002: Evolution of the generative mind. In Sternberg, R. J. and Kaufman, J. C. (eds), *The Evolution of Intelligence.* Mahwah, NJ: Lawrence Earlbaum Associates, 117–144.

Corballis, M. C. 2003: Recursion as the key to the human mind. In Sterelny, K. and Fitness, J. (eds), *From Mating to Mentality: Evaluating Evolutionary Psychology.* New York: Psychology Press, 155–171.

DeLoache, J. S. 1987: Rapid change in the symbolic functioning of very young children. *Science*, 238, 1556–1557.

Döhl, J. 1966: Manipulierfahigkeit und 'Einsichtiges' Verhalten eines Schimpansen bei komplizierten Handlungsketten [Manipulability and 'insightful' behaviour of a chimpanzee in complicated behaviour chains]. *Zeitschrift für Tierpsychologie*, 23, 77–113.

Döhl, J. 1968: Uber die Fahigkeit einer Schimpansin, Umwege mit selbststandigen Zwischenzielen zu uberblicken [The ability of a female chimpanzee to overlook intermediate goals]. *Zeitschrift für Tierpsychologie*, 25, 89–103.

Döhl, J. 1969: Versuche mit einer Schimpansin uber Abkurzungen bei Umwegen mit selbststandigen Zwischenzielen [Experiments with a chimpanzee on using shortcuts in detour problems with subgoals]. *Zeitschrift für Tierpsychologie*, 26, 200–207.

Dunbar, R. I. M. 2003: Why are apes so smart? In Kappeler, P. M. and Pereira, M. E. (eds), *Primate Life Histories and Socioecology*. Chicago: University of Chicago Press, 285–298.

Gagnon, S. and Doré, F. Y. 1992: Search behavior in various breeds of adult dogs (*Canis familiaris*): Object permanence and olfactory cues. *Journal of Comparative Psychology*, 106, 58–68.

Glickman, S. and Sroges, R. 1966: Curiosity in zoo animals. *Behaviour*, 26, 151–187.

Greenfield, P. M. 1991: Language, tools and brain: the ontogeny and phylogeny of hierarchically organized sequential behavior. *Behavioral and Brain Sciences*, 14, 541–595.

Hare, B., Call, J., Agnetta, B. and Tomasello, M. 2000: Chimpanzees know what conspecifics do and do not see. *Animal Behaviour*, 59, 771–785.

Hare, B., Call, J. and Tomasello, M. 2001: Do chimpanzees know what conspecifics know? *Animal Behaviour*, 61, 139–151.

Hayes, C. 1951: *The Ape in our House*. New York: Harper.

Hopf, S. 1970: Report on a hand-reared squirrel monkey (*Saimiri sciureus*). *Zeitschrift für Tierpsychologie*, 27, 610–612.

Jensvold, M. L. A. and Fouts, R. S. 1993: Imaginary play in chimpanzees. *Human Evolution*, 8, 217–227.

Jerison, H. J. 1973: *Evolution of the Brain and Intelligence*. New York: Academic Press.

Kawai, N. and Matsuzawa, T. 2000: Numerical memory span in a chimpanzee. *Nature*, 403, 39–40.

Köhler, W. 1917/1927: *The Mentality of Apes*. London: Routledge & Kegan Paul.

Kuhlmeier, V. A. and Boysen, S. T. 2001: The effect of response contingencies on scale model task performance by chimpanzees (*Pan troglodytes*). *Journal of Comparative Psychology*, 115, 300–306.

Kuhlmeier, V. A., Boysen, S. T. and Mukobi, K. L. R. P. 1999: Scale-model comprehension by chimpanzees (*Pan troglodytes*). *Journal of Comparative Psychology*, 113, 396–402.

Leslie, A. M. 1987: Pretense and representation in infancy: the origins of 'theory of mind'. *Psychological Review*, 94, 412–426.

Matevia, M. L., Patterson, F. G. and Hillix, W. A. 2002: Pretend play in a signing gorilla. In Mitchell, R. W. (ed.), *Pretending and Imagination in Animals and Children*. Cambridge: Cambridge University Press, 285–304.

Mithen, S. 1996: *The Prehistory of the Mind*. London: Thames and Hudson.

Natale, F. and Antinucci, F. 1989: Stage 6 object-concept and representation. In Antinucci, F. (ed.), *Cognitive Structure and Development in Non-human Primates*. Hillsdale, NJ: LEA, 97–112.

Natale, F., Antinucci, F., Spinozzi, G. and Poti, P. 1986: Stage 6 object-concept in non-human primate cognition: a comparison between gorilla (*Gorilla gorilla gorilla*) and Japanese macaque (*Macaca fuscata*). *Journal of Comparative Psychology*, 100, 335–339.

Nimchinsky, E. A., Gilissen E., Allman J. M., Perl D. P., Erwin J. M. and Hof P. R. 1999: A neuronal morphologic type unique to humans and great apes. *Proceedings of the National Academy of Sciences, USA*, 96, 5268–5273.

Parker, C. E. 1974a: Behavioral diversity in ten species of nonhuman primates. *Journal of Comparative and Physiological Psychology*, 95, 930–937.

Parker, C. E. 1974b: The antecedents of man the manipulator. *Journal of Human Evolution*, 3, 493–500.

Passingham, R. E. 1982: *The Human Primate*. San Francisco: Freeman.

Patterson, C. and Linden, E. 1981: *The Education of Koko*. New York: Holt, Rinehart and Winston.

Perner, J. 1991: *Understanding the Representational Mind*. Cambridge, MA: Bradford/MIT.

Piaget, J. 1954: *The Construction of Reality in the Child*. New York: Basic Books.

Poss, S. R. and Rochat, P. 2003: Referential understanding of videos in chimpanzees (*Pan troglodytes*), orangutans (*Pongo pygmaeus*), and children (*Homo sapiens*). *Journal of Comparative Psychology*, 117, 420–428.

Povinelli, D. J. and Eddy, T. J. 1996: What young chimpanzees know about seeing. *Monographs of the Society for Research in Child Development*, 61(2).

Reader, S. M. and Laland, K. N. (eds) 2003: *Animal Innovation*. Oxford: Oxford University Press.

Russon, A. E. 2002: Pretending in free-ranging rehabilitant orangutans. In Mitchell, R. W. (ed.), *Pretending and Imagination in Animals and Children*. Cambridge: Cambridge University Press, 229–240.

Russon, A. E. 2003: Innovation and creativity in forest-living rehabilitant orangutans. In Reader, S. M. and Laland, K. N. (eds), *Animal Innovation*. Oxford: Oxford University Press, 279–306.

Savage-Rumbaugh, E. S. 1986: *Ape Language; From Conditioned Response to Symbol*. New York: Columbia University Press.

Savage-Rumbaugh, E. S. and Macdonald, K. 1988: Deception and social manipulation in symbol-using apes. In Byrne, R. W. and Whiten, A. (eds), *Machiavellian Intelligence: Social Expertise and the Evolution of Intellect in Monkeys, Apes and Humans*. Oxford: Oxford University Press, 224–237.

Scott, F. and Baron-Cohen, S. 1996: Imagining real and unreal things: evidence of a dissociation in autism. *Journal of Cognitive Neuroscience*, 8, 371–382.

Shannon, C. E. and Weaver, W. 1964: *The Mathematical Theory of Communication*. Urbana: University of Illinois Press.

Sterelny, K. 2003: *Thought in a Hostile World: The Evolution of Human Cognition*. Oxford: Blackwell.

Suddendorf, T. 1998: Simpler for evolution: secondary representation in apes, children, and ancestors. *Behavioral and Brain Sciences*, 21, 131.

Suddendorf, T. 1999: The rise of the metamind. In Corballis, M. C. and Lea, S. E. G. (eds), *The Descent of Mind: Psychological Perspectives on Hominid Evolution*. London: Oxford University Press, 218–260.

Suddendorf, T. 2003: Early representational insight: Twenty-four-month-olds can use a photo to find an object in the world. *Child Development*, 74, 896–904.

Suddendorf, T. 2004: How primatology can inform us about the evolution of the human mind. *Australian Psychologist*, 39, 180–187.

Suddendorf, T. and Fletcher-Flinn, C. M. 1997: Theory of mind and the origins of divergent thinking. *Journal of Creative Behavior*, 31, 59–69.

Suddendorf, T. and Fletcher-Flinn, C. M. 1999: Children's divergent thinking improves when they understand false beliefs. *Creativity Research Journal*, 12, 115–128.

Suddendorf, T. and Whiten, A. 2001: Mental evolution and development: Evidence for secondary representation in children, great apes and other animals. *Psychological Bulletin*, 127, 629–650.

Suddendorf, T. and Whiten, A. 2003: Reinterpreting the psychology of apes. In Sterelny, K. and Fitness, J. (eds), *From Mating to Mentality: Evaluating Evolutionary Psychology*. New York: Psychology Press, 173–196.

Swartz, K. B., Sarauw, D. and Evans, S. 1999: Comparative aspects of mirror self-recognition in great apes. In Parker, S. L., Mitchell, R. W. and Boccia, M. L. (eds), *The Mentalities of Gorillas and Orangutans*. Cambridge: Cambridge University Press, 283–294.

Tanner, J. 1985: Koko and Michael, gorilla gourmets. *Gorilla*, 9, 3.

Tinbergen, N. 1963: On aims and methods of ethology. *Zeitschrift für Tierpsychologie*, 20, 410–433.

Tomasello, M. and Call, J. 1997: *Primate Cognition*. New York: Oxford University Press.

Torigoe, T. 1985: Comparison of object manipulation among 74 species of non-human primates. *Primates*, 26, 182–194.

de Waal, F. B. M. 1986: Deception in the natural communication of chimpanzees. In Mitchell, R. W. and Thompson, N. S. (eds), *Deception: Perspectives on Human and Non-human Deceit*. Albany: State University of New York, 221–244.

Waddell, P. J. and Penny, D. 1996: Evolutionary trees of apes and humans from DNA sequences. In Lock, A. and Peters, C. R. (eds), *Handbook of Symbolic Evolution*. Oxford: Oxford University Press, 53–73.

Ward, W. C. 1968: Creativity in young children. *Child Development*, 39, 737–754.

Whiten, A. 1996: Imitation, pretence and mindreading: Secondary representation in comparative primatology and developmental psychology? In Russon, A. W., Bard, K. A. and Parker, S. T. (eds), *Reaching into Thought: The Minds of the Great Apes*. Cambridge: Cambridge University Press, 300–324.

Whiten, A. 1998: Imitation of the sequential structure of actions by chimpanzees (*Pan troglodytes*). *Journal of Comparative Psychology*, 112, 270–281.

Whiten, A. 2000: Chimpanzee cognition and the question of mental re-representation. In Sperber, D. (ed.), *Metarepresentations*. Oxford: Oxford University Press, 139–167.

Whiten, A. and Byrne, R. W. 1988a: The manipulation of attention in primate tactical deception. In Byrne, R. W. and Whiten, A. (ed.), *Machiavellian Intelligence: Social Expertise and the Evolution of Intellect in Monkeys, Apes and Humans*. Oxford: Clarendon Press, 211–223.

Whiten, A. and Byrne, R. W. 1988b: Tactical deception in primates. *Behavioral and Brain Sciences*, 11, 233–273.

Whiten, A. and Byrne, R. W. 1991: The emergence of metarepresentation in human ontogeny and primate phylogeny. In Whiten, A. (ed.), *Natural Theories of Mind:*

Evolution, Development and Simulation of Everyday Mindreading. Oxford: Basil Blackwell, 267–281.

Whiten, A. and Byrne, R. W. (eds) 1997: *Machiavellian Intelligence II: Extensions and Evaluations*. Cambridge: Cambridge University Press.

Whiten, A., Custance, D. M., Gomez, J.-C., Teixidor, P. and Bard, K. A. 1996: Imitative learning of artificial fruit processing in children (*Homo sapiens*) and chimpanzees (*Pan troglodytes*). *Journal of Comparative Psychology*, 110, 3–14.

Wildman, D. E., Uddin, M., Grossman, L. I. and Goodman, M. 2003: Implications of natural selection in shaping 99.4% nonsynchronous DNA identity between humans and chimpanzees: enlarging genus *Homo*. *Proceedings of the National Academy of Sciences, USA*, 100, 7181–7188.

Wrangham, R. and Peterson, D. 1996: *Demonic Males*. London: Bloomsbury.

3

Memes, Minds, and Imagination

SUSAN BLACKMORE

Abstract. Two assumptions are often made about the human capacity for creative imagination: first, that it evolved because it serves a biological function; second, that consciousness is necessary for or is the driving force behind it. I suggest that both of these assumptions are false. I shall argue, instead, that human creativity, like biological creativity, is the result of an evolutionary process, but one based on memes rather than genes. Once our hominid ancestors were capable of imitation, a new replicator was let loose and evolved, driving human brains to become ever better at copying, storing, and recombining memes. This coevolution between the memes and their copying machinery led to modern imaginative minds which have evolved, not primarily because they were biologically adaptive, but because they were advantageous for the memes. The driving force behind human creativity is not therefore consciousness, but the power of the evolutionary algorithm. Its function is not biological but memetic.

INTRODUCTION

THE HUMAN IMAGINATION IS A FOUNT OF CREATIVITY. We can imagine things that we have never seen or heard, imagine multiple possible outcomes of events that have not yet happened, and even imagine things that are impossible in the real world. Sometimes we put these imaginings into action and change the world we live in. Humans appear to be unique in this capacity for creativity and imagination. This is not to say that these abilities came out of nowhere. Clearly they did not. Most animals are capable of learning, and arguably both classical and operant conditioning involve some capacity for imagination. For example, my cat deciding whether to go out has learned

Proceedings of the British Academy **147**, 61–78. © The British Academy 2007.

what lies outside, the blackbird on the lawn has learned that the cats lurk behind the hedge, and even the pestilential snail has a simple mental map of the garden. Whether they can all be said to 'imagine' the garden is a moot point, but they certainly store information about it for making decisions.

In a big step up from ordinary learning, some species display insight in their capacity for solving novel problems. For example, New Caledonian crows use and make tools in the wild, and in captivity have been shown to solve problems requiring invention. One crow, provided with straight wire, spontaneously bent it into a hook to retrieve food from a narrow container (Weir *et al.* 2002). Whether this counts as imagination or not is a tricky question, but apparently she was able to consider the consequences of using different shaped wires for the task and act accordingly. Although most primates are probably incapable of such feats, some apes use tools, and chimpanzees not only use and make tools but also have simple cultures, passing on ways of getting food or water, or using tools (Whiten *et al.* 1999).

All these skills may have been available to our hominid ancestors, but modern humans are different. Turner (in Chapter 10) calls this the 'grand difference'. Jacob Bronowski (1988) referred to the 'specifically human gift' for 'calling to mind the recollection of absent things'. Our minds are constantly busy with ideas, suppositions, and plans. We use language with its infinite capacity for creative recombination. And we have created vast cultures that have not only spread around the whole planet but are so powerful that they are changing that planet itself and interfering with every ecosystem. As Mithen points out (Chapter 1), this development has had deleterious as well as beneficial effects for humankind. Essential to this extraordinary development is not only the capacity for learning, but the ability to play with ideas in the mind—to try out new combinations and imagine their consequences. This is the sense in which I shall use the term 'imagination'.

Human culture, and its continuing evolution, depend on this capacity for recombination. For culture to evolve two abilities are critical: its carriers must be able to accurately copy the inventions or discoveries of others, otherwise existing design features will be lost; and they must be able to combine them in novel ways, otherwise culture remains static. We humans are remarkably good at both, and we now sustain extraordinarily complex cultural evolution. But why?

Why do we have imaginative minds? Why are we so creative? Indeed why do we have culture at all? The answer is usually taken to be obvious—that culture, creativity, and imagination have evolved because they are biologically adaptive. I suggest that this answer is wrong and that there is a better alternative.

THE FUNCTION OF IMAGINATION AND CULTURE

Most theories start with a simple assumption; that imagination must have served a biological function. In this view, early hominids with a better capacity for imagination would have had a reproductive advantage and so passed on genes for that ability. In this way, genes underlying imaginative capacity would have spread, leading ultimately to the human imaginative mind. For example, Wilson claims that 'innovation is a concrete biological process' (Wilson 1998, p. 236), and such arguments are common in evolutionary psychology (Pinker 1997). Mithen (1996 and Chapter 1) presents a more complex account. His seven steps involve several different processes, and he emphasizes the importance of culture and the extended mind, but his underlying assumption is that the human imagination evolved because it was biologically adaptive.

Similar arguments can be applied to the products of imagination. Theories of gene–culture coevolution treat human artefacts as aspects of their phenotype, and consider their adaptive value in terms of their effect on gene frequencies. For example, Cavalli-Sforza and Feldman treat 'cultural activity as an extension of Darwinian fitness' (1981, p. 362) and on Wilson's famous 'leash principle', 'genetic natural selection operates in such a way as to keep culture on a leash' (Lumsden and Wilson 1981, p. 13). More recently, Miller (2000) has argued that the human mind was shaped by sexual selection, with cultural products such as art, music, or science acting as sexual displays; for him these cultural products are also aspects of the human phenotype, and are more like peacocks' tails than independently evolving systems. In Chapter 11, Boyer asks whether cultural products are themselves adaptations. The only alternative he offers is that they are mere by-products constrained only by relevance.

There is, however, another possibility—that all these cultural products are part of a new evolving system that is piggy-backing on the old: the 'grand difference' is not explicable entirely in biological terms because we humans are the products of two replicators not one—of memes as well as genes. In this alternative view, culture is seen to have evolved for its own sake, rather than for the benefit of us or our genes.

MEMES AS REPLICATORS

A replicator is defined as information that is copied with variation and selection (Dawkins 1976). The concept arises from the principles of universal Darwinism, according to which evolution must occur whenever there is variation, selection, and heredity. In other words, evolution happens whenever something is copied, multiple copies are made with variations, and only some of the variants survive to be copied again (Dawkins 1976; Dennett 1995). This iterative process produces design whose function is the replication of that information. This is what is meant by the concept of 'selfish replicators'. Our most familiar replicator is the gene, but in 1976 Dawkins speculated about the possibility of other replicators and pointed out that, in culture, information is copied between people by imitation and teaching, and is subject to variation and selection. He called this new replicator the meme (to rhyme with gene); examples include stories, songs, games, financial systems, scientific theories, music, and the arts. The root definition of a meme is 'that which is imitated' (from the Greek *mimeme*; but see Blackmore 1998; Aunger 2000). In other words, a meme is not some independently existing ethereal entity: it is whatever it is that people copy between each other, or to and from artefacts such as books, images, or computers.

There has been much disagreement over whether memes fit the requirements for being a replicator. For example, Sperber (2000) queries the nature of the copying process, and Gil-White (2005) argues that memes are not replicated at all (see also Aunger 2000; Blackmore 2005). Richerson and Boyd (2005) argue that cultural variants are not replicators on the grounds that they are not faithfully reproduced, and are not particulate, independent 'bits'. However, neither of these is a requirement for being a replicator. For example, perfect copying may be desirable, and replicators are more effective the higher the copying fidelity, but poor quality replicators may still count as replicators, and it is an empirical question just how high the copying fidelity must be for an evolutionary process to take off. Similarly, digital copying and recombination make for a more effective evolving system, and arguably all such systems evolve towards digital versions as genes have done, but this does not mean that crude analogue copying cannot sustain any evolution, nor that continuously varying memes, such as gestures or dances, cannot count as replicators; they may be just rather poor quality ones. Following Dawkins (1976) and Dennett (1995), I conclude that memes are replicators because they are information that is copied with variation and selection.

As an example, consider urban legends. Countless stories are told by people all over the world every day. Most of these are boring or relevant to only a few people; they are forgotten and die out quickly. Some are repeated among groups of friends or in families and so have a longer life, while others are copied all over the world and achieve the status of legends. These stories clearly fit the definition of a replicator.

First there is heredity. These stories are not created anew by each person who tells them, but spread like infections from person to person across the globe, originally by word of mouth, but now by radio, television, telephone, and email. Each person must be able to recall and store the story accurately enough to be able to retell it to the next.

Second, there is variation. This occurs through misremembering or imprecise copying, and by elaboration of the story or recombining it with elements from other stories. In this way many variants appear and may be at large in the population of stories being passed around. Such legends as the phantom hitchhiker, the Kentucky fried rat, or the poodle in the microwave, all have variants (Brunvand 1999). For example, there are tales of microwaved cats, dogs, hamsters, and even tortoises, and some of these creatures die an agonizing death while others explode all over the ignorant owner who thought she could dry its fur in her new oven. In British versions the owner is nearly always an American; in American versions she is from South Africa, or from another, often Southern, state.

Finally, selection occurs because some variants are more frequently copied than others. This may be because they are emotionally more powerful, funnier, easier to recall, or for any other reason that gives them the edge in the competition to be stored and passed on. The result of all this competition is that some variants end up being far more common than others. This is memetic selection.

The same principles of copying with variation and selection apply to all the written material in the world—think of the competition between newspapers to be sold, or between books to be published, displayed in bookshops, bought, read, and recommended to others. It applies to behaviours such as eating with a knife and fork rather than with chopsticks, to driving on the right rather than on the left, or to drinking tea with milk rather than with lemon. It applies to the competition between paintings to be displayed, plays to be performed, scientific theories to be tested and published, and political systems to prevail. In all these cases, and many more, multiple variants are created and then subjected to the ruthless competition to thrive in human culture.

The underlying principle of memetics is that, as true replicators, memes compete to be copied for their own sake. The results of that competition shape human minds and culture, but that is not their function—the function of memes is nothing other than their own replication. Memes may be copied for any reason at all, including biological value, ease of copying, ease of remembering, emotional appeal, or many other factors but, as Dennett puts it 'The first rule of memes, as it is for genes, is that replication is not necessarily for the good of anything; replicators flourish that are good at ... replicating!' (Dennett 1991, p. 203).

Memes that harm their carriers or their carrier's genes may be likened to viruses or parasites; email viruses and chain letters are simple examples that waste resources for no gain to the person who copies them, but there are many more virulent ones. Suicide bombers and martyrs may be infected with memes which thrive even when, or indeed because, their carriers kill themselves. Dawkins (1993) calls religions 'viruses of the mind' because of the way in which these stable and long-lived memeplexes use tricks, such as promising heaven and threatening eternal punishment, to induce their hosts to protect and propagate them at the hosts' expense. Viral memes may be especially interesting as examples of selfish replicators, but it is important to remember that most memes are not viruses in this narrow sense. Viral memes are a small subset of the meme pool which includes neutral memes and useful or life-enhancing ones, as well as some that are viral in some circumstances and helpful in others. All these compete to be stored in human brains or artefacts, and then to be recombined, varied, and copied again.

HUMANS AS MEME MACHINES

Memetics provides an explanation of human evolution that is quite different from that of purely gene-based theories or conventional theories of gene–culture coevolution. In this view, what makes us uniquely human— what makes the 'grand difference'—is not intelligence per se, nor symbolic capacities, nor tool use, but our capacity for imitation.

Imitation is often thought to be a simple or childish process, whereas creativity is thought to be difficult. After all, kids find imitation so easy that they even have a game, 'Simon Says', in which the whole point is *not* to imitate unless you hear the words 'Simon says'. The fun of the game is in laughing at those poor players who just cannot control themselves and end up imitating when they should not. In fact, I shall argue, imitation is the hard part and creativity its consequence. Imitation is cognitively very demanding which is why so very few species are capable of it. Human children only find it easy—and we adults take it for granted—because humans are so good at it. The advent of imitation was, I suggest, the turning point in hominid evolution; the new ability that turned us from gene machines into meme machines. All evolutionary processes depend on an accurate copying mechanism, and that mechanism tends to evolve towards higher and higher fidelity. Imitation may not have started as very accurate at all, but it was still the essential copying process without which cultural evolution could never have taken off. Only once human imitation was sufficiently accurate (and we do not yet know exactly how accurate that is) could memetic evolution begin. Once it began, increasing creativity was inevitable.

Imitation, as a new form of social learning, may have originally evolved because it was biologically adaptive (see, e.g., Richerson and Boyd 2005), but I suggest that once it did so the world was changed forever and there was no going back. The possibility of imitation, and hence copying with variation and selection, let loose a second replicator: memes. And once memes appeared the environment for human genes was irrevocably changed.

These early memes may have been new ways of hunting or carrying food, new sounds or gestures, ways of lighting fire, or making clothes or ornaments. We cannot know for sure, but we can assume that once such behaviours could be copied, some of them would be accurately and frequently copied and would spread in the newly emerging meme pool, while others would fail and die out. In this way the new replicator would begin evolving in its own right and for no purpose other than itself. As Dawkins put it 'Once this new evolution begins, it will in no necessary sense be subservient to the old' (Dawkins 1976, pp. 193–194). Whether the evolving memes helped or harmed their carriers would not be the ultimate arbiter, but just one of many factors influencing memetic success.

In this view, the function of imagination cannot be understood without reference to memes; cultural products are not seen as by-products or as adaptive to genes, but as replicators in their own right. They can be thought of as a parasite or symbiont living and evolving along with the human brains that copy them, and forcing those brains to adapt to their presence. This transforms our view of human nature and, I believe, makes far more sense of why we are so different from other species.

Dennett (1995) describes the importance of different replicators in his image of the Tower of Generate-and-Test. On the ground floor are Darwinian creatures, selected by death; on the second floor are Skinnerian creatures whose behaviour is selected by learning; on the third floor are Popperian creatures whose ideas can be selected in their imagination; and on the top floor are Gregorian creatures whose memes are selected in culture. In each case there is a replicator and a selective process going on, and evolution occurs as a result, but the last step is a dramatic one because the replicator escapes from the individual out into the social world. Humans are the only species to have truly made the leap to being Gregorian creatures. They are the product of two interacting replicators, genes and memes.

This coevolution of memes and genes is a two-way process. Genes influence the selection of memes because they build the copying machinery of the human body and brain. But memes influence genes too, in a process I have referred to as memetic drive. Once a species is capable of imitation, memes start evolving; those of high fidelity, fecundity, and longevity outperform the rest, leading to increasing numbers and varieties of memes, and changes in the dominant memes. This memetic evolution, with all its various products, changes the environment in which genetic selection takes place. Depending on the direction the memetic evolution happens to take, genes may be forced to follow, and in this sense they are driven by the memes (Blackmore 1999, 2001).

This theory differs from most theories of gene–culture coevolution because of the final step. The process works like this. Before there were many memes, the major pressures on hominid genes came from the physical environment and from other individuals. But once memetic evolution took off, status, survival, and reproductive chances were affected by the memes a person acquired. This would create a need for new strategies concerning whom to copy and whom to mate with. For example, it might pay to mate with those who were capable of imitating the currently most popular memes. So, if wearing skins as clothes was frequently copied (i.e. it was a successful meme) then people who were poor at copying clothes-wearing would be at a disadvantage. If there were genetic differences between people in how good they were at acquiring this skill then these genes would spread in the gene pool, gradually increasing people's ability.

Note that wearing clothes has a biological advantage in terms of warmth and protection, so the spread of clothing and the ability to copy clothing could be explained biologically. However, the interesting point is this. Once the ability to imitate increases in the population, then more behaviours and artefacts can be copied. So memetic evolution increases. Inevitably people will copy all sorts of memes, not just clothes, including those that are biologically useful and those that are not. Unless certain memes are positively lethal to their carriers (and even then, under some circumstances), they may thrive along with the useful ones. In most theories of gene–culture coevolution this is as far as the argument goes, but memetics takes a further step.

If acquiring the latest memes provides a genetic advantage, then genes for acquiring those memes will increase. This means an inherited improvement in the ability to copy whichever memes have been successful in the memetic competition. In other words, the direction of memetic evolution drives the direction taken by the genes. Genes are forced to build brains that can copy the most successful memes. Since memes thrive for memetic, not just biological, reasons, this means we can only understand the design of the human brain by considering memes as well as genes.

In this way we can see culture not as a biological adaptation, but as a new parasite made possible by the advent of imitation. I have argued that language itself began as a memetic parasite that then coevolved to become a symbiont with its human carriers (Blackmore 1999). Indeed we can see all of culture as a new organism parasitic on the old. Like other parasites it may initially have been dangerous but then evolved to become less so; it might even be like the bacteria that originally invaded other organisms and then evolved to become indispensable organelles, so that now we are dependent upon being infected with culture.

It may be that the memetic parasite is initially so dangerous that it can kill any species that acquires it before it has time to adapt. This may have happened to other species in the past, in which case we humans were lucky to have survived the danger phase long enough to coevolve with our culture. This may be an extreme hypothesis and it may be false, but it follows directly from taking memetics seriously—that is, from seeing memes as spreading because they can and not necessarily because they are adaptive for their carriers. In this view, having survived the advent of the new replicator, human brains evolved to become ever better meme machines, copying, storing, and recombining memes with increasing fidelity. Examples of this process may include not only the evolution of the big brain and language (Blackmore 1999) but our enjoyment of art, science, and religion, and our capacity for imagination.

THE ORIGINS OF ART AND MUSIC

There are many theories of the origins of art and almost all rely on biological functions of some kind. For example, Ramachandran and Hirstein (1999) propose eight laws of aesthetic experience, and these derive directly from the structure of perceptual systems that evolved for biological purposes. Zeki describes one of the functions of art as 'an extension of the major function of the visual brain', that is, a search for the enduring features of objects and situations (Zeki 1999, p. 79), and Solso (2003) attributes artistic appreciation to a consciousness that evolved for other purposes.

Music provides an especially interesting example. Pinker declares that 'As far as biological cause and effect are concerned, music is useless' (Pinker 1997, p. 528), and Dennett (1999) says we 'cannot avoid the obligation to explain how such an expensive, time-consuming activity came to flourish in this cruel world'. Miller (2000) provides an explanation, citing music as an example of a sexual display, but this, in common with other biologically based theories, treats the music as part of a person's phenotype, rather than as a new system evolving in its own right. Mithen (in Chapter 1) suggests that music began as part of a holistic communication system that remained when language evolved separately into a system with words and grammar. The important difference is that for Mithen the functions of language and music are communication, the expression of emotions and the facilitation of group bonding. In other words they have biological functions and are advantageous for the organisms and their genes. On a memetic theory the primary function of memes is the survival and proliferation of the musical memes themselves.

Dennett (1999) imagines how music might have begun—a Just-So story about the first ever infectious sounds:

> One day one of our distant hominid ancestors sitting on a fallen log happened
> to start banging on with a stick—*boom boom boom*. For *no good reason at all*.
> This was just idle diddling, a by-product, perhaps, of a slightly out-of-balance
> endocrine system. This was, you might say, mere nervous fidgeting, but the
> repetitive sounds striking his ears just happened to feel to him like a slight
> improvement on silence . . .
>
> Now introduce some other ancestors who happen to see and hear this drum-
> mer. They might pay no attention, or be irritated enough to make him stop or
> drive him away, or they might, again *for no reason*, find their imitator-circuits
> tickled into action; they might feel an urge to drum along with musical Adam.

Dennett explains that it does not matter why either the first person or the imitators did what they did—it might have been for good biological reasons or
it might have been because of some quirk in the design of their brains or the
weather that day. The important point is that the drumming was copied, and
so with a community of other imitators around, the sounds began to spread.
Among all the different drummings, some proved more infectious than others. It did not matter why—maybe because they were easier to remember,
sounded nicer, or were less harmful—the point is that once they could be
copied they were copied, and so the drumming virus was born.

Dennett supposes that soon some of the hominids began humming, and
humming memes spread in the meme pool. At first the copying might have
been inaccurate and new variants rare, but even so the number and variety of
musical memes gradually increased, and the competition hotted up. Memes
now had to be more catchy, easier to hum, or more likely to gain attention in
order to find themselves preserved in the meme pool. Individual brains
changed too because everyone now lived in a music-filled culture and they
learnt to hum some of the tunes, with some learning faster and learning more
tunes than others, and some being good at recombining tunes they heard to
make new variants. As Dennett himself says, this is only a Just-So story. We
cannot know what really happened, but the point is this: once there were
creatures capable of imitation something like this must have happened. Of all
the many behaviours carried out, some would have been copied more than
others. If any proved especially copyable, given the oddities of the hominid
brain and the specifics of the environment, then those would spread, and so
memetic evolution would be up and running.

The next step, which Dennett does not consider, is memetic drive. If
drumming and humming became popular, and people who were good at it
acquired status, then the pressures on hominid genes would change. It would
now pay to have a brain that is good at copying drumming and humming,
when previously it did not. Any genes that contribute to that ability are now
favoured and so, gradually, hominid brains are redesigned. The coevolutionary process then continues indefinitely. Improvements to the copying machin-

ery mean that more sounds can be created, copied, and imaginatively recombined, and that in turn means further redesign and so on. If this is how music evolved then we can easily understand why we modern humans have the sort of brains (and ears and hands) that help us enjoy making and listening to music. Once we know a few songs or melodies, we can easily elaborate them into new ones, or combine motifs from different ones in our imagination. We are like that, not because music serves any biological function, but simply because, at some point in the past, musical memes infected our ancestors and helped to redesign their brains. Those brains are now designed to remember, hum, sing, play, and pass on music; they are skilled at mixing up all the fragments they hear to make new ones and at using the schemes and musical tricks they come across to develop them further. This is what it means to have a musical imagination. If quite different memes had happened to thrive at that time, our brains would have ended being designed quite differently. We are musical creatures not because of music's survival value for our genes but because of the replicator power of musical memes.

Another example of memetic drive in action could be the power of religious belief. It is a curious fact that humans seem to be naturally religious creatures (Boyer 2001; Newberg and D'Aquili 2001). Even today most people in the world believe in a god. This is true even in highly educated and technologically advanced societies such as the USA, where a 2003 Harris poll found that 79% believed in God. By contrast, Britain has one of the lowest levels of religious belief and observance, with a 2004 BBC poll showing just under half of people claiming to believe in God. Even so, this is a large proportion, and enormous amounts of money and effort are devoted to religious observance. The resources consumed are even larger if one includes cults, New Age groups and non-theistic religions as well. All this demands explanation.

Most theories of the origins of religious belief treat it as a natural consequence of having a brain designed for other purposes. For example, Pinker (1997) describes how religious concepts arise from our evolved perceptual capacities and from limitations in our understanding of the world. Boyer (2001 and Chapter 11) argues that religion consists of by-products of normal mental functioning evolved for other purposes. In contrast, Ehrlich argues that 'Organized religion thus seems to have evolved to help stabilize hierarchical social structure' (Ehrlich 2000, p. 256). There may indeed be biological value in being religious; for example, membership of certain religious groups confers social advantages and reduces fear of death. On the other hand levels of violent crime are much higher in the religious USA than in less religious Britain, so religious belief is no panacea for social ills. On a memetic theory of the evolution of religiosity this is not surprising. Indeed we might expect religions to flourish even if they cause severe hardship and suffering.

Religions provide one of the most powerful examples of infectious meme-plexes. In his analysis of 'viruses of the mind' Dawkins (1993) uses Roman Catholicism as an example, pointing out all the tricks that this highly success-ful and long-lived memeplex uses to get itself copied and safely stored. Hidden within the complex of stories and dogmas are powerful instructions to pass on the whole package, both to one's children and to others. This instruction is backed up by untestable threats and promises, including heaven, hell, and eternal damnation. Doubt is to be fought against and belief admired, which helps prevent intelligent children from questioning the whole idea. Giving money to the poor is encouraged, and so is giving money to the church itself. This makes possible the fabulous buildings, wonderful music, extravagant paintings, and other glories which instil awe and delight in church-goers—so encouraging them to spend time in church, to encourage others to come too, and to spread the memes still further.

As with the origins of musical ability, I have argued that memetic drive is responsible for our deep-seated religious tendencies: the long history of coevolution between religious memes and human brains has resulted in brains that are designed to be good at copying, storing, and manipulating the kinds of religious memes that happened to survive. If this is so it is not sur-prising that religions persist in the face of contemporary education and sci-entific understanding which make most religious claims seem ridiculous. Incidentally, music plays a significant role here. Having evolved a delight in music we enjoy singing and listening to others sing. A religious memeplex can then use this evolved capacity to spread itself by using the music to carry the viral words. We sing 'Praise my soul the King of heaven', 'Now thank we all our God', 'All things bright and beautiful . . .', 'Jesus Christ is risen today . . .'. Curiously I have no trouble thinking up countless examples of hymns I learnt in my childhood. They are certainly long-lived memes.

Note that phrases like 'the religion uses X' or 'religions want X' are short-hand. They do not imply that the memes have plans or intentions—obvi-ously they do not because memes are only the behaviours, words, and sounds that are copied. These phrases can be unpacked as 'religions that have X are copied more often than those that do not'. In this way memetics explains how and why the great religions of the world are structured the way they are, and have survived so long and irrevocably infected so many people. It can also explain how their power shifts with changing cultures, and why other newer religions are taking over in some places, including secular 'religions' such as Transcendental Meditation, Landmark Education, and New Age beliefs.

Our early ancestors would not have had such complex and highly evolved religious memeplexes to deal with, but the same principles apply. If some people adopted rituals to help hunting or relieve the pain of famine or death, and others copied them, then variations of these rituals would compete to be copied. The same would apply to any other aspect of religious behaviour or tradition. Some of these religious memes would thrive at the expense of less fit memes, and those successful ones would very slowly drive genes to provide machinery good at copying them. In other words the human brain would gradually be redesigned for religious behaviour just as it was for language and musical ability. There need have been no biological advantage to religious behaviour at all. Whether there was or not is beside the point—so long as the memes did not actually kill off too many of their carriers. The point is that the religious memes themselves could have forced our brains to end up the way they are.

THE COEVOLUTION OF REPLICATORS AND THEIR COPYING MACHINES

I have suggested that human brains were redesigned by the second replicator, memes, which drove them to become better and better meme machines. This process can be seen as an example of a more general process in which replicators evolve along with the machinery that copies them. For example, genes did not arise on this planet fully designed along with nuclear RNA, messenger RNA, ribosomes, and all the other complex paraphernalia of their replication. All of this slowly evolved into the exquisitely high-fidelity system we see today (Maynard Smith and Szathmáry 1999).

This is not surprising. If there was variation in copying systems as well as in the replicators themselves, those copying systems producing higher-quality replicators would outperform the others and take more of the available resources. In this way the whole system would evolve into a more effective evolutionary system, with stable and safe storage, high-fidelity copying, and variation produced by the controlled recombination of elements rather than by degradation and errors.

The equivalent in human evolution was the coevolution of memes along with the brains, voices, hands, and bodies that copied them. But this process has not stopped there. The same process can be seen in the evolution of printing presses along with the books and papers they copy, cameras along with the images they produce, and computers, along with the documents, images, spreadsheets, and other products they manipulate. In the world wide web we see a system comparable with (though nowhere near as fine as) the biological system; enormous amounts of information are safely stored, copied with almost one hundred per cent fidelity, and available for recombining with other bits of information in the system. This process is still going on and is sustaining increasingly fast evolution of both the information and the system itself. The web itself is now a fount of creativity.

We can now return to the question of why humans have such imaginative and creative minds. All these examples of coevolution produced systems that were increasingly creative, and had ever better methods for recombining old designs to produce new ones; from the biological system to the world wide web. In each case the copying machinery became ever better at copying the kinds of information that had been successfully copied in the past, from the copying of DNA sequences to the copying of html texts. The human brain is just one intermediate stage in this sequence of coevolutionary processes; it is a machine designed by its coevolution with memes to copy memes, store them, and mix them up to produce new ones. The answer to the question why we have imaginative minds is that meme–gene coevolution designed them.

CONSCIOUSNESS, CREATIVITY, AND EVOLUTION

Before Darwin, no one could understand how living things could evolve unless someone designed them—hence Paley's famous argument for the existence of God. Our intuitions tell us that clever designs require a conscious designer and, as Dennett (1995) points out, our experience seems to confirm this. We always see fancy things making less fancy things. We do not see a pot making a potter, or a web making a spider, but always the other way around. Then Darwin came along and turned this intuition on its head. His great insight was to realize that natural selection could mindlessly design all of the living world without a designer and without a plan. Simple, dumb, mindless processes can, given enough time and materials, create the cleverest things in the world.

Some people still find this shift hard to make today, as is seen in the continuing antagonism to Darwinism in many parts of the world, and the success of creationism and intelligent design as religious alternatives to Darwinism. Then there are various theories that try to sneak a role for intelligence or consciousness back into evolution. For example, Teilhard de Chardin (1959) proposed that all life is striving towards higher consciousness, and Julian Huxley believed that evolution was pulled along by consciousness as well as driven from behind by blind processes (Pickering and Skinner 1990). More recently, Wilber (1997) describes the inevitable progress from insentience to superconsciousness, and Hubbard (1997) urges us to take conscious control of our future in 'conscious evolution'. However, with these exceptions, most people have managed to make the Darwinian shift from thinking that evolution needs a designer to realizing that biological creativity is a bottom-up process in which simple things produce complex results with neither a conscious designer nor a plan.

This same shift has not been made in thinking about human creativity. In popular discourse there is a common tendency to speak of creative people as individual conscious designers who deliberately, and from the top down, create something new using the power of their imagination. In this view, creativity and consciousness are closely associated, as can be seen in the numerous popular books, business plans, and self-help tapes that encourage you to increase your consciousness and creativity, or learn to be creative through enhanced creative awareness.

The same idea, that consciousness can exert power or create design, can be found in philosophy and psychology. For example, Searle (1992) claims that consciousness is caused by brains and that it serves to increase creativity and flexibility. Mithen (1996) argues that consciousness plays an integrating role, bringing separate aspects of the mind together and so allowing for greater creativity. These suggestions fit with the common intuition that novel thinking is difficult and that difficult tasks require consciousness.

This emphasis on consciousness meets with several problems, not least the fact that consciousness itself is impossible to define and poorly understood. The term is mostly used in contemporary science and philosophy to refer to subjective experience, or 'what it's like to be' something (Blackmore 2003). Taking this definition, it is hard to understand how subjective experiences themselves could act as a force or have any function at all—a serious problem for theories of the evolution of consciousness, but also for any theory that makes consciousness the power behind creativity.

Attempts to link creative imagination to consciousness run into another problem if they imply that when we imagine something it must be 'displayed' in consciousness, or be consciously visible to the mind's eye, or in some other way come 'into consciousness'. These phrases all imply versions of what Dennett (1991) calls the 'Cartesian theatre'—the mythical time or place in the mind or brain where things come together and consciousness happens. This cannot exist, according to Dennett, not only because there is no observer inside the brain but because there is no centre of operations, nor indeed a centre of any kind, and there is no finishing line beyond which previously unconscious processes suddenly become conscious ones. The brain is a massively parallel system with no special inner sanctum where information comes to be turned into the contents of consciousness.

The idea that consciousness is essential for creativity conflicts with another odd and interesting fact. This is that many creative writers, thinkers, scientists, and artists, claim that their best work just 'comes' to them. They have no idea how they do it, and indeed often feel that 'they' did not really do it at all. It is as though the poem, the solution to the scientific problem, or the painting just shaped itself without any conscious effort, or even any awareness on the part of the creator. Some describe this feeling of total immersion as a state of 'flow' (Csikszentmihalyi and Csikszentmihalyi 1988) in which the self seems to disappear. This kind of selfless creativity seems at odds with the idea that consciousness is the force behind creativity. Yet these artists may be right and the common intuition that consciousness causes creativity may be wrong.

I suggest that it is time to give up this old and false intuition, just as we (reluctantly) gave up the need for a creator God. The shift needed here is exactly the same shift that was made in the mid-nineteenth century when Darwin explained how natural selection works. Instead of hanging on to the intuition that clever design needs a conscious designer, we should apply the principle of universal Darwinism to ourselves as well.

Memetics does just this, and so provides a new way of thinking about human creativity. In this new view, the process of copying with variation and selection is the only creative design force in the universe. This simple iterative process, along with processes of self-organization and random change, not only designed all living things, but all human inventions as well. Neither biological evolution nor human creative imagination is a top-down process in which a clever conscious mind thinks up new ideas and puts them into effect; both are mindless processes in which new products emerge because old ones are copied with variation and selection. All human creativity results from memetic evolution; from the reiterative process of recombination and selective imitation of behaviours and artefacts. It may not feel that way, but then our intuitions about the way the mind works have not proven a reliable guide to how they really work, so this should not unduly surprise us.

In this Darwinian view we human beings are not creative because we have specially powerful conscious minds, or creative inner selves, but because we are capable of selective imitation. And those of us who are the most creative are those who are best at accurately copying and storing the memes we come across, recombining them in novel ways, and selecting appropriately from the myriad new combinations created. Incidentally this makes the (so far untested) prediction that creativity should be positively correlated with the ability to imitate, rather than some people being creative while others are just copiers. In this new view, we humans are the copying machines—the meme machines—that form part of a new evolutionary process: the true creative power behind human imagination is memetic evolution.

To some people, this view may seem depressing or dehumanizing, with its emphasis on selective imitation and away from the power of consciousness. Yet it provides a unifying view of creative design. As information explodes, the web expands, and human life becomes ever more complex and full of cultural creations, we can see the same process at work as that which designed the living world. Everything was, and still is, designed by the power of that familiar mindless process, the evolutionary algorithm. This is a beautiful, if daunting, view of our place in the world.

References

Aunger, R. A. (ed.) 2000: *Darwinizing Culture: The Status of Memetics as a Science*. Oxford and New York: Oxford University Press.

Blackmore, S. J. 1998: Imitation and the definition of a meme. *Journal of Memetics— Evolutionary Models of Information Transmission*, 2 (http://www.cpm.mmu.ac.uk/ jom-emit/1998/vol2/blackmore_s.html).

Blackmore, S. J. 1999: *The Meme Machine*. Oxford, Oxford University Press.

Blackmore, S. 2001: Evolution and memes: The human brain as a selective imitation device. *Cybernetics and Systems*, 32, 225–255.

Blackmore, S. J. 2003: *Consciousness: An Introduction*. London: Hodder and Stoughton; New York: Oxford University Press.

Blackmore, S. J. 2005: Even deeper misunderstandings of memes: Commentary on Gil-White. In Hurley, S. and Chater, N. (eds), *Perspectives on Imitation: From Mirror Neurons to Memes*, Volume 2. Cambridge, MA: MIT Press, 406–409.

Boyer, P. 2001: *Religion Explained*. New York: Basic Books.

Bronowski, J. 1988: The reach of the imagination. In Eastman, A. (ed.), *The Norton Reader*. New York: Norton, 194–201.

Brunvand, J. H. 1999: *Too Good to be True: The Colossal Book of Urban Legends*. New York: Norton.

Cavalli-Sforza, L. L. and Feldman, M. W. 1981: *Cultural Transmission and Evolution: A Quantitative Approach*. Princeton, NJ: Princeton University Press.

Csikszentmihalyi, M. and Csikszentmihalyi, I. S. (eds) 1988: *Optimal Experience: Psychological Studies of Flow in Consciousness*. Cambridge: Cambridge University Press.

Dawkins, R. 1976: *The Selfish Gene*. Oxford: Oxford University Press (new edition with additional material, 1989).

Dawkins, R. 1993: Viruses of the mind. In Dahlbohm, B. (ed.), *Dennett and his Critics: Demystifying Mind*. Oxford: Blackwell.

Dennett, D. 1991: *Consciousness Explained*. Boston: Little, Brown.

Dennett, D. 1995: *Darwin's Dangerous Idea*. London: Penguin.

Dennett, D. 1999: The evolution of culture. Charles Simonyi Lecture, Oxford, February 17 and at http://www.edge.org/3rd_culture/dennett/dennett_p2.html

Ehrlich, P. R. 2000: *Human Natures: Genes, Cultures, and the Human Prospect*. Washington, DC: Island Press.

Gil-White, F. J. 2005: Common misunderstandings of memes (and genes): The promise and the limits of the genetic analogy to cultural transmission processes. In Hurley, S. and Chater, N. (eds), *Perspectives on Imitation: From Mirror Neurons to Memes*. Cambridge, MA: MIT Press.

Hubbard, B. M. 1997: *Conscious Evolution: Awakening the Power of our Social Potential*. Novato, CA: New World Library.

Lumsden, C. J. and Wilson, E. O. 1981: *Genes, Mind and Culture*. Cambridge, MA: Harvard University Press.

Maynard-Smith, J. and Szathmáry, E 1999: *The Origins of Life: From the Birth of Life to the Origin of Language*. Oxford and New York: Oxford University Press.

Miller, G. 2000: *The Mating Mind: How Sexual Choice Shaped the Evolution of Human Nature*. London: Heinemann.

Mithen, S. 1996: *The Prehistory of the Mind*. London: Thames and Hudson.

Newberg, A. and D'Aquili, E. 2001: *Why God Won't Go Away: Brain Science and the Biology of Belief*. New York: Ballantine.

Pickering, J. and Skinner, M. (eds) 1990: *From Sentience to Symbols: Readings on Consciousness*. London: Harvester Wheatsheaf.

Pinker, S. 1997: *How the Mind Works*. Harmondsworth: Penguin.

Ramachandran, V. S. and Hirstein, W. 1999: The science of art: A neurological theory of aesthetic experience. *Journal of Consciousness Studies*, 6–7, 15–51.

Richerson, P. J. and Boyd, R. 2005: *Not by Genes Alone: How Culture Transformed Human Evolution*. Chicago: University of Chicago Press.

Searle, J. R. 1992: *The Rediscovery of the Mind*. Cambridge, MA: MIT Press.

Solso, R. L. 2003: *The Psychology of Art and the Evolution of the Conscious Brain*. Cambridge, MA: MIT Press.

Sperber, D. 2000: An objection to the memetic approach to culture. In Aunger, R. A. (ed.), *Darwinizing Culture: The Status of Memetics as a Science*. Oxford and New York: Oxford University Press, 163–173.

Teilhard de Chardin, P. 1959: *The Phenomenon of Man*. London: Collins; New York: Harper.

Weir, A. A. S., Chappell, J. and Kacelnik, A. 2002: Shaping of hooks in New Caledonian crows. *Science*, 297, 981.

Whiten, A., Goodall, J., McGrew, W. C., Nishida, T., Reynolds, V., Sugiyama, Y., Tutin, C. E. G., Wrangham, R. W. and Boesch, C. 1999: Cultures in chimpanzees. *Nature*, 399, 682–685.

Wilber, K. 1997: An integral theory of consciousness. *Journal of Consciousness Studies*, 4(1), 71–92.

Wilson, E. O. 1998: *Consilience: The Unity of Knowledge*. New York: Knopf.

Zeki, S. 1999: Art and the brain. *Journal of Consciousness Studies*, 6–7, 76–96.

Part II

DEVELOPMENT OF IMAGINATION IN CHILDREN

Part II

DEVELOPMENT OF IMAGINATION
IN CHILDREN

4

Autonomy and Control in Children's Interactions with Imaginary Companions

MARJORIE TAYLOR, STEPHANIE M. CARLSON,
AND ALISON B. SHAWBER

Abstract. Although many children describe their imaginary companions as primarily friendly and compliant, imaginary companions can also be experienced as unfriendly, mean, bossy, aggressive, and/or frightening. Such negative accounts of imaginary companions suggest that children do not always experience their imaginary companions as completely under control. In this chapter we report a study investigating the extent of negative characteristics in children's descriptions of imaginary companions. The participants were 89 preschool children who described their imaginary companions (46 invisible friends and 43 personified objects). The descriptions were coded for disobedient or otherwise difficult behaviour attributed to the imaginary companions. Thirty-six per cent of the children described their imaginary companions as consistently compliant and agreeable, 35 per cent gave some indication that the imaginary companions did not always do or say what the children wanted, although they were mostly friendly and compliant, and 29 per cent described their imaginary companions as noncompliant in ways that suggested the children experienced the companion to some extent as being out of their conscious control. Three reasons for some children's experience of lack of control over their imaginary companions were discussed: noncompliance as an emotive, illusion of independent agency, and individual differences in inhibitory control. Noncompliant and/or troublesome imaginary companions occur frequently enough to be considered normative, and provide insight into what is on children's minds as well as how children process information that is generated in imagination versus what is perceptually experienced.

Proceedings of the British Academy **147**, 81–100. © The British Academy 2007.

IN THEIR PRETEND PLAY, young children exhibit a striking ability and inclination to imagine and act out the roles of other people and creatures. They have long conversations on the phone with imaginary friends, animate their stuffed animals, dolls, and action figures, and enact elaborate pretend scenarios. Much of the research on these types of role play has focused on social contexts in which young children's activities are scaffolded by mature play partners (parents, older children) or coordinated with the pretending of peers (e.g. Kavanaugh *et al.* 1983; Howes 1985; Howe *et al.* 2005). In social contexts, children tend to engage in '*what is*' pretending in which they replicate or reconstruct real-life activities, often with direct instructions from a parent or other play partner (Dunn and Dale 1984; Miller and Garvey 1984; Engel 2005). However, role play also happens when children are alone. Private role play is believed to be particularly conducive to '*what if*' pretending in which the child transforms reality to his or her own specifications (Bretherton 1989; Engel 2005). Given its idiosyncratic and generative nature, private role play provides unique information about children's interpretations and emotional responses to events in their lives.

In this chapter we discuss children's private role play with imaginary companions, characters that are created by children and interacted with and/or talked about on a regular basis. Although imaginary companions are sometimes integrated into play with other children or with family routines (e.g. setting a place at the dinner table for an imaginary companion), this type of sustained and elaborated role play frequently occurs in a solitary context (Hoff 2005a). Imaginary companions are fascinating in and of themselves, but they also can be used as a vehicle for shedding light on a variety of interesting questions in social and cognitive development. For example, Gleason (2002) has argued that the relationships that children invent in role play with imaginary companions are informative about their concepts of what friendships are and how they function. It is interesting, however, that sometimes imaginary companions are not all that friendly. They can be mean, bossy, aggressive, and/or frightening.

In this chapter we consider explanations for why some children create imaginary companions with negative characteristics and discuss how research on this topic has the potential of providing new information about the distinction between automatic and controlled processes in consciousness and the relation between inhibitory control and pretend play. However, before turning our attention to the special case of imaginary companions who are noncompliant and/or troublesome, we briefly review some of the general findings of research in this area.

OVERVIEW OF RESEARCH ON
CHILDREN'S IMAGINARY COMPANIONS

In the past, imaginary companions have sometimes been described as relatively rare and as possibly reflecting problems such as extreme shyness or emotional inadequacies (e.g. Svendson 1934; Bender and Vogel 1941; Benson and Pryor 1973; Myers 1976). Ames and Learned (1946) believed the general phenomenon was normative, but certain types (e.g. invisible animals) reflected adjustment problems. Even Piaget did not have a positive view of this type of pretending, reminding his readers that 'In reality, the child has no imagination, and what we ascribe to him as such is no more than a lack of coherence' (1962, 131). Other authors were discouraging about the possibility of conducting research on this topic, claiming that children are secretive about their imaginary companions and will not discuss them with adults (Hurlock and Bernstein 1932). In contrast to these claims, the past twenty years of research indicates that the creation of imaginary companions is a common and generally healthy type of play that children are happy to describe to an interviewer and that tends to be associated with positive characteristics in children (for a review see Taylor 1999).

Prevalence and Developmental Course

Estimates of the incidence of imaginary companions vary depending upon the definition of 'imaginary companion' (e.g. stuffed animals are sometimes included as well as invisible companions) and the source of the information (the children who create them, their parents, or adults recalling their childhood companions). In our research, we interview both children and parents about the children's imaginary companions, cross-check the information, and conduct follow-up interviews as necessary. By having two sources of information and asking follow-up questions, we avoid some of the interpretive problems that arise in this area of research (e.g. children describing a real friend instead of an imaginary one, making up an imaginary friend on the spot in response to the interview, describing a stuffed animal that is treated more as a transitional object than an imaginary companion, etc.). Our definition of imaginary companion includes special toys (referred to as personified objects) as well as invisible friends, if the description of the toy indicates that the child treats it as having a distinct personality and has interacted with it (e.g. talking, listening) on a regular basis (see Gleason *et al.* 2000 for a discussion of the similarities and differences between invisible imaginary companions and those based on toys). On the basis of several studies using this methodology and definition, we estimate that about a

84 *Marjorie Taylor, Stephanie M. Carlson, and Alison B. Shawber*

third of preschool children have imaginary companions; about half are based on toys (personified objects) and half are invisible (Taylor and Carlson 1997).

Imaginary companions tend to be associated with the preschool years (e.g. Piaget 1962; Hughes, 1999), but there have been several reports of imaginary companions created by older children and recent research provides evidence that imaginary companions continue beyond the preschool years. For example, Pearson *et al.* (2001) interviewed children aged 5–12 and found that 28 per cent of them had imaginary companions. Hoff (2005a) reports that 20.3 per cent (14 of a sample of 69) of Swedish fourth graders (9–10 years old) described having *current* imaginary companions. Taylor *et al.* (2004) re-contacted a sample of 100 second-grade children who had been assessed as preschoolers and found that a substantial number of these school-aged children were *currently* playing with imaginary companions (31 per cent). (The majority of imaginary companions created in middle childhood were invisible.) According to Taylor *et al.*, by the age of 7 years, about 65 per cent of children have had an imaginary companion (either personified objects, PO, or invisible friends, IF) at some point in their lives. If only invisible friends are considered, 37 per cent of children have had one by age 7 (see Table 4.1). These results speak to both the continuity of imaginary companions beyond the preschool years, and the generativity of this phenomenon — a substantial number of children were continually inventing new imaginary companions for a period of years.

Characteristics of Children who have Imaginary Companions

On many measures of personality, intelligence, and behaviour, children with imaginary companions do not seem very different from children without

Table 4.1. Imaginary companion (IC) status at Time 1 (when children[a] were aged 3–4 years), between Time 1 and Time 2, and Time 2 (when children were 6–7 years) (Taylor *et al.* 2004).

| Type of IC | Period when child reported playing with imaginary companion | | |
	Time 1	Between Time 1 and Time 2	Time 2
Invisible friends	13	14	20
Personified objects	18	3	10
Both IF and PO	–	1	1
Total ICs	31[b]	18	31

[a]$n = 100$.

[b]16 of these children had an imaginary companion only at Time 1. To calculate the total percentage (65 per cent) of 7-year-old children who had an imaginary companion at some point in their lives, those 16 children were added to the 18 children who had an imaginary companion between Time 1 and Time 2, and the 31 children who had an imaginary companion at Time 2.

them (Taylor *et al.* 2004). However, when differences are found, they tend to favour the children who have imaginary companions. For example, in comparison with children who do not have imaginary companions, children who create imaginary companions are more sociable and less shy (Singer and Singer 1990; Mauro 1991; Seiffge-Krenke 1993, 1997; Shawber and Taylor 2006), more creative (Schaefer 1969; Hoff 2005a), participate in more family activities (Manosevitz *et al.* 1973), and have advanced theory of mind skills (Taylor and Carlson 1997). Note, however, there are a few studies in which children with imaginary companions are described as lower in social competence (Harter and Chao 1992; Bouldin and Pratt 1999) and self-image (Hoff 2005a).

During the preschool years, girls are more likely than boys to have imaginary companions. However, this sex difference should not be interpreted as suggesting that preschool boys are less imaginative or less interested in elaborated role play. Carlson and Taylor (2005) found that boys and girls were equally likely to engage in elaborated role play, but the form of the role play differs as a function of sex. Whereas girls are more likely than boys to have imaginary companions, boys are more likely than girls to create a character that is acted out rather than treated as a companion (i.e. a pretend identity). Another important caveat about the sex difference in incidence of imaginary companions is that it is limited to the preschool years; by age 7, boys and girls are equally likely to report having imaginary companions (Taylor *et al.* 2004).

One interesting difference between children with and without imaginary companions, which is particularly relevant to the issues addressed later in this chapter, relates to inhibitory control—the ability to suppress thought processes that interfere with goal-directed behaviour. Inhibitory control is a key component of 'executive function', the hallmark of prefrontal brain activity that serves to monitor and control thoughts, actions, and emotions (Posner and Rothbart 2000). Individual differences in executive function are increasingly recognized as playing a critical role in children's cognitive and social development (e.g. Mischel *et al.* 1989; Hughes 1998; Kochanska *et al.* 2000; Zelazo *et al.* 2003; Carlson *et al.* 2004a). In a recent study of 104 typically developing children aged 3 and 4, Carlson and Davis (2005) found that children who have imaginary companions (26 per cent of this sample) showed evidence of greater inhibitory control on the two main types of inhibitory control tasks: delay-of-gratification and attention-conflict. On the delay-of-gratification task (Mischel *et al.* 1989), children with imaginary companions were able to wait alone 20 per cent longer in order to receive a larger snack than children without imaginary companions. This finding is consistent with Singer's (1961) report of a relation between fantasy proneness and waiting ability in school-age children. Attention-conflict was assessed with the dimensional change card sort in which children are asked to sort cards featuring bidimensional symbols according to one dimension (e.g. colour) and then according to another dimension (e.g. shape) (Zelazo *et al.* 2003). Carlson and Davis found that children with imaginary companions were more flexible at switching their focus of attention and controlling actions than those without imaginary companions. It is important to note that in this sample, children who had imaginary companions did not differ from other children significantly in terms of age or verbal ability. These differences in performance on inhibitory control measures point to an intriguing relation between executive control processes and imagination that we will return to later in our discussion.

Characteristics of Imaginary Companions

In our research we have collected hundreds of descriptions of imaginary companions and have been struck by the diversity and richness of children's creations. Our research indicates that there is no 'typical' imaginary companion; the animals and people who populate children's fantasy lives come in all sizes, ages, genders, and species, including Martians, ghosts, angels, superheroes, and monsters, as well as invisible girls and boys. Sometimes the character is completely made-up and sometimes it is based on a real person/animal (e.g. an invisible version of a cousin who lives far away). Imaginary companions also differ in their vividness, personality development, the extent to which they have some basis in the real world, and the length of time they inhabit children's imagination. Sometimes imaginary companions are stable, long-lived, and played with regularly; other pretend friends have a much more transitory existence, drifting in and out of the child's fantasy life. In our research, we have encountered children whose lives were crowded with imaginary people and animals, none of which lingered for any length of time. Other children had only one or two imaginary companions at a time, but they updated their friends frequently, for example, trading in a blue-eyed blond boy named Tompy for a small female mouse named Gadget. Some children keep the same imaginary companions for years with few changes.

Attention to the content of children's descriptions is instructive because imaginary companions are custom-designed by children to meet their own needs and thus can be used as a source of information about children's interests, concerns, emotions, and understanding of their world (Harter and Chao 1992). The descriptions also provide clues about the diverse functions served by this type of pretend play (Hoff 2005b). In the remainder of this chapter, we focus on a feature of children's descriptions that we find particularly intriguing and potentially informative: children's frequent complaints about the undesirable personality characteristics and undesirable behaviour of their imaginary companions.

THE SPECIAL CASE OF THE TROUBLESOME AND
NONCOMPLIANT IMAGINARY COMPANION

When adults think about the attractions of having an imaginary companion, they tend to focus on the joys of having a friend who is always supportive and helpful, agrees with what you say, does what you want, keeps your secrets, and is consistently loving and good company. It seems reasonable to assume that a made-up friend would not suffer from the moodiness, stubbornness, and other flaws of real friends. However, descriptions of imaginary companions often include pretend friends who are disobedient, bossy, argumentative, and unpredictable (Jersild et al. 1933; Bender and Vogel 1941; Taylor 1999; Taylor and Carlson 2002). Some imaginary companions do not go away when the child wishes they would, but instead follow the child around in a way that is described as annoying. Others do not show up when they are wanted. They come and go on their own schedule (rather than according to the child's wishes) and do not always want to play what the child wants to play. They talk too loudly, do not share, or do not do as they are told.

Children's complaints about their imaginary companions raise some fascinating questions. We are particularly interested in the possibility that some children actually experience their imaginary companions as autonomous beings who are not completely under their control. This idea is counterintuitive because it seems reasonable to assume that children, who are the authors or the puppet masters, have complete control over the things that the imaginary companion says and does. Some researchers have suggested that control over the actions and words of another is at the root of the appeal of this type of fantasy (Benson and Pryor 1973). Yet at least some of the descriptions of noncompliant imaginary companions we have collected suggest a perceived lack of control (also see Hoff 2005b) and we believe there is empirical support for taking children at their word about the unruly behaviour of their imaginary companions (Taylor et al. 2003).

Our first step in investigating children's control over their imaginary companions was to ask children more specifically about it. Up to this point, our observations of the negative attributes and uncontrollable behaviours of imaginary companions were based on children's responses to general questions ('What do you like to do when you play with your pretend friend?'; 'What do you like/not like about your pretend friend?'). In a study designed to examine the wilder and darker side of imaginary companions more systematically, we asked specific questions about negativity and control. The participants in this study were 89 preschool children (mean age = 4 years, 5 months; 47 girls and 42 boys), all of whom were identified as having imaginary companions on the basis of interviews with the children and their parents (46 invisible friends and 43 personified objects). After the children provided general descriptions of their imaginary companions, they were asked:

- You know, friends get along most of the time, but sometimes they don't get along. Do you ever have fights or argue with your friend?
- Does your friend ever try to boss you around or make you do things that you do not want to do?
- Does your friend ever surprise you with things he or she says or does?
- Does your friend always do what you want him/her to do?
- Does he or she always play what you want to play?

The coding of children's control over imaginary companions was based on the entire interview (not just the questions listed above) because descriptions of unruly behaviour were elicited by the general questions as well as by the more specific ones. Two coders rated children's responses on a three point scale from a score of 1 (the imaginary companion is described as very obedient and compliant with no indication he or she is ever argumentative or difficult) to a score of 3 (the imaginary companion is wilful and difficult with ideas of his/her own that are sometimes at odds with what the child wants).

Of the 89 children, 32 (36 per cent) described their imaginary companions as models of compliance and agreeableness. For example, 'Shadow the Shark' (despite his name) could not have been more loyal, friendly, and supportive. Thirty-one children (35 per cent) gave some indication that the imaginary companions did not *always* do or say what the child wanted, although they were mostly friendly and compliant. However, 26 children (29 per cent) described their imaginary companions as noncompliant and gave specific examples of their unruly behaviour. These are imaginary companions who have to be reprimanded ('Stop bothering me!'), locked out ('When he is bad I just lock the door'), and punished. For six children, the difficulty of their interactions with the imaginary companion was the predominant theme in the description (see Table 4.2 for examples of compliant and noncompliant imaginary companions).

Table 4.2.   Examples of noncompliant and compliant imaginary companions.

Noncompliant imaginary companions

Roger, a tiny invisible boy (child is female, 41 months)

E: Do you ever have fights with Roger?
C: When he is bad I just lock the door.

E: Does Roger ever get bossy, bother you, or make you do things you do not want to do?
C: Yes, when I'm trying to eat my lunch and he bothers me and I say, 'Don't Roger, don't!'

E: What do you not like about Roger?
C: When he's got my toys and I say, 'That's mine, that's mine' and he lays down.

Boo, an invisible ghost (child is male, 43 months)

E: How did you meet Boo?
C: He came to my house and I said, 'Please don't eat my daddy'.

E: When you want to play with Boo, how do you get him to come?
C: He usually takes something and eats it and I get really mad.

E: Does Boo ever surprise you with the things he says or does?
C: He turns on the music and it sucks him in.

E: Does Boo do whatever you say?
C: Yes, I vacuum him up because he is naughty.

E: What is special about Boo?
C: He goes under the table and bites my foot.

Examples of compliant imaginary companions

Shadow the Shark, a shark based on the child's shadow (child is male, 52 months)

E: When you want to play with Shadow the Shark, how do you get him to come?
C: He just comes with me, he's right by my side.

E: When you and Shadow the Shark are together, what do you like to do?
C: Draw, do the same things I do, eats, blocks light.

E: Can Shadow the Shark do anything you don't know how to do?
C: Yes, I can do anything he can do.

E: Does Shadow the Shark help you sometimes?
C: Yes, he's right on my side.

E: Do you help Shadow the Shark sometimes?
C: Yes, I'm right on his side.

Sally, an invisible girl (child is female, 51 months)

C: Sally is my best friend. She zooms everywhere I go!

E: Where does Sally go when she is not with you?
C: She always wants to be with me.

E: Do you ever have fights or argue with Sally?
C: No, never.

E: Does Sally ever try to boss you around or make you do things that you don't want to do?
C: No, never.

E: Does Sally always play what you want to play?
C: Yes, she always shares.

E: Does Sally ever help you do things?
C: Yes, she helps me sweep, mop and rake.

E: Does Sally ever help you feel better?
C: Yes, when I'm feeling sad she makes me feel happy because she gives me things.

In summary, this analysis using specific questions about autonomy revealed that almost a third of children with imaginary companions described them as noncompliant in ways that suggested the children experienced the companion to some extent as being out of their conscious control. Note that it is possible that our study underestimates the perceived autonomy of imaginary companions because we focused on negativity in the children's descriptions. This was because behaviours that are described as undesirable are more unambiguously consistent with a perceived lack of control than behaviours that are desirable or neutral. However, perceived autonomy does not *require* that the imaginary companion's behaviour be vexing to the child. Hoff provides some positive descriptions of imaginary companions that suggest some degree of perceived autonomy. For example, some children reported that their imaginary companions taught them things that they did not know before ('he can teach me about where he was before, when he didn't know who I am') (2005a, 175).

WHY DO CHILDREN CREATE
NONCOMPLIANT IMAGINARY COMPANIONS?

What should we make of the unruly character of many imaginary companions? First of all, we do not consider these types of imaginary companions to be evidence of psychopathology. It is important to be clear about this point because imaginary companions have sometimes been described by adult and adolescent patients as the first manifestations of the 'alters' of their dissociative identity disorder (Dell and Eisenhower 1990; Putnam 1997). More specifically, Silberg (1998) suggested that lack of control over the actions of imaginary companions characterizes dissociative children's interactions with them. However, lack of control in the context of dissociative psychopathology is only one of a number of other characteristics that Silberg lists. For example, children with dissociative disorders tend to be confused about whether the imaginary companion is real or imaginary, believe that the imaginary companion can take over the body, feel the need to protect the privacy of the imaginary companion's identity, and often report conflicts between imaginary companions that leave the child confused about how to behave.

We have not seen these characteristics in our normative samples. On the contrary, the children in our studies have openly shared details about imaginary companions with parents and researchers and have shown age-appropriate reality monitoring. For example, Taylor *et al.* (1993) found that children with and without imaginary companions were equally competent at distinguishing mental images from reality, such as what someone could do with the *thought* of a cookie versus a real cookie (Wellman and Estes 1986). Furthermore, in the sample of 89 children in which more systematic details were collected about noncompliant imaginary companions, we also coded the valence of children's affect during the interviews about the pretend friend (positive, neutral, or negative). Silberg's research suggests that children with dissociative disorders would show distress when describing an imaginary companion's uncontrollable behaviour. However, the children in our study were mostly neutral in their affect when they described these behaviours and, in general, there were no differences in affect among the three groups of children who described compliant, intermediate, and noncompliant imaginary companions. Thus, children do not seem to be truly upset by their imaginary companions' naughty or disobedient behaviour. We saw no evidence of genuine anger in children's interviews. These findings, along with the sizeable frequency of descriptions of unruly imaginary companions in our research, suggest that psychopathology is an unlikely explanation for this phenomenon.

Silberg (1998) is careful to point out that there is no empirical research investigating the clinical differentiation between normative imaginary companions and dissociative projections. We suspect that children's feelings of being bossed or annoyed by imaginary companions have been underestimated in nonclinical samples. Here we explore three alternative explanations that focus on either the child's choice of *content* or the *process* involved in generating the actions and words of the imaginary companion. We do not mean to suggest that only one of the three explanations is correct. For some children a number of factors might result in the creation of a noncompliant and/or troublesome imaginary companion. It is possible that all three accounts have some validity for at least some children some of the time.

Noncompliance as an Emotive

Negative behaviours in a child's imaginary companion have sometimes been interpreted in terms of psychodynamic defence mechanisms (Nagera 1969; Bach 1971). This is not our orientation, but it is possible that the behaviour of the imaginary companion might reflect the child's preoccupation with thoughts about disobedience, being punished, and related aspects of bad behaviour. On this view, an unruly imaginary companion is not fundamentally different from a loyal and compliant one; both reflect the child's thoughts about behaviour that are explored via the role play fantasy. This account is consistent with Bretherton's (1989) emphasis on pretend play as facilitating emotional mastery and Ariel's (2002) discussion of pretend play as an avenue for children to explore and express *emotives*, emotionally arousing themes that have significance for a person for an extended period. (Ariel gives the example of physical vulnerability as a frequent emotive that is explored in pretend play; also see Dunn and Hughes 2001.) According to Ariel (2002), emotive themes might be particularly likely to emerge in the child's solitary play. When alone, children's pretending is guided by their personal network of associations among thoughts, feelings, and emotions, whereas in collaborative play, particularly with older children and adults, pretend play often is partially structured by the other person.

It makes sense to us that at least for some children, the issues of independence, rule breaking, and disobedience could be preoccupying in this way. Thus, for some children, the exciting thing about having an imaginary companion is their contact with a disobedient, mischievous creature who gets into trouble. We suspect that children would experience contact with a real friend who acted this way to be more troubling. However, mulling over the dark side of a pretend companion is a potentially adaptive method of coping with the real-life themes and challenges that children normally experience.

Illusion of Independent Agency

According to the emotive explanation described above, the noncompliance is actually desired by the child and presumably part of what the child controls in the imaginary companion's behaviour. However, it is also possible that the noncompliance occurs at least in some cases as a by-product of the processes underlying this type of role play. In this account, reports of autonomy in imaginary companions are taken more seriously as accurate descriptions of what the children experience. There is precedent for this type of experience in research with adult fiction writers who frequently describe autonomy in their characters, a phenomenon referred to as the *illusion of independent agency* (Taylor *et al.* 2003).

The illusion of independent agency (IIA) occurs when a fictional character is experienced by the person who created it as having independent thoughts, words, desires, and/or actions (i.e. as having a mind and will of its own). Taylor *et al.* (2003) have found that this illusion often characterizes the reports of adult fiction writers describing the process of creative writing and their relationships with the characters in their novels (also see Watkins 1990). The essence of this conceptual illusion is the sense that the characters are independent agents not directly under the author's control. In some descriptions, the events of the story seem to be dictated by the characters and the writer's job becomes merely to observe the story as it unfolds, almost as one would experience a dream. At times, the characters rebel against the author's vision of a story, as described in E. M. Forster's comments on the process of writing a novel:

> The characters arrive when evoked, but full of the spirit of mutiny. For they have these numerous parallels with people like ourselves, they try to live their own lives and are consequently often engaged in treason against the main scheme of the book. They 'run away,' they 'get out of hand': they are creations inside of a creation, and often inharmonious towards it; if they are given com-

plete freedom they kick the book to pieces, and if they are kept too sternly in check, they revenge themselves by dying, and destroy it by intestinal decay. (1927/1985, pp. 66–67)

Although the illusion of independent agency is a specific type of experience that occurs in the context of creative writing, Taylor *et al.* (2003) point out a number of connections to recent investigations of automatic and controlled processes in cognitive and social psychology. For example, Wegner and colleagues have provided growing evidence that people often fail to recognize their own causal role in outcomes in which they do play a part (Ansfield and Wegner 1996; Wegner and Wheatley 1999; Aarts *et al.* 2005). This research has focused on perceptions of involuntary behaviour in the motor realm (e.g. people are unaware of the small movements they have produced that make a dowsing rod twitch), but it opens the door to the possibility that a person could be unaware of the thought processes giving rise to a sense of what a character is saying or doing (also see research on reality monitoring; Johnson *et al.* 1993).

The findings of research on skill acquisition might also be relevant to the illusion of independent agency (Dreyfus and Dreyfus 1986). When a person first starts to operate within a domain—driving a car, playing chess, or making medical diagnoses—judgements and behaviour come slowly with lots of conscious, effortful thinking and reasoning. With increased expertise, however, the process becomes automated, freeing the person's conscious attentional capacity for other tasks. Perhaps someone who pretends a lot—a child who regularly plays with an imaginary companion or an adult who day after day thinks about the world of a novel—could be described as developing expertise in the domain of fantasy. Thus, it is possible that the process of imagining the companion or the fictional world might become automated until it is no longer consciously experienced. As the person readies him- or herself for the imaginative act, the fantasy characters present themselves automatically. Their words and actions begin to be perceived, listened to, and recorded rather than consciously created. As a result, the imagined characters are experienced as speaking and acting independently.

To what extent is it appropriate to draw a connection between the adult reports of autonomy in fictional characters and children's reports of autonomy in imaginary companions? Clearly caution is warranted, yet we are intrigued by the possibility that sustained experience resulting in the automation that comes with expertise might account for the illusion in both children and adults. Alternatively, expertise might be less crucial for the illusion to occur in children. According to Wilson, children are particularly likely to, 'act on automatic pilot, with their adaptive unconscious guiding their behavior in sophisticated ways before they are aware of what they are doing or why they are doing it' (2002, 56). In any case, we are hopeful that it will be possible to develop hypotheses and gain understanding of the phenomenology of childhood fantasy by investigating parallels in the experiences of adults, who are better able to describe their fantasy activities than young children.

Individual Differences in Inhibitory Control

Our third explanation extends the second, process-oriented explanation by focusing on the finding that some children are more prone than others to experience their imaginary companions as uncontrollable. Although pretence and executive control are positively related on average (high pretence paired with high inhibitory control), a subset of high-fantasy individuals with relatively poorer ability to control thought processes might be particularly prone to experience the illusion of independent agency and to describe their fictional characters as being out of their conscious control. Specifically, individuals who have facility in creating fantasy representations at a high level of activation might come to experience those representations as if they are not self-generated, especially if they have relatively weaker self-control skills.

In general, having an imaginary companion was associated with enhanced inhibitory control skills (Carlson and Davis 2005), but Carlson *et al.* (2004b) found an interesting difference between children who reported a lack of control over their imaginary companions and children whose imaginary companions were more compliant. These subgroups did not differ on age, sex, or verbal ability; however, the children with unruly imaginary companions did not do as well as the other children on a Stroop-like measure of executive function called Grass/Snow. On this task, children are told to point to a white card when the experimenter says 'grass' and to point to a green card when she says 'snow' (Carlson and Moses 2001). Children with imaginary companions who provided evidence of the illusion of independent agency had significantly *more difficulty* inhibiting a prepotent response on this task. They tended to err by pointing to the green card for 'grass' and the white card for 'snow' after the first few trials. This result suggests that children who are more prone to interference from perceptual stimuli might be more likely to experience their imaginary companions as acting autonomously. The bottom-up phenomenology of the fantasy might override top-down cognitive control and reflection for these children.

This interpretation is highly speculative, but it would be interesting to pursue future research investigating the relation between inhibitory control and the experience of imaginary companions. Another future direction of research would be to examine self-awareness and its relation to both imaginative activities and conscious control of thought processes. Along with dramatic gains in inhibitory control in the preschool period, children become increasingly capable of reflecting on their own thought processes, feelings, and behaviours (Kopp 1982; Harter 1999). Research on executive control in problem-solving tasks has shown that preschoolers go through a period of 'knowing' the correct answer verbally, but nevertheless making the dominant (but incorrect) response behaviourally, perhaps because they cannot yet control their attention and resist interference from distracting stimuli. Only later in development do knowledge and controlled behaviour line up (e.g. on the Dimensional Change Card Sort, see Zelazo *et al.*, 2003; Diamond *et al.* 2005). Children's developing awareness and reflection upon their efforts to control thoughts and behaviours may contribute to their understanding of their imaginative processes, and vice versa.

CONCLUSION

Having an imaginary companion is a common occurrence in both early and middle childhood that is associated with a number of positive characteristics in cognitive and social development. It is hypothesized to play an adaptive role in development and may serve many of the same functions as social role play with parents, siblings, and peers (Harris 2000). However, because imaginary companions are most often self-created, they can provide a unique window into *what* is on children's minds as well as *how* they process information that is generated in imagination versus perceptually experienced.

The main goal of this chapter was to illuminate a relatively unexplored aspect of children's private role play—autonomy and control in interactions with imaginary companions. We have found that a substantial number of children with imaginary companions (almost a third) describe their imaginary companions as noncompliant—they come and go of their own accord, engage in bad behaviour, and do not 'listen' to their creator. This phenomenon is inconsistent with the historical belief that an imaginary companion is attractive for children precisely because it is one of the few things in life that a child gets to control completely. Indeed, some of the parents in our research expressed concern about these 'bad' imaginary companions. However, noncompliant and/or troublesome imaginary companions occur frequently enough to be considered normative, do not seem to be truly distressing to children and do not appear to be accompanied by symptoms of a dissociative disorder such as poor reality monitoring.

Instead, we favoured three explanations for seemingly uncontrollable imaginary companions. On the first account, the negative attributes of the pretend friend simply reflect the emotional themes and challenges that children encounter on a regular basis. On the second account, the imaginary character is experienced as though it is autonomous—the illusion of independent agency—as a result of the process of activating the fantasy with such frequency. Similar to the illusion of independent agency reported by adult fiction writers, expert pretenders develop automatic and unconscious thought processes that may contribute to this illusion. The third explanation builds on the second by suggesting that in combination with high levels of *activation* of the fantasy, relatively low levels of *inhibition* of one's own thoughts and actions may predispose some individuals to have difficulty consciously controlling the products of their imagination. In support of this possibility, we reported that the subset of children who described uncontrollable imaginary companions performed more poorly than other children on a measure of inhibitory control, even though children with imaginary companions as a whole showed greater inhibitory control than those without them (Carlson *et al.* 2004b).

These explanations are not mutually exclusive. Note, for example, that a balance between activation of fantasy and inhibition of reality or perceptual cues that signal 'real' may be at play in the mind of creators of fictional characters. Furthermore, it is theoretically possible that even compliant imaginary companions would be experienced as if they are autonomous and out of the child's conscious control according to the information processing explanations—highly vivid, self-generated fantasy of any kind could lead to this phenomenon. We focused on negative attributes in children's descriptions of autonomous imaginary companions because they provide more overt signs of it, but this might not be merely a coincidence. It may be that negative emotional content is more conducive to the information processing features that contribute to the illusion of independent agency. Consider, for example, that both children with imaginary companions and adult fiction writers would be far more likely to experience an imagined character as autonomous if its intentions, desires, and beliefs are at odds with one's own than if they are in complete harmony. Thus, the negative valence of the content might contribute to or enhance the illusion of independent agency. Finally, although the expertise and inhibitory control explanations are complementary in some respects, they also make somewhat different predictions. For example, on the expertise account, older children who on average have spent more time with their imaginary companions would be more likely to experience them as autonomous than younger children who had had less time to develop expertise. In contrast, the inhibitory control account predicts that older children who on average have better executive functioning skills would be less likely to experience their imaginary companions as autonomous. We believe that research that disambiguates the interaction between content and process in perceived lack of control over imagined characters will be exciting as a new direction in the study of imagination in pretenders of all ages.

References

Aarts, H., Custers, R. and Wegner, D. M. 2005: On the inference of personal authorship: Enhancing experienced agency by priming effect information. *Consciousness and Cognition*, 14, 439–458.

Ames, L. B. and Learned, J. 1946: Imaginary companions and related phenomena. *The Journal of Genetic Psychology*, 69, 147–167.

Ansfield, M. E. and Wegner, D. M. 1996: The feeling of doing. In Gollwitzer, P. M. and Bargh, J. A. (eds), *The Psychology of Action*. New York: Guilford Press, 482–506.

Ariel, S. 2002: *Children's Imaginative Play*. Westport, CT: Praeger Publishers.

Bach, S. 1971: Notes on some imaginary companions. *Psychoanalytic Study of the Child*, 26, 159–171.

Bender, L. and Vogel, B. F. 1941: Imaginary companions of children. *American Journal of Orthopsychiatry*, 11, 56–65.

Benson, R. M. and Pryor, D. B. 1973: When friends fall out: Developmental interference with the function of some imaginary companions. *Journal of the American Psychoanalytic Association*, 21, 457–468.

Bouldin, P. and Pratt, C. 1999: Characteristics of preschool children with imaginary companions. *The Journal of Genetic Psychology*, 160, 397–410.

Bretherton, I. 1989: Pretense: The form and function of make believe play. *Developmental Review*, 9, 383–401.

Carlson, S. M. and Davis, A. C. 2005: *Executive Function and Pretense in Preschool Children*. Poster presented at the annual meeting of the Jean Piaget Society, Vancouver, BC.

Carlson, S. M. and Moses, L. J. 2001: Individual differences in inhibitory control and children's theory of mind. *Child Development*, 72, 1032–1053.

Carlson, S. M. and Taylor, M. 2005: Imaginary companions and impersonated characters: Sex differences in children's fantasy play. *Merrill-Palmer Quarterly*, 51, 93–118.

Carlson, S. M., Mandell, D. J. and Williams, L. 2004a: Executive function and theory of mind: Stability and prediction from age 2 to 3. *Developmental Psychology*, 40, 1105–1122.

Carlson, S. M., Taylor, M. and Maring, B. L. 2004b: Sustained interactions with imaginary others. In Subbotsky, E. and Taylor, M. (co-convenors), *Causation in Non-physical Domains: Magical Thinking and Human Communication*. International Society for the Study of Behavioral Development, Ghent, Belgium.

Dell, D. F. and Eisenhower, J. W. 1990: Adolescent multiple personality disorder: A preliminary study of eleven cases. *Journal of the American Academy of Child and Adolescent Psychiatry*, 29, 359–366.

Diamond, A., Carlson, S. M. and Beck, D. M. 2005: Preschool children's performance in task switching on the Dimensional Change Card Sort task: Separating the dimensions aids the ability to switch. *Developmental Neuropsychology*, 28, 689–729.

Dreyfus, H. L. and Dreyfus, S. E. 1986: *Mind over Machine*. New York: The Free Press.

Dunn, J. and Dale, N. 1984: I a daddy: 2-year-olds' collaboration in joint pretend with sibling and with mother. In Bretherton, I. (ed.), *Symbolic Play: The Development of Social Understanding*. New York: Academic Press, 131–158.

Dunn, J. and Hughes, C. 2001: 'I got swords and you're dead!': Violent fantasy, anti-social behavior, friendship and moral sensibility in young children. *Child Development*, 72, 491–505.

Engel, S. 2005: The narrative worlds of *what is* and *what if*. *Cognitive Development*, 20, 514–525.

Forster, E. M. 1927/1985: *Aspects of the Novel*. New York: Harcourt Brace.

Gleason, T. 2002: Social provisions of real and imaginary relationships in early childhood. *Developmental Psychology*, 38, 979–992.

Gleason, T., Sebanc, A. and Hartup, W. 2000: Imaginary companions of preschool children. *Developmental Psychology*, 36, 419–428.

Harris, P. L. 2000: *The Work of the Imagination*. Oxford: Basil Blackwell.

Harter, S. 1999: *The Construction of the Self*. New York: Guilford Press.

Harter, S. and Chao, C. 1992: The role of competence in children's creation of imaginary friends. *Merrill-Palmer Quarterly*, 38, 350–363.

Hoff, E. 2005a: Imaginary companions, creativity, and self-image in middle childhood. *Creativity Research Journal*, 17, 167–180.

Hoff, E. 2005b: A friend living inside me: The forms and functions of imaginary companions. *Imagination, Cognition and Personality*, 24, 151–189.

Howe, N., Petrakos, H., Rinaldi, C. M. and LeFebvre, R. 2005: "This is a bad dog, you know. . .": Constructing shared meanings during sibling pretend play. *Child Development*, 76, 783–794.

Howes, C. 1985: Sharing fantasy: Social pretend play in toddlers. *Child Development*, 56, 1253–1258.

Hughes, C. 1998: Finding your marbles: Does preschoolers' strategic behavior predict later understanding of mind? *Developmental Psychology*, 34, 1326–1339.

Hughes, F. P. 1999: *Children, Play and Development* (3rd edn). Needham Heights, MA: Allyn and Bacon.

Hurlock, E. B. and Burnstein, M. 1932: The imaginary playmate: A questionnaire study. *Journal of Genetic Psychology*, 41, 380–391.

Jersild, A. T., Markey, F. V. and Jersild, C. L. 1933: *Children's Fears, Dreams, Wishes, Daydreams, Likes, Dislikes, Pleasant and Unpleasant Memories*, Volume 12. New York: Teachers College, Columbia University.

Johnson, M. K., Hashtroudi, S. and Lindsay, D. S. 1993: Source monitoring. *Psychological Review*, 114, 3–28.

Kavanaugh, R. D., Whittington, S. and Cerbone, M. J. 1983: Mothers' use of fantasy in speech to young children. *Journal of Child Language*, 10, 45–55.

Kochanska, G., Murray, K. T. and Harlan, E. T. 2000: Effortful control in early childhood: Continuity and change, antecedents, and implications for social development. *Developmental Psychology*, 36, 220–232.

Kopp, C. B. 1982: Antecedents of self-regulation: A developmental perspective. *Developmental Psychology*, 18, 199–214.

Manosevitz, M., Prentice, M. and Wilson, F. 1973: Individual and family correlates of imaginary companions in preschool children. *Developmental Psychology*, 8, 72–79.

Mauro, J. 1991: The friend that only I can see: A longitudinal investigation of children's imaginary companions. Unpublished doctoral dissertation, University of Oregon.

Miller, C. and Garvey, C. 1984: Mother–baby role play. In Bretherton, I. (ed.), *Symbolic Play*. New York: Academic Press. 101–131.

Mischel, W., Shoda, Y. and Rodriguez, M. L. 1989: Delay of gratification in children. *Science*, 244, 933–938.

Myers, W. A. 1976: Imaginary companions, fantasy twins, mirror dreams and depersonalization. *Psychoanalytic Quarterly*, 45, 503–524.

Nagera, H. 1969: The imaginary companion: Its significance for ego development and conflict resolution. *The Psychoanalytic Study of the Child*, 24, 89–99.

Pearson, D., Rouse, H., Doswell, S., Ainsworth, C., Dawson, O., Simms, K., Edwards, L. and Falconbridge, J. 2001: Prevalence of imaginary companions in a normal child population. *Child: Care, Health and Development*, 27, 12–22.

Piaget, J. 1962: *Play, Dreams and Imitation*. London: Routledge and Kegan Paul.

Posner, M. I. and Rothbart, M. K. 2000: Developing mechanisms of self-regulation. *Development and Psychopathology*, 12, 427–441.

Putnam, F. 1997: *Dissociation in Children and Adolescents*. New York: Guildford Press.

Schaefer, C. E. 1969: Imaginary companions and creative adolescents. *Developmental Psychology*, 1, 747–749.

Seiffge-Krenke, I. 1993: Close friendship and imaginary companions in adolescence. *New Directions for Child Development*, 60, 73–87.

Seiffge-Krenke, I. 1997: Imaginary companions in adolescence: Sign of a deficient or positive development? *Journal of Adolescence*, 20, 137–154.

Shawber, A. B. and Taylor, M. 2006: Individual differences in children's sociability and their play with imaginary companions. In Taylor, M. (Chair), *Developmental and Clinical Perspectives on Imaginary Companions*. Symposium presented at the annual meeting of the Jean Piaget Society, Baltimore, MD.

Silberg, J. L. 1998: Interviewing strategies for assessing dissociative disorders in children and adolescents. In Silberg, J. A. (ed.), *The Dissociative Child*. Lutherville, MD: Sidran Press, 47–68.

Singer, J. L. 1961: Imagination and waiting ability in young children. *Journal of Personality*, 29, 396–413.

Singer, D. G. and Singer, J. L. 1990: *The House of Make-believe: Children's Play and Developing Imagination*. Cambridge, MA: Harvard University Press.

Svendsen, M. 1934: Children's imaginary companions. *Archives of Neurology and Psychiatry*, 2, 985–999.

Taylor, M. 1999: *Imaginary Companions and the Children Who Create Them*. New York: Oxford University Press.

Taylor, M. and Carlson, S. M. 1997: The relation between individual differences in fantasy and theory of mind. *Child Development*, 68, 436–455.

Taylor, M. and Carlson, S. M. 2002: Imaginary companions and elaborate fantasy in childhood: Discontinuity with nonhuman animals. In Mitchell, R. W. (ed.), *Pretense in Animals and Humans*. Cambridge: Cambridge University Press, 167–182.

Taylor, M., Cartwright, B. S. and Carlson, S. M. 1993: A developmental investigation of children's imaginary companions. *Developmental Psychology*, 29, 276–285.

Taylor, M., Hodges, S. D. and Kohanyi, A. 2003: The illusion of independent agency: Do adult fiction writers experience their characters as having minds of their own? *Imagination, Cognition and Personality*, 22, 361–380.

Taylor, M., Carlson, S. M., Maring, B. L., Gerow, L. and Charley, C. 2004: The characteristics and correlates of high fantasy in school-aged children: Imaginary companions, impersonation and social understanding. *Developmental Psychology*, 40, 1173–1187.

Watkins, M. 1990: *The Development of Imaginal Dialogues: Invisible Guests*. Boston, MA: Sigo Press.

Wegner, D. M. and Wheatley, T. (1999: Apparent mental causation: Sources of the experience of will. *American Psychologist*, 54, 480–492.

Wellman, H. M. and Estes, D. 1986: Early understanding of mental entities: A reexamination of childhood realism. *Child Development*, 57, 910–923.

Wilson, T. 2002: *Strangers to Ourselves: Discovering the Adaptive Unconscious*. Cambridge, MA: Harvard University Press.

Zelazo, P. D., Müller, U., Frye, D. and Marcovitch, S. 2003: The development of executive function in early childhood. *Monographs of the Society for Research in Child Development*, 68 (3, Serial No. 274).

5

Imagination and Testimony in Cognitive Development: The Cautious Disciple?

PAUL L. HARRIS AND MELISSA KOENIG

Abstract.   Although the imagination is often associated with the contemplation of non-existent possibilities, it is also deployed to think about various non-observable but real events that are learned about via others' testimony rather than direct observation. We ask whether children gullibly believe whatever they are told about matters that they cannot verify for themselves. Emerging evidence shows that even preschool children are cautious in their trust. In particular, they seek out and endorse information from hitherto reliable informants. They also show some differentiation among different types of non-observable entity. In particular, they exhibit more credence in invisible, scientific entities (e.g. germs) than in invisible, non-scientific entities (e.g. God).

IMAGINATION AND TESTIMONY

THE IMAGINATION IS OFTEN CONCEPTUALIZED as a mental faculty dedicated to the contemplation of what has never existed or what does not yet exist. Thus, it is in our imagination that we ruminate about what might have been, daydream about alternatives to our present commitments, and construct plans for a possible future. On this view, the imagination does not make much contact with reality. Once we engage with actual objects and events, it is assumed that our imagination quietly leaves the stage so that more rational, objective processes of observation and ratiocination can take over. However, on close inspection, this view of the imagination is too restrictive. Consider our ideas about the past. Our sense of identity is connected to what we know about our parents, the family and community in which they were raised, and the historical events that directly touched their lives, and indirectly our own. Thus, we situate our own biography in a particular socio-historical complex that

Proceedings of the British Academy **147**, 101–120. © The British Academy 2007.

depends on the vicissitudes and migrations that we have been told about. We think of ourselves as English, or Corsican, or Asian-American, as the case may be. Yet we have not witnessed the past events that infuse our identity. Rather, we accept the reality of the family stories and the larger historical narrative in which those family stories are embedded.

This example illustrates a wider point: the phenomenal world in which we situate our lives reaches far beyond what we can experience first hand. We construct that larger world on the strength of others' testimony. That testimony informs us about events in the past, as just illustrated. It also informs us about ongoing events that are too distant or too small for us to observe first hand. Finally, for most of humanity, at least, it informs us about metaphysical events that are not amenable to straightforward empirical observation.

Adults presumably make sense of this vast sea of testimony with the help of their imagination. Just as we process an entirely fictional narrative by means of the imagination, so too we rely on our imagination to contemplate events that take place in those narratives where fact and fiction are interwoven, as well as those that lay claim to complete veracity. By implication, the imagination is not dedicated only to the consideration of non-actual events but rather to the innumerable events—whether actual or merely fictional—that we have not witnessed for ourselves.

On this alternative view, the imagination is also critical for the normal process of cognitive development. Psychologists have often made the claim that children actively explore the world, construct their own theories and interpretations of what they have observed, and slowly revise those theories in the light of further, first-hand exploration. In key areas—the understanding of space, quantity, and probability, for example—children are assumed to be self-sufficient in constructing their own ideas. Indeed, they often resist the corrections and suggestions offered by adults. Thus, children can be characterized as stubborn autodidacts. However, although this account may apply to domains in which children can gather first-hand, observational data for themselves, it is not easy to apply to domains in which children can make few pertinent observations (Harris 2002). Yet children do show conceptual development in such domains.

Consider three quite recent ideas in human history: that the Earth is a sphere, that mental processes are intimately linked to the brain, and that species were not abruptly created but gradually evolved. Recent developmental research shows that each of these ideas can be understood and accepted by young children. For example, across various questions (e.g. 'If you walked for many days in a straight line would you fall off the edge of the world?' or 'Some children think the sky is all around; other children think the sky is only on top. Point (on a globe) to where the sky really is'), the majority of British

6- to 7-year-olds display an understanding of the spherical shape of the Earth. Australian children display a comparable level of understanding at 4–5 years—not because their first-hand experience of the shape of the Earth is more informative but presumably because they are more often exposed to comments about differences between the hemispheres than their British cousins (Siegal *et al.* 2004). Children also have some understanding of the contemporary view that the brain is critical for mental processes. For example, North American 7- and 8-year-olds appreciate that swapping one's brain with a toddler—but not swapping one's heart—would have dire effects on one's ability to think and count (Johnson 1990). They even realize that the brain is intimately connected to our sense of who we are (Johnson 1990; Gottfried *et al.* 1999; Corriveau *et al.* 2005). For example, when invited to think about the consequences of transplanting their own brain to a pig, the majority of 7- and 8-year-olds concluded that the pig would no longer admit to being a pig but would claim to be a child. Finally, between the ages of 8 and 11 years, children begin to acknowledge that, for example, the first dinosaurs were not instantly created and did not just mysteriously appear on Earth, but gradually evolved. This developmental shift, it must be acknowledged, is not universal. It is displayed by children in non-fundamentalist communities. Their peers in fundamentalist American communities subscribe, almost exclusively, to a Creationist account at both ages (Evans 2000).

Summarizing across these three different lines of investigation it is clear that young children have the ability to assimilate claims that would have been rejected as implausible in earlier centuries. Children's understanding does not appear to be confined to a verbal parroting of claims that they do not actually understand. Even when they are asked novel questions that they are unlikely to have discussed explicitly (e.g. 'If you walked for many days in a straight line would you fall off the edge of the world?' or 'How would a brain transplant with a toddler affect your ability to think?'), children answer consequentially. Yet their answers are presumably not grounded in their own first-hand experience. Countless generations of adults never arrived at such claims on the basis of their first-hand experience—and even contemporary children vary in their replies depending on the type of community in which they are raised and the testimony that they hear.

The most plausible interpretation of children's acceptance of these claims is, we think, straightforward. Children construct, in their imagination, a representation—a working model—that incorporates the claims that they have heard. Thus, they begin to imagine a spherical Earth, or an organ inside the head that sustains the processes of thinking and remembering, or species that change gradually over successive generations. This interpretation of various key aspects of cognitive development raises intriguing and unanswered questions about the nature of cognitive development. We first spell out our interpretation in more detail and then turn to those larger implications.

Although the standard view of cognitive development, as we described earlier, emphasizes the way that children explore and observe the world, it is plausible to suppose that children are also equipped to learn from other people's testimony. Particularly in those domains where they cannot make the relevant observations for themselves, it is likely that children listen in a trusting fashion to what adults tell them. It might be objected that children will have insuperable difficulties in making sense of claims about processes and events that they cannot observe for themselves but that objection seems implausible. After all, with the help of their imagination, children, like adults, readily become absorbed in, and appear to make sense of, a variety of narratives (Harris 2000). Many of these narratives—for example, historical accounts and fairy tales—describe events and processes that children have not observed themselves. Granted such an ability to understand narratives about unobservables, there is no reason to suppose that children will have any special difficulty in understanding factual or scientific claims about unobservables.

This does not mean that children will automatically assimilate the full implications of all that they are told about the Earth, the brain, or evolution. There is still, no doubt, a major role for conceptual development. So, for example, it may take some time for the child to realize that the brain is not just an organ that energizes or activates mental processes (akin to a replaceable battery) but rather an organ whose organization is intimately connected to, and indeed inseparable from, the specificity of each individual's thought processes. However, in that respect, conceptual hurdles to the child's learning via testimony need not be any different from those that stand in the way of the child's learning via first-hand observation. In each case, critical pieces of information may be ignored or distorted if they strain the child's existing conceptual system. Our point is simply that there is no reason to think that learning via testimony is any more obstacle-strewn than learning via first-hand experience. Indeed, it is reasonable to entertain a hypothesis first advanced by Thomas Reid to the effect that learning via testimony is a straightforward human endowment—as critical to human cognition as learning via first-hand experience.

Yet if Reid's plausible hypothesis is adopted, we need to consider some of its implications. Reid (1764/1967) himself pointed to one important implication:

> It is evident, that, in the matter of testimony, the balance of human judgment is by nature inclined to the side of belief; and turns to that side of itself when there is nothing put in the opposite scale . . . In a word, if credulity were the effect of reasoning and experience, it must grow up and gather strength, in the

same proportion as reason and experience do. But if it is a gift of nature, it will be the strongest in childhood, and limited and restrained by experience; and the most superficial view of human life shows, that the last is really the case, and not the first.

In a nutshell, Reid argues that we begin life with an undue readiness to believe testimony and that in the course of development we gradually become more cautious in what we believe. In the next two sections, we argue that the course of development is more complicated. Children do not shift from credulity to caution. In the first place, they show signs of caution very early in life and second, in line with the view that Reid summarily rejects, there is good reason to conclude that the scope of children's credulity expands, as their reason and experience expand.

SIGNS OF EARLY CAUTION

When infants hear an interlocutor name an object, they typically turn to look at the named object, if it is visible. This selective looking can be used to assess lexical comprehension in the second year of life. For example, if infants are shown two pictures—a picture of a cat and a cow—and hear an adult name one of them, they will look selectively at the named picture (Oviatt 1980; Meints *et al.* 1999). It is also possible to use infants' selective looking to probe their reactions to an adult who misnames an object. Koenig and Echols (2003) studied infants' looking patterns when they had heard an adult produce either a true assertion (e.g. 'That's a shoe', said when a picture of a shoe was shown on the screen) or a false assertion (e.g. 'That's a dog', said when a picture of a shoe was shown on the screen). When the speaker named the picture correctly, the standard pattern of looking emerged: infants mainly looked at the named referent, sometimes at the speaker, and very occasionally at their parent who was seated behind them. However, when the informant named the picture incorrectly, infants spent less time looking at the named picture and more time looking at the speaker—as if puzzled by her behaviour. Figure 5.1 illustrates this shift in the pattern of looking.

Further evidence that infants registered the speaker's mistake emerged when infants' own remarks were analysed. Having heard the speaker name the pictured object, they frequently named it themselves. The names that they supplied were typically correct. So, in response to a picture of a shoe, they said 'shoe'. Importantly, they did not copy the mistake made by the incorrect speaker. For example, if the speaker had incorrectly said, 'That's a dog', they still produced the correct name. Not only did infants resist the inaccurate speaker in this fashion, there were indications that they intended to offer a correction. When different conditions of the experiment were compared,

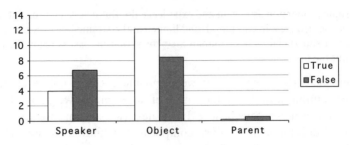

Figure 5.1. Mean looking (in seconds) at speaker, pictured object, and parent as a function of type of assertion.

infants were especially likely to name the object correctly when the speaker (i) had been wrong and (ii) was gazing forward and looking at the object in question—as if intending to name it. If the speaker produced the correct name or was facing away from the picture, infants were less likely to offer the correct name. By implication, infants were sensitive to whether or not the speaker was seeking—but failing—to name an object visible to him or her (as in the gazing-forward condition) and offered corrections accordingly.

Further evidence that very young children resist and even rebut assertions that they regard as inaccurate was obtained by Pea (1982). Children of 18, 24, 30, and 36 months listened to two different speakers. As in the experiments of Koenig and Echols (2003), one made true assertions (e.g. 'That's the dog', said of a toy dog) and the other made false assertions (e.g. 'That's the cat', said of a toy dog). Pea plotted the frequency of simple denials—'No'—following each of these two types of assertion. Figure 5.2 shows the proportion of such responses as a function of age and type of assertion. From 30 months, it is clear that toddlers deny false claims much more often than true ones.

Summing across the studies conducted by Koenig and Echols (2003) and by Pea (1982) it seems clear that children resist false assertions almost as soon

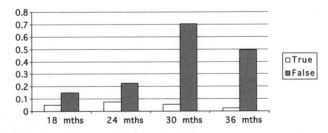

Figure 5.2. Proportion of denials as a function of age and type of assertion.

as they can talk: at 16 months, they stare at an inaccurate speaker, supply what appear to be corrections and by the age of 30 months, they issue explicit denials. Contrary to Reid's favoured proposal, we have important evidence that children place their own experience in the balance when weighing a piece of testimony virtually from the outset. Having previously learned what an object is called, they resist alternative descriptions. The weighing process that Reid associates with mature judgement appears to be built into the very foundations of the child's communication system.

Still, it might be objected that the kind of situation explored so far is relatively uncommon. More specifically, children will typically hear claims about situations or events that they themselves have no way of checking. In the experiments just described, children already knew the standard names for the objects in question—hence their resistance to the mistaken speaker. Yet how could children exercise caution when they have no prior knowledge to weigh in the balance alongside the testimony that they are being offered?

We have recently explored children's recourse to one strategy that they might plausibly use in such circumstances. Suppose that children are confronted by two speakers, one accurate and one inaccurate. The evidence just reviewed strongly suggests that children will be able to recognize the truth of the assertions made by the one and the falsity of the assertions made by the other. Suppose further that children now hear these same two speakers make an assertion about some unknown entity or situation—for example, one speaker might call an unfamiliar object a 'modi' whereas the other might call it a 'toma'. Will children display selective trust in one of the two speakers? More specifically, in deciding what the unfamiliar object should be called will they be more swayed by the hitherto accurate speaker than the hitherto inaccurate speaker? This was the question posed by Koenig *et al.* (2004). Children aged 3 and 4 years heard one speaker accurately name three familiar objects and another speaker name the same three objects inaccurately. In two so-called explicit judgement trials, children were asked to identify which of the speakers had been right/wrong in what they had said. Children also entered a test phase in which the two speakers offered conflicting, novel names for three unfamiliar objects. The basic pattern of results was very straightforward. The majority of children did well on the two explicit judgement trials—they correctly picked out the right/wrong speaker. These children—in contrast to the minority who made a mistake on one or both of the explicit judgement trials—went on to show selective trust. They were more likely to adopt the names supplied by the hitherto accurate speaker. By implication young children not only recognize that someone has said something true or false, they can go on to form a reliability judgement about the person, a reliability judgement that is based on the speaker's past record. This strategy would obviously help children to avoid being misled about novel situations. They trust informants who have been reliable in the past.

In a related experiment, we have tried to establish how far such selective trust extends and whether it varies with age (Clément *et al.* 2004). Children aged 3 and 4 were again introduced to two speakers—puppets, in fact. One named the colour of three different objects correctly whereas the other named the colours incorrectly. In the test phase, children saw the interviewer place a further object in a box but they were not able to see its colour. Both puppets then peeked into the box and made a different claim about the colour of the object inside, one saying, for example, that it was red and the other saying that it was green. When children were asked for their opinion, the findings were similar to those obtained by Koenig *et al.* (2004). Children were likely to show trust in the hitherto accurate speaker. In addition, the results confirmed a trend that had been apparent in that earlier study: 4-year-olds showed more selectivity than 3-year-olds.

We also probed just how far children would extend their trust in the reliable speaker. On a follow-up trial, children watched the interviewer place an additional object in the box. This time, however, children were allowed to see its colour briefly before it disappeared. As before, the two speakers peeked into the box and each made a different claim about its colour—in neither case corresponding to what children had just seen for themselves. Accordingly, children were faced with a choice of whether to trust their first-hand experience or the claim made by the hitherto reliable speaker. The majority of children went with their original experience. Thus, this experiment confirmed that young children diagnose the accuracy of a speaker and come to trust an accurate speaker—but only up to a point. When their own recent observational experience can be weighed in the balance, it is their own experience that wins.

In the two studies described so far, children were given information by an accurate and an inaccurate informant and they then chose whom to trust. In follow-up studies, we asked if children are proactive in their trust. More specifically, do children seek out information from a hitherto reliable speaker? Children aged 3 and 4 were familiarized on three trials either with an accurate versus an inaccurate speaker or alternatively with an accurate versus an ignorant speaker (who admitted to not knowing). In the test phase, children were shown unfamiliar objects and asked if they knew their names. When children admitted to not knowing, they were prompted to get help from one of the two speakers and to indicate which speaker they would like to help them. Irrespective of whose help they asked for, both speakers suggested a name and children were free to choose which to endorse.

Four-year-olds discriminated between the two speakers—they sought help from the accurate rather than the inaccurate speaker and from the informed rather than the ignorant speaker. In addition, they endorsed the two speakers in a selective fashion—more often accepting information provided by the accurate or the informed speaker. Three-year-olds were less selective when faced with a choice between an accurate and an inaccurate speaker but, like the 4-year-olds, they generally preferred to seek and accept help from an informed as opposed to an ignorant speaker (Koenig and Harris 2005).

Summing up this series of experiments, we can tentatively identify three sequential stages. At stage 1, children weigh the claims that they hear against what they already know and they resist those that do not accord with their past experience. They evince puzzlement, corrections, and denials. At around 3 years of age, children appear to move beyond this proposition-based evaluation. They start to focus on the person who has made the claim. They are ready to seek out, and willing to accept, information from a speaker who has supplied accurate information in the past rather than professed ignorance. Conversely, however, they do not differentiate between an accurate and an inaccurate speaker. In the third stage, at around 4 years of age, children start to make this more subtle distinction. Faced with two speakers who have both supplied information in the past, they are inclined to seek and accept help from the more accurate of the two. Note that at both stages two and three, young children are making trait-like attributions. After a very short interaction with an interlocutor, they form an impression of his or her trustworthiness.

These findings raise many questions. Two are especially intriguing. First, we would like to know just how broad in scope children's attributions are. On the one hand, children might make a fairly narrow assessment of the epistemic competence of the two informants. For example, they might conclude that the speakers differ only in their mastery of a few words of English. Alternatively, they might reach the much broader conclusion that the two speakers differ not just in their knowledge of a few words of English but in their overall conceptual knowledge of the world. A second question concerns the nature of the observed age change. We have found that 3-year-olds, like 4-year-olds, can accurately indicate who has just been wrong but, unlike 4-year-olds, 3-year-olds do not readily extrapolate from that past record of inaccuracy to anticipate the person's future inaccuracy. One plausible interpretation of this age change is that 4-year-olds recognize that false labels imply a mistaken and epistemically unreliable informant whereas 3-year-olds are at a loss to interpret the mistakes made by the inaccurate informant, and therefore draw no prognosis from them. Certainly, this interpretation fits a much larger body of research showing that 4-year-olds are better than 3-year-olds at understanding how someone might misconstrue or mistakenly represent a situation (Harris 1996; Wellman et al. 2001).

UNDERSTANDING ONTOLOGY

We now turn to children's understanding of ontology, where, as we shall try to show, children continue to face the question of what testimony they can trust. In making ontological judgements, children might in principle adopt either of two different stances. They might adopt an empirical strategy that we can roughly characterize as follows: 'What exists is what I have observed'. Alternatively, they might adopt a more trusting strategy: 'What exists is what I have been told about'. One way to explore which strategy children adopt is to ask them directly about what entities exist, and to include among those entities some that children cannot observe for themselves but will have heard people talk about. If children systematically adopt the empirical strategy then they should deny that such entities exist. If they trust others' testimony, then they should claim that such unobservable entities do exist.

In a recent study, we asked a younger group of 4- to 5-year-olds and an older group of 7- to 8-year-olds about three different types of entity: so-called *real* entities such as rabbits and giraffes; so-called *scientific* entities such as germs and oxygen; and *impossible* entities such as flying pigs and barking cats (Harris and Pons 2003). Children were asked with respect to each entity whether such things actually exist. For this *existence* question, we anticipated that children would readily assert the existence of the real entities and deny the existence of impossible entities. Our major focus was on how they would respond to the so-called scientific entities. Presumably, children have never seen any germs. Hence, if they rely on the empirical strategy, they should be quite sceptical about their existence. On the other hand, if they rely on a more trusting strategy, they should be willing to acknowledge their existence. Figure 5.3 shows the mean number of times (out of 3) that children in each age group gave a 'yes' response to the existence question for the three types of entity.

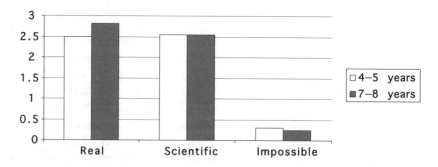

Figure 5.3.   Mean number of 'yes' responses to existence question (maximum = 3) as a function of age and type of entity.

Figure 5.3 indicates, as expected, that children accepted the existence of real entities and denied the existence of impossible entities. In addition, however, they readily asserted the existence of scientific entities. Indeed, as Figure 5.3 reveals, they appeared to be just as convinced of the existence of entities that they had never seen—germs, for example—as they were of entities that they probably had seen—rabbits, for example.

We also asked children an *appearance* question about each entity. More specifically, we asked children whether they knew what each entity looked like. Figure 5.4 shows the mean number of times (out of 3) that children in each age group gave a 'yes' response to the appearance question for the three types of entity.

Inspection of Figure 5.4 reveals, unsurprisingly, that children claimed to know what the real entities looked like but generally admitted to not knowing what the impossible entities looked like. The important finding again concerned children's responses with respect to invisible scientific entities such as germs, oxygen, and vitamins. Children frequently acknowledged that they did not know what such entities look like. Drawing together the findings presented in Figures 5.3 and 5.4, then, we can say that children's ontological judgements are not exclusively guided by an empirical strategy. Not only do they claim that unobservable entities exist, they also admit to not knowing what such entities look like. By implication, children can conceptualize the existence of a category of entities even if they are unable to recognize instances of the category in question. Note that, in this respect, children are no different from adults. We also conceptualize entities that we would not recognize instances of. For example, we may have a non-technical appreciation of what a cancerous cell is like but few of us would recognize such a cell were we to see it.

As a final probe, we asked children to explain their existence claims—to tell us why they thought that a particular entity exists. Children's replies fell into three main categories: they mentioned a potential *encounter* (e.g. 'I saw

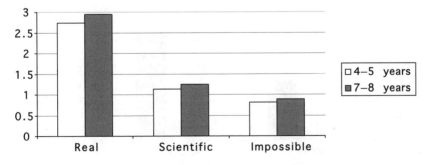

Figure 5.4. Mean number of 'yes' responses to appearance question (maximum – 3) as a function of age and type of entity.

them at the zoo' or 'My uncle has one'), the *source* of their knowledge about the entity (e.g. 'Because I know that—my Mum and Dad told me' or 'I learnt that at school'), or they offered some *generalization* about the entity in question (e.g. 'Because animals can have germs' or 'They can give you diseases'). The frequency with which children produced these three types of explanation for real entities and for scientific entities is illustrated in Figure 5.5 (for 4- to 5-year-olds) and in Figure 5.6 (for 7- to 8-year-olds). (Explanations for impossible entities were not informative—and are not included in these two figures.)

Inspection of these two figures shows that for real entities, both age groups mostly explained their existence judgements by referring to an actual or potential encounter. Such explanations were much less frequent for scientific entities. Instead, both age groups mainly explained their existence judgements by producing a generalization about the entity in question. Interestingly, explicit references to a knowledge source—such as parents or school—were relatively uncommon for both categories.

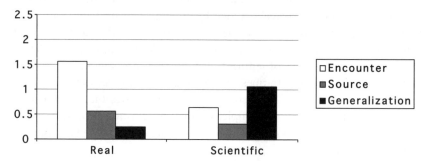

Figure 5.5. Mean number of encounter, source, and generalization explanations offered by 4- to 5-year-olds for real and scientific entities.

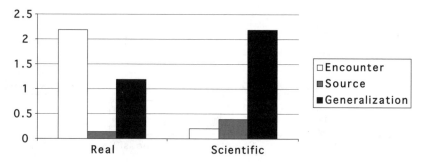

Figure 5.6. Mean number of encounter, source, and generalization explanations offered by 7- to 8-year-olds for real and scientific entities.

Summing up, these findings strongly suggest that children do not adopt a narrowly empiricist stance toward ontological matters: they accept the existence of entities that they cannot observe for themselves. Consistent with their reliance on other people's testimony rather than first-hand encounter, children admit that that they know little about the visible properties of such entities yet they make various generalizations about them—generalizations that are presumably based on what other people have told them.

At first sight, however, there is one outcome that does not fit this line of interpretation. If children place so much credence in what people tell them, why do they rarely mention those sources in their explanations? Recall that source explanations—references to information provided by other people— were rarely produced by either age group, whether for real entities or for scientific entities. We suspect that this is not because children do not actually depend on such sources—it is hard to see how they could learn about germs and oxygen in any other fashion. A more plausible explanation lies in children's 'amnesia' for sources. In a clever series of experiments, Taylor and her colleagues have shown that young children are often unaware that someone has just told them something—even though they retain the information itself. For example, when preschoolers were introduced to a fact that they did not know (e.g. tigers' stripes provide camouflage), they were likely to claim immediately afterwards that they had known the new fact for a long time. Thus, they often failed to acknowledge that they had only just been told the new fact (Taylor *et al.* 1994; Esbensen *et al.* 1997). Granted the rapid onset of this source amnesia for recent items of knowledge, it is not surprising that children fail to acknowledge the source of items of knowledge that they have probably retained over much longer periods.

In a follow-up study, we asked two additional questions about children's ontological judgements (Harris *et al.* 2005). First, we asked whether children take any kind of reference to an unobservable entity as an indication that the entity exists. Consider, for example, the many creatures or beings that children hear adults refer to: God, mermaids, giants, Santa Claus, dwarves, witches, ghosts, and so forth. Arguably, insofar as children come to believe in the existence of unobservable entities such as germs, so too they might come to believe in the existence of a large panoply of extraordinary beings. An alternative hypothesis, however, is also feasible. When adults talk about germs, they typically take for granted the existence of such entities and in addition they call attention to some real-world process in which such entities have a causal role. As mentioned earlier, children's justifications frequently involved a generalization and such generalizations often included a reference to causal processes. Surveying the set of extraordinary beings just listed, it is likely that adults' discourse will situate some of them in real-world causal processes. For example, in talking to children many adults, at least in western

Christian communities, will comment on the way that God and Santa Claus can bring about observable outcomes in the real world. By contrast, few adults are likely to suggest that mermaids, giants, dwarves, witches, or ghosts can bring about such outcomes. These beings may be attributed causal powers in the context of fairy stories but adults do not connect them to the world that children actually inhabit. If children are sensitive to this variation in the pattern of testimony, this should emerge in their existence judgements. More specifically, they should be inclined to accept the existence of God and Santa Claus but deny the existence of mermaids and ghosts.

A further question builds on the above line of speculation. Let us assume that children accept the existence of scientific entities. Let us also accept, for the moment, that children accept the existence of what we might dub credible beings—God and Santa Claus—but deny the existence of incredible beings—mermaids and ghosts. In that case, we can probe potential parallels or differences in the way that children conceptualize the existence of scientific entities—germs and oxygen—as compared with credible beings—God and Santa Claus. Two possible outcomes can be envisaged. First, whatever broad similarities emerge in children's ontological judgements about these two types of unobservables, children might still have some embryonic intuition about the differential status of scientifically established entities such as germs as compared with extraordinary beings such as God. On the other hand, young children might know very little about the specialized, scientific consensus that surrounds the existence of germs and oxygen—or alternatively, the absence of a similar consensus concerning the existence of God—or the Santa Claus.

In summary, we designed an experiment to differentiate between three possible outcomes: (i) young children indiscriminately accept the existence of all unobservable entities; (ii) they make a broad dichotomy between unobservable but 'real' entities on the one hand and unobservable but incredible entities on the other; (iii) they go beyond a broad dichotomy between the 'real' and the incredible by differentiating among 'real' entities; more specifically, they distinguish between scientific entities on the one hand (e.g. germs) and credible beings on the other (e.g. God). Figure 5.7 summarizes these three hypothetical outcomes.

Children aged 5–6 years were asked about three types of entity: credible entities (e.g. God, Tooth Fairy), scientific entities (e.g. germs, oxygen), and incredible entities (e.g. mermaids, ghosts). To obtain a relatively thorough profile of their conception of these different types of entity, they were asked the existence question, as in the previously described experiment; children were also asked to indicate their confidence in that existence judgement; and, they were asked about what other people would say about the existence of such entities. Figure 5.8 shows how often—for each type of entity—children affirmed the existence of a given entity, how confident they were of that affir-

All unobservables exist: God = Germs = Mermaids

Some unobservables really exist, others are fictional: God = Germs > Mermaids

Some unobservables do exist, some may exist, others are fictional: Germs > God > Mermaids

Figure 5.7. Three potential outcomes when children are asked to judge the existence of three types of unobservable entity (credible beings, e.g. God; scientific entities, e.g. germs; and incredible beings, e.g. mermaids).

mation, and how often they judged that other people would make the same affirmation.

Inspection of Figure 5.8 immediately reveals one straightforward result. Children offer a different pattern of judgement for incredible entities as compared to both credible and scientific entities. With respect to those latter entities, children often assert their existence and express confidence in that assertion. By contrast, children mostly deny the existence of incredible entities and express confidence in that denial. Children are also cautious about asserting that other people believe in the existence of such incredible entities. Looking back, then, at Figure 5.7, we can eliminate the first hypothesis. Children do not regard the unobservable domain as a single, undifferentiated territory. They can separate 'real' entities from those that are simply fictional. To the extent that children have not had a first-hand encounter with either type, their differentiation confirms their sensitivity to variation in the pattern of discourse surrounding these entities. As noted earlier, it is likely that children are sensitive to the fact that everyday remarks about credible and scientific entities implicate them in actual events. By contrast, references to ghosts

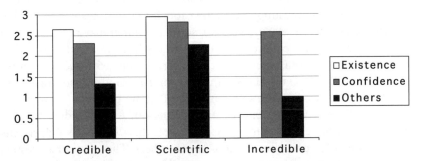

Figure 5.8. Mean number of existence, confident, and 'other people' judgements offered by 5- to 6-year-olds for credible (e.g. God, Santa Claus), scientific (e.g. germs, oxygen), and incredible entities (e.g. mermaids, ghosts).

and mermaids will likely be confined to fictional narratives and will rarely imply that such creatures can make a difference to any real-world outcomes.

Further inspection of Figure 5.8 confirms an additional important point. Children are also starting to make a distinction between credible entities on the one hand and scientific entities on the other. Statistical analysis confirms that, compared with credible entities, children are more likely to assert that scientific entities exist, more likely to express confidence in that judgement, and more likely to say that other people believe in their existence. Looking back once more at Figure 5.7, therefore, we may eliminate the second hypothesis and turn to the third: young children accept both scientific entities and credible beings as real and doubt the existence of incredible beings. Nevertheless, they appear to be more confident of the existence of scientific entities than credible beings.

There are two distinct classes of explanation for this final result. One class of explanation again focuses on the type of discourse that children hear, in this case concerning scientific entities as compared to credible beings. The other class of explanation focuses on the ways in which children conceptualize scientific entities and credible beings. We will consider each class of explanation in turn.

The discourse that surrounds scientific entities is likely to differ in at least three ways from the discourse that surrounds credible beings. First, although adults' comments will probably implicate each of them in real-world causal processes, comments about credible beings might be confined to special or 'marked' occasions such as an act of worship or a particular time of the year. By contrast, comments about germs are likely to be in the context of mundane or routine events. Second, children may sometimes hear adults or peers explicitly assert the existence of extraordinary beings or explicitly assert faith in their existence (e.g. 'There really is a Santa Claus' or 'I believe in God'). Paradoxically, such assertions might lead children to consider the possibility that credible beings do not exist. By contrast, the existence of germs and oxygen will be routinely presupposed ('Don't touch that—it has germs') rather than asserted ('There really are germs'), so that children may never question their existence. Finally, children may occasionally hear doubtful or sceptical remarks, especially from other children concerning the existence of credible beings such as Santa Claus, the Tooth Fairy, or even God. By contrast, they are unlikely to ever hear such scepticism voiced about germs or vitamins.

In sum, for several different reasons, the discourse surrounding credible beings might lead children to be less sure of their existence judgements and more inclined to attribute scepticism to others. That discourse, despite taking the same general form, is more qualified or equivocal with respect to credible beings compared with scientific entities. As a result, a fissure between the two types might emerge in children's minds. They start to express occasional ontological doubts themselves and to acknowledge the doubts of other people.

As mentioned, a different class of explanation focuses on children's conceptualization, particularly their ideas about causality. The causal processes attributed to germs or oxygen should not violate children's understanding of causation in any flagrant fashion. Admittedly, children cannot observe those processes—they have to accept the testimony that they are given. Still, there is nothing in that testimony to indicate that such entities have extraordinary or magical powers. The situation is different for credible beings. Recent research shows that 5-year-olds understand that God—unlike ordinary mortals—can form true beliefs even in the absence of any relevant perceptual access (Barrett *et al.* 2001). Similarly, 5-year-olds understand that God's existence—again unlike that of ordinary mortals—is not constrained by the biology of the life cycle: God was never a baby, does not get older, and will not die (Giménez *et al.* 2005). Thus, young children recognize God's extraordinary powers. Comparable research has not been carried out on children's conception of Santa Claus and the Tooth Fairy but it is plausible to assume that children also recognize their special powers. After all, both of these beings somehow know where you live, enter unseen into your home, and often figure out what gift you would like or when you deserve a gift without your telling them. To the extent that young children are lead to attribute extraordinary powers to credible beings such as God or Santa Claus—but not to scientific entities such as germs or oxygen—it is plausible that they come to have occasional doubts about the former or, at least less certitude when compared with the latter.

How might we test between these two classes of explanation, the one implying that children are guided by others' discourse and the other implying that children come to their own, relatively autonomous conclusions guided by their assessment of causal likelihood? One plausible avenue of research is cross-cultural investigation. Consider a child growing up in an isolated, small-scale community that is relatively cut off from contact with the outside world. In such an isolated community of this type, it is likely that the type of discourse that children hear concerning credible beings such as the ancestors will lack the features mentioned earlier. References to the ancestors will be routine rather than confined to special, marked occasions. Adults will not assert their faith in the ancestors—they will simply take them for granted. Finally, in such a homogeneous community, children are unlikely to hear anyone express doubt about the existence of the ancestors. At the same time, children growing up in such a community are likely to acknowledge that the ancestors, notwithstanding certain resemblances to ordinary human beings, have special powers and demands—they may cause illness unless placated and they do not age like ordinary people. Accordingly, if children are guided by discourse, they should express no doubt about the existence of the ancestors in such a community. On the other hand, if children are prompted to doubt the existence of special beings by virtue of their extraordinary, non-human powers, then such doubts should be quite pervasive.

CONCLUSIONS

We may reasonably describe young children as cautious disciples. First, contrary to the thrust of much classic work on cognitive development, it is evident that children accept various claims about hidden or unobservable aspects of the world such as the shape of the Earth, the function of the brain and the origin of species. In that sense, children can reasonably be described as disciples. Nevertheless, right from the start—or at least from the start of language comprehension—children also show certain signs of caution. Contrary to the thrust of Reid's proposal, infants, toddlers, and young children weigh incoming testimony against what they have previously observed or what they have previously heard. By the age of 3–4 years, they also assess speakers not just with respect to the truth of their current claims but also in the light of their past history of informedness and accuracy. The final set of data on children's ontological judgements similarly reinforces the claim that children are cautious. The evidence shows when children are faced with testimony about unobservables, they are attuned to ways in which that testimony is organized. Not only do they distinguish fictional from non-fictional assertions, they show some budding differentiation among different types of unobservable.

Nevertheless, it goes almost without saying that children's caution offers no royal road to the truth. Children may come to accept all sorts of false, but widespread, claims. Still, we can at least note that children show no special signs of gullibility in this respect. If they are prone to mistake testimony for truth, they are probably no different from adults. The imagination enables us to understand, and make sense of testimony, but by itself it provides no firm basis for distinguishing between collective truth and collective illusion.

References

Barrett, J. L., Richert, R. A. and Driesenga, A. 2001: God's beliefs versus mother's: The development of non-human agent concepts. *Child Development*, 72, 50–65.
Clément, F., Koenig, M. and Harris, P. L. 2004: The ontogenesis of trust in testimony. *Mind and Language*, 19, 360–379.

Corriveau, K. H., Pasquini, E. S. and Harris, P. L. 2005: 'If it's in your mind, it's in your knowledge': Children's developing anatomy of identity. *Cognitive Development*, 20, 321–340.

Esbensen, B. M., Taylor, M. and Stoess, C. 1997: Children's behavioral understanding of knowledge acquisition. *Cognitive Development*, 12, 53–84.

Evans, E. M. 2000: Beyond Scopes: Why creationism is here to stay. In Rosengren, K., Johnson, C. N. and Harris, P. L. (eds), *Imagining the Impossible: Magical, Scientific and Religious Thinking in Children*. Cambridge: Cambridge University Press.

Giménez, M., Guerrero, S. and Harris, P. L. 2005: Intimations of immortality and omniscience in early childhood. *European Journal of Developmental Psychology*, 2, 285–297.

Gottfried, G. M, Gelman, S. A. and Schultz, J. 1999: Children's understanding of the brain: From early essentialism to biological theory. *Cognitive Development*, 14, 147–174.

Harris, P. L. 1996: Desires, beliefs and language. In Carruthers, P. and Smith, P. K. (eds), *Theories of Theories of Mind*. Cambridge: Cambridge University Press, 200–220.

Harris, P. L. 2000: *The Work of the Imagination*. Oxford: Blackwell.

Harris, P. L. 2002: What do children learn from testimony? In: Carruthers, P., Stich, S. P. and Siegal, M. (eds), *The Cognitive Basis of Science*. Cambridge: Cambridge University Press, 316–334.

Harris, P. L. and Pons, F. 2003: Germs, angels, and giraffes: Children's understanding of ontology. Poster presented at the Biennial Meeting of the Society for Research in Child Development, Tampa, Florida (24–27 April).

Harris, P. L., Pasquini, E. S., Duke, S., Asscher, J. and Pons, F. 2005: Germs and angels: The role of testimony in young children's ontology. *Developmental Science*, 9, 76–96.

Johnson, C. N. 1990: If you had my brain, where would I be? Children's understanding of the brain and identity. *Child Development*, 61, 962–972.

Koenig, M. and Echols, C. 2003: Infants' understanding of false labeling events: The referential roles of words and the speakers who use them. *Cognition*, 87, 179–208.

Koenig, M. and Harris, P. L. 2005: Preschoolers mistrust ignorant and inaccurate speakers. *Child Development*, 76, 1261–1277.

Koenig, M., Clément, F. and Harris, P. L. 2004: Trust in testimony: Children's use of true and false statements. *Psychological Science*, 10, 694–698.

Meints, K., Plunkett, K. and Harris, P. L. 1999: When does an ostrich become a bird? The role of typicality in early word comprehension. *Developmental Psychology*, 35, 1072–1078.

Oviatt, S. L. 1980: The emerging ability to comprehend language: An experimental approach. *Child Development*, 51, 97–106.

Pea, R. D. 1982: Origins of verbal logic: Spontaneous denials by two- and three-year-olds. *Journal of Child Language*, 9, 597–626.

Reid, T. 1764/1997: *An Inquiry into the Human Mind on the Principles of Common Sense*. Edinburgh: Edinburgh University Press.

Siegal, M., Butterworth, G. E. and Newcombe, P. A. 2004: Culture and children's cosmology. *Developmental Science*, 7, 308–324.

Taylor, M., Esbensen, B. M. and Bennett, R. T. 1994: Children's understanding of knowledge acquisition: the tendency for children to report that they have always known what they have just learned. *Child Development*, 65, 1581–1604.

Wellman, H. M., Cross, D. and Watson, J. 2001: Meta-analysis of theory-of-mind development: The truth about false belief. *Child Development*, 72, 655–684.

Part III

MIND INTO CULTURE: PERSPECTIVES ON MUSICAL IMAGINATION

6

Imagining Things:
Mind Into Music (And Back Again)

NICHOLAS COOK

Abstract. Most people would probably sign up to the description of music as a culture of the aural imagination. But such a formulation could equally encompass Romantic conceptions of music as the audible trace of unfettered fantasy, and the post-war avant-garde view of it as the last word in rational construction: in this way it begs more questions than it addresses. In this chapter I focus on the inherent limits of all imaginative models of music, and the role of the remainder that lies beyond them—the excess of actual over imagined experience. Drawing examples from the composer Roger Reynolds and from a recent project investigating the performance of contemporary piano music, I argue that imaginative models of music are best understood not as attempted comprehensive specifications (as music theorists have generally seen them), but as spurs or prompts to performative action. Seen this way, music constitutes a model of how people can work together towards a common vision and yet retain their own autonomy: it shows how individual imagination is consummated in social action.

IMAGINING MUSIC

A GREAT DEAL OF WRITING ABOUT MUSIC has as its real topic the way in which music is imagined by composers, performers, or listeners. But the word 'imagination' is not particularly common in musicological or music-theoretical discourse. There is, for instance, no 'theory of musical imagination'—except in the sense that all music theory might be said to be just that.

I can make the point in terms of established practices of musical analysis. In the second half of the twentieth century, one approach came to dominate the rest as a means to understand the inner workings of 'common practice'

Proceedings of the British Academy **147**, 123–146. © The British Academy 2007.

music, that is to say music of the western 'art' tradition from roughly Bach to Brahms: this was Schenkerian analysis, a method developed by the *fin de siècle* Viennese pianist, teacher, and editor Heinrich Schenker. His system, which was disseminated throughout North America after the Second World War by a group of devoted followers, involved identifying musical lines that were elaborated at successive hierarchical levels: an entire movement might be circumscribed by a linear descent from the third to the tonic, for example, with each of those notes being elaborated ('prolonged' in Schenkerian terminology) through its own linear patterns, each note of which might itself be further prolonged, and so forth. The system gave rise to a reductive process of analysis—you began with the music and stripped away successive layers of prolongation until you were left with the descent from third to tonic—and the structural cohesiveness which the analysis revealed was seen by Schenker and his adherents as an indication of the music's quality.

Not everybody was impressed, however. Writing before Schenkerian analysis was exported to North America, the composer Arnold Schoenberg —who had developed his own system of analysis—made fun of Schenker when he peered at his analytical graph of the 'Eroica' Symphony, looking for his favourite passages, and eventually found them in the tiny notes at the bottom. Nowadays Schenkerian analysis is more frequently caricatured as reducing the masterworks—all the masterworks—to 'Three Blind Mice' (it is a fact that the third-to-tonic descent is much the most frequent 'background' structure in Schenkerian analysis). This criticism is a frivolous one, obviously, but the same point has frequently been made in a more serious context. The pianist and writer Charles Rosen (1971, p. 38), for example, complained that 'the analysis moves in one direction, away from what is actually heard and toward a form which is more or less the same for every work. It is a method which, for all it reveals, concentrates on a single aspect of music and, above all, makes it impossible to bring the other aspects into play'. And the influential musicologist Joseph Kerman, who quoted this passage from Rosen, agreed, complaining of Schenker's 'determination to seek the essence of all tonal music in an invariable abstract formula rather than in its infinite, concrete, magnificent variety. . . . Schenker was ready to strip away not only salient details of individual compositions, but also distinctions between compositions, composers, and periods. . . . Indeed, he was ready to strip away most of music history' (Kerman 1985, pp. 84–85).

Such complaints were perfectly understandable in the context of the rigid and dogmatic manner in which Schenkerian theory was disseminated by the first-generation disciples, who (as is often the way with disciples) displayed a kind of fundamentalist zeal that interpreted any engagement with other ways of thinking about music as a betrayal. All the same, responses such as Rosen's and Kerman's can be seen as embodying a basic misunderstanding. A

Schenkerian reduction is not like a stock cube, concentrating the essence and individuality of an individual composition. Its purpose is rather to stimulate and support a particular way of experiencing or 'hearing' the music, a particular understanding of it that is at the same time conceptual and perceptual. The graph has no more inherent meaning than a recipe does, but is a means by which meaning is created through the act of listening to the music in an analytically informed manner. Or to put it another way—and this is the point I am driving at—the purpose of the analysis is to prompt an imaginative hearing of the music, a hearing of it as the unfolding of a cohesive, hierarchical structure. The act of preparing an analysis may move, as Rosen put it, from the audible surface of the music to what Schenkerians often call the 'underlying' structure, but the realization of the analysis through an act of analytically informed listening involves a constant oscillation between structure and surface, analytical graph and score, music as conceptualized and music as heard. The analysis may 'strip away' the salient details of the music, as Kerman put it, but only so that they will be put back again in the act of experiencing the music in light of the analysis.

In this way, what was missing from Rosen's and Kerman's accounts of Schenkerian analysis was the role of the imagination, and the same might be said for the culture of western 'art' music in general during the second half of the twentieth century, at least to the extent that it was represented within academia. Campus composers, who in North America often held joint appointments in composition and theory, were widely criticized for writing music that represented, so to speak, analysis in reverse: it illustrated the ramifications of theoretical models of music in much the same way that a research paper might expound them (there is also a parallel with the way in which performance was seen as concerned with the 'reproduction' of compositional structures). It is easy and probably correct to see this as the consequence of music being incorporated within a research-led culture in which the only credible model of theory was the scientific one, and so the idea that the purpose of theory might be to prompt acts of imagination—that there should be some kind of imaginative gap between theory and practice—came to seem woolly and old-fashioned. Those outside the increasingly closed circles of campus composition and theory tended to react by going to the opposite extreme and denying that music had anything at all to do with intellectual understanding.

THE 'NEW' MUSICOLOGY

By around 1980 there was, then, a rather arid standoff between an over-theorized musical culture within academia and an under-theorized one outside it. As might be expected, the situation changed under the influence of different strains of postmodernist thought in the final two decades of the century. This was evident in compositional crossovers involving not only historical musical styles (particularly nineteenth-century Romanticism) but also popular and 'world' musics—and equally it was reflected by developments within musicology.

Kerman's 1985 book, from which I have already quoted, was an attack on what he termed 'positivist' musicology: a discipline that he saw as preoccupied with the clutter of past music—with editing musical manuscripts or theoretical texts, taxonomical classification of instruments, and the like—but as swerving away from fundamental, humanly interesting questions about what music meant or what its value (or values) might be. He called instead for a 'critical' approach, meaning this in the sense of literary criticism, but the response to his call by a younger generation of musicologists—what became generally known as the 'New' musicology—took the term 'critical' in a different sense, one deriving rather from Frankfurt School critical theory. Writers such as Susan McClary and Lawrence Kramer did indeed engage with issues of musical meaning, adopting what might be (and was) called a broadly hermeneutical approach, but at a basic level they worked to an agenda that closely conformed to Adorno's conception of music as social text. Music, Adorno claimed, 'presents social problems through its own material and according to its own formal laws—problems which music contains within itself in the innermost cells of its technique' (Martin 1995, p. 100): it follows that meaning is located within the musical text, and is to be retrieved from it through an act of interpretation that lies somewhere between decoding and hermeneutic dialogue. This, of course, is a very different understanding of musical meaning from the 'production of culture' approach characteristic of contemporary sociology, with its emphasis on how meaning is performed through social activity, with music being seen as a particularly rich context for such activity (DeNora 2003; see also Chapter 7).

The net result of this is that the rethinking of musicology that took place in the 1990s changed less than one might have expected. If 'New' musicology is to be more long-lasting than New Labour, then a second stage of rethinking may be necessary: one that moves beyond the dominant textualism which characterized the 'New' as much as the old discipline, and that views musical texts not as self-sufficient entities but as the traces of social actions and the acts of imagination inherent in them. (The same applies, of course, to the other musical traces I referred to—theoretical texts, musical instruments, and so forth.) And there are two very obvious sources on which such a rethinking might draw. One is the field of interdisciplinary performance studies, with its emphasis on the acts of negotiation through which meaning is constructed in real-time performance; there is a real sense in which this kind of perspective will need to be adopted if musicologists are ever to think of music as primarily a performing art, rather than a marginal form of literature that can, if wished, be presented in performance (in the manner of poetry readings). The other is the study of material culture, as represented in the work of Daniel Miller or Steven Mithen.

In Chapter 1, Mithen asks how, in terms of evolutionary development, it was possible for the domain-specific constraints on human thought to be over-ridden, resulting in the cognitive fluidity definitive of imagination, and answers: 'The types of thoughts made possible by cognitive fluidity . . . could be effectively maintained, manipulated, and transmitted only by down-loading such thoughts into material culture' (he mentions paintings, sculpture, and later writing: Chapter 1, page 21). He then gives an example: counterfactual images such as the Hohlenstein-Stadel 'man-lion' are hard to describe or even recall, because they are not supported by the domain-specific modes of cognition evolved to cope with the real world. To overcome this, Mithen continues, it is necessary to 'down-load that thought into either a representational or a symbolic image to act as a "cognitive anchor"'. So objectified, the thought becomes both enduring and accessible to manipulation. And Mithen cites Matthew Day's characterization of religious thought, according to which its ritualistic and material expressions are not 'thin cultural "wrap arounds" that dress up real cognitive processes going on underneath' (Day 2004, pp. 116–117) but integral to the thought itself. The applicability of such an approach to musical scores, instruments, and the rest is evident enough: they are not mere trappings but the actual traces of past acts of imaginative listening, and equally—like Schenkerian graphs—they can script future acts of imaginative listening (which may or may not coincide with past ones, though most probably not).

Before developing and illustrating these ideas, however, I would like to call attention to two consequences of this comparison between the study of material culture and that of music. The first is the implication that musical compositions might be thought of as embodying some kind of counterfactual reality, as—to appropriate a term from Kramer (1990, pp. 85–93)—'impossible objects': blends of the attributes of real-world objects and experiences but in non-real-world combinations, which rely for their facticity—for the possibility of maintaining them as cultural objects—on the mediation of notation or other systems of musical representation. (In this way scores, like other material objects, are not 'thin cultural "wrap arounds"' but concretizations of musical thought.) The second is that, seen this way, the reconstruction of past acts of imagination and the scripting of new ones become the basic subject matter of musicology. I am not proposing in this chapter that musicology should become about imagination, but suggesting that it always was, only unknowingly.

HEARING AS

But what kind of acts of imaginative listening might be 'down-loaded' into musical artefacts and how might they relate to one another? In my book *Music, Imagination, and Culture* (Cook 1990)—the only one with the word 'imagination' actually in the title—I explored an approach to the imaginative process in music based on the idea of 'aspect perception', a Wittgensteinian notion developed in relation to aesthetic perception by Roger Scruton (1974), which is most succinctly exemplified by the idea of 'seeing as', or in this context 'hearing as' (or simply 'hearing' in inverted commas). I quote Rosen's complaint that Schenkerian analysis 'concentrates on a single aspect of music and, above all, makes it impossible to bring the other aspects into play': it would be better to say that, in foregrounding a particular aspect of music, Schenkerian analysis leads you to hear the music 'as' prolongation. In other words you hear the music—the whole of the music—from the aspect of pro-longation, understanding its other aspects in terms of how they relate to pro-longation (which is not the only way to hear music, and may not necessarily be a profitable way to hear any given piece of music, but cannot be accurately described as making it impossible to bring other aspects into play).

But of course analytical acts of 'hearing as' are just one example of an indefinite number of couplings of sound and image. One important system of musical imagery, which I discussed in my book and has also been described by, among others, Baily (1985), Sudnow (1978), and Yung (1984), derives from instrumental or vocal performance: each instrument sets up a different kinesthetic topography, a different manner of physical engagement with sound production, and in so doing emphasizes certain aspects of the music while de-emphasizing others. It is not simply a question of what is playable on the piano, guitar, or saxophone: it is the way in which different topographies and modes of physical engagement lead one to formulate and manipulate musical thoughts in different ways, transform them in fact into *different* musical thoughts. You can play counterpoint on a guitar, for instance, but the instrument lends itself to strumming and so promotes a homophonic conception of texture and rhythm in a way that the piano does not (though you may sometimes hear Bach's keyboard fugues played that way, which is to say badly); again, the permanently visible topography of the piano promotes the concern with tonal architecture that characterizes music of the 'common practice' style (most composers of which were themselves keyboard players), in a way that the voice does not. But then, the voice pro-motes a sensitivity to the influence of context, to local inflection and orna-mentation, which the basically permutational principle of the keyboard does not (on the piano you are always playing the same notes, only in different sequences). And the same applies to other systems of imagery: scores make large-scale pitch relationships explicit in a way they are not for most listeners, while omitting the inflections of pitch, timing, and dynamics that are central to the art of performance; by contrast, verbal representations of music arguably convey certain aspects of emotional nuance but capture large-scale musical processes only in the most abstract and formulaic manner. It also applies to the homologies between sounds and other aspects of experience which invoke an indefinite number of further imaginative correlates, whether shared across a culture or specific to the individual. Each correlation of sound with instrumental kinesthesis, notation, word, or other life experience promotes a different act of 'hearing as', in short a different 'hearing'—or, as we shall see in relation to composition, a different determination of what there is to hear.

Seen in this manner, then, any musical artefact is the trace of multiple acts of imaginative hearing, the complexity and overlapping nature of which is such that it will probably be impossible in any one case to fully retrieve them. What we are talking about here is very similar to the fluidity that results, in Mithen's account, from the interaction of different, domain-specific modes of cognition. It is also amenable to formulation in terms of conceptual blending (Turner in Chapter 10), that is to say the mapping of schemata from one cognitive domain to another. The conceptual integration networks developed by conceptual blending theorists, which model the potential for mapping within any specific conjunction of domains, have been applied to music by a number of writers (see especially Zbikowski 2002). However the sedimentation of cognitive schemata laid down in a musical artefact such as a score—normally a highly overdetermined construct, in that a musical experience lasting say half an hour may have been designed over a period of weeks or months—is such that comprehensive modelling in such terms will almost certainly be unachievable. If this argument holds water, then the approach I adopted in my 1990 book might be seen as a pragmatic short cut: I emphasized the disparity between any given representation of music—including scores, analytical models, and the rest—and the experience for which it stands, seeing the gap between the two as a site for aesthetically crucial, but theoretically irrecoverable, activity. (It is of course exactly this gap that closed in the campus composition of the post-war period.) My aim in the remainder of this chapter is to provide concrete illustration of this through two brief case studies, both involving contemporary 'art' music: the first focuses on the compositional process that culminates in the score, the second on the transformation of the score into a performance.

There is, however, an aspect of conceptual blending theory that is fundamental to my argument. Cross-domain mappings result in emergent meaning, in other words meaning that is not inherent in any source domain but is generated by the blend. That is precisely what I wish to claim about both composition and performance. Performers in the western 'art' music tradition reproduce the music they are performing, of course, in the sense that they play the notes specified by the composer, but I shall emphasize the creative nature of the interaction between performance and score, an interaction that must be created anew on each occasion of performance: I shall argue that performance is not so much specified as prompted by the score. Again, like conceptual artists, modernist (or postmodernist) composers typically develop their work from a variety of different ideas or sources, whether musical, verbal, visual, numerical, or all of these: I shall argue, or rather I shall let the composer Roger Reynolds argue for me, that composition is best understood as a kind of improvisatory process that takes place in the gaps between these different representations, or between them and the emerging sound image. Composition may proceed through a successive elaboration of models, as Schenkerian analysis suggests, but there is an important sense in which the term 'model' can be misleading: what is involved here is not the empirical testing of increasingly developed representations of the music against known criteria, but a determination of what the criteria might be, of what there is to be represented. In music as in other domains of culture, imaginative minds are, as a matter of course, creative minds.

IMAGE INTO SCORE: ROGER REYNOLDS

It is a consequence of the prevailing textualist orientation of the discipline to which I have already referred that musicologists tend to know much less about actual musical practices than is the case of ethnomusicologists, who for the last fifty years have been working to a broadly anthropological agenda. An illustration of this is the lack of ethnographic or even detailed introspective accounts of the compositional process, or so at least the Pulitzer Prize winning composer Roger Reynolds claims: there is, he complains, 'an almost complete silence regarding the ways in which recognized figures actually go about their work' (Reynolds 2002, p. 83).[1] This is the lack which he sets out

---

[1] The main exception to this (though for obvious reasons involving documentary rather than ethnographic or introspective methods) is Beethoven, on the basis of whose sketches—that is, short-hand music notations of his works in progress—a substantial literature on the compositional process has come into being (see, e.g., Cooper 1990). There is however a problem in treating this as a source of information on the creative process in general, quite apart from the historical distance of Beethoven from the concerns and practices of contemporary composition: what makes it possible to study Beethoven's creative process is the quite exceptional extent to which he relied on such written-down sketches—in short, its abnormality.

to rectify in his book *Form and Method: Composing Music*, which forms the basis of the following discussion.[2]

For Reynolds, what he calls the 'impetus' behind a composition is often visual: *Versions/Stages I–V* (1986–91), he tells us, is a study in the changing relationships between formal structure and material realization inspired by Monet's series of paintings of Rouen Cathedral, while a particular spatial disposition of computer-processed sound in *Personae* (1990) was suggested by the pattern of rushing snowflakes during a winter drive (Reynolds 2002, p. 81). The most striking translation from visual to sound image, however, is provided by his *Symphony[Myths]* (1990), which is based on a peculiar rock formation on the shore of Honshu (Japan): a large and a small rock surrounded by the sea but linked by a braided rope, with between them a still smaller rock that is often hidden under the waves (Figure 6.1). Reynolds translates this image into music in a number of different ways. There is a story that the two main rocks represent male and female gods, who were separated from one another but have been symbolically rejoined by the rope, while the third is a 'spirit rock': Reynolds not only explores the expressive ramifications of these stories but also links them to other myths, such as the 'clashing rocks' from the story of Jason and the Argonauts. Then again, he uses the height above the sea of the two main rocks (in feet) as reference points for the numerical series used to organize various aspects of the music (more on this shortly). He also attempts to convey the large rocks' massiveness through layered ostinati—superimposed repeating patterns which give rise to a musical texture that is continually changing, but within a larger, unchanging framework.

But there is more to it than that. Reynolds draws a sketch of the two main rocks (Figure 6.2). Then he elaborates this into a more schematic but still readily recognizable representation whose coordinates are time and pitch height (you can see the rope on the left side of Figure 6.3). Next, he progressively formalizes the representation until it eventually reaches a condition of notational specificity (see Figure 6.4, where the circles numbered 1 and 5 mark the sections corresponding to the two rocks; Figure 6.5, which shows the passage from sections 1 to 5 in more detail; Figure 6.6, in effect a blow-up of section 1 (the first rock), with the note-to-note detail beginning to emerge; and Figure 6.7, further development of the beginning of this section). Admittedly, this extended process of abstraction from visual image to compositional structure is something of a special case: Reynolds (2002, p. 30) introduces it as 'a form that is more explicitly wedded to its subject, that

[2] Adapted from my review of the book ('Form and Method: Composing Music (The Rothschild Lectures) by Roger Reynolds') originally published in *Music Perception* 22/2 (2004), 357–64; © Regents of the University of California.

Figure 6.1. A photograph of the Japanese rock formation *Futami ga ura*. Copyright (©
2002) from *Form and Method: Composing Music* by Roger Reynolds, Ex. 13. Reproduced by
permission of Routledge/Taylor & Francis Group, LLC.

actually attempts the direct *musical manifestation* of a more physical model'
(more, that is, than the compositions he has talked about up to then). All the
same, you only have to flick through the many sketches reproduced in
Reynolds's book to see the extent to which graphic representations not only
serve as a shorthand for intended musical effects (a means of down-loading
a perhaps counterfactual reality, in Mithen's terms), but also contribute to
determining what it is that is intended. It is evident that they 'speak back', as
it were, to the composer, becoming an arena for the making of compositional
decisions, and in this way playing a full role in the process of interaction
between intent and realization, between composer and page, through which
the composition comes into being. At the risk of repeating myself, the representations are not just representations, but stages in the process of determining what is to be represented.

I also want to claim that the same applies to Reynolds's parallel use of
mathematical imagery. He explains that in *Symphony[Myth]* he based the
series on the height of the rocks (29 and 13 feet, as shown in Figure 6.3) not
simply because the rocks happened to be that height, but because, as he puts
it, 'the proportion has attractive features. If, for example, their relative height
had been 30:15, I would have bypassed this datum' (Reynolds 2002, p. 61).
Here the criteria are obvious enough—a simple arithmetical proportion has
no potential for interesting development—but in another, similar situation

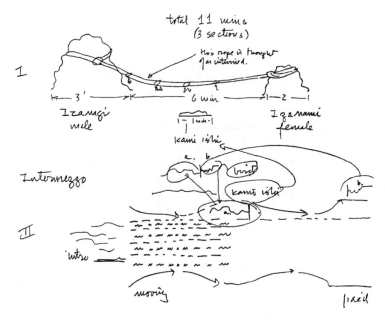

Figure 6.2.   The first sketch of the overall form of *Symphony[Myths]*. Copyright (© 2002) from *Form and Method: Composing Music* by Roger Reynolds, Ex. 16. Reproduced by permission of Routledge/Taylor & Francis Group, LLC.

(the selection of a pitch series in his *Variation* for solo piano) Reynolds explains that 'Although a very considerable amount of time goes into exploring alternative rows, the process by which one possibility is discarded and another is more extensively searched remains for me a very personal one, resistant to objectification' (2002, p. 46). Mathematical relationships, it appears, feel or look right or wrong: they speak back to him in the same way that the visual images do. And so, not content with working with multiple numerical sequences, Reynolds invokes computer-based algorithms that redistribute the terms of the series in order to create further effects of transformation, the outputs of which can equally well be translated (usually through approximations) into notational terms or directly realized in the electroacoustic domain.

All this means that a careless reading of *Form and Method* might convey the impression that Reynolds falls into that discredited tradition of post-war campus composers to which I have already referred: composers who explored sophisticated (or sometimes not so sophisticated) mathematical models, which they then translated into sound at the last minute, so to speak, with the consequence that there was little or no interaction between mathematical conception and musical realization—little or no scope, in short, for imagination. But in reality Reynolds's book is a sustained polemic against such

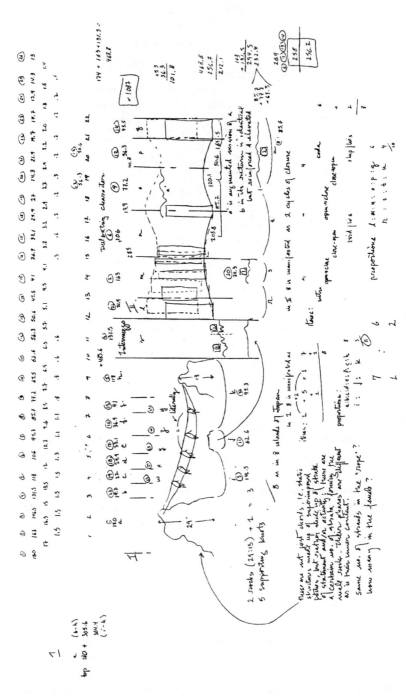

Figure 6.3. A second more refined laying-out of the overall form of *Symphony[Myths]*. Copyright (© 2002) from *Form and Method: Composing Music* by Roger Reynolds, Ex. 17. Reproduced by permission of Routledge/Taylor & Francis Group, LLC.

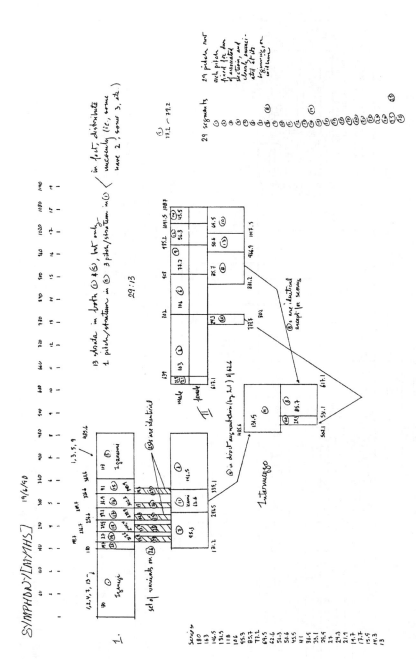

Figure 6.4. The formalized plan for *Symphony[Myths]* with proportional specifics. Copyright (© 2002) from *Form and Method: Composing Music* by Roger Reynolds, Ex. 18. Reproduced by permission of Routledge/Taylor & Francis Group, LLC.

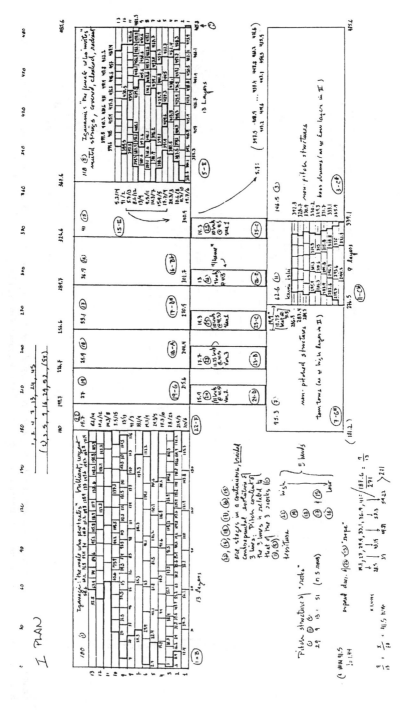

Figure 6.5. First movement plan for *Symphony[Myths]*. Copyright (© 2002) from *Form and Method: Composing Music* by Roger Reynolds, Ex. 19. Reproduced by permission of Routledge/Taylor & Francis Group, LLC.

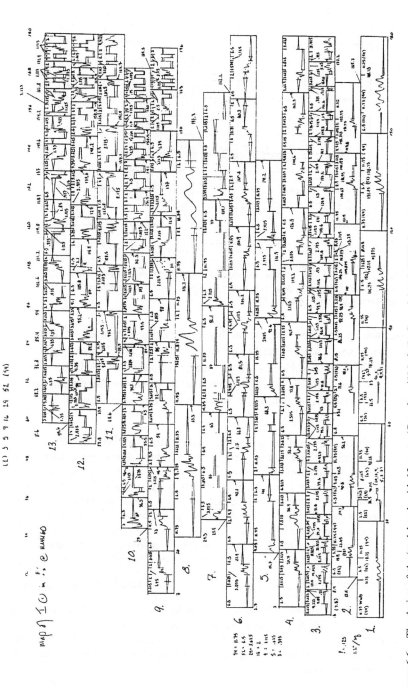

Figure 6.6. The design of the 'male' rock with 13 strata (*Symphony*/[*Myths*]). Copyright (© 2002) from *Form and Method: Composing Music* by Roger Reynolds, Ex. 21. Reproduced by permission of Routledge/Taylor & Francis Group, LLC.

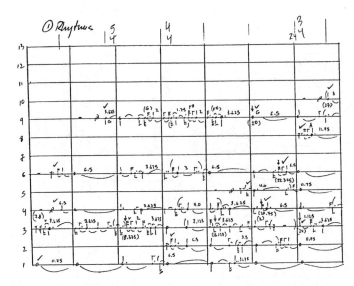

Figure 6.7. A detail of the 'male' rock design (*Symphony[Myths]*). Copyright (© 2002) from *Form and Method: Composing Music* by Roger Reynolds, Ex. 96. Reproduced by permission of Routledge/Taylor & Francis Group, LLC.

approaches, as may be seen from his disparaging reference to the 'rote architectonicisms' that resulted from the 'numerical absolutism of the 50's' (Reynolds 2002, p. 20). He says it over and over again: of itself, no rule, no system, no algorithm is likely to give rise to humanly interesting music. Because this point is so central, it is worth quoting what Reynolds says at some length:

> I should emphasize, if it is not already evident, that I am not implying (because I do not believe) that the direct translation of physical concepts or their mathematical representation into musical terms holds much promise for most composers. My goal, my interest in such things, is far more limited: *a certain plausibility*, an 'acceptable' proposal to which useful aesthetically directed responses can be made. Evidently, anyone can simply sit down and *invent* an eccentric pattern of relationships. Anyone is free to do so. What I have found is this: if one can identify an external source of proportions, a resource that is acceptable, it may carry with it valuable bonuses. (Reynolds 2002, p. 27)

And at another point he goes on to spell out what these bonuses might be:

> I believe that while plausible notions about form and its contents are necessary, they are certainly not sufficient to confer inevitable merit. It is the quality of and the reasonable coherence of the many small decisions and adjustments the composer makes while working that lend to the music its ability to engage us dimensionally. (Reynolds 2002, p. 41)

One might paraphrase this by saying that the mathematical, visual, or other constructs are of value not for what they *are* but for what they *do*. They present possibilities for further action which the composer may accept or reject, for any compositional realization represents but a tiny subset of what might have been done: as Reynolds says, 'The process only proposes, the composer decides what will find its way into the score' (2002, p. 55). They define a terrain within which the composer responds to stimuli (at one point Reynolds refers to mathematical processes as a 'spur' as well as a 'guide'; 2002, p. 72), and it is often the approximations or contradictions which they introduce— their failure to map seamlessly onto the requirements of the moment—that prompt the myriad intuitive decisions of which the compositional process ultimately consists, or as Reynolds puts it 'the freeing of local invention for more intuitional vibrancy' (2002, p. 41). In this way—though Reynolds does not put it like this—composition might be described as a highly structured and sequential process of improvisation, for 'The point [of such givens] is that one is able to think about different aspects of creation at different stages, not in one, unmanageably congested, here and now' (Reynolds 2002, p. 28).

SCORE INTO PERFORMANCE: *ÊTRE-TEMPS* FOR PIANO

There is of course one respect in which Reynolds's compositions are quite the opposite of improvisation: they are conventional, fully notated scores (sometimes supplemented by a tape to be played as part of the performance). The processes of imagination that took place in the privacy of the composer's study—processes of which Reynolds has allowed us a privileged and possibly partial glimpse—belong to the music's history, and only the score remains as the final record of the creative act. As the embodiment of the autonomous musical work, the score—the authoritative score, the score as the composer intended it, or rather as musicologists judge that the composer intended it—has traditionally been the focus of musicological analysis: scores have been seen as having inherent meaning, and as a result performance, like poetry reading, has been seen as a kind of supplement. What I want to do now is undermine this idea of the autonomous work as embodied in the score, and the correlative conception of performance as in essence a process of reproduction, by showing how scores—some scores at least—work by prompting creative, that is, inherently meaningful responses in the real time of performance.

Here I am drawing on a collaborative project with the pianist Philip Thomas, the composer Bryn Harrison, and the music psychologist and theorist Eric Clarke (Clarke *et al.* 2005). In 2002 Thomas commissioned a piano piece (*être-temps*) from Harrison, and Clarke documented the entire process of creating the performance, from the initial play-through up to the premiere. The documentation also included interviews that Clarke conducted with both Thomas and Harrison, and a session at an early stage of the process in which Thomas worked with Harrison on issues of interpretation; it is from this session, and the two interviews, that I draw the following quotations. In his interview, Harrison drew on a quotation from Jasper Johns, the New York-based painter and friend of John Cage:

> BRYN HARRISON: Jasper Johns said that 'sometimes they see and paint it, some-times they paint it to see it', and I really like that quote, because I think in some ways the way that I'm dealing with rhythm and the setup on the page, it's not purely deterministic in my point of view, even though you know, it's carefully regulated on the page but in some ways I'm writing it to hear it, as much as I'm hearing it to write it.

To put this another way, a composition is not the translation into notes of a prior experience: rather the experience is constructed by virtue of the compositional process—which links with the claim I made, in relation to Reynolds, that compositional imagery is less about representing the music than deciding what there is to represent. In the same way, the manner in which the music should be played is not implicit in it, just waiting to be drawn out by the performer: interpretations are created through the process of rehearsal, and there is no law to say that the composer knows better than anyone else how the music should go. At least that was Harrison's view:

> BRYN HARRISON: I think the thing I've learnt is that you don't have to have the answers to every question as well, I think you know, when I first started getting performances and I'd go and attend rehearsals, you know I was, well I was probably scared stiff for one thing, but there was always this feeling that any question that a player had you had to feel you immediately knew the answer to that question, and of course you've got to trust their judgement as well.

The analytical issue, then, is how to leave space for the performer—and I am suggesting that this can be done by seeing the score not as something to be reproduced in performance, but as something that prompts performance, where the term 'performance' is understood as a real-time social event which generates a particular auditory trace. (If it seems odd to think of a solo performance as a social event, that is because you have forgotten the audience.) In order to make my point I need to explain a little about the way in which *être-temps* is notated, or rather I can quote the composer's own explanation of it:

> BRYN HARRISON: The way that I'm working now is very much with using what I describe as kind of time frames where I actually draw a sort of grid, or if I've got some pre-made that I just photocopy and use over and over again, and they're basically grids of different shapes and sizes, into which I kind of plot a

kind of series of rhythms, and then look for the closest approximate sort of irregular, irrational ratio to sort of contain that material, so it may be that I create a rhythmic series and then I'll use it again but in a different time grid, so that it either expands or contracts the material, or rhythms tend to work across the bar, so you get sort of interesting sort of elongations and contractions of rhythmic material.

For example, on the second page of the score (Figure 6.8), the same pattern 3/8, 5/16, 3/16, 5/16 appears in every system. Harrison comments specifically on this passage:

> BRYN HARRISON: On page 2 of the score, bars 23–26 have this kind of broken arpeggiated passage and then you get the same thing again coming in just at the end of bar 30 through to 34/35, and it's the same, basically the same rhythmic material and the same pitch material, but because it's offset by the different series of bars it allows me to sort of contract and expand the material within a new given set of time signatures.

In other words, because the material is inserted into a different metrical grid, or more precisely into a different place within the metrical grid, not only will the durations fit differently, resulting in the contractions and expansions Harrison talked about, but also their notational expressions will change. For instance, the high F on the downbeat of bar 25 reappears on the fourth beat in bar 32, and this means that it prompts a different kind of interpretive act, a different performance, even if the material is in some abstract sense the same. What is at issue here was thrown into relief when Thomas, the pianist, criticized a certain musician's attempt to simplify Brian Ferneyhough's notations, on the grounds that to do this misses the whole point of the notation:

> PHILIP THOMAS: He transcribed a section of a performance into something almost as banal as 6/8 and he transcribed it rhythmically as if Ferneyhough's notation had no, was just needlessly complex, and it is a completely ridiculous notion, because it's as if rhythmic notation affects duration alone, but of course it doesn't, and of course if you played his transcription it would sound entirely different from what Ferneyhough had written, the effect would be completely different.

Then what exactly is the function of the elaborate rhythmic notation that Harrison uses? In his interview with Clarke, Thomas talked about passages of this kind:

> ERIC CLARKE: But God, I mean it's, does he really want it so, I mean, you know, like the second bar of page 6, you've got a 3 in the time of 2, within a 6 in the time of 5, within a 5/16 bar. . .

> PHILIP THOMAS: Oh, but that's not complicated, really, that's, forget the six in the space of five, so if you played it without the six in the space of five it would be [sings], and six in the space of five simply means it's a little bit faster, so those

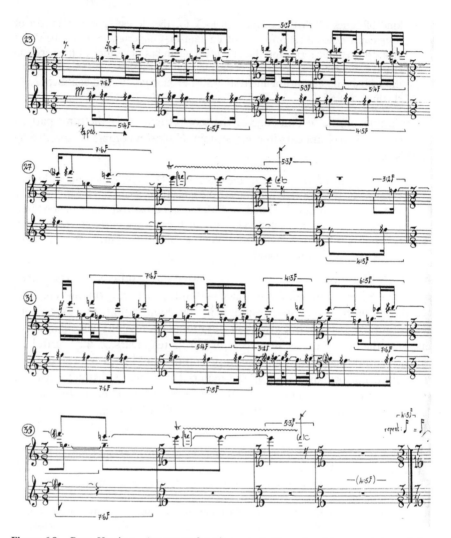

Figure 6.8. Bryn Harrison, *être-temps* for piano, p. 2. Reproduced by permission of the composer.

two bars would be [sings], you just simply nudge the beat on a bit faster. . . I mean it's correct as I, I mean, hearing it on the Disklavier,[3] if someone was going to really meticulously see the timings of that, then it would be different every time, I'm not going to be, it's not going to be exact. . . I hope no one listens to music really hearing things as they are, 6 in the space of 5, it's a bit of a, it's just a notational device which encourages me to just move on a little bit here.

The issue of rhythmic accuracy also cropped up during the session in which Thomas and Harrison worked together on the performance:

PHILIP THOMAS: Do you think it's accurate? I think I'm pretty accurate.

BRYN HARRISON: As far as I can tell, I'm struggling to tell.

PHILIP THOMAS: You kind of do it so much, I've practised it, and then you get used to it, and it gets compromised again, so I've got to keep kicking myself in the arse to kind of take it apart again, I think that's the problem, I've got to keep unravelling it.

BRYN HARRISON: Otherwise you get used to the sound and keep imitating yourself in a slightly inaccurate way really.

In this way, just playing the music accurately, in the sense of reproducing the rhythmic specifications in the score, is not sufficient, and indeed may not be necessary (or even possible). Harrison is not thinking of the score as a kind of text to be reproduced in performance, in the sense that a hi-fi system reproduces a recording; that kind of fidelity is not at issue. He is asking for the music to be recreated—I think it would be fair to say reimagined—every time it is performed: the score functions less like a literary text than a theatrical script, not so much specifying as prompting the act of performance in real time.[4] The performance emerges from the imaginative gap between score and experience. There is, then, a sense in which Thomas was improvising even when he was playing from the music.

MUSIC AS SOCIAL ACTION

In this chapter I have tried to document the inherent limits of all images for music, from analyses to sketches to scores, and the gap that opens up between them and the real-time experience of music, whether on the composer's, the performer's, or the listener's part. I have tried to show how, in composition, mathematical, visual, or other constructs act as 'spurs' (in Reynolds's word)

---

[3] Piano manufactured by Yamaha and incorporating a digital recording and playback facility.
[4] On the distinction of text and script see Cook (2003, p. 206).

or 'prompts' (in mine) to the ultimately improvisatory creative act that brings the piece into being as a performable entity. And I have tried to show how the same kind of process is replicated in performance. But of course it might be objected that I have stacked the odds by choosing my examples from avant-garde and hence anomalous works, so documenting the exceptions that in reality prove the opposite rule. I have two answers to that objection. In the first place, to describe Reynolds's brand of modernism—a tradition now a century old—as 'avant-garde' is pushing the term rather further than it will comfortably stretch: how long does an anomaly have to last before it becomes the norm? In the second place, I could have made the same kind of argument I made in relation to Thomas's performance of *être-temps* just as well, and perhaps more easily, by talking about classical chamber music. Doing that now will allow me, by way of conclusion, to introduce something which my case studies have not featured: the social dimension of musical imagination.

Consider a performance of a classical string quartet: to give concreteness to the exercise, Figure 6.9 shows a passage from Mozart's Quartet in G major, K. 387, but virtually any page of virtually any classical chamber music would do as well.[5] The quartet may well play the notes exactly as Mozart wrote them. And yet they *do not* play them exactly as Mozart wrote them, because every note in the score is subject to the contextual negotiation of intonation, precise dynamic value, articulation, timbral quality, and so forth. For example, the performers stay in time not because each accommodates his or her playing to an externally defined beat (as when studio musicians record to a click track), but because each is continuously listening to the others, accommodating his or her timing to the others', and this gives rise to a shared, communal temporality: this is music that, in Ingrid Monson's words, has 'as one of its central functions the construction of social context' (Monson 1996, p. 186).[6] Mozart's score choreographs a series of ongoing social engagements between the players, setting up a shared framework or goal (a shared mission, if you like) but delegating detailed decisions to be made in real time by the relevant individuals in light of local circumstances—to be improvised, that is to say, like so much in everyday life. In short, it prompts the emergence of social meaning. And seeing music of the western 'art' tradition this way underlines its continuities with other musical traditions in which this social dimension is more overt (see Cross in Chapter 7).

[5] The following is adapted from Cook (2004), where the implicit analogy with management theory is further explored.
[6] Note however that Monson presents this as a description of jazz in contradistinction to the classical tradition.

Figure 6.9.   Mozart, Quartet in G major, K. 387, bars 118–135.

Music is sometimes seen as a prime example of the authoritarian impulse in western art, of the desire to create an imaginative structure so complete, so compelling, as to allow the individual no space for interpretation: it is because of this, as well as Wagner's anti-semitism, that we sense there is some kind of path from *The Ring* or *Parsifal* to the Third Reich. But I would like to counterpose this idea with its opposite. Understood in the manner I've been describing—as script rather than text—music provides perhaps the most transparent model we have of how people can work together towards a common vision and yet retain their own autonomy. The performance of music does not just convey the vision (or audition) of a better society: it enacts it, while the music lasts. Music may be a triumph of individual imagination, but it is consummated in social action.

References

Baily, J. 1985: Music structure and human movement. In: Howell, P., Cross, I. and West, R. (eds), *Musical Structure and Cognition*. London: Academic Press, 237–258.

Clarke, E., Cook, N., Harrison, B. and Thomas, P. 2005: Interpretation and performance in Bryn Harrison's être-temps. *Musicae Scientiae*, 9, 31–74.

Cook, N. 1990: *Music, Imagination, and Culture*. Oxford: Clarendon Press.

Cook, N. 2003: Product or process? Music as performance. In: Clayton, M., Herbert, T. & Middleton, R. (eds), *The Cultural Study of Music: A Critical Introduction*. London: Routledge, 204–214.

Cook, N. 2004: Making music together, or improvisation and its others. *The Source: Challenging Jazz Criticism*, 1, 5–25.

Cooper, B. 1990: *Beethoven and the Creative Process*. Oxford: Clarendon Press.

Day, M. 2004: Religion, off-line cognition and the extended mind. *Journal of Cognition and Culture*, 4, 101–121.

DeNora, T. 2003: *After Adorno: Rethinking Music Sociology*. Cambridge: Cambridge University Press.

Kerman, J. 1985: *Musicology*. London: Fontana [published in the US as *Contemplating Music: Challenges to Musicology*].

Kramer, L. 1990: *Music as Cultural Practice, 1800–1900*. Berkeley: University of California Press.

Martin, P. 1995: *Sounds and Society: Themes in the Sociology of Music*. Manchester: Manchester University Press.

Monson, I. 1996: *Saying Something: Jazz Improvisation and Interaction*. Chicago: University of Chicago Press.

Reynolds, R. 2002: *Form and Method: Composing Music*. New York: Routledge.

Rosen, C. 1971: Art has its reasons. *New York Review of Books*, 17 June, 38.

Scruton, R. 1974: *Art and Imagination*. London: Methuen.

Sudnow, D. 1978: *Ways of the Hand: The Organization of Improvised Conduct*. London: Routledge and Kegan Paul [revised edn 2001].

Yung, B. 1984: Choreographic and kinesthetic elements in performance on the Chinese seven-string zither. *Ethnomusicology*, 28, 505–517.

Zbikowski, L. 2002: *Conceptualizing Music: Cognitive Structure, Theory, and Analysis*. New York: Oxford University Press.

7

Music, Science, and Culture

IAN CROSS

Abstract. 'Music' as a product and a process of the imagination
can appear to be fundamentally different things to the sciences
and to musicology. For the sciences, music is complexly patterned
sound or the experience of such structured sound. For current
musicology and ethnomusicology, musics cannot be dissociated
from the cultural contexts in which they occur, yielding meaning-
centred as opposed to structure-centred approaches. Although
these different conceptions of music have afforded valuable
insights, the methods and, in particular, the objects of study of
the sciences and of musicology seem irreconcilable. This chapter
suggests that a radical redefinition of 'music' may provide ways of
understanding music as both biologically grounded structure and
as culturally embedded practice. It will investigate some of the
consequences and potential implications of this radical redefinition, among which is the possibility that the modern human
capacity for culture may have been supported and consolidated by
the emergence of human musicality.

INTRODUCTION

IN THE WESTERN TRADITION, from the Romantic era to the present day, listening to music can be seen to have stimulated and exercised the human
imaginative faculty. From the rhapsodic exaltations of Beethoven's works by
E. T. A. Hoffman in the early nineteenth century to the sexualized condem-
nations of those self-same works by Susan McClary in the late twentieth
century, music has embodied values and manifested features that have
elicited imaginative and creative responses in listening. Of course, in addition, music is self-evidently the *product* of such acts in composition and in
performance.

Yet, outside the western tradition—and even in some strands within it—
engagement with music has taken, and continues to take, forms that cannot
easily be assimilated to the discrete roles of listener, composer, and performer.

Proceedings of the British Academy **147**, 147–165. © The British Academy 2007.

For many, perhaps most, world cultures, music has been and is an active and interactive medium of experience and expression: music appears to be a participatory art in which the roles of listener and performer—and sometimes composer—are united in dynamic sequences of musical acts. From this perspective music seems to allow space for the individual mind to engage fluidly with its surroundings and with itself, as well as coordinating and shaping collective action and interaction in ways that enhance the likelihood of the emergence of individually and socially imaginative minds. It is even possible that active engagement with and in music underpins the developmental and evolutionary emergence of imagination.

This conception of music and its relationship to human powers of individual and social imagining requires that music be considered both from scientific and from cultural perspectives. However, in the imaginations of the scientist and of the musicologist 'music' appears to be fundamentally different types of phenomena. For the sciences music seems to be complexly patterned sound structure. For musicology, and this is particularly evident in ethnomusicology, the complexly patterned sound structures of music cannot be separated out from the cultural contexts within which they are embedded. This creates a particular difficulty for our scholarly imaginings of music in the present day: which music are we dealing with? We appear to have at least two different conceptions of music that are mutually irreducible, each bearing radically divergent implications. Yet both conceptions seem to be productive, and it does not seem that one should supplant the other.

One possible way of reconciling these radically divergent conceptions of music is to attempt to redefine music in a way that is consonant with both the notion of a biologically grounded structure and that of a culturally contingent interactive behaviour. This chapter will propose a broad operational definition of music that may be applicable cross-culturally, and that seems to be evident in the behavioural predispositions of all human infants. Starting from this broad definition it seems that activities, behaviours, and cognitions that are broadly interpretable as musical are efficacious in individual development and in social interaction; indeed, it can be suggested that such human behaviours and cognitions arose through, and may have been adaptive in, processes of evolution.

MUSIC IN SCIENCE

Over the last half century music has been an increasingly significant focus of scientific exploration. Within the fields of acoustics, psychoacoustics, computer science, cognitive psychology, and, most recently, neuroscience, the overwhelming majority of this research has tended to treat music as complexly patterned structures in sound or as the experience of such structures. For the human sciences concerned with understanding our experience of music, the sonic structures that we experience in music are conceived of as related to or even determined by the workings of our physiologies and neuro-physiologies. In other words, for the human sciences, music appears to have biological foundations: it is grounded in human biology.

Scientific research on music has been extraordinarily productive. An immense amount has been learned about the behaviour of musical sounds—for instance, how musical instruments operate as physical systems to produce musical sounds. We are gaining an ever more comprehensive understanding of how ears and minds, and computational models of these, process musical sounds. And neuroscience is beginning to disentangle many of the complex-ities of the neurophysiological processes involved in the experience and pro-duction of musical sound. To give examples of the types of research to which I am referring, I shall briefly review two different scientific approaches to music, one being perhaps the most substantial and long-running research programme in the cognitive psychology of music, and one being a single study that appears to have significant implications for the place of music in the human world.

When someone listens to a piece of tonal music, it seems that some tones are more stable or important than others, some are more legitimate or allow-able than others. How might such impressions arise in a listener's mind? Are there any generalized principles of the functioning of mind that could be discovered which could explain this? Over the last two decades, Carol Krumhansl and her colleagues have carried out numerous experiments to explore this phenomenon (Krumhansl 1990; Krumhansl and Toivianen 2003). Most of the individual experiments are quite simple; they involve pre-senting listeners with a pattern of tones and then a single tone, and asking lis-teners to judge how well the single tone fitted into the preceding pattern. From the results of many of these experiments, a general pattern has emerged that suggests that listeners actively pick up the regularities of the music to which they have been exposed. As a listener hears a piece unfolding in time, certain pitches will appear more important than others, perhaps because they occur more frequently, or because they sound for a longer proportion of the piece than do other pitches. Over the course of the piece these pitches will become referential for the listener, serving as fixed points around which the other tones of the piece are organized. As the listener hears more and more pieces in which pitches are organized in the same way, they will build up a cognitive schema (the workings of which are unlikely to be conscious) within which certain pitches will be more stable and will fit better in certain musical contexts than others. Hence listeners' implicit or unconscious knowl-edge of regularities in music comes to shape and guide the ways in which they

subsequently experience music. While many aspects of this research programme have been criticized, there is no doubt that the overall programme
has greatly contributed to our understanding of the human experience of
musical pitch.

Here music is being treated as, in essence, complex sonic structure. A similar treatment of music underlies a recent study (Drayna *et al.* 2001) that
claims to demonstrate that there is a significant genetic component to human
musicality, particularly in respect of the perception of musical pitch. In this
research Drayna and his collaborators used large numbers of identical and
non-identical twins to test whether or not individuals with the same genetic
attributes would show similar patterns of judgements in identifying tunes
that were presented either in canonical versions or in versions into which
wrong notes had been introduced. The logic of the approach is that comparisons between identical and non-identical twin pairs offer a method for
evaluating the contribution of genetic inheritance to a human characteristic,
while holding the effects of environment constant. Patterns of judgement
were much closer between members of identical twin pairs than between
members of non-identical twin pairs. The experimenters interpreted these
superior 'concordance' levels in identical twins as demonstrating that the
capacity to discriminate between distorted and correct versions of tunes is
71% due to genes and only about 29% amenable to environmental influences.
The study has since been used to claim that music, or musical ability, is
largely genetic, and one of the scientists involved was reported in the press as
suggesting that there is really no need to give access to music lessons for all
as only a certain percentage will be predisposed to be musical. For anyone
concerned with music and music education, the basis for such claims really
does require close scrutiny.

In fact this research appears to have several flaws that severely undermine
its credibility. In part these relate to its treatment of the musical materials,
which takes no account of the vast body of research conducted since the
1960s that bears on the cognitive processes involved in discriminating
between tunes. In particular, research such as that of Dowling (1978) demonstrates that melodic contour (pattern of ups-and-downs) constitutes a significant dimension in melodic cognition that is partly independent of specific
pitch patterning. Hence it would be entirely expected that changes in a tune
that preserve its contour though altering the actual pitches might not be
noticed by many listeners, and indeed certain of the 'distorted tunes' used in
the experiment preserved contour, while others did not. As Judy Edworthy
(1985) cogently points out, what Ingrid Bergman sings and what Sam plays
in response to her injunction 'Play it, Sam', in the film *Casablanca* are two
quite different sequences of musical pitches, yet both share the same contour
and have been happily accepted by generations of film-goers as versions of

As Time Goes By. So it appears that the most the results of the experiment would allow the researchers to claim is that for some listeners the identities of tunes are more closely bound to the specific pitches used than is the case for other listeners and that this might have some genetic basis.

However, even here a problem arises in that the methods and some of the statistical procedures employed in the experiment itself appear to be flawed. The experimenters start from the assumption that a significant proportion of human beings are simply non-musical and employ a particular statistical procedure (the probandwise concordance) in analysing their results that is effectively grounded in this assumption rather than being capable of testing it. The probandwise concordance is used to explore 'familial resemblance for dichotomous traits' (Plomin *et al*. 1997, p. 288), such as *either* suffering from *or* not suffering from a specific disorder; here, 'musicality' is being conceived of as a capacity which is *either* possessed *or* is not possessed at all, an assumption that is severely at odds with almost all the available evidence, and, indeed, with the experimenters' own finding of a continuous rather than a dichotomous distribution of test scores. This treatment of musicality as an 'either/or' capacity cannot be justified on any 'pure' scientific or methodological grounds, but seems to be motivated by the exigencies of twin studies where the categorical presence or absence of a capacity or a disorder provides evidence that is much more easily interpretable in genetic terms than does continuous variation in degree of ability or illness.

Here we have two applications of the sciences to music, one successful, one unsuccessful (at least as far as I am concerned). But because of the power that is accorded to 'scientific' knowledge in the present day, the results of both Krumhansl's research programme and the seemingly 'hard' (but problematic) genetic evidence provided in Drayna's experiment are quite likely to impact critically on any political considerations of music's value or significance.

MUSIC IN MUSICOLOGY

Somewhat ironically, it is relatively rare for scientists concerned with music to make explicit claims about music's identity or value. In treating music as complexly patterned and non-linguistic sound, science glosses over any problematic aspects of music's identity while leaving its prospective value an open question (though implicitly affording music a lesser status than speech, simply on the grounds of the evidently greater instrumental utility of language than of music). However, issues of identity and value are at the core of contemporary musicology's engagement with the idea of music. Within musicology, music is seen not as just complexly patterned sound but as a dynamic social process embedded in its historical and cultural contexts and understandable only in terms of those contexts.

While this view of music has been become increasingly prevalent within the study of western music history, it is perhaps easier to understand just to what extent music cannot be dissociated from the cultural practices that enmesh it by examining its manifestations in a non-western context. A complex example can be found in the ethnomusicological research of Steven Feld on the music of the Kaluli peoples of Papua New Guinea (Feld 1982). Feld focused on Kaluli music as displayed in the *gisalo* ceremony, a funerary ceremony which is rehearsed and 'composed' for performance by a medium, and can elicit very strong reactions on the part of the audience; in fact, the audience may, if moved too much to tears against their will, actually cause physical harm to the performer (a contingency that is accepted as very much part of the job by the performer).

The melody that the performer uses derives from the call of the *muni* bird, one of the common birds of the Papuan rainforest. In the Kaluli belief system those who die join the realm of the birds, and the *muni* bird is the central numinous entity in the main Kaluli myth of 'the boy who turned into a *muni* bird' and thus joined the departed spirits. The performer in the *gisalo* ceremony employs the song of the *muni* to retell the history of the person who has died, hence straddling and joining the two realms of the living and of the dead. The structure of the *muni* song is very simple (it is one of the least interesting aspects of the *gisalo* ceremony!), and the use of that particular musical pitch structure makes little sense in its own right; for the Kaluli, the song's structure, identity, and efficacy in mourning are inextricably bound both to its sacred connotations and to its place in the ecology of the local environment. Thus it is inappropriate to think of the 'music' of the *gisalo* ceremony simply as a complex sonic structure that is separable from the ceremony, its associated belief systems and its rainforest environs; it certainly does not help us understand what is 'musical' about the *gisalo* ceremony. Indeed, in certain societies such as traditional Navaho (McAllester 1954, quoted in Magrini 2000, p. 325) there does not seem to be a term that translates into our term 'music', even though we can identify practices in that society that to us seem to be 'musical'. Music makes sense only in social context: it has been claimed by Philip Bohlman (2000) that 'expressive practices do not divide into those that produce music and those that produce something else, say ritual or dance. Music accumulates its identities. . . from the ways in which it participates in other activities'. Hence for musicology and ethnomusicology music appears to be inextricable from the cultural contexts in which it occurs.

It must be said that the claims being made here about what music is for the sciences, and for musicology, are to some extent caricatures. In the present day, the sciences often treat music as more than just sound structures, considering, for instance, its emotional import. Similarly, musicology, in exploring music in cultural context, often focuses on the complexly patterned sonic structures that constitute one aspect of music. I am claiming, nonetheless, that the general trend within the sciences and the humanities is to treat music as two quite disparate phenomena. The trend within the sciences is partly motivated by the reductionism inherent in most scientific method (it is virtually impossible to explore anything in terms of science without 'stripping it down' so that different and clearly defined aspects of a problem can be explored by the application of rigorous scientific method). In contrast, within musicology an increasing awareness of the different forms that music takes, and the diverse roles that it plays in different cultures and at different times, has led to an increasing concern to explore and explain music as manifested in, and as emergent from, dynamic social and historical processes.

THE NEED FOR A BROAD DEFINITION OF MUSIC

At the extremes, music for the sciences and music for musicology appear to be two different things. Yet, as the volume of scientific research on music increases it becomes more and more evident that the sciences must at some point address music as grounded not only in biology but also in culture. And musicology, in particular ethnomusicology, has seen an increasing need to deal with music not only as a cultural but also as a biologically grounded phenomenon. There is, then, recognition of the requirement for some reconciliation between these two views, of music as structure, and of music as cultural practice.

One strategy for arriving at such a reconciliation is to explore the common features of 'music' across cultures in an attempt to specify the nature of the human faculty for music. Specification of these common features could constitute the basis for generalizable claims about music that could make it more amenable to scientific investigation. At the same time, if these features can be shown to be unconditionally present in all manifestations of 'music' across cultures, this could provide a means whereby interpretive and cultural explorations of music could ground their accounts in human biology while maintaining a focus on sociohistorical dynamics. Hence a broad definition of music seems to be required from both scientific and humanistic perspectives.

Underlying this approach is the assumption that all human beings can, universally, engage in music and musical behaviours, and if there is one message that comes out of musicological research it is that although musics may be various and manifest themselves in cultural contexts in quite strange and different ways, all societies of which we know appear to engage in activities that could be said to be musical. Indeed, in many cultures musicality and a

capacity actively to engage in musical activity is expected of all members of
the culture. Even in contemporary western culture, where the practice of
music appears to be a highly specialized activity requiring considerable
expertise, the capacity to engage with music through dance and through listening that embodies a degree of understanding is expected to be more or less
shared by all. In other words 'something like music' appears to be humanly
universal, but what precisely is this 'something like music'?

First of all a broad account of music would have to address the fact that
music is often, if not always, indissociable from aspects of dance. Music
has not only a sonic but also a motoric dimension. Indeed the structure of
its sonic patterns may be as much determined by the actions that produce
them as by any abstract considerations of sonic design, as John Blacking
(1961, 1976) pointed out (see also Baily 1985; Nelson 2002). While this
motoric dimension may not be evident in the 'passive' listening behaviours
of a western concert audience, the *acquisition* of the capacity to listen and
respond appropriately to concert music is likely to have involved movement, as we shall see. And in any case, a recent meta-review of the neuroscientific literature (Janata and Grafton 2003) has shown that even 'passive'
listening to music can involve activation of brain regions concerned with
movement.

In the second place, musical behaviours (and I include listening in these)
are generally not only active but interactive. Both the listening experience and
active musical performance (or dance) involve abstraction of, and orientation
to, temporal aspects of music's structure, usually in the form of pulse (Drake
and Bertrand 2001). While this is rarely overtly evident in the western concert
hall other than in the actions and interactions of the performers, outside the
confines of the concert hall, the 'action' and 'interaction' dimensions of musical participation can be less covert and may be extremely ostentatious.
Indeed, in many non-western contexts active and collective entrainment with
the sonic structure of the music seems to be as much a part of the music as is
the sonic structure itself, perhaps evidenced in the lack of distinction made in
certain societies between what in the west might be separately categorized as
music and as dance (Gourlay 1984). The intelligibility of the sonic structure
of music may even depend on its contextualization in collective movement, as
is evident in, for example, many of the musical practices of the *campesino*
culture of Northern Potosí in Bolivia (Stobart and Cross 2000). In this
society musical rhythms can appear to be very 'four-square' and relatively
simple. However, when the musical rhythms of the instrumental performers
are analysed—or better, heard and experienced—against the rhythms produced by the dancers, they suddenly appear potent and complex; indeed, the
only way to learn to play the instruments in the 'right' way is to learn—to
entrain—to the steady and simple beat of the dance. While this capacity to

entrain to a pulse, most simply evidenced in our ability to tap along with a piece of music, may appear simple and 'primitive', its underlying neurobiology appears complex (see, e.g., Molinari *et al.* 2003). Indeed, it may be that this seemingly basic capacity (in fact, suite of capacities) is itself unique to humans among mammalian species (Merker 2002).

In the third place, music is a strangely mutable and flexible phenomenon. Whereas in language it is usually possible to specify the subject of an utterance with some precision, this is almost never the case for music. Although a particular piece of music may be able consistently to evoke certain feelings, or to bear certain cultural associations (and may even be able to cue particular suites of words that relate to these: see Koelsch *et al.* 2004), the meaning or significance of a musical behaviour or of a piece of music can rarely be pinned down unambiguously; music appears to be inherently ambiguous (Kramer 2003). As Langer (1942) puts it:

> music at its highest, though clearly a symbolic form, is an unconsummated symbol. Articulation is its life, but not assertion; expressiveness, not expression. The actual function of meaning, which calls for permanent contents, is not fulfilled; for the *assignment* of one rather than another possible meaning to each form is never explicitly made. (Langer 1942, p. 195)

This ambiguity has been conceived of as valuable within social and political contexts: as Devereux and LaBarre (1961, p. 369) put it, 'In addition to viewing art as a harmless safety valve, society and the artist alike consider the artistic utterance as *unrepudiable* in form but *repudiable* as to content . . .'. In effect, one and the same piece of music can bear quite different meanings for performer and listener, or for two different listeners; it might even bear multiple disparate meanings for a single listener or participant at a particular time. Music has a sort of 'floating intentionality' (the word 'intentionality' here simply means 'aboutness'): it gathers meaning from the contexts within which it happens and in turn contributes meaning to those contexts.

So music appears to involve not just sound but also action; music appears to involve not only action but also interaction; and music appears to be fluid in the meanings that it can bear at any time. From these considerations the following might constitute a first attempt at a broad definition of music: *music embodies, entrains and transposably intentionalizes time in sound and action* (Cross 2003a).

MUSIC, MEANING, AND LANGUAGE

This broad definition of music is offered as a hypothesis; it may require reformulation, or it may be completely wrong. It is not intended as a constitutive definition, but rather as a more adequate and explicit operational definition

than those that have tended to be employed in exploring music from a scientific perspective. And while it leaves much about music undefined, it can
certainly be used to identify aspects of the human faculty for music that are
of interest, such as how it relates to, but is distinct from, other human
communicative capacities such as language. Briefly, music as defined here
overlaps considerably with language, a suggestion that fits well with much
recent neuroscientific research (see, e.g., Patel 2003; Koelsch *et al.* 2004).
Language has an embodied, motoric component, most evident in the sign
languages employed by many deaf and partially hearing people, often spontaneously produced by them, but also evident in the para-linguistic gestures
that are part of everyday speech. Language too is interactive, although the
ways in which entrainment occurs to the temporal characteristics of the
stream of speech in conversation may be by means of mechanisms somewhat
distinct from those employed in music. And of course language also means;
it has a conceptual-semantic dimension. However, here we see a difference
between language and music.

In most everyday situations language is used in ways that are susceptible
to multiple interpretations; nevertheless, language is capable of being used so
as unambiguously to convey meaning. Language is capable of expressing
semantically decomposable propositions unambiguously, although this may
only be absolutely so in the limiting cases where the inferential context for the
recovery of the propositional content of a linguistic statement can be made
wholly explicit, as, for instance, in the case of a linguistic gloss on the content
of a theorem in the domain of formal logic. Perhaps the canonical semantically decomposable proposition is 'the cat sat on the mat', a statement that
conveys a quite specific and more or less complex meaning, at least for someone who can identify which cat and which mat is intended. And language can
be employed so as to pinpoint the range of possible cats and mats intended
to theoretically infinite degrees of complexity and, indeed, significance, as in
'the old white cat from next door spent some time sitting on the mat outside
our back door', or in the rather more complex and consequential 'the old
white cat from next door which the vet this morning identified as carrying a
life-threatening virus that can infect humans appears to have entered our
house last night by means of the cat-flap which you foolishly left open and by
the copious traces of white hair left behind it seems that at the least it sat on
our Bokhara rug which we conventionally refer to as the mat . . .'.

While music can be constituted of structures that are as complex and
multi-levelled as are those of language, music cannot even express simple
and unambiguous propositions such as 'there exists a cat'. One could *sing*
'the cat sat on the mat', but one could not *play* it. While language in everyday use is often ambiguous, language *can* be used unambiguously; music
appears to embody a necessary ambiguity (Cross 2005), and one can conceive

of language and music as occupying opposite poles on a continuum of specificity of meaning. This ambiguity, or open-endedness in meaning, of music
can be thought of as affording conceptual and social spaces within which
individual and collective imaginings can take place, and the last part of this
chapter will explore the possible functions of music's ambiguity for individuals and for groups and societies, as well as exploring briefly the biological basis for the appearance of musicality. This will entail the adoption of
developmental and evolutionary perspectives, within which the emergence
of music and the emergence of the human capacity for culture seem to be
intimately intertwined.

FUNCTIONS OF MUSICALITY

Humans are very unusual animals, even for primates. We are socially
extremely flexible, being able to interact in complicated ways and form complex social groupings that have no analogues in other species (Foley 1995).
While language, with its powers of articulating and communicating complex
states of affairs, is self-evidently one of the principal factors that drives and
sustains such inter-personal versatility (see, e.g., Plotkin 2002), activities with
the attributes of music can be conceived of as playing a crucial role in
enabling and in maintaining social flexibility. The potential for music-like
activities to entrain collective behaviour, together with their ambiguity, provides a means whereby groups can coordinate their interaction within a
framework that allows the meaning of any musical act to vary from participant to participant without undermining the integrity of the collective
musical behaviour. Music can thus serve as a 'minimal-risk' medium for the
exploration of types of social interaction and thereby serve to reinforce
human social flexibility. These properties of music-like activities might be
considered most efficacious in children's musical interactions, which afford
the exploratory value of play whilst structuring interaction in time and min-
imizing the risk of conflict by virtue of the ambiguity inherent in musical
behaviours. Here it might be that social flexibility is not just being maintained
but formed, the musical behaviours effectively underlying the gestation of
social flexibility. One only has to encounter a group of children interacting
verbally and unambiguously rather than musically to see (and hear) how
quickly conflict is likely to emerge in linguistic rather than musical interaction!
   Intimately related to human social flexibility is, of course, human intellectual flexibility. In contrast to other animals individual humans seem to have
an almost unconstrained ability to acquire, integrate, and manipulate information, not only in our dealings with each other but also in our dealings
with the physical world. We appear to possess a powerful domain-general

intellectual capacity. Yet, over the past twenty years, an increasing weight of evidence indicates that human infants and children are not general-purpose learning devices. It seems, rather, that they are primed to pick up certain types of information rapidly and efficiently in ways that differ according to the nature of the information being handled (see Spelke 1999). So, for example, the behaviours of even a very young infant will show that it has well-formed and veridical expectations about the likely behaviours of animate objects that differ from those that it exhibits in respect of the behaviours of inanimate objects. These capacities emerge too rapidly in infancy to be explained on the basis of general-purpose learning mechanisms, and seem to be specific to the particular domains in respect of which they are displayed. A seemingly precocious ability to generate appropriate expectations concerning the behaviour of objects in the physical world may well not be matched by a similar level of ability in dealing with the behaviour of animate objects, even though the level of informational complexity in the latter domain may be judged to be matched to that in the former. A domain-general intelligence does not seem to underlie many infant behaviours.

But somehow in the course of development children seem to acquire the capacity to deal with information in a domain-general way; for example, in a drawing task where they are required to draw a house or a man that 'doesn't exist', children of different ages demonstrate different levels of ability to 'move flexibly across representational categories' (Karmiloff-Smith 1992, p. 161) in the drawings that they produce. As in the field of social relations, language is likely to play a major role in the emergence of this domain-general intellectual flexibility (Pinker 1994), in the richness of semantic and syntactic representations that it affords. But music can also be conceived of as playing a significant role in this process. Over the past ten years a considerable amount of research has demonstrated that caregiver–infant interactions in many cultures have musical or proto-musical attributes, incorporating exaggerated pitch contours and periodic rhythmic timings in their structure, involving turn-taking and a close linkage between sound and movement, with similar or the same 'musical' interactions occurring in a wide variety of contexts. Even very young infants can engage in music-like or *proto-musical* behaviours (Trehub 2003) which involve not only sound perception and production but also movement, and they are highly motivated to do so. Individual musical behaviours in childhood have been characterized as fundamentally exploratory and children seem to be predisposed to engage in music-like activities from birth (Trevarthen 1999). It is notable that in the earliest years proto-musical and proto-linguistic behaviours appear to be indistinguishable: the infant's early manifestations of linguistic capacity and of musicality are more likely to co-occur than to be displayed separately (Papousek 1996). In the course of the infant's development, linguistic and proto-musical behaviours can be thought of as gradually differentiating out from this common suite of complex and communicative behaviours; linguistic behaviours become increasingly bound by considerations of relevance (after Sperber and Wilson 1986) so as to constrain the extent to which they can substitute one for another in the linguistic contexts in which they are deployed. However, proto-musical and musical behaviours are likely to retain a degree of 'floating intentionality': for the child, they are likely to continue to be appropriate to a wide range of dissimilar situations and types of information, their individual and social functionality being closely tied to their effective ambiguity.

Music's floating intentionality, its potential for its meaning or aboutness to be transposed from one situation to another, allows that one and the same musical act might be co-opted by an infant or child in dealing with information in two quite different domains. So, for example, a child might experience a melody in terms of a temporal pattern that actualizes either the increase and decrease in muscular tension involved in singing it, or the flight of a thrown ball that happens to co-occur with the melody or even the pattern of actions of the ball's thrower; indeed, the experience of the melody might simultaneously involve more than one of these types of events. Hence the experience of the melody may allow an experience that combines or integrates the (visual) flight of the ball, the (haptic) pattern of tension and release, and the visual and social action of the thrower, underpinning the emergence of a rich and dynamic 'connotative complex' (to use Leonard Meyer's 1956 term) that is associable with the melody—that constitutes a matrix for *meanings* for the music (see Cross 2005).

For a child, then, music may help in the emergence of a capacity to relate or to integrate information across domains, and assist in the development of a domain-general competence, a suggestion given support by some (very tentative and culture-specific) evidence for a positive correlation between IQ and engagement in musical activities (Schellenberg 2004). Early musical, or rather, proto-musical, behaviours may be functional in individual development in giving rise to a *metaphorizing* capacity (Cross 2003b). The attributes of music that may facilitate this transposition of its significances and hence allow the *redescription* of information across domains (Karmiloff-Smith 1992) may lie in its capacity to mirror forms of emotional and cognitive dynamics (Cross 1999). Alternatively, it may be that positive emotions evoked in an infant's or child's engagement with music are directly beneficial in cognitive processing, particularly in affording the conditions for rich integration of representations and enhanced exploratory behaviour (see Damasio 1995, pp. 163–165). Music as broadly defined seems likely to play crucial roles for humans in individual and social development and a predisposition to engage in music-like activities seems to be part of our biological heritage.

MUSIC IN EVOLUTION

That biological heritage is, by and large, a consequence of the operation of
evolutionary processes, and it can be suggested that music, as broadly
defined, may have played a significant role in human evolution (Cross 1999).
The intellectual and social flexibility that marks out modern humans appears
to have emerged in the hominid lineage sometime within the last seven million
years, the likely date of the last common ancestor of humans and of our
nearest relatives, the chimpanzees and bonobos (see Chapter 2).

The first evidence of that flexibility seems to emerge some two to two and
a half million years before the present (BP) with the appearance of *Homo
habilis*, a small-brained hominid which seems to have been the first to use and
conserve stone tools. Subsequent to *Homo habilis* there emerges *Homo
ergaster* or *erectus* (around two million BP), with a much wider range and
geographical dispersion, extending the hominid range for the first time out of
Africa. Between 500,000 and 700,000 BP, *Homo heidelbergensis* appears in the
archaeological record, the predecessor of both the Neanderthals, who appear
some 250,000–350,000 BP and ourselves, modern *Homo sapiens*, who seem to
have emerged as an African species some 150,000–200,000 BP (for a more
detailed account see Chapter 1). While successive hominid species from
ergaster to ourselves exhibit progressively more complex skills, it is only with
modern *Homo sapiens* that we find the unambiguous capacity to engage in
symbolic activities that indicate the possession of a flexible and cross-domain
intellectual capacity (see Chapter 1), the earliest of that evidence consisting
of engraved pieces of ochre found in South Africa and dated to 77,000 BP
(Henshilwood *et al.* 2002). And again, only with modern *Homo sapiens* do we
find unambiguous evidence for musicality, in the form of musical instruments
(d'Errico *et al.* 2003).

The earliest musical instrument yet found is a bone pipe from
Geissenklösterle in southern Germany, dated to between 36,000 and 40,000
BP, and a large assemblage of musical bone pipes has been found in Isturitz
in southern France covering a time-span of some 15,000–20,000 years and
first appearing at around 30,000 BP. These are, for the time, extraordinarily
sophisticated objects, and it is notable that the dates to which the earliest is
attributed is around the time of the earliest appearance of modern humans
in Europe. In other words, almost as soon as modern humans reach Europe
they are leaving traces of sophisticated musical behaviours, which strongly
suggests that humans brought music with them out of Africa, and to me, and
to many others, strongly suggests that musicality constitutes a specific and
unique attribute of modern humans.

It is unlikely, however, that all the elements of musicality sprang into existence with modern humans. Different capacities which are components of

musicality seem to arise at different times in the hominid evolutionary record. As Morley (2002) points out, there is a strong likelihood that *Homo ergaster* employed complex sequences of vocal signals to communicate affect or emotional state in order to regulate social interactions. *Ergaster*, like modern humans, had a barrel-shaped chest which would have given it fine control over breath duration and pressure; all its predecessor species had 'pyramid'-shaped rib cages, which allow much less control of breath pressure and duration, and hence limit the capacity to produce complex and extended sequences of vocalizations. With *Homo heidelbergensis* we find something equivalent to the modern human vocal tract, which would allow the articulation of the full range of vocal sounds (including musical sounds) of which modern humans are capable. But on the basis of the archaeological evidence, it appears that an integrated musicality arose only with modern humans. I have suggested that music is likely to be efficacious among present-day populations in achieving and maintaining social versatility and in the emergence through childhood of generalized and flexible intellectual capacities. It seems likely that music may have played this role from the earliest appearance of our species and that modern *Homo sapiens* achieved and stabilized their potent social and intellectual abilities in part through their use of music-like behaviours.

It is possible that the emergence of musical capacities in modern *Homo sapiens* relates to a biological feature which occurs with the appearance of modern humans and which differentiates us from our predecessor species: an increase in the length of the juvenile state in modern humans. We take longer to attain adulthood than did members of our predecessor species. On the basis of a strong and positive correlation between complexity of social organization and proportion of lifespan spent as a juvenile in a large sample of primate species, Joffe (1997) has suggested that an extension of the juvenile stage effectively acts to increase the proportion of the lifespan that can be devoted to acquiring flexible social competences. In the hominid lineage, there appears to be a general trend for the duration of the juvenile period to increase between successive species (Dean *et al.* 2001). In modern humans, the trend towards extension of the juvenile period is taken to extremes: our childhoods are generally longer in absolute terms than were those of any of our predecessor species, and the modern human juvenile period incorporates more, and more complex, phases of growth and development than do those of any of our extant primate relatives (Bogin 1999). It is quite likely that these changes led to a need to incorporate aspects of childhood modes of thought and behaviour into the adult repertoire simply to accommodate the greater likelihood of having to deal with children in populations where (other things being equal) a greater proportion than before would have consisted of children. Music would appear to be an ideal mechanism for mediating between childhood and adult patterns of thought and behaviour, at least in part because of its ambiguity: the exploratory dimension of musical behaviours coupled to the indefiniteness of the meanings that these can bear would have provided a means of assimilating the forms and the positive value of something like social and individual play into the adult repertoire while providing a means of regulating its expression (Cross 2003b).

CONCLUSIONS

In conclusion, I am proposing that music is more than just structured sound, and that music is not just a contingent outcome of social and historical forces. Music derives from our evolutionary history and is rooted in our biological being. And music employs structured sound and action in social interaction in ways that can be sensitive to, and supportive of, the underlying dynamics of human cultures: *music embodies, entrains, and transposably intentionalizes time in sound and action.*

This broad definition of music severely under-specifies the role of cultural context in shaping music and in endowing it with meanings. Its value for musicology, if any, lies in its insistence that music has a biological basis that must be acknowledged in exploring the vicissitudes of music in culture, and as I mentioned earlier, this biological basis is indeed coming to constitute the research focus of a growing number of ethnomusicologists and of musicologists concerned with issues in the performance of music in contemporary western cultures.

The implications of this definition for scientific studies of music are perhaps more far-reaching, and relate to its insistence that the scientific exploration of music must address music as structured sound and action, must explore music as interaction and must take account of the culturally contingent meanings of music which, after all, make it worth pursuing for most of us. In the sciences (as in musicology) recent research trends are encouraging. An increasing number of studies, even at the neurophysiological level, focus on relations between musical structure and musical meaning, usually in the context of emotion, and such studies are also beginning to focus on music in interaction. Intriguingly, recent research that aims to redefine the neuroscientific understanding of *amusia*—a quite rare set of neurological conditions in which central nervous system dysfunctions lead to deficits in musical capacities—has incorporated the study of music in action into this redefinition (Ayotte *et al.* 2001).

It may seem redundant to consider the implications of the broad definition of music for the contemporary practice of music, as the broad definition under-determines in the extreme the forms that music may take, being intended to encompass examples as disparate as Cage's *4'33''* and the song-lines of the Pitjantjatjara Aboriginals of Australia. But it may be worth noting that this broad definition almost encourages a promiscuity in the activities, and types of activity, that can and should be explored in the musical domain. If music is as comprehensively grounded in action, interaction, and multiplicity of meanings as the definition would suggest, then recent trends in music towards interactivity and multi-media events can be regarded as representing not so much a forward progression, but a turn back towards music's roots.

And what, finally, of the implications of this broad definition for the politics of music in the wider world? Well, whatever one makes of them; after all, politics has seldom been pursued on the basis of fact or informed understanding. However, if this view of music is anywhere near correct, it would suggest that music is worth pursuing both for its own sake and for the potential benefits that it may well afford for our sociality and for our intellect; indeed, the evolutionary story told here implies that music is at least one of the reasons why we *have* imaginative minds.

References

Ayotte, J., Peretz, I. and Hyde, K. 2001: Congenital amusia: a group study of adults afflicted with a music-specific disorder. *Brain*, 125, 238–251.

Baily, J. 1985: Music structure and human movement. In Howell, P., Cross, I. and West, R. (eds), *Musical Structure and Cognition*. London: Academic Press, 237–258.

Blacking, J. 1961: Patterns of Nsenga *kalimba* music. *African Music*, 2(4), 3–20.

Blacking, J. 1976: *How Musical is Man?* London: Faber.

Bogin, B. 1999: *Patterns of Human Growth* (2nd edn). Cambridge: Cambridge University Press.

Bohlman, P. 2000: Ethnomusicology and music sociology. In Greer, D. (ed.), *Musicology and Sister Disciplines*. Oxford: Oxford University Press, 288–298.

Cross, I. 1999: Is music the most important thing we ever did ? Music, development and evolution. In S. W. Yi (ed.), *Music, Mind and Science*. Seoul: Seoul National University Press, 10–39.

Cross, I. 2003a: Music and biocultural evolution. In Clayton, M., Herbert, T. and Middleton, R. (eds), *The Cultural Study of Music: A Critical Introduction*. London: Routledge, 19–30.

Cross, I. 2003b: Music and evolution: causes and consequences. *Contemporary Music Review* 22(2), 79–89.

Cross, I. 2005: Music and meaning, ambiguity and evolution. In Miell, D., MacDonald, R. and Hargreaves, D. (eds), *Musical Communication*. Oxford: Oxford University Press, 27–43.

Damasio, A. 1995: *Descartes' Error: Emotion, Reason and the Human Brain*. London: Picador.

Dean, C., Leakey, M. V., Reid, D., Schrenk, F., Schwartzk, G. T., Stringer, C. and
    Walker, A. 2001: Growth processes in teeth distinguish modern humans from
    Homo erectus and earlier hominins. *Letters to Nature: Nature*, 414(6), 628–631.
Devereux, G. and LaBarre, W. 1961: Art and mythology. In Kaplan, B. (ed.), *Studying
    Personality Cross-culturally*. Evanston: Row, Peterson, 361–403.
Dowling, W. J. 1978: Scale and contour: Two components of a theory of memory for
    melodies. *Psychological Review*, 85, 341–354.
Drake, C. and Bertrand, D. 2001: The quest for universals in temporal processing in
    music. *Annals of the New York Academy of Science*, 930, 17–27.
Drayna, D., Manichaikul, A., de Lange, M., Snieder, H. and Spector, T. 2001: Genetic
    correlates of musical pitch recognition in humans. *Science*, 291, 1969–1972.
Edworthy, J. 1985: Melodic contour and musical structure. In Howell, P., Cross, I. and
    West, R. (eds), *Musical Structure and Cognition*. London: Academic Press,
    169–188.
d'Errico, F., Henshilwood, C., Lawson, G., Vanhaeren, M., Tillier, A.-M., Soressi, M.,
    Bresson, F., Maureille, B., Nowell, A., Lakarra, J., Backwell, L. and Julien, M.
    2003: Archaeological evidence for the emergence of language, symbolism, and
    music—an alternative multidisciplinary perspective. *Journal of World Prehistory*,
    17(1), 1–70.
Feld, S. 1982: *Sound and Sentiment: Birds, Weeping, Poetics and Song in Kaluli
    Expression*. Philadelphia: Publications of the American Folklore Society.
Foley, R. A. 1995: *Humans before Humanity*. Oxford: Blackwell.
Gourlay, K. A. 1984: The non-universality of music and the universality of non-music.
    The World of Music, 26(2), 25–36.
Henshilwood, C. S., d'Errico, F., Yates, R., Jacobs, Z., Tribolo, C., Duller, G. A. T.,
    Mercier, N., Sealy, J. C., Valladas, H., Watts, I. and Wintle, A. G. 2002: Emergence
    of modern human behavior: middle Stone Age engravings from South Africa.
    Science, 295(15), 1278–1280.
Janata, P. and Grafton, S. T. 2003: Swinging in the brain: Shared neural substrates for
    behaviors related to sequencing and music. *Nature Neuroscience*, 6(7), 682–687.
Joffe, T. H. 1997: Social pressures have selected for an extended juvenile period in
    primates. *Journal of Human Evolution*, 32(6), 593–605.
Karmiloff-Smith, A. 1992: *Beyond Modularity*. London: MIT Press.
Koelsch, S., Kasper, E., Sammler, D., Schultze, K., Gunter, T. and Frederici, A. 2004:
    Music, language and meaning: Brain signatures of semantic processing. *Nature
    Neuroscience*, 7(3), 302–307.
Kramer, L. 2003: Musicology and meaning. *Music Times*, 144(1883), 6–12.
Krumhansl, C. L. 1990: *The Cognitive Foundations of Musical Pitch*. Oxford: Oxford
    University Press.
Krumhansl, C. L. and Toivianen, P. 2003: Tonal cognition. In Peretz, I. and Zatorre,
    R. (eds), *The Cognitive Neuroscience of Music*. Oxford: Oxford University Press,
    95–108.
Langer, S. 1942: *Philosophy in a New Key*. Cambridge, MA: Harvard University Press.
Magrini, T. 2000: From music-makers to virtual singers: New musics and puzzled
    scholars. In Greer, D. (ed.), *Musicology & Sister Disciplines*. Oxford: Oxford
    University Press, 320–330.

Merker, B. 2002: Principles of interactive behavioral timing. In Stevens, C., Burnham, D., McPherson, G., Schubert, E. and Renwick, J. (eds), *Proceedings of the 7th ICMPC, Sydney*. Adelaide: Causal Productions, 149–152.

Meyer, L. B. 1956: *Emotion and Meaning in Music*. London: University of Chicago Press.

Molinari, M., Leggio, M. L., De Martin, M., Cerasa, A. and Thaut, M. H. 2003: Neurobiology of rhythmic motor entrainment. *Annals of the New York Academy of Sciences: The Neurosciences and Music*, 999, 313–321.

Morley, I. 2002: Evolution of the physiological and neurological capacities for music. *Cambridge Archaeological Journal*, 12(2), 195–216.

Nelson, S. 2002: Melodic improvisation on a twelve-bar blues model: an investigation of physical and historical aspects, and their contribution to performance. Unpublished PhD, City University London, Department of Music, London.

Papousek, H. 1996: Musicality in infancy research: biological and cultural origins of early musicality. In Deliège, I. and Sloboda, J. A. (eds), *Musical Beginnings*. Oxford: Oxford University Press, 37–55.

Patel, A. D. 2003: Language, music, syntax and the brain. *Nature Neuroscience*, 6(7), 674–681.

Pinker, S. 1994: *The Language Instinct*. London: Allen Lane.

Plomin, R., DeFries, J. C., McClearn, G. E. and Rutter, M. 1997: *Behavioral Genetics* (3rd edn). New York: W.H. Freeman and Company.

Plotkin, H. 2002: *The Imagined World Made Real: Towards a Natural Science of Culture*. London: Allen Lane.

Schellenberg, E. G. 2004: Music lessons enhance IQ. *Psychological Science*, 15(8), 511–514.

Spelke, E. 1999: Infant cognition. In Wilson, R. A. and Keil, F. C. (eds), *The MIT Encyclopedia of Cognitive Sciences*. Cambridge, MA: MIT Press, 402–404.

Sperber, D. and Wilson, D. 1986: *Relevance: Communication and Cognition*. Oxford: Blackwell.

Stobart, H. F. and Cross, I. 2000: The Andean Anacrusis? Rhythmic structure and perception in Easter songs of Northern Potosí, Bolivia. *British Journal of Ethnomusicology*, 9(2), 63–94.

Trehub, S. E. 2003: Musical predispositions in infancy: an update. In Peretz, I. and Zatorre, R. (eds), *The Cognitive Neuroscience of Music*. Oxford: Oxford University Press, 3–20.

Trevarthen, C. 1999: Musicality and the intrinsic motive pulse: evidence from human psychobiology and infant communication. *Musicae Scientiae, Special Issue*, 155–215.

Part IV

IMAGINATION, COGNITION, AND CREATIVE THINKING

8

A Claim on the Reader[1]

GREGORY CURRIE

Abstract. Imaginative engagement with a narrative has two aspects. We can ask what it is that we imagine, and we can ask how we imagine it. Answering the second question requires the notion of a point of view; narrative readers imagine the events of the story from a certain point of view, which involves having certain kinds of responses to the events and to the characters who act them out. I argue that narratives often prescribe a certain point of view for imaginative engagement, just as they prescribe what is to be imagined. They generally do not do this by explicit direction; an imaginative point of view is best understood as something of which the narrative is expressive. Narratives may be expressive in this way without our having to think of them as intended by their authors to be so.

How does the narrative's being expressive of a point of view provide the motivation necessary for the reader to adopt that very point of view? The question has no simple answer, and I concentrate on one of many relevant factors: the reader's tendency to respond imitatively to their own imaginative construction of the narrative maker's mind. I embed the discussion within a general view of the relations between language and communication: a view which denies that communicative content can be derived from—or is even systematically related to—the meanings of the words and sentences in a text or utterance.

---

[1] The ideas in this chapter are further developed in my 2007 article, where the idea of a point of view for imagining is replaced by that of an imaginative framework. While the difference is not wholly terminological, what I say here translates without much alteration into talk of frameworks.

Proceedings of the British Academy **147**, 169–186. © The British Academy 2007.

INTRODUCTION

THE PRIMATOLOGIST FRANS DE WAAL (1998) describes some interesting chimpanzee behaviour at the Yerkes Primate Center:

> . . . infants sometimes get a finger stuck in the compound's fence . . .. One older juvenile came over to reconstruct the event. Looking me in the eyes, she inserted her finger into the mesh, slowly and deliberately hooking it around, and then pulled as if she, too, had gotten caught. Then two other juveniles did the same at a different location, pushing each other aside to get their fingers in the same tight spot they had selected for this game. Long ago these juveniles themselves may have experienced the situation for real, but here their charade was prompted by what had happened to the infant.

How much do these chimps have in common with the readers of Henry James? Like the chimps, readers of James, and of other authors, depend on imitative tendencies inherited, presumably, from a common ancestor. True, the readers do not imitate James's voice or gestures, about which they may know little. Theirs is an imitation of mind, not of behaviour. Their imitation may also be less conscious than that of a chimp exploring the wire mesh; de Waal seems to suggest that the chimps knew what they were doing, whereas the readers of James, I suspect, generally do not. But imitation may be conscious or unconscious; it may involve action or behaviour, or thought and feeling alone. Imitation is not the whole story about engagement with imaginative narratives; taken as a whole, the activity calls upon a range of mental acts up to and including the most sophisticated forms of reasoned reflection well beyond the capacity of any chimp. But unconscious, or barely noticed, imitation is part of the story, and it is a part that has not been much investigated.

IMAGINATION AND IMITATION

With a writer such as James, or any other of distinction, the capacity to create a story is matched by a capacity to place us, the readers, in relation to the events and characters of the story; it is the remarkable combination of story-making and reader-placing that explains James's distinctive qualities as a writer, and the distinctive kind of imaginative experience to which his stories give rise. Indeed, the story-making and reader-placing skills are hard to separate and in some cases there is little we could find in the way of intrinsic interest in the bare facts of the story that would account for its attractions. How interesting is it to hear of a middle-aged man in search of younger man embroiled in an affair in Paris, or of a young woman in search of marriage for her friends, or, for that matter, a sea captain in search of a whale? We cannot answer these questions without knowing a good deal about where we readers are expected to stand in relation to these events. Good story-makers get us to make the effort of imagining the events of their stories by providing a satisfying *way* for us to imagine these things—what, in an extended sense, we might call a point of view from which to imagine them.[2]

How do story-tellers do this? Not, generally, by issuing explicit directions about the relevant point of view; such efforts would, most likely, alienate rather than draw in the reader, reminding us of the vast pretence that fictional stories involve and amounting to what James himself described as 'the betrayal of a sacred office' (James 1884, p. 662; James has Trollope in mind here). Anyway, instructions about how to do things can be very ineffective; you may attend all the lectures in Bicycle Riding 101, completing all the written exercises, and still be unable to ride a bike at the end of it. Some activities benefit from the presence of a model to imitate. Most of us are not lucky enough to have James present to read to us, but this, as I have indicated, would not provide the sort of model I have in mind. Instead, our act of reading, and our attempt to understand what we read, generates a mental model—a representation of a certain guiding persona or mental economy—which we are then apt to imitate.[3] This may involve us in adopting certain ways of gathering information from the narrative, attending preferentially to certain aspects of what occurs, thinking through certain events and their consequences, particularly with attention to how those events affect certain characters, exploring the possible future ramifications of those events for the characters. It will also involve us in responding in certain ways to those events, evaluating them in certain ways and experiencing certain emotions. It is a matter of adopting a point of view.

The next section says more about the idea of point of view. After that, I say something about the kind of imagining we characteristically engage in when reading fictional narratives, and about how this sort of imagining is done from a point of view. The following section argues that readers, in the process of understanding the events and characters of a narrative, are required to focus on the mind of the author. Finally, I argue that this mind, as we reconstruct it in our imaginative exploration of the story, is one we are naturally prone to imitate.

---

[2] Point of view has been analysed in great detail by theorists of narrative, largely with the aim of describing the role of the narrator. These studies are somewhat tangential to my interest here, which is in the adoption of point of view by the reader. Also, I do not attempt here to disentangle the complex relations between the narrator and the author, which narrative theorists are keen to distinguish. These are refinements for another occasion.

[3] For a brilliant account of the relations between literary style and the expressed persona see Jenefer Robinson (1985).

POINT OF VIEW

Each of us occupies a point of view, and the point of view we occupy influences both our access to things in the world and our responses to those things. Where I am standing influences what I can see. This is an aspect of my point of view I am normally able to change with ease. I simply move to another place, from which I can see more or fewer or different things, or the same things from another angle. However I move and wherever I am, what I see or hear or otherwise experience is experienced by me from a point of view—the one I occupy at that time. If I want to specify the content of my visual perception I have to say not merely what I see but from which point of view I see it. Point of view belongs to the very content of my experience.

We speak also of point of view when we have in mind something more stable than position in space-time: a person's way of thinking about, responding to and evaluating what goes on around them.[4] Changes in these aspects of point of view, Pauline conversions aside, tend to be more difficult to effect. At the limit they involve character-defining traits, alteration to which might make us wonder whether we are dealing with 'the same person'. It will be helpful for us to distinguish between a rather inclusive sense of *point of view*, which covers all these kinds of cases, and a narrower notion of *perspective*, which I shall use when talking specifically about perceptual experience.

The existence of points of view raises questions about objectivity which are among the most difficult in philosophy (Moore 1997). The perceptual case is relatively unproblematic. We think of our experiences as the joint product of how things really are, and our own individual perspectives, and we can generally distinguish between changes in appearances that are due to changes in things themselves, and changes in appearances that are due to changes in our perspectives. We recognize that there is no inconsistency between the different descriptions we give of the things we see, so long as those differences are a product merely of difference in perspective; that way we retain a grip on the idea of an objective world. Other cases are harder; we do not easily distinguish between things being important from our point of view and their being important in themselves, though reflection can sometimes convince us that something we insisted is intrinsically important is in fact merely important from our point of view. And over a range of cases—colours, moral and aesthetic values, for example—debate rages as to whether these things are projections we make reflective of our points of view, or whether they are properties of things to which we are sensitive in ways determined by the distinctively human points of view we occupy.

---

[4] Adrian Moore uses 'point of involvement' to refer to points of view of this kind (1997).

One indication that we are not entirely the prisoners of our points of view is our capacity to imagine how things would appear from points of view other than our own. Sometimes this imagining is memory based, as when we vividly recall the look of a painting we once saw, or the sound of a B flat played on a bassoon. But we can imagine things we have not seen or heard, and fictions regularly put us in touch with events which are thoroughly imaginable despite their telling us of the exploits of non-existent people involved in events which never happened. The point of view that we take on in imagination may be more than a merely spatial one: adopting it can mean that we find ourselves valuing things and responding to things in ways that are different from, perhaps alien to, the ways we normally respond to and value things. It is sometimes a mark of quality in a fictional narrative that it helps us to adopt, in imagination, a point of view that is not merely different from our own, but alien to it in some way. We may see that as morally enlarging, either because it reveals merit in a point of view to which we were previously insensitive, or because it helps us to understand, from the inside, the attractions of a distorted way of seeing things.

Sometimes we are made uncomfortable by the sorts of shifts in point of view such a narrative brings about. Oscar Wilde said that one must have a heart of stone to read the death of Little Nell without laughing. But few of us, I suspect, do laugh, however cheap we think the pathos of Dickens's narrative.[5] We feel a strong pull in the direction of reacting as Dickens so obviously wants us to, though we may resent its effects on us. Dickens may not tell us how to react; instead he sets a tone in his writing which makes tears seem a natural and appropriate reaction. The tone he sets is difficult to cast aside. Or we may be disconcerted by the author's having placed us in a position where the appropriate (and tempting) reaction to tragic events is amusement, as is often the case with Evelyn Waugh. That Dickens and Waugh, in their very different ways, succeed so often in having us respond in ways that contradict the pull of natural inclination or better judgement is an indication of how important for understanding the attractions of narrative is this idea of point of view. Authors have claims on the reader, and these claims can be hard to ignore.

With a writer as bafflingly complex as Henry James, we do not find such easy indications of the point of view we are expected to adopt, and one might wonder whether the notion applies at all in such a case. But as I use it, the expression 'point of view' allows within its scope a style of responding that fastidiously avoids the coarser emotions or unqualified endorsement, looking always to the bracing, upward path of moral understanding—a journey

---

[5] 'Cheap pathos' is Henry James's phrase, but from a review of *Our Mutual Friend* (James 1865).

some of us find daunting, knowing that when James comments on a conversation between Strether and Madame de Vionnet by remarking that 'she had driven in by a single word a little golden nail', it will be very easy to become disorientated.[6] *The Ambassadors* draws the reader to a point of view at once less constraining and more demanding than those of *The Old Curiosity Shop* and *Decline and Fall*.[7]

How is it that we come to adopt, at least on some occasions, these unfamiliar, troublesome, sometimes alien points of view in our imaginative exploration of a novel? The examples from Dickens and Waugh, where we sometimes end up complicit in a way of responding we resent, suggest that this is not wholly a matter of choice. I do not mean that, once in the grip of a narrative we have no capacity to exercise our judgement in understanding it, or our will in disengaging from it. It is merely that the point of view from which we make these judgements, or exercise our will, is generally not wholly of our choosing. We may, as in the case with Little Nell, find this in some ways a negative experience, rather like finding ourselves imitating the hectoring manner of a despised pedagogue or the swagger of a bully. But what this means for our engagement with the narrative will vary greatly between cases. Sometimes the discomfort of the point of view means we disengage altogether; other times, we think the discomfort is worthwhile in order that we should be in a position to appreciate other merits of the work; we may be ambivalent, feeling discomfort along with guilty pleasure; a sly wink from the author suggesting the point of view is meant ironically may help. Perhaps the work seems to offer no coherent point of view, or has us jump inconsistently from one to another. There are no rules to guide us, and no reduction of our often richly complex and cerebral engagements with literature to the imitation of an authorial point of view. I say only that adoption of point of view by imitation is one factor to take account of.

IMAGERY, SUPPOSITION, AND NARRATIVE IMAGINING

Narratives come in many forms but here I focus exclusively on literary ones; much of what I will say generalizes to other cases. Literary narratives are, I claim, associated with a distinctive kind of imagining which I shall call *non-perspectival narrative imagining*. The present section explains that notion, and distinguishes it from cases of imagistic imagining and from what is sometimes called supposition or assumption.

---

[6] *The Ambassadors*, Book Six, III.
[7] Martha Nussbaum points to the ways in which James both implicates readers in 'love's guilty partiality of vision' while asking them to retain 'a keen awareness of what the characters lose

If I visualize a chair, my imagining has built into it a certain perspective, just as my perceptual experience of a chair does. In order to describe the content of my imagining I have not merely to describe the chair imagined, but to specify the perspective from which the chair would be seen, if one were seeing it rather than forming an image of it. Imagery in other modes is perspectival in less obvious ways; a tactile image involves a relation between the object and the part of one's body which makes contact with the object, and so the object is presented in a certain relation to the subject. Having an image differs from perception in various ways; one is that the perspective of the image does not present itself as my actual perspective.[8] In this a mental image resembles a picture, which presents its content from a perspective that is not that of the viewer, though the perspective of the picture may be one the viewer is encouraged to imagine occupying. This is perhaps one reason why the otherwise very unhelpful view that mental images are mental pictures has some attractions; its difficulties are well known, but we have to keep reminding ourselves of them in order not to slip back into the pictorial fallacy.

Other kinds of imagining are not intrinsically perspectival kinds of imagining. Suppose, as I read a story by Sir Arthur Conan Doyle, I imagine that Holmes struggled with Moriarty at the Reichenbach Falls. A full specification of what I imagine is then given by a sentence that expresses this proposition; we need specify nothing about any perspectival relations I would have had if it really had been true that Holmes struggled with Moriarty at the Reichenbach Falls. My imagining may be accompanied by a perspectival mental image of the Reichenbach Falls, with perhaps two figures out of Sidney Paget's illustrations locked together in struggle. But that would be incidental to imagining that Holmes struggled with Moriarty at the Reichenbach Falls.[9] Nonetheless, issues of point of view still arise for these

---

from view' (1990, p. 51). On how some of James's evaluations 'mingle with and tend to dilute the demands of morality' see John (1997).

[8] On this and other differences between imagery and perception see McGinn (2004, Chapter 1).

[9] I say this despite there being evidence that imagery plays a role in my comprehending the story I am reading. This is particularly true of what is called *motor imagery* or 'simulated movement'. Comprehending language involves, it seems, a high level of activation in bodily systems that control movement; we simulate movements appropriate to the kind and direction of movement described, even when no movement is literally implied ('prices went up') (see, e.g., Glenberg and Kashak 2002; Hauk *et al.* 2004). Some researchers claim that these simulation processes are 'important to the immediate construal of meaning and [are] not just an afterthought to understanding' (Gibbs 2006). The picture suggested by these results is of a very active, though not consciously controlled, bodily engagement with narrative in which we form motor images of actions and movements congruent with the events represented in the narrative as we encounter their representations. But for my purposes we need merely to distinguish between the processes that lead

sorts of imaginings. We can imagine Holmes's adventure with engaged excitement, analytical admiration, amused detachment, or a complex mixture of these and other responses.

I said that readers of Conan Doyle's story imagine that Holmes struggled with Moriarty at the Reichenbach Falls. With such circumscribed propositional contents, we often say that we suppose or assume them. Should this difference in terminology suggest a real distinction between kinds of mental acts? In my view, the difference is not one between kinds of mental acts, but between the larger contexts in which such acts take place.[10] We find it useful to distinguish between imagining in the service of argument, where we regularly imagine single propositions in order to deduce things from them or to work out what would be true if they were true, and imagining where we engage with some extended narrative by having a connected series of such imaginings, though there may be no sharp distinction to be drawn between these cases. It is this second kind of case that I am interested in here; I shall call it 'narrative imagining'. In the former kind of case we often speak of supposition or assumption, and are more likely to reserve 'imagining' for narrative imagining. Narrative imagining has an extended, dynamic, and affective quality generally lacking in the reasoning case. In narrative, we typically describe events and their causes, and our imagining of those events and their causes are themselves causally connected in intricate ways, constituting a seamless flow of imaginative activity. These patterns of causal connection between imagining make imaginings prone to generate certain kinds of emotions. Emotions typically have a pattern of development, which has itself been described as a 'narrative shape', and they are likely to be generated and developed in response to dynamical sequences of imaginings where we imagine one thing being caused by another and itself having further consequences.[11] The use of imagination in reasoning, where there are fewer extended dynamical connections between the imaginings, tends to have less noticeable emotional impact.[12]

In summary, the narrative imaginings of a reader are likely to be non-perspectival, yet still done from a point of view; they form a connected and coherent system of imaginings that reflects the coherence of the narrative, and generate emotional responses which themselves often have a narrative

---

to imaginings that are appropriate to a narrative—processes that may themselves involve perspectival imaginings—and those imaginings themselves, which are not perspectival; they are imaginings the contents of which have no inbuilt perspective.

[10] For a contrary view see Gendler (2000).

[11] On the narrative shape of emotions see de Sousa (1987).

[12] Emotion might not be absent in the reasoning case, depending on the content of what you are reasoning about. But it will lack the kind of congruence we find in the narrative case between the unfolding of the events we imagine occurring, and the shape of the emotion itself.

shape. But how is it that these imaginings bring us into very intimate contact with the mind of the author? For the hour of reading, or for however long it is, we are unlikely to be focusing on the author; if we are absorbed, it is by the events and characters of the story, and our imaginings concern those events and those characters. What is the relation between engagement with the events of the narrative and engagement with the mind of its maker? Answering this question will take a little scene-setting, about which I shall have to be brief and dogmatic.[13]

UNDERSTANDING STORIES AND UNDERSTANDING UTTERANCES

The first business of the reader is to grasp the events of the story; without this, narrative engagement is impossible. In practice such a grasp is a matter of degree and is often less than ideal. We rarely comprehend the story in all relevant detail, but the less we grasp of the story the less we can claim to have engaged with the narrative. I say that this kind of understanding requires the reader to be highly sensitive to features of the mind of the author. For we generally take something to be part of the story if the text provides us with evidence that the author *intended* it to be part of the story. The idea that the text of a narrative is somehow a 'self-standing representation', from which competent readers, possessed of the relevant code, can read off the events of the story, is false.[14] It is not even an approximation to the truth. This is not a claim proprietary to the study of narrative; it is a general thesis about the relations between the words and sentences we use to convey a message, and what our hearers need to grasp in order to understand the message itself. Communicative content is, in virtually every case, far richer than the purely linguistic content of an utterance; there is not even any systematic relation between the two which would enable us to take linguistic content and then to apply rule-governed processes of explication that would deliver communicative content.[15] Being more explicit sometimes helps, but it does so because it

[13] I develop these ideas in more detail in Currie (forthcoming).
[14] For criticism of the code view of communication see Sperber and Wilson (1995) Chapter 1 Section 1.
[15] Recent theorists who emphasize the gap between semantic content and communicated content include Sperber and Wilson (1995), Carston (2002), Borg (2004), and Cappelen and Lepore (2005). A contrary opinion is that of Jason Stanley and his collaborators, who have argued for the existence of implicit syntactic structure in ordinary language sentences as a way of combating the view that 'once syntactic and semantic inquiry is finished, it will turn out that the semantic content of a sentence relative to a context is not a good guide to what speakers typically use that sentence to communicate' (King and Stanley 2005; see also Szabó and Stanley (2000)).

gives us better clues to the speaker's intentions, not because it enables us to bypass them. Language is an aid to communication; it assists us in ensuring that communication takes place, which means ensuring that a speaker's intentions are understood. All sorts of other things are important as well: facial expression, intonation, things which are otherwise manifest in the context of utterance, general principles about what people want, think, and feel. Language may well be the most important one of these factors: the most subtle, the one with the greatest capacity to enhance our understanding of each other. But that is, in the end, all that language is: an aid to mindreading. Recovering the content of a narrative—or any other communicative form— from the text provided means taking the text to be a set of indications as to what the utterer intends to convey—generally in the case of a narrative, a unified and coherent set of causal-intentional relations between characters.[16] Thus the reader's task is, from the beginning, an inquiry into the mind of the narrative's maker.[17] The story is represented in the narrative by the author's choice of words and sentences being *expressive of* his or her decisions about what that story is. Narratives get their story contents by having certain sorts of expressive contents. Expressive content is primary.

This can seem an unlikely view if one is looking at a page of reported speech in a novel; what is more obvious in such a case than that the words of the narrative directly report exactly what the characters said?[18] In that case the correspondence between the text and the story content is as close as any-one could wish. True, an author can speak with the voice of an unreliable narrator. But we should not conclude from this that the normal case is one where we make complicated inferences from the text to the story's account of what was said—no more than the possibility of fake barns should persuade us that we never see real barns, but merely infer their existence from the

---

[16] By 'text' here I mean the words and sentences used; they need not be written down or provided with any other enduring form.

[17] For some, this will be a worryingly intellectual way of putting the reader's task. They deny that intersubjective understanding depends on our inquiries into the minds of others; Shaun Gallagher says that 'Ordinarily, in everyday encounters, and in the pragmatic and social contexts that characterize our everyday encounters with others, we perceive their movements, gestures, facial expressions, and speech acts as meaningful and intentional, without worrying about their minds or about how to explain or predict their actions' (Gallagher 2006). I do not follow Gallagher and others in believing that inference to mental states is largely dispensable with, but we need not debate this here. My claim is only that understanding a story requires understand-ing the narrative-maker's intentions, and those who think that these intentions can be read off from the text itself are at liberty to agree with me about that—as long as they do not hold that we read off those intentions by applying semantic rules.

[18] Some narratives consist only of directly reported speech; the novels of Ivy Compton-Burnett approximate to this. But in Compton-Burnett's novels the story content extends well beyond the facts of reported speech, and the reader is required to reconstruct the motives behind that speech. That requires us to ask what Compton-Burnett intends her characters' motivations to be.

appearances. To this I say that the case of directly reported speech is a special one—a case where, in normal circumstances, the words of the text serve as instances of the words spoken by the characters. Where narratives describe objects and events, characters, and actions, there is no such close correspondence between the structure of words and the entities described. The words are important of course; without them we would be severely limited in what we could convey in a narrative (a wholly pictorial one, for example, or a dumb show). What the words provide is a marvellously subtle and flexible way of indicating what it is the narrative-maker *wants* to convey by way of description.

Another way to put the point is to say that the text expresses, or is an expression of, the author's story-telling intentions: his or her intentions to make this or that part of the story. In this sense, successful expression depends on our recognition of what the speaker intends to express. Yet we allow that things can be expressive without being the expression of an intention, and without there being any intention to express anything. A speaker may carefully choose his or her words in order to express certain views about current events, and in his or her act of speaking thus may express a profoundly pessimistic outlook, without intended to express that outlook, of which he or she may even be unaware. People's facial expressions and bodily postures regularly express their mental states, without being chosen to express them. So an author, in the process of crafting a text to make it expressive of certain story-telling intentions, may also and unintentionally express attitudes, emotions, moods, feelings, and evaluations of those events—may, in other words, express a point of view (see Vermazen 1986).

I do not say that the expression of point of view in narrative is never intentional; self-conscious authors often carefully craft their texts so as to convey mood, evaluation, and other aspects of point of view. But the mechanisms by which points of view are successfully conveyed do not depend on their being intended. In order to succeed in conveying these aspects of point of view, it is not generally the case that the reader has to see them as having been intended, and it may be that point of view is more easily conveyed if readers are not aware of, or at least do not consciously focus on, the fact that these expressive aspects of the text were intended. Readers, made highly sensitive to the mind of the narrative's maker by their efforts to understand the story itself, will often simply take over the emotional and evaluative aspects of that mind and will, in the process, adopt or move significantly in the direction of, the canonical point of view for that story. That, at least, is my claim. In the next section I outline a theory of how this occurs. I conclude this section with a brief illustration of how one aspect of point of view can be expressed through the act of representing a narrative's events.

Mood—as opposed to more specific emotional states—is an important ingredient in point of view, making certain emotional and evaluative responses to specific events more likely than others. Noël Carroll asks how it is that works of art create a mood in their audiences, suggesting that this often happens through a kind of overflow; we experience a specific emotion as a result of reading about the actions or sufferings of a character, and such emotions often leave one with an associated and relatively sustained mood (Carroll 2003). I do not doubt that this is part of the explanation, but works of various kinds are capable of creating mood more directly than this. Carroll mentions the famously mood-setting introduction to Dickens' *Bleak House*; here I consider the case of *Little Dorrit*, with its opening description of Marseilles. Very quickly, and well before we learn the fate or doings of any character, a certain mood is set by the descriptive choices Dickens makes; he speaks of the 'staring' white walls and streets, 'tracts of arid road' and dust 'scorched brown'. The intense heat, the water within the harbour, the blistered boats are what is represented, but their mode of representation expresses a certain, not easily described, mood of sombre oppression, though summer heat bearing down on a city lends itself equally to anything from a sense of anxious expectation to comic indolence. This seems to me one of those very common instances where mood is conveyed imitatively; we have a sense of the narrator's mood, as expressed through his act of representation, and we quickly catch that mood ourselves; we need no specific, emotion-generating event in the story to create the mood.

MECHANISMS OF IMITATION

On my account then, imitation plays a significant role in providing the reader with an appropriate point of view from which to engage with the events of the narrative. There is nothing new in the idea that imitation is a subtle and powerful agent for generating and controlling feeling and action. Adam Smith placed a great deal of weight on imitation in expounding his theory of sympathy, and at the beginning of the twentieth century the social thinker Gabriel Tarde thought it 'the fundamental social fact' (Tarde 1903).[19] It is now widely held that there is a developmentally significant connection between the capacity of infants to imitate and the capacity to understand mental states (see, e.g., Gopnik and Melzoff 1993; Goldman 1992). A less positive note is struck by the idea that unconscious imitation plays a significant causal role in the production of violent and antisocial acts—the very

---

[19] For a summary of current evidence for this idea see Dijksterhuis (2005).

strong evidence for which seems to be unknown to or ignored by liberal opponents of censorship (see, e.g., Hurley 2006).

We might be tempted to think of imitation as a matter simply of conforming our behaviour to that of another. Such a conception would not be very useful to our present study; I have noted that, whatever readers do, they do not copy the behaviour the writers engage in when writing their novels. Tarde was very clear that imitation is not fundamentally a matter of behaviour, but of conforming one's state of mind to that of another, though he did not illuminate matters much by calling it the 'action at a distance' of one mind on another. Current usage in psychology tends to reserve 'imitation' for the re-enactment of goal-directed behaviour, while the mere reproduction of a bodily movement is called 'response priming'. It makes sense also to speak of imitation where there is little or no discernible behaviour. Take, for example, the discovery of systems of so-called 'mirror neurons' in primates including, very probably, humans, which apparently fire both when the subject is making a movement and when the subject sees a conspecific moving in the same way (see, e.g., Rizzolatti *et al.* 1996, 2001). The activation of these neurons in response to observed movement constitutes a simulation or 'implicit imitation' of the movement itself. Mirror neurons may be part of a much more complex system which enables us to identify and understand intentional movements by others (Gallese and Goldman 1998).

Imitation is sometimes consciously undertaken, as when one imitates another's voice for comic effect. But if someone is sad, their unconscious posture or their facial expression may express their sadness, and we may 'catch' their sadness simply through being exposed to this expressive feature. In this case of course we are exposed to the person directly, and not to an artefact of their making; does the same mechanism hold in the artefactual case? I believe so. We can be made to have feelings of sadness by various sorts of indications of sadness, and facial expression is just one particularly effective means of achieving this. If my child draws a sad-looking face, and I see the drawing as expressive of her own sadness, I am likely to have feelings of sadness myself. And I need not assume that she drew the face in order that it be an expression of her sadness.

There is an objection to my claimed parallel between the adoption of narrative point of view and the empathic spread of sadness. The case of my child's drawing is different from the case of a novel and its author in at least the following respect. My child is, I assume, genuinely sad about something that has happened, or which she at least thinks has happened. But what kind of sadness is the author's work expressive of when we know that the story is invention—and know that the author knows that also? Indeed we may know from various sources that the author was not sad at all during the process of writing—a point often made in criticism of crude versions of the expressive theory of art according to which works of art communicate to their audiences emotions genuinely felt by artists. And so we know that the novel itself is not really expressive of the author's sadness, since she was not after all, sad.

To this I say that there is plenty of evidence that we are easily provoked to adopt alien moods, feelings, styles of thinking, and even ways of moving our bodies merely by imagining certain kinds of mental states; belief in the reality of the mind thus imagined is not required. The author's mind is real enough of course, but we need to recall that the interpretation of narrative is not an exercise in biography. The mind we are looking for is the mind accessible to us through our imaginative engagement with the narrative itself: the mind of what is sometimes called the implied author.[20] Narratives, like other artefacts, can seem to be strongly expressive of mental states, creating for us a vivid picture of a persona with whose mind we engage imaginatively—a mind arresting enough to occlude the real, perhaps duller or at any rate less salient persona of the agent who actually created the object. The point is general: paintings can seem to be the product of angry strokes of the brush even when we know how carefully the paint was applied, and on a good day the world can seem to be the creation of a benevolent deity, even for those otherwise convinced of its wholly accidental character.[21] Interpreting things in the world as the product of imagined agents is something that seems to be built in to our very perceptual systems. Paolo Viviani and colleagues have shown how certain motion-illusions can be explained on the assumption that we process the motion as if it were the product of agency. In one experiment, subjects were shown an isolated point of light moving in an ellipse. The point moved at a varying angular velocity which was perceived by subjects to be constant, as long as the irregularities were consistent with irregularities that would be produced if the point had been moved by a human hand; it seems that we register the motion as regular as long as irregularities are biomechanically explicable (Viviani and Stucchi 1992).[22] We may know that the movement is not the effect of any human agency, yet it seems to us to be so.

Is there specific evidence concerning the imitation of points of view? There certainly is evidence that we can easily be made to imitate aspects of another person's way of solving problems—ways which seem to reflect rather

[20] Here we make contact with an extensive literature on the so-called *implied author*. The *locus classicus* is Booth (1983). For a selection of essays relating to the idea of an implied author and to such related notions as that of a postulated author, see Irwin (2002).

[21] Vermazen (1986) argues that expression in the artistic case should be relativized to a fictional persona, the agent who seems to have made the work, rather than the agent who did make it and whose brush technique may be quite deliberate and certainly not caused by anger.

[22] I am indebted here to Scoyles (1999). See also Maynard (2003) on the ways that elements within a picture 'carry information about how and why they were produced' (p. 80); see also Michael Podro's comments, reproduced in Maynard's note 44.

large-scale aspects of a person's overall emotional and evaluative response to the world. Recent work in social psychology has produced some quite surprising results which indicate the extent to which a merely imagined persona can influence us, without our even realizing it, in ways that we might have thought of as beyond the reach of such influences. Two Dutch social psychologists, Ap Dijksterhuis and Ad van Knippenberg, asked subjects to imagine a 'typical professor' for five minutes, 'and to list the behaviors, lifestyle, and appearance attributes of this typical professor'. Subjects thus primed turned out to do better on trivial pursuits questions than did subjects who had not been asked to engage in any imaginative task; subjects who had been asked instead to imagine soccer hooligans did worse (Dijksterhuis and van Knippenberg 1998).[23]

What brought about these surprising results? It is unlikely, of course, that the participants in these experiments actually became more intelligent while imagining a professor, or more brutish when imagining a soccer hooligan. Dijksterhuis and van Knippenberg suggest the following explanation: Intelligence is likely to be linked in the minds of participants with such traits as concentration, the use of varied strategies, confidence in one's abilities, and careful and rational thoughts. These are likely, therefore, to be prominent elements within a mental model built up through the act of imagining a professor, since professors are generally thought of as intelligent. The effect of the task, then, is to cause participants to call up their knowledge of intelligence and its more obvious facets, and then to cause them to exercise (for them) untypical levels of epistemic effort by way of an attempt to imitate the levels exemplified by the model, much as the vivid example of an athletic triumph might make you run that little bit harder during your daily exercise. The mind is, without your conscious awareness, adjusting its level of activity in various areas as a result of your contemplation of an imaginary mind in which those levels are habitually high. You are unconsciously imitating the characteristics of a mind you imaginatively construct, much as you unconsciously imitate the bodily movements and posture of those around you.

I mentioned the vivid example of an athlete. It is perhaps not surprising that vivid exemplars are a prompt to imitation, and theories of moral education have taken this idea for granted. But it is striking that in the experiments of Dijksterhuis and van Knippenberg no vivid examples were provided; participants were not, for example, shown film of highly accomplished professors looking thoughtful or expounding complex thoughts, nor were they given details of the biographies of particularly successful academics. They

---

[23] Dijksterhuis and van Knippenberg drew on suggestive earlier work by Bargh *et al.* (1996). Thanks to Tamar Szabó Gendler who drew my attention to these and other studies. See her (2006) for a detailed analysis of research in this area.

were merely asked to imagine 'a professor' for a few moments; a very vague request with no 'props' to make the imagination keen. It is all the more remarkable, then, that their experiments produced the effect they did. Sustained imaginative engagement with a vividly expressed and highly individuated mental economy through a long and detailed narrative can therefore be expected to have even stronger and more detailed imitative consequences.

As I noted above, these experiments depend on the subject's knowledge of features of what it is they are asked to imagine: the mechanisms by which the effects are achieved must, in some way, operate at the conceptual level rather than via the primitive operations that bring about, say, imitative smiling in infants. This was brought out vividly in a version of the experiment conducted on psychology students who were asked to imagine 'a neuropsychological patient' and were then asked to perform a test—the Tower of Hanoi—which such patients do badly on (Turner *et al.* 2005). The students' performance was adversely affected—partly because they, unlike the rest of us, happened to know that such patients do not perform well. This knowledge, providing them with a way of thinking of someone as having impaired epistemic capacities, then led them, without conscious awareness, to reduce their own epistemic efforts roughly in line with those of the imagined exemplar.

In these experiments and, I believe, in the case of narrative understanding, we are observing the combined effect of high-level conceptual abilities and low-level, automatic responses. In the experiments, the subject's knowledge of professors, soccer hooligans, and neuropsychological patients are creating detailed mental models which then are responded to imitatively, but without personal control or even conscious awareness. With narratives, readers bring to bear vast quantities of real-world knowledge in constructing a picture of the author's mind on the basis of what they read. But their imitative response to that mind may see them pulled in the direction of a point of view they have not chosen and that they may have some difficulty in resisting.

The picture suggested by these results, taken in conjunction with the theory I have outlined, is one of a cycle of complex imaginative activity: we read, and we try to understand; in trying to understand we start to construct a picture of the agent behind what we read, and of the point of view this agent occupies; the construction triggers our imitative tendencies and we become, temporarily, like the imagined agent—or at least more like it than we were before. Becoming more like it, we come to read from a point of view like that of the imagined agent, thus affecting in subtle or even in substantial ways our understanding of what we read, leading to alterations to the model and corresponding adjustments to our imaginative point of view. The process may settle into an equilibrium state—comfortable or not—well before the reading experience is over. It may, with the most demanding of works, leave us in a permanently unresolved tension as further reading brings ever new aspects of the authorial persona to light.

References

Bargh, J. A., Chen, M. and Burrows, L.1996: The automaticity of social behavior: Direct effects of trait concept and stereotype activation on action. *Journal of Personality and Social Psychology*, 71, 230–244.

Booth, W. 1983: *The Rhetoric of Fiction* (2nd edn). Chicago: University of Chicago Press.

Borg, E. 2004: *Minimal Semantics*. Oxford: Oxford University Press.

Cappelen, H. and Lepore, E. 2005: *Insensitive Semantics*. Oxford: Blackwell.

Carroll, N. 2003: Art and mood: preliminary notes and conjectures. *The Monist*, 86, 521–555.

Carston, R. 2002: *Thoughts and Utterances*. Oxford: Blackwell.

Currie, G. 2007: Narratives and their frameworks. In Hutto, D. D. (ed.), *Narrative and Understanding Persons*, Royal Institute of Philosophy Supplement. Cambridge: Cambridge University Press.

Currie, G. forthcoming: *Narrative Thinking*. Oxford: Oxford University Press.

Dijksterhuis, A. 2005: 'Why we are social animals'. In Chater, N. and Hurley, S. (eds), *Perspectives on Imitation*, volume 2. Cambridge, MA: MIT Press, 207–220.

Dijksterhuis, A. and van Knippenberg, A. 1998: The relation between perception and behavior or how to win a game of Trivial Pursuit. *Journal of Personality and Social Psychology*, 74, 865–877.

Gallagher, S. 2006: 'Logical and phenomenological arguments against simulation theory'. In Hutto, D. and Ratcliffe, M. (eds), *Minding our Practice: Folk Psychology Re-assessed*. Dordrecht: Springer Publishers, 63–78

Gallese, V. and Goldman, A. I. 1998: Mirror neurons and the simulation theory of mindreading. *Trends in Cognitive Sciences* 2, 12, 493–501.

Gendler, T. S. 2000: The puzzle of imaginative resistance. *Journal of Philosophy*, 97, 55–81.

Gendler, T. S. 2006: Imaginative contagion, *Metaphilosophy*, 37, 183–203.

Gibbs, R. 2006: Metaphor interpretation as embodied simulation. *Mind and Language*, 21, 434–458.

Glenberg, A. and Kashak, M. 2002: Grounding language in action. *Psychonomic Bulletin & Review, 9*, 558–565.

Goldman, A. 1992: Empathy, mind and morals. *Proceedings and Addresses of the American Philosophical Association*, 66, 17–41.

Gopnik, A. and Meltzoff, A. N. 1993: The role of imitation in understanding persons and developing a theory of mind. In Baron-Cohen, S., Tager-Flusberg, H. and Cohen, D. J. (eds), *Understanding Other Minds: Perspectives from Autism*. Oxford: Oxford University Press, 335–366.

Hauk, O., Johnsrude, I. and Pulvermuller, F. 2004: Somatotopic representation of action words in human motor and premotor cortex. *Neuron,* 41, 301–307.

Hurley, S. 2006: Bypassing conscious control: Media violence, unconscious imitation, and freedom of speech. In Pockett, S., Banks, W. and Gallagher, S. (eds), *Does*

186   *Gregory Currie*

Consciousness Cause Behavior? An investigation of the Nature of Volition. Cambridge, MA: MIT Press, 301–337.

Irwin, W. (ed.) 2002: *The Death and Resurrection of the Author.* Westport, CT: Greenwood.

James, H. 1865: Review of *Our Mutual Friend, The Nation* (New York), 21 December.

James, H. 1884: The art of fiction. *Longman's Magazine* 4.

John, E. 1997: Henry James: Making moral life interesting. *The Henry James Review,* 18, No. 3, 234–242.

King, J. and Stanley, J. 2005: 'Semantics, pragmatics and the role of semantic content'. In Szabó, Z. G. (ed.), *Semantics vs Pragmatics.* Oxford: Oxford University Press, 111–164.

Maynard, P. 2003: Drawing as drawn: An approach to creation in an art. In B. Gaut and P. Livingstone (eds), *The Creation of Art.* Cambridge: Cambridge University Press, 53–88.

McGinn, C. 2004: *Mindsight.* Harvard, MA: Harvard University Press.

Moore, A. 1997: *Points of View.* Oxford: Oxford University Press.

Nussbaum, M. (1990) *Love's Knowledge.* Oxford: Oxford University Press.

Rizzolatti, G., Fadiga, L., Gallese, V. and Fogassi, L. 1996: Premotor cortex and the recognition of motor actions. *Cognitive Brain Research,* 3(2), 131–141.

Rizzolatti, G., Fogassi, L. and Gallese, V. 2001: Neurophysiological mechanisms underlying the understanding and imitation of action. *Nature Reviews Neuroscience,* 2, 661–670.

Robinson, J. 1985: Style and personality in the literary work. *Philosophical Review,* 94, 227–247.

Scoyles, J. 1999: Language and imitation: Informational processing and the elementary units of speech. In *Proceedings of the AISB'99 Symposium on Imitation in Animals and Artifacts,* 6–9 April, 1999, Edinburgh.

de Sousa, R. 1987: *The Rationality of Emotion.* MIT Press, Cambridge, MA.

Sperber, D. and Wilson, D. 1995: *Relevance: Communication and Cognition* (2nd edn). Oxford: Blackwell.

Szabó, Z. G. and Stanley, J. 2000: On quantifier domain restriction. *Mind and Language,* 15, 219–261.

Tarde, G. 1903: *The Laws of Imitation,* translated by E. C. Parsons with introduction by F. Giddings. New York: Henry, Holt and Co.

Turner, R. N., Forrester, R., Mulhern, B. and Crisp, R. J. 2005: Impairment of executive abilities following a social category prime. *Current Research in Psychology,* 11, 29–38.

Vermazen, B. 1986: Expression as expression. *Pacific Philosophical Quarterly,* 67, 196–224.

Viviani, P. and Stucchi, N. 1992: Biological movements look uniform: Evidence of motorperceptual interactions. *Journal of Experimental Psychology: Human Perception and Performance,* 18, 603–623.

de Waal, F. 1998: No imitation without identification. *Behavioral and Brain Sciences,* 21, 689.

9

Mental Imagery and Creative Thought

DAVID G. PEARSON

Abstract. Mental imagery is often cited as playing an important role during creative thought, but the exact nature of its contribution remains controversial. This chapter will outline some of the anecdotal evidence supporting a link between imagery and creative thought, and also review evidence from a number of experimental studies that have examined the use of imagery under controlled conditions. I will argue that laboratory studies have revealed a number of factors that can influence how well imagery can facilitate creative insights. I will also discuss the extent to which representational theories of imagery have largely failed to directly account for the phenomenology that is associated with imagery experience.

THE TERM 'MENTAL IMAGERY' is used to describe a quasi-perceptual state of consciousness in which the mind appears able to simulate or re-create sensory-like experience. Such images can be experienced either as veridical memories of perceptual experience (e.g. the details of the face of a loved one) or as fantastical objects or events that have never been directly perceived (e.g. a green elephant). There can be considerable differences in how individuals subjectively experience imagery in terms of its vividness, detail, and frequency of occurrence (Marks 1973; Reisberg *et al.* 2003), and in some cases an individual may report no experience of quasi-perceptual imagery at all (Galton 1880; Abelson 1979). However, despite such variation in the phenomenological aspects of imagery it appears to be a regular feature of everyday consciousness for the majority of people, particularly under circumstances in which some form of perceptual judgement has to be made in the absence of an external referent. For example, if people are asked whether an elephant possesses a long or a short tail, many respond by visualizing the appearance of an elephant from memory (Farah *et al.* 1988). In addition to visual imagery, individuals can experience auditory imagery (Reisberg 1992), olfactory imagery (Stevenson and Case 2005), gustatory imagery (Tiggemann and

Proceedings of the British Academy **147**, 187–212. © The British Academy 2007.

Kemps 2005), and haptic imagery (Juttner and Rentschler 2002). In other words, mental imagery can be created for all of the sensory modalities, with visual and auditory imagery usually reported as the most frequent (Betts 1909; Tiggemann and Kemps 2005). What links all forms of imagery is an apparent correspondence between the conscious experience of holding an image in mind and the conscious experience associated with perceiving that particular stimulus in the real world. The quasi-perceptual phenomenology of mental imagery is both its most defining and its most controversial feature (Pylyshyn 2004; Kosslyn *et al.* 2006).

Mental imagery has a long history of association with imagination and creative thought, and the experience of imagery has been linked to successful performance across a wide range of different creative tasks, including the visualization and development of scientific models (Miller 1984), the conceptual stage of architectural design (Purcell and Gero 1998; Reed 1993), and many aspects of general everyday problem-solving (Finke 1990; Kaufmann 1988). Some of the best anecdotal accounts of imagery facilitating imaginative thought come from scientists, particularly those working in the fields of physics, chemistry, and engineering. Albert Einstein was a particularly strong supporter of the use of imagery or 'visualization' as a powerful technique for reasoning about theoretical problems in physics. Einstein combined visual thinking with 'thought experiments' (from the German *gedankenexperiment*), in which he reflected on the consequences of imagined scenarios. At the age of 16 in 1895 Einstein conceived a classic thought experiment in which he imagined an observer attempting to match the velocity of a wave of light (Gardner 1993). This was followed in 1907 by another thought experiment in which he imagined an observer jumping from the roof of a house and simultaneously dropping a stone. This led Einstein to establish a 'principle of equivalence', which later became a key aspect of his general theory of relativity (Miller 2000). When Einstein was asked to provide an account of his scientific reasoning he offered the following description:

> The words of the language, as they are written or spoken, do not seem to play any role in my mechanism of thought. The psychical entities which seem to serve as elements in thought are certain signs and more or less clear images which can be 'voluntarily' reproduced and combined. . ..From a psychological viewpoint this combinatory play seems to be the essential feature in productive thought. (Reproduced in Gardner 1993, p. 105)

Many other scientists have attached a similar importance to imagery when attempting to describe the nature of their creative thought. Michael Faraday used imagery as a means to visualize lines of electromagnetic force (Gooding 1991), while the inventor Nikola Tesla described using images to mentally assemble and manipulate designs for complex electric motors (Miller 2000).

The physicist Richard Feynman was a strong supporter of the use of visualization as part of scientific reasoning (Miller 1984), as is Stephen Hawking, who in the collection *Black Holes and Baby Universes and Other Essays* writes:

> I was sure that nearly everyone was interested in how the universe operates, but most people cannot follow mathematical equations—I don't care much for equations myself. This is . . . because I don't have an intuitive feeling for equations. Instead, I think in pictorial terms, and my aim in the book was to describe these mental images in words, with the help of familiar analogies and a few diagrams. (Hawking 1993, p. 35)

One of the most famous examples of mental imagery apparently supporting scientific discovery is that of Friedrich August von Kekulé's solution to the molecular structure of benzene (Weisberg 1986; Gardner 1993; Miller 2000). Kekulé proposed in 1865 that benzene consisted of a ring of six carbon atoms, and gave the following account for how this insight was gained:

> I turned my chair to the fire and dozed. Again the atoms were gambolling before my eyes. . ...My mental eye, rendered more acute by repeated visions of this kind, could now distinguish larger structures, of manifold conformation; long rows, sometimes more closely fitted together; all twining and twisting in snakelike motion. But look! What was that? One of the snakes had seized hold of its own tail, and the form whirled mockingly before my eyes. As if by a flash of lightening I awoke. (Reproduced in Weisberg 1986, p. 32)

This account of the discovery of the benzene ring has been widely interpreted as demonstrating that a mental image of a snake biting its own tail directly inspired Kekulé to the insight that the carbon atoms were linked together within a circular structure. However, some authors have disputed whether this account should be taken at face value. Wotiz and Rudofsky (1954; discussed in Miller 2000) have claimed that the story was fabricated by Kekulé while writing a preface to a lecture delivered in Berlin in 1890, and that it is notable that there is no previous record of it during the thirty years prior to this. Even if the account is based on real circumstances rather than a romanticized notion of scientific insight, Weisberg (1986) has pointed out that Kekulé may have used the term 'snakelike' figuratively rather than descriptively, and that some details of the account may have become distorted during translation from the original German into English.

This case illustrates that however compelling such anecdotal accounts may appear to be, they must be treated with a degree of caution as unequivocal evidence in favour of a functional role for mental imagery during imaginative thought. However, the frequency with which imagery is mentioned during anecdotal accounts of creative thought is impressive, and not only limited to scientific fields such as physics and chemistry. Imagery also features in accounts of musical composition (Mozart 1789; reproduced in Vernon 1970), writing (Nin 1969; Richardson 1969), painting (Finke 1986), sculpture (Samuels and Samuels, 1975), and architectural design (Goldschmidt 1991, 1992; Purcell and Gero 1998).

EXPERIMENTAL STUDIES OF MENTAL SYNTHESIS

If mental images do provide a foundation for creative discovery and insight, then these processes should be amenable to study under controlled experimental conditions. A common thread through many of the anecdotal reports described above is that mental images are actively manipulated and interpreted as part of creative thought. For example, Einstein makes reference to what he called 'combinatory play' (Gardner 1993), while Lawson describes reasoning during creative design as involving a 'highly organised mental process capable of manipulating many kinds of information, blending them all into a coherent set of ideas, and finally generating some realisation of those ideas' (Lawson 1980, 6). This process of combining ideas into new constructs can be described by the term *mental synthesis* (Thompson and Klatzky 1978; Finke and Slayton 1988). Mental synthesis has been experimentally studied using a wide variety of different methodological techniques, including an influential programme of research on 'creative cognition' conducted by the psychologist Ronald Finke and colleagues (Finke 1989, 1990; Finke *et al.* 1992).

Guided Mental Synthesis

Finke *et al.* (1989) conducted a series of visual synthesis experiments in which participants were required to mentally manipulate simple alpha-numeric and geometric symbols in response to a sequence of verbal instructions provided by the experimenter. If the sequence of instructions was followed correctly then the resulting mental image was designed to resemble a familiar object or scene. Figure 9.1 provides an example of these instructions and the corresponding mental images they were intended to produce. At the end of each experimental trial, participants were asked to draw their image on a piece of paper to establish whether they had followed the verbal instructions correctly or not. Finke *et al.* were interested in establishing whether their participants would be able to recognize the emergent patterns in their mental images without reliance on any form of external picture or sketch.

Imagine a 'D'

Imagine a 'J'

Rotate the 'D' 90
degrees to the left

Place the 'D' directly on
top of the 'J'

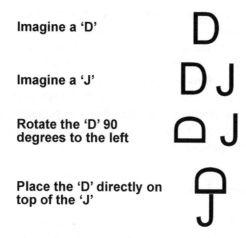

Figure 9.1. Sample trial from Finke *et al.* (1989).

Their results showed that participants were able to correctly follow the verbal instructions for 60% of the experimental trials. For these correctly manipulated images, 70% were identified by participants as resembling a recognizable object or scene. A further 21% of trials were classified as 'partial transformations', in which an error had occurred in following one or more of the instructions (for example, in the trial illustrated in Figure 9.1 the letter D could be rotated 90 degrees to right rather than left). Out of these trials only 13% were correctly identified as resembling a recognizable figure. On the remaining 19% of trials participants failed to follow the instructions correctly and created images very different from the final intended state. Under these circumstances the number of correct identifications fell to zero.

The clear implication from these findings is that the participants were able to reinterpret their images as resembling familiar objects or scenes without any additional support from an external perceptual source. In other words, the mental image itself was sufficient to provide the basis for the discovery. A potential criticism of this interpretation is that participants might have guessed the identity of the final pattern on the basis of the initial geometric and alpha-numeric symbols rather than the synthesized mental image. However, this interpretation seems unlikely considering that participants' ability to correctly recognize the final pattern dropped sharply if they failed to correctly follow the verbal instructions. Finke *et al.* also conducted a control study in which they asked participants to try to guess the identity of the final pattern after each instruction was given, rather than waiting until all of the image manipulations had been carried out. They found that none of the participants was able to correctly recognize the pattern after the first instruction. After the second, only 4% of trials were correctly identified. After the final instruction was issued, participants had correctly followed the instructions for 66% of the trials. Out of these, 48% were correctly identified as a recognizable object or scene, in comparison to only a single correct identification if the instructions had been followed incorrectly. These results are consistent with the interpretation that it is the mental images that are forming the basis for recognizing the emergent patterns, rather than some alternative guessing strategy that is not dependent on the mental manipulation and interpretation of the presented symbols.

The Creative Synthesis Task

One limitation of this type of procedure for examining mental synthesis is that participants manipulate their images in response to explicit instructions, rather than spontaneously making the mental discoveries on their own. This is very different from how imagery is often described within anecdotal reports of creative reasoning in which individuals have full control over the image manipulations. In addition, the Finke *et al.* procedure restricts participants' ability to make creative interpretations of the synthesized images, as the potential emergent properties have been already predetermined by the experimenter ahead of testing.

An alternative experimental paradigm that allows participants to make less constrained mental discoveries is the *creative synthesis task* devised by Finke and Slayton (1988). Participants were first presented with a set of 15 alpha-numeric and geometric symbols (Figure 9.2) which were learnt until they could be accurately imaged in response to the verbal description alone. For each experimental trial participants were then verbally presented with three symbols randomly selected from the stimuli set of 15 (i.e. 'square, capital "P", number "8"'). They were asked to form visual images of the symbols and were allowed two minutes to try to mentally combine the symbols into a novel recognizable pattern. Participants were not allowed to leave any symbols out or distort their overall shape (e.g. stretch the square into a rectangle), but were otherwise free to combine the symbols in any way they wished, including making changes to their size and orientation. If participants believed they had been successful in creating a recognizable pattern from the selected symbols, they first recorded its verbal description on paper, and then drew the synthesized image from memory (thus ensuring that any discoveries were not supported by the act of sketching). Once all data had been collected the degree of correspondence between each verbal description and its corresponding drawing of the image was independently rated to provide a measure of how recognizable the synthesized patterns actually were.

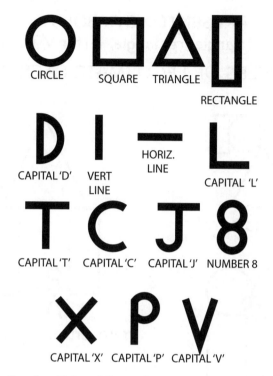

Figure 9.2.   Stimuli set from Finke and Slayton (1988).

Finke and Slayton found that participants were able to produce a recognizable pattern on 40% of the experimental trials. This suggested that individuals were readily able to discover emergent properties by carrying out manipulations using mental imagery, even within a restricted timeframe of only two minutes. My own experience of conducting studies using a similar creative synthesis procedure is that participants are often highly surprised by their ability to mentally create recognizable patterns from the symbols, and that a number of diverse and creative patterns can result from a single set of randomly selected symbols. Figure 9.3 provides examples from such a study of the synthesized patterns produced in response to a trial comprising five randomly selected symbols.

WORKING MEMORY PROCESSES AND MENTAL SYNTHESIS

Mental synthesis is a complex activity which requires that information is not only retained within short-term memory, but also actively *manipulated* as part of the creative discovery process. Mental synthesis can therefore be

PRESENTED SYMBOLS
'rectangle, triangle, rectangle, letter V, number 8'
EXAMPLES OF LEGITIMATE PATTERNS

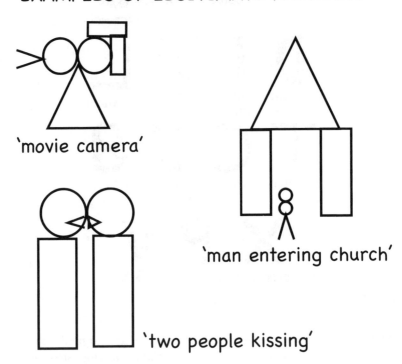

'movie camera'

'man entering church'

'two people kissing'

Figure 9.3.   Sample synthesized patterns from Pearson *et al.* (1999).

usefully considered as a form of *working memory procedure* (Pearson 2001; Pearson *et al.* 2001). The term working memory is used to describe temporary memory systems that are involved in tasks such as reasoning, learning, and understanding (Baddeley 1990). Examples of everyday tasks that rely on working memory include performing mental arithmetic or remembering a shopping list. One of the most influential models of working memory is the multi-component approach first proposed by Baddeley and Hitch in 1974. This model as originally stated comprised three separate, limited-capacity components: the phonological loop, the visuospatial sketchpad, and the central executive. The phonological loop and sketchpad are modality-specific 'slave systems' that enable individuals to retain verbal speech-based material and visuospatial material respectively. Both are controlled by the central executive, a modality-free system that coordinates the activities of the two slave systems, and is also assumed to be involved in strategy selection and the planning of complex cognitive tasks.

Over the thirty years since publication of the model these three components have been modified to some extent from their original conception. The phonological loop has been fractionated into two separate but interrelated components: a passive phonological store containing information that is rehearsed by an active articulatory mechanism closely linked to the production of speech (Baddeley and Lewis 1981; Baddeley 1986). The importance of the phonological loop has been demonstrated for the performance of reading (Baddeley and Lewis 1981), mental arithmetic (Logie *et al.* 1994), and the acquisition of a second language (Van den Noort *et al.* 2006). A similar distinction has been made within the visuospatial component between a passive visual store and an active spatial 'inner scribe' mechanism (Logie 1995; Logie and Pearson 1997) believed to be involved both in the planning and execution of movement, and also in actively maintaining the contents of the visual store. The visuospatial component of working memory has been shown to play an important role during memory for the position of objects (Cattaneo *et al.* 2006), the generation of visual mental images (Baddeley and Andrade 2000), and memory for sequences of movements (e.g. ballet moves; Rossi-Arnaud *et al.* 2004).

The concept of the central executive has also undergone considerable development in recent years, with increased attempts to specify in more detail the extent and limitations of its functioning (Baddeley 1996; Logie *et al.* 2004). Its roles are believed to include strategic cognitive control, the coordination of tasks carried out in parallel, and scheduling and planning during multi-tasking (Baddeley and Logie 1999; Logie *et al.* 2004; Law *et al.* 2006). Baddeley (2000) has also proposed a fourth component of the working memory system—the episodic buffer—which acts to bind together information from working memory and long-term memory into unitary multimodal episodic representations. The operation of the episodic buffer has been studied in the context of prose recall (Jefferies *et al.* 2004), and the integration of verbal and visual information in working memory (Zhang *et al.* 2004). The present version of Baddeley's model incorporating the episodic buffer is shown in Figure 9.4.

Towards a Model of Creative Synthesis

Pearson *et al.* (1999) conducted a series of studies that attempted to interpret participants' performance on the Finke and Slayton creative synthesis task using the multi-component framework of working memory proposed by Baddeley and colleagues (Baddeley and Hitch 1974; Baddeley 1986, 1996,

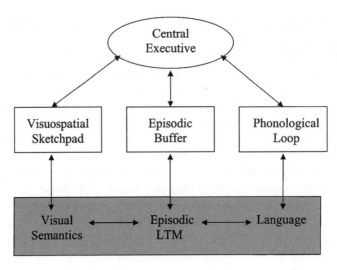

Figure 9.4.   Illustration of multi-component model of working memory (from Baddeley 2000).

2000). Participants were asked to carry out mental synthesis in conjunction with secondary tasks that were designed to selectively target the resources of the spatial, visual, and verbal components of the working memory system. This was based on the so-called dual-task principle whereby tasks that both compete for the mental resources of the same component will interfere with each other to a significantly greater extent than tasks that involve the resources of separate components (Baddeley 1986, 1990). For example, a concurrent verbal task such as articulatory suppression (continuously repeating a word or phrase out loud to inhibit the active silent rehearsal of verbal material) will interfere with verbal short-term memory to a greater extent than visuospatial short-term memory. In contrast a concurrent visuospatial task (tapping buttons in a repeating sequence) can produce the opposite pattern, interfering with visuospatial short-term memory to a greater extent than verbal short-term memory (Smyth *et al.* 1989; Smyth and Scholey 1994).

Performance of the creative synthesis task is usually characterized as relying solely on visuospatial cognitive resources (Finke 1990; Anderson and Helstrup 1993).Within the working memory framework, mental synthesis would therefore be expected predominantly to involve the resources of the visuospatial sketchpad component (Baddeley 1986). However, Pearson *et al.* (1999) found that concurrent articulatory suppression produced higher levels of interference than either the spatial or visually based secondary tasks, causing participants not only to fail to produce a recognizable pattern, but also to fail to accurately recall the symbols that had been originally presented. This apparently important relationship in the creative synthesis task between the verbal storage of symbols in working memory and participants' ability to produce a recognizable mentally synthesized pattern informed the model of creative synthesis reproduced in Figure 9.5. It is based on a visual cache–visual buffer model of mental imagery, in which the imagery visual buffer is considered functionally separate from a visual short-term 'cache' that temporally stores visual representations in a non-image based form (Pearson 2001). Operations utilizing the visual buffer are supported by the visual cache, which acts as a temporary back-up store for representations that are no longer being maintained in the form of a conscious mental image. On each trial of the creative synthesis task the selected symbols are presented to participants via their verbal descriptions. Initially they gain direct access to the phonological store component of working memory and are maintained there by the operation of an active rehearsal mechanism; the articulatory loop (Baddeley and Lewis 1981; Baddeley *et al.* 1984). Participants then generate visual images of the symbols from long-term memory using the stored verbal representations, but continue to maintain the representations within the loop so as to provide a memory back-up for the symbols that is separate from the use of visual imagery. Concurrent articulatory suppression interferes with the verbal rehearsal of the presented symbols, thereby placing a greater load on the other components of the working memory system and reducing participants' overall performance on the creative synthesis task.

The model depicted in Figure 9.5 also allows for the visual cache to store material during synthesis as a back-up store for the visual buffer, in a fashion analogous to the way in which the phonological loop is used to maintain the identity of the symbols being manipulated via mental imagery. During performance of the creative synthesis task the consciously experienced representation within the visual buffer is continuously changing as a result of the transformations and manipulations carried out by the participant. The visual cache provides a temporary storage area in which abandoned or intermediate stages in the synthesis process can be maintained, and if necessary regenerated back into the visual buffer as a mental image when required. For example, a participant may try to mentally combine a rectangle, circle, and the letter 'D' into a representation of a car, but then abandon this mental image in favour of an alternative approach. However, later on in the trial they may decide to revisit the earlier attempt at making a car. In this case the visual cache would maintain sufficient information to allow the earlier representation to be restored as a conscious mental image within the visual buffer.

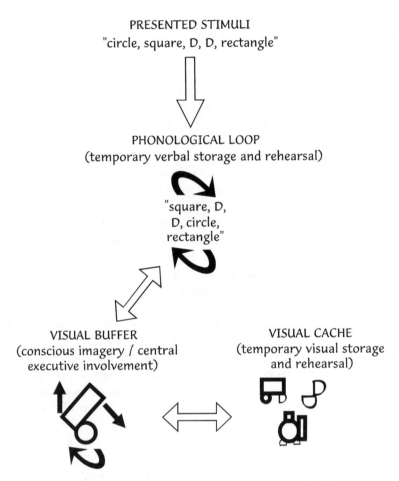

Figure 9.5. Model of mental synthesis performance (from Pearson *et al.* 1999).

Visual and Verbal Routes to Mental Images

If this model is accurate then it predicts that the method by which stimuli are presented to participants during mental synthesis may have a considerable influence on their subsequent task performance. Visual rather than verbal presentation of the symbols would allow them to be generated directly into the visual buffer from short-term memory, removing the need to generate images from long-term memory using verbal representations stored within the phonological loop. This prediction is based on the observation that there are two distinct routes by which a mental image can be created within the mind. In one instance an image can be directly created from immediate perceptual information in the form of a 'visual trace'. For example, you can look at a painting, form a mental image of it, then maintain this image as you look away or close your eyes. Alternatively, an image can be created entirely from previously stored representations in long-term memory. For example, you can read the word 'elephant' and then form an appropriate mental image based on your previous experience of what an elephant looks like. A number of studies have demonstrated significant differences in cognitive performance between images generated either from visual traces or from long-term memory. For example, Cornoldi et al. (1998) found differences in the number and type of visual characteristics recalled by participants for mental images of geometric patterns that were formed either from visual traces or from long-term memory. For instance, in images generated from long-term memory the colour of the patterns was much less accurately retained than for images created directly from visual traces.

Similar findings have been reported by Hitch et al. (1995) using a mental synthesis procedure. Participants were asked to mentally synthesize a pattern based on two sequentially presented line drawings which were either congruent or incongruent in terms of their black and white contrast (Figure 9.6). In one condition participants generated an image of the first drawing as a visual trace and then attempted to mentally combine it with the second drawing. In another condition the drawings were pre-learnt and then generated from long-term memory before being mentally combined. Participants' performance became impaired if the contrast between the drawings was incongruent, but only for the condition in which synthesis was based on visual traces created directly from perceptual experience. There was no effect of congruency if one of the images of the line drawings was generated from long-term memory instead. However, synthesis using images based on long-term memory did become sensitive to congruency effects if participants were also required to carry out concurrent articulatory suppression. Hitch et al. argue from these findings that visual images generated from short-term memory preserve surface perceptual information to a greater extent than images generated from long-term memory, which rely more heavily on abstract non-perceptual information. The re-establishment of a congruency effect using articulatory suppression, however, implies that this loss of surface perceptual information is caused by verbal processing, and need not be an inherent feature of images generated from long-term memory representations.

Similar findings have been found by Brandimonte et al. (1992) using an image reinterpretation task, which involved mentally subtracting one element from a composite pattern and then attempting to reinterpret what remained as a recognizable outline. Brandimonte et al. found that performance was improved when original learning of the composites was accompanied by articulatory suppression, which they suggested blocked verbal recoding of perceptual information in long-term memory. Such results suggest that verbal

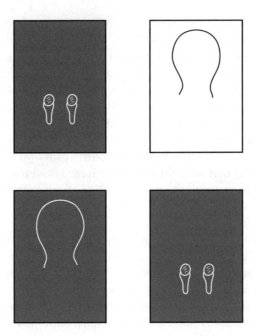

Figure 9.6. Sample stimuli from Hitch *et al.* (1995).

representations can significantly impair the ability to make novel discoveries on the basis of mental imagery alone, and that concurrent articulatory suppression can remove this effect by preventing the use of verbal recoding during imagery. Verbal recoding is an extremely common and automatic cognitive strategy adopted by participants to help retain visual information, and is the bane of researchers attempting to investigate visual memory in isolation from linguistic processing (Wilson *et al.* 1989; Della Sala *et al.* 1999). However, it is questionable whether articulatory suppression can completely block the verbal processing of visual information in the manner suggested by Brandimonte *et al.* (Reisberg 1996; Pearson *et al.* 1999). For example, you can repeatedly say the word 'go' out loud as quickly as possible and still look around the room and mentally label the objects that you can see. It is more likely that concurrent suppression instead induces a strategy shift in participants and discourages them from using verbal recoding as a means to retain visual information. For example, using a similar image subtraction procedure to Brandimonte *et al.*, Intons-Peterson (1996) has demonstrated that performance declines when linguistic processing is encouraged using manipulated instructions and experimental procedures, and increases when instead the purely visual aspects of the task are emphasized.

Visual Trace Imagery and Transformational Complexity

A study conducted by Pearson and Logie (2004) directly examined the effect
of manipulating the type of imagery (visual trace or long-term memory) on
performance of the Finke and Slayton creative synthesis task. In one condition participants completed the task as normal, and were verbally presented
with a random selection of symbols on each trial. Because only the verbal
labels were presented, all corresponding visual images would have to be generated from long-term memory. In a second condition the symbols were visually presented to participants on printed cards, allowing the images to be
generated from immediate perceptual experience. We found no significant difference in the number of recognizable patterns produced with verbal and
visual presentation, suggesting that the capacity limitations of working
memory remain constant irrespective of the modality of stimulus presentation. However, there were clear differences in performance between the visual
and verbal conditions in terms of *transformational complexity*; a measure
devised by Anderson and Helstrup (1993) to estimate the number of mental
transformations necessary in order to produce a synthesized pattern from the
set of symbols originally presented. Patterns are scored in terms of changes
in size and orientation of the symbols, as well as embedding of one or more
symbols in each other. Figure 9.7 illustrates two synthesized patterns that
score differentially in terms of transformational complexity. Participants in
the visual presentation condition produced patterns that displayed a significantly greater degree of mental manipulation and transformation than participants in the verbal presentation condition. This suggests that mental
synthesis carried out with images generated directly from visual traces is
more effective than synthesis with images generated from long-term memory,
and is consistent with Hitch *et al.*'s contention that visual trace images offer
greater preservation of surface perceptual features than comparable images
generated instead from long-term memory.

Image Reference Frames

Another possibility is that images generated directly from perceptual experience may be less susceptible to constraints imposed by *image reference
frames* than images generated from long-term memory. Reisberg (1996;
Reisberg and Logie 1993) has argued that images and percepts, unlike external pictures, cannot be inherently ambiguous. While perceptual processes can
interpret an external representation relatively flexibly, an internally generated
mental image is interpreted within a specific frame of reference, which by
specifying information such as orientation and figure/ground organization,

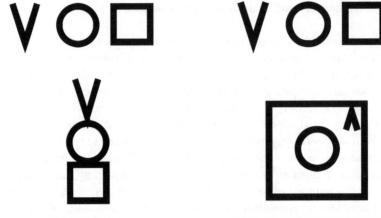

SPACEMAN
Low transformational complexity

WASHING MACHINE
High transformational complexity

Figure 9.7. Illustration of synthesized patterns with high and low transformational complexity created from the same set of presented symbols (data from Pearson and Logie 2004).

help determine how an image should be (correctly) interpreted. For example, Figure 9.8 illustrates an ambiguous figure which can be perceived as representing either a duck or a rabbit (adapted from Jastrow 1899). Interpreting the figure as a rabbit involves a reference frame in which the orientation of the figure runs from left to right, with the right side representing the front of the rabbit and the left side the back. In contrast, the alternative interpretation as a duck involves a different reference frame in which the perceived orientation of the figure is reversed. Reisberg argues that while discoveries and manipulations that are compatible with an existing reference frame can be made fairly easily, discoveries that are incompatible can be extremely difficult to make if based only on an internal mental image. However, this limitation can potentially be overcome by converting the mental image into an external representation via sketching or drawing, which may support restructuring by allowing the frame of reference in which the mental image is interpreted to be changed. A dramatic demonstration of this was made by Chambers and Reisberg (1985) using the Jastrow ambiguous duck–rabbit figure. They found that none of their participants was able to reinterpret the figure successfully using a mental image created from a brief visual presentation of the figure. Those who initially saw the figure as a rabbit were unable to see their mental image as representing anything else, and vice versa for those who first saw the figure as representing a duck. However, all of the participants were able successfully to reinterpret the figure once they were allowed to draw their mental image on a sheet of paper.

Figure 9.8.   The Jastrow ambiguous duck–rabbit figure (from Chambers and Reisberg 1985).

Constraining effects of frames of reference may be even stronger in images generated from long-term memory because they are more dependent on abstract non-perceptual information, and also preserve surface perceptual features to a lesser extent than images generated directly from perception. This may account for why mental synthesis carried out using images generated from long-term memory shows less evidence of mental manipulation and transformation than synthesis carried out using images generated from visual traces (Pearson and Logie 2004). There are also limitations imposed by the process of verbal recoding discussed previously. In an early demonstration of this, Carmichael *et al.* (1932) showed that the verbal label associated with an ambiguous figure at the time when it was remembered could substantially alter the way in which it was subsequently recalled from visual memory (Figure 9.9).

Brandimonte and Gerbino (1993) have further demonstrated that participants' ability to reinterpret ambiguous figures using mental imagery alone is increased if articulatory suppression is performed at the initial presentation of the figure. They argue that this is because suppression discourages a verbal recoding strategy from being applied as an image is generated within the visual buffer, thus allowing the visual properties of the image to be interpreted more clearly. However, Reisberg (1996) suggests instead that the act of requiring participants to perform a concurrent secondary task may induce strategy shifts that are not directly linked to verbal recoding. As argued previously, if you carry out articulatory suppression yourself by repeatedly saying the word 'go' out loud, you can still mentally label objects in the environment around you. It would therefore seem unlikely that suppression can entirely block verbal recoding from taking place when stimuli are visually presented. Instead it may cause you to adopt an encoding strategy that emphasizes surface perceptual features more than occurs without suppression taking place.

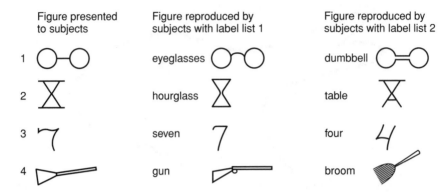

Figure 9.9. Sample data from Carmichael *et al.* (1932) depict the effects of verbal labels on memory for ambiguous figures. Participants initially viewed the same set of figures paired with different verbal labels (lists 1 and 2).

Mental Imagery and Intrusive Thoughts

The broad pattern of findings that has emerged from this literature implies that verbal processing may sometimes be detrimental to an individual's ability to use mental imagery as a basis for imaginative thought. This is consistent with arguments put forward by Shepard (1978), who stated that an extensive reliance on language might place a limitation on an individual's creative ability. Shepard noted that many anecdotal accounts of imaginative thinking such as those provided by Einstein disavowed the use of verbal strategies, particularly during early stages of creative thought.

The implications of employing verbal processing during the encoding of perceptual information into memory extend well beyond the study of mental synthesis processes alone. For example, the experience of intrusive mental images linked to a past trauma is a key symptom associated with post-traumatic stress disorder (Ehlers and Clark 2000), and intrusive imagery has also been demonstrated to occur as part of normal memory functioning (Bywaters *et al.* 2004). Holmes *et al.* (2004) examined the occurrence of memory intrusions in a group of non-clinical participants who watched a film depicting traumatic events (police footage of road traffic accidents). Participants watched the film either on its own, or while concurrently performing a visuospatial or a verbal secondary task. Holmes *et al.* found that participants who performed a concurrent visuospatial task showed a significant reduction in the occurrence of reported memory intrusions compared with those who only watched the film, while those who performed a verbal secondary task displayed a significant *increase* in the number of intrusions. These findings are consistent with the earlier proposal that interfering with verbal processing during encoding may increase the amount of perceptual information in representations stored in long-term memory. In the case of recall from autobiographical memory, greater perceptual information may directly lead to an increase in the likelihood of trauma-linked imagery intrusions to occur (Brewin *et al.* 1996; Kosslyn 2005b). In contrast performance of a concurrent visuo-spatial task may lessen the encoding of perceptual information into memory, thereby directly reducing the amount of subsequent memory intrusions (Holmes *et al.* 2004; Stuart *et al.* 2006). This suggests that the same conditions that enhance imaginative thought by augmenting the encoding and storage of perceptual information in memory, may have potentially damaging consequences if the emotional valence of the associated images is both negative and high.

THE PHENOMENOLOGY OF IMAGERY

At the beginning of this chapter I reviewed a number of famous anecdotal accounts that appear to imply that mental imagery can directly facilitate creative discovery and insight during reasoning. Although the accuracy of such accounts on their own should be regarded with caution, supporting evidence for a functional role for imagery in creative thought is provided by experimental studies of the ability to reinterpret and manipulate images in the absence of external perceptual support. Work by Finke and others has shown that individuals can create novel and recognizable patterns using imagery while under highly constrained circumstances, with frequency of success as high as 60% of experimental trials. This suggests that the ability to detect emergent properties within mental images is relatively common across the population as a whole, and is not something restricted solely to exceptional thinkers such as Einstein, Faraday, or Tesla. However, research has also demonstrated that there are a wide range of factors that can influence how successfully images can support creative reinterpretations. Images generated from long-term memory are processed differently from images generated directly from immediate perceptual experience. In addition, image reference frames and the occurrence of verbal encoding and other linguistic-based processes also markedly interact with how images are manipulated and combined during imaginative thought.

While these experimental findings on imagery may appear compelling, there still remains considerable controversy in psychology regarding the *causal* role played by imagery during cognition. Over the past forty years this debate has focused primarily on the nature of the mental representations which underlie imagery. One of the most developed theories has been proposed by Stephen Kosslyn (1980, 1994, 2005a), who argues that visual mental images rely on depictive representations that are qualitatively distinct from the mental representations that support language. Opponents of this view, most notably Zenon Pylyshyn, argue instead that there is nothing unique or special about mental images, and that imaginative thought utilizes exactly the same type of propositional language-based representations as all other forms of reasoning (Pylyshyn 1973, 1981, 2002). Initial exchanges between Kosslyn and Pylyshyn during the 1970s have been characterized as the so-called 'Imagery Debate' (Tye 1991), with more recent publications demonstrating that this debate is far from reaching any kind of resolution (Pylyshyn 2004; Kosslyn *et al.* 2006). Importantly, however, the ongoing debate focuses on the *representational* nature of imagery, rather than the conscious experience associated with holding an image in mind. In his critique of depictive theories, Pylyshyn is careful not to deny the experiential nature of imagery itself, although he argues that we are 'deeply deceived by our subjective experience of mental imagery' (Pylyshyn 2002, p. 158).

In a review of attitudes towards imagery and mental representation Thomas (1989) has distinguished between 'experiential iconophobia' (denying conscious perceptual-like imagery can occur) and 'functional iconophobia' (accepting imagery may occur but arguing it fulfils no cognitive function). Thomas notes that even arch-behaviourists such as B. F. Skinner and John Watson were not true experiential iconophobes. Watson in particular is well known for his savage critique of the scientific value to psychology of mental imagery. However, anecdotal reports suggest that prior to his development of behaviourism he may actually have experienced quite vivid mental images. Knight Dunlop, an early colleague of Watson, wrote:

> I had already discarded the old doctrine of 'images'. Watson, however, still accepted it. He, he said, used visual imagery very effectively in designing his apparatus. Watson had not at that time developed his behaviorism and his thinking was, to a large extent, along conventional lines. (Dunlap 1932, p. 45; reproduced in Thomas 1989)

Watson himself wrote in 1913:

> Until a few years ago, I thought that centrally aroused visual sensations were as clear as those peripherally aroused. I had never accredited myself with any other kind. However, closer examination leads me to deny in my own case the presence of imagery in the Galtonian sense (Watson, 1913, p. 173, footnote 2).

Later he goes on to write that mental images 'rarely come to consciousness in any person who has not groped for imagery in the psychological laboratory' (Watson 1913, p. 174, continuation of footnote 2). It is interesting to speculate whether Watson's developing theoretical ideas caused him to stop consciously experiencing imagery as he had previously or, instead, whether he came to reinterpret the subjective nature of his imagery experience. A study conducted by Daniel Reisberg, Stephen Kosslyn, and myself suggests that, in the absence of clear empirical evidence, theoretical beliefs may indeed be linked to the phenomenological experience of imagery (Reisberg *et al.* 2003). We contacted a number of researchers who were active during the 'Imagery Debate' of the 1970s and ascertained their theoretical beliefs regarding imagery, as well as their subjective ratings for the vividness of their own mental images. Evidence was found for a relationship between theoretical belief and personal experience, with those who experienced mental images as vivid and picture-like more likely to be sympathetic towards depictive theories of imagery, and to regard imagery as a valuable topic for further research.

As the phenomenological nature of imagery is itself not judged to be controversial, what function might it play during creative thought? I would argue that its main value lies in the ability to create simulations of the *conscious experience* of perception. This is different from stating that imagery simulates perception itself, which has been the focus of much research and argument. Such simulations allow us to anticipate the perceptual consequences of various actions. To give a mundane example: if I am trying to decide what colour of paint to buy in order to decorate my living room, I can use imagery to visualize what the room might look like painted in a particular shade. This image can then allow me to form an aesthetic judgement of how I and others might react to such a colour scheme. This function can be considered separately from issues of whether the image is truly depictive or the extent of overlap with actual perceptual processes in the brain. In other words, the fact that images are experienced consciously *as if* they were quasi-perceptual entities is in itself of functional importance, irrespective of the type of representational system that may underlie them.

Of course, such mental simulations cannot totally predict true perceptual experience, as scores of badly decorated rooms can testify. Nonetheless, they provide artists and designers with a valuable facility that allows them to anticipate the potential sensory impact that a work might have prior to expending the effort to actually create it. Indeed, in the case of the composer Ludwig van Beethoven (who suffered from profound hearing loss during his later life), aural imagery provided the only means to anticipate how his artistic work might be perceived. Imagery is also valuable in allowing simulations to be experienced of events that would be impossible to perceive in reality, such as the scientific visualizations described by Einstein and Hawking. This allows visual metaphors to be created and explored for concepts that may be too difficult to reason with entirely at an abstract level. Of course, it could be argued that the phenomenology associated with imagery is epiphenomenal, and not directly causative of the reasoning processes involved. However, this is a hypothesis, not an excuse for excluding the experiential nature of imagery from further explanation. Obviously the associated phenomenology must be

generated by processes within the brain, and these processes need to be
accounted for. In addition, experimental evidence demonstrates that the act
of forming a mental image places a considerable drain on general-purpose
executive resources that also play a key role during working memory operations, reasoning, and general decision-making (Grossi *et al.* 1994; Pearson
et al. 1996, 1999; Bruyer and Scailquin 1998; Rudkin *et al.* 2007). Therefore, if
mental images fulfil no useful function during cognition, it begs the question
as to why the brain expends so much cognitive effort to create them within
conscious experience.

In conclusion, there are many good reasons to suggest that imagery
plays an important role during creative thought, although the true functional importance remains controversial. The challenge for future research
will be to move beyond arguments concerning the representational status of
imagery in cognition, and instead move towards a greater understanding
and explanation of the associated and highly distinctive phenomenology
itself.

References

Abelson, R. P. 1979: Imagining the purpose of imagery. *Behavioral and Brain Sciences*,
    2, 548–549.
Anderson, R. E. and Helstrup, T. 1993: Visual discovery on mind and on paper.
    Memory and Cognition, 21, 283–293.
Baddeley, A. D. 1986: *Working Memory*. Oxford: Oxford University Press.
Baddeley, A. D. 1990: *Human Memory: Theory and Practice*. Hove, UK: LEA.
Baddeley, A. D. 1996: Exploring the central executive. *Quarterly Journal of
    Experimental Psychology: Human Experimental Psychology*, 49A, 5–28.
Baddeley, A. D. 2000: The episodic buffer: A new component of working memory?
    Trends in Cognitive Sciences, 4(11), 417–423.
Baddeley, A. D. and Andrade, J. 2000: Working memory and the vividness of imagery.
    Journal of Experimental Psychology: General, 129(1), 126–145.
Baddeley, A. D. and Hitch, G. J. 1974: Working memory. In Bower, G. (ed.), *The
    Psychology of Learning and Motivation*, Vol. VIII. New York: Academic Press,
    47–90.
Baddeley, A. D. and Lewis, V. J. 1981: Inner active processes in reading: The inner
    voice, the inner ear and the inner eye. In Lesgold, A. M. and Perfetti, C. A. (eds),
    Interactive Processes in Reading. Hillsdale, NJ: LEA, 107–129.
Baddeley, A. D. and Logie, R. H. 1999: Working memory: the multiple component
    model. In A. Miyake and P. Shah (eds), *Models of Working Memory*. Cambridge,
    MA: Cambridge University Press, 28–61.
Baddeley, A. D., Lewis, V. J. and Vallar, G. 1984: Exploring the articulatory loop.
    Quarterly Journal of Experimental Psychology, 36, 233–252.
Betts, G. H. 1909: *The Distribution and Functions of Mental Imagery*. New York:
    Teachers College, Columbia University.
Brandimonte, M. and Gerbino, W. 1993: Mental image reversal and verbal recoding:
    When ducks become rabbits. *Memory and Cognition*, 21, 23–33.

Brandimonte, M., Hitch, G. J. and Bishop, D. 1992: Verbal recoding of visual stimuli impairs mental image transformations. *Memory and Cognition*, 20, 449–455.

Brewin, C. R., Dalgleish, T. and Joseph, S. 1996: A dual representation theory of posttraumatic stress disorder. *Psychological Review*, 103, 670–686.

Bruyer, R. and Scailquin, J. C. 1998: The visuospatial sketchpad for mental images: testing the multicomponent model of working memory. *Acta Psychologica*, 98(1), 17–36.

Bywaters, M., Andrade, A. and Turpin, G. 2004: Intrusive and non-intrusive memories in a non-clinical sample: the effects of mood and affect on imagery vividness. *Memory*, 12, 467—478.

Carmichael, L., Hogan, H. P. and Walter, A. A. 1932: An experimental study of the effect of language on the reproduction of visually perceived forms. *Journal of Experimental Psychology*, 15, 73–86.

Cattaneo, Z., Postma, A. and Vecchi, T. 2006: Gender differences in memory for object and word locations. *Quarterly Journal of Experimental Psychology*, 59(5), 904–919.

Chambers, D. and Reisberg, D. 1985: Can mental images be ambiguous? *Journal of Experimental Psychology: Human Perception and Performance*, 11, 317–328.

Cornoldi, C., De Beni, R., Giusberti, F. and Massironi, M. 1998: Memory and imagery: A visual trace is not a mental image. In Conway, M. A., Gathercole, S. E. and Cornoldi, C. (eds), *Theories of Memory*, Vol. II. Hove: The Psychology Press, 87–108.

Della Sala, S., Gray, C., Baddeley, A., Allamano, N. and Wilson, L. 1999: Pattern span: A tool for unwelding visuo-spatial memory. *Neuropsychologica*, 37(10), 1189–1199.

Ehlers, A. and Clark, D. M. 2000: A cognitive model of posttraumatic stress disorder. *Behaviour Research and Therapy*, 38(4), 319–345.

Farah, M. J., Hammond, K. M., Levine, D. N. and Calvanio, R. 1988: Visual and spatial mental imagery: Dissociable systems of representation. *Cognitive Psychology*, 20, 439–462.

Finke, R. A. 1986: Mental imagery and the visual system. *Scientific American*, 254, 88–95.

Finke, R. 1989: *Principles of Mental Imagery*. Cambridge, MA: MIT Press.

Finke, R. 1990: *Creative Imagery: Discoveries and Inventions in Visualization*. Hillsdale, NJ: Lawrence Erlbaum.

Finke, R. and Slayton, K. 1988: Explorations of creative visual synthesis in mental imagery. *Memory and Cognition*, 16, 252–257.

Finke, R., Pinker, S. and Farah, M. J. 1989: Reinterpreting visual patterns in mental imagery. *Cognitive Science*, 13, 51–78.

Finke, R., Ward, T. B. and Smith, S. M. 1992: *Creative Cognition: Theory, Research, and Applications*. Cambridge, MA: MIT Press.

Gardner, H. 1993: *Creating Minds*. New York: Basic Books.

Galton, F. 1880: Statistics of mental imagery. *Mind*, 5, 301–318.

Goldschmidt, G. 1991: The dialectics of sketching. *Creativity Research Journal*, 4(2), 123–143.

Goldschmidt, G. 1992: Serial sketching: Visual problem solving in design *Cybernetics and Systems*, 23(2), 191–219.

Gooding, D. 1991: Faraday was a hands-on scientist. *Physics Education*, 26, 307–312.

Grossi, D., Becker, J. T. and Trojano, L. 1994: Visuospatial imagery in Alzheimer-disease. *Perceptual and Motor Skills*, 78(3), 867–874.

Hawking, S. W. 1993: *Black Holes and Baby Universes and Other Essays*. London: Bantam Press.

Hitch, G. J., Brandimonte, M. A. and Walker, P. 1995: Two types of representation in visual memory: Evidence from the effects of stimulus contrast on image combination. *Memory and Cognition*, 23, 147–156.

Holmes, E. A., Brewin, C. R. and Hennessy, R. G. 2004: Trauma films, information processing, and intrusive memory development. *Journal of Experimental Psychology: General*, 133(1), 3–22.

Intons-Peterson, M. J. 1996: Linguistic effects in a visual manipulation task. *Psychologische Beitrage*, 38(3/4), 251–278.

Jastrow, J. 1899: The mind's eye. *Popular Science Monthly*, 54, 299–312.

Jefferies, E., Ralph, M. A. L. and Baddeley, A. D. 2004: Automatic and controlled processing in sentence recall: The role of long-term and working memory. *Journal of Memory and Language*, 51(4), 623–643.

Juttner, M. and Rentschler, I. 2002: Imagery in multi-modal object learning. *Behavioral and Brain Sciences*, 25(2), 197–198.

Kauffman, G. 1988: Mental imagery and problem solving. In Denis, M., Engelkamp, J. and Richardson, J. T. E. (eds), *Cognitive and Neuropsychological Approaches to Mental Imagery*. Dordrecht: Martinus Nijhoff Publishers.

Kosslyn, S. M. 1980: *Image and Mind*. Cambridge, MA: Harvard University Press.

Kosslyn, S. M. 1994: *Image and Brain: The Resolution of the Imagery Debate*. Cambridge, MA: MIT Press.

Kosslyn, S. M. 2005a: Mental images and the brain. *Cognitive Neuropsychology*, 22(3–4), 333–347.

Kosslyn, S. M. 2005b: Reflective thinking and mental imagery: A perspective on the development of posttraumatic stress disorder. *Development and Psychopathology*, 17(3), 851–863.

Kosslyn, S. M., Thompson, W. L. and Ganis, G. 2006: *The Case for Mental Imagery*. New York: Oxford University Press.

Law, A. S., Logie, R. H. and Pearson, D. G. 2006: The impact of secondary tasks on multitasking in a virtual environment. *Acta Psychologica*, 122(1), 27–44.

Lawson, B. 1980: *How Designers Think*. Westfield, NJ: Eastview Editions.

Logie, R. H. 1995: *Visuo-spatial Working Memory*. Hove: LEA.

Logie, R. H. and Pearson, D. G. 1997: The inner eye and the inner scribe of visuo-spatial working memory: Evidence from developmental fractionation. *European Journal of Cognitive Psychology*, 9(3), 241–257.

Logie, R. H., Gilhooly, K. J. and Wynn, V. 1994: Counting on working memory in arithmetic problem solving. *Memory and Cognition*, 22(4), 395–410.

Logie, R. H., Cocchini, G., Della Sala, S. and Baddeley, A. D. 2004: Is there a specific executive capacity for dual task coordination? Evidence from Alzheimer's disease. *Neuropsychology*, 18(3), 504–513.

Marks, D. F. 1973: Visual imagery differences in the recall of pictures. *British Journal of Psychology*, 64, 407–412.

Miller, A. I. 1984: *Imagery in Scientific Thought: Creating 20th Century Physics*. Boston, MA: Birkhauser.

Miller, A. I. 2000: *Insights of Genius: Imagery and Creativity in Science and Art*. Cambridge, MA: MIT Press.

Nin, A. 1969: *The Diary of Anais Nin 1931–1934*. New York: Harvest Books.

Pearson, D. G. 2001: Imagery and the visuo-spatial sketchpad. In Andrade, J. (ed.), *Working Memory in Perspective*. Hove: The Psychology Press.

Pearson, D. G. and Logie, R. H. 2004: Effects of stimulus modality and working memory load on mental synthesis performance. *Imagination, Cognition, and Personality*, 23(2/3), 183–191.

Pearson, D. G., Logie, R. H. and Green, C. 1996: Mental manipulation, visual working memory, and executive processes. *Psychologische Beitrage*, 38, 324–342.

Pearson, D. G., Logie, R. H. and Gilhooly, K. 1999: Verbal representations and spatial manipulation during mental synthesis. *European Journal of Cognitive Psychology*, 11(3), 295–314.

Pearson, D. G., De Beni, R. and Cornoldi, C. 2001: The generation, maintenance, and transformation of visuo-spatial mental images. In Denis, M., Logie, R. H., Cornoldi, C., De Vega, M. and. Engelkamp, J. (eds), *Imagery, Language, and Visuo-Spatial Thinking*. Hove: The Psychology Press.

Purcell, A. T. and Gero, J. S. 1998: Drawings and the design process. *Design Studies*, 19(4), 389–430.

Pylyshyn, Z. W. 1973: What the mind's eye tells the mind's brain: A critique of mental imagery. *Psychological Bulletin*, 80, 1–24.

Pylyshyn, Z. W. 1981: The imagery debate: Analogue media versus tacit knowledge. *Psychological Review*, 87, 16–45.

Pylyshyn, Z. W. 2002: Mental imagery: In search of a theory. *Behavioral and Brain Sciences*, 25, 157–238.

Pylyshyn, Z. W. 2004: *Seeing and Visualising: It's Not What You Think*. Cambridge, MA: MIT Press.

Reed, S. K. 1993: Imagery and discovery. In Roskos-Ewoldsen, B., Intons-Peterson, M. J. and R. Anderson (eds), *Imagery, Creativity and Discovery: A Cognitive Perspective*. Amsterdam: North-Holland.

Reisberg, D. 1992: *Auditory Imagery*. Hillsdale, NJ: LEA.

Reisberg, D. 1996: The nonambiguity of mental images. In Cornoldi, C., Logie, R. H., Brandimonte, M. A., Kaufmann, G. and Reisberg, D. (eds), *Stretching the Imagination: Representation and Transformation in Mental Imagery*. New York: Oxford University Press.

Reisberg, D. and Logie, R. H. 1993: The ins and outs of visual working memory: Overcoming the limits on learning from imagery. In Intons-Peterson, M., Roskos-Ewoldsen, B. and Anderson, R. (eds), *Imagery, Creativity, and Discovery: A Cognitive Approach*. Amsterdam: Elsevier, 39–76.

Reisberg, D., Pearson, D. G. and Kosslyn, S. M. 2003: Intuitions and introspections about imagery: The role of imagery experience in shaping an investigator's theoretical views. *Applied Cognitive Psychology*, 17, 147–160.

Richardson, A. 1969: *Mental Imagery*. London: Routledge.

Rossi-Arnaud, C., Cortese, A. and Castari, V. 2004: Memory span for movement configurations: The effects of concurrent verbal, motor and visual interference. *Current Psychology of Cognition*, 22(3), 335–349.

Rudkin, S. J., Pearson, D. G. and Logie, R. H. 2007: Executive processes in visual and spatial working memory tasks. *Quarterly Journal of Experimental Psychology*, 60(1), 79–100.

Samuels, M. and Samuels, N. 1975: *Seeing with the Mind's Eye*. New York: Random House.

Shepard, R. N. 1978: Externalization of mental images and the act of creation. In Randhawa, B. S. and Coffman, W. E. (eds), *Visual Learning, Thinking, and Communication*. New York: Academic Press.

Smyth, M. M. and Scholey, K. A. 1994: Interference in spatial immediate memory. *Memory and Cognition*, 22, 1–13.

Smyth, M. M., Pearson, N. A. and Pendleton, L. R. 1989: Movement and working memory: Patterns and positions in space. *Quarterly Journal of Experimental Psychology*, 40(A), 497–514.

Stevenson, R. J. and Case, T. I. 2005: Olfactory imagery: A review. *Psychonomic Bulletin and Review*, 12(2), 244–264.

Stuart, A. D. P., Holmes, E. A. and Brewin, C. R. 2006: The influence of a visuospatial grounding task on intrusive images of a traumatic film. *Behaviour Research and Therapy*, 44(4), 611–619.

Thomas, N. J. T. 1989: Experience and theory as determinants of attitudes toward mental representation: The case of Knight Dunlop and the vanishing images of J.B. Watson. *American Journal of Psychology*, 102, 395–412.

Thompson, A. L. and Klatzky, R. L. 1978: Studies of visual synthesis: Integration of fragments into forms. *Journal of Experimental Psychology: Human Perception and Performance*, 4(2), 244–263.

Tiggemann M. and Kemps, E. 2005: The phenomenology of food cravings: The role of mental imagery. *Appetite*, 45(3), 305–313.

Tye, M. 1991: *The Imagery Debate*. Cambridge, MA: The MIT Press.

Van den Noort, M. W. M. L., Bosch, P. and Hugdahl, K. 2006: Foreign language proficiency and working memory capacity. *European Psychologist*, 11(4), 289–296.

Vernon, P. E. (ed.), 1970: *Creativity*. Harmondsworth: Penguin Books Ltd.

Watson, J. B. 1913: Psychology as the behaviorist views it. *Psychological Review*, 20, 158–177.

Weisberg, R. W. 1986: *Creativity: Genius and Other Myths*. New York: W.H. Freeman and Company.

Wilson, J. T. L., Wiedmann, K. D., Hadley, D. M. and Brooks, D. N. 1989: The relationship between visual memory function and lesion detected by magnetic resonance imaging after closed head injury. *Neuropsychology*, 3, 255–265.

Wotiz, J. H. and Rudofsky, S. 1954: Kekulé's dream: Fact or fiction? *Chemistry in Britain*, 20, 720–723.

Zhang, D., Zhang, X., Sun, X., Li, Z., Wang, Z., He, S. and Hu, X. 2004: Cross-modal temporal order memory for auditory digits and visual locations: An fMRI study. *Human Brain Mapping*, 22, 280–289.

10

The Way We Imagine[1]

MARK TURNER

Abstract. Conceptual integration is a basic mental operation, in which input conceptual arrays are 'blended' to produce compressed, memorable conceptual packets, congenial to human thought, often with emergent structure not available from the input conceptual arrays. The highest form of conceptual integration is 'double-scope' integration. Double-scope integration is the hallmark of the distinctively human imagination. A double-scope integration network has input conceptual arrays with different, often clashing, organizing frames and an organizing frame for the blend that includes parts of each of those organizing frames and emergent structure of its own. In such networks, both organizing frames make central contributions to the blend, and their sharp differences offer the possibility of rich clashes. Far from blocking the construction of the network, such clashes offer conceptual challenges. The resulting blends can turn out to be highly imaginative.

BLENDING AND THE HUMAN MIND

FIFTY THOUSAND YEARS AGO, more or less, during the Upper Paleolithic, unmistakable archeological evidence began to accumulate of a remarkable set of human singularities: art, science, religion, refined tool use, advanced music and dance, fashions of dress, language, and mathematics. Human beings began to demonstrate an unprecedented ability to be imaginative in whatever they encountered. Cognitively modern human beings throughout

---

[1] This chapter draws on Turner, M. 2004: 'The origin of Selkies', *Journal of Consciousness Studies*, 11(5–6), 90–115.

Proceedings of the British Academy **147**, 213–236. © The British Academy 2007.

the world since that time have demonstrated this remarkable ability, as a routine part of what it means to be human.

In *The Way We Think*, Gilles Fauconnier and I proposed that this change happened in the following way (Fauconnier and Turner 2002). The basic mental operation of conceptual integration, also known as 'blending', has been present and evolving in various species for a long time. Modern human beings evolved not an entirely different kind of mind, but instead the capacity for the strongest form of conceptual integration, known as 'double-scope' blending. It is the engine of the human imagination.

What is blending and why is it so important? (Technical introductions to the nature and mechanisms of blending can be found in Fauconnier 1997; Fauconnier and Turner 1998, 2002; Turner 2001, 2003. See also Goguen 1999.) Let us begin with an example. A man is participating in a wedding. He is consciously enacting a familiar mental story, with roles, participants, a plot, and a goal. But while he is fulfilling his role in the wedding story, he is remembering a different story, which took place a month before off the Cycladic island of Despotico, where he and his girlfriend, who is not present at the wedding, went diving in the hopes of retrieving sunken archeological treasures from the newly discovered Temple of Apollo and Artemis. Why, cognitively, should he be able mentally to activate and interleave these two stories? There are rich possibilities for confusion, but in all the central ways, he remains unconfused. He does not mistake the bride for his girlfriend, for the treasure, for the fish, for the temple, or even for Artemis. He does not swim down the aisle or speak as if through a snorkel.

Human beings go beyond merely imagining stories or concepts that run counter to the present environment. We can also connect them and blend them to make a third mental array. The man at the wedding can make analogical connections between his girlfriend and the bride and between himself and the groom, and blend these counterparts into a daydream in which it is he and his girlfriend who are being married at this particular ceremony. This blended story is manifestly false, and he should not make the mistake, as he obediently discharges his duties at the real wedding, of thinking that he is in the process of marrying his girlfriend. But he can realize that he likes the blended story, and so formulate a plan of action to make it real. Or, in the blended story, when the bride is invited to say 'I do', she might say, 'I would never marry you!' Her response might reveal to him a truth he had sensed intuitively but not recognized.

DOUBLE-SCOPE BLENDING

The most imaginative blending networks are double-scope networks. In a double scope network, the two inputs have different (and often clashing) organizing frames, and the blend has an organizing frame that receives projections from each of those organizing frames. The blend also has emergent structure of its own that cannot be found in any of the inputs. Sharp differences between the organizing frames of the inputs offer the possibility of rich clashes. Far from blocking the construction of the network, such clashes offer challenges to the imagination. The resulting blends can turn out to be highly imaginative.

The imagination is not arbitrary or accidental. It has elaborate constitutive principles and governing principles (Fauconnier and Turner 2002). It cannot be explained as the sparks of crossed wires, the mere loss of separation between supposedly modular capacities. It is much too systematic for such an explanation to be plausible. In addition, imaginative blending operates with as much systematicity within individual conceptual domains as it does across domains.

The ability for highly imaginative double-scope blending seems to be available to children very early. For example, in Crockett Johnson's (1983) *Harold and the Purple Crayon,* written for 3-year-olds, Harold uses his purple crayon to draw, and whatever he draws is real, although the result is clearly a child's sketch.

His world is a blend of spatial reality and its representation. In the blend, the representation is fused with what it represents. When Harold wants light to go for a walk, he draws the moon, and so he has moonlight. The moon stays with him as he moves. This blend has two inputs. One input has elements of the real spatial world as we experience it and perceive it. One of those elements is the moon. The other input to the blend has conventional knowledge about drawing. In the input with the real moon, the moon cannot be created by drawing and it does not come into existence at someone's will. In the input with drawing, a drawn moon cannot emit moonlight or float along in the sky as the artist's companion. But in the blend, there is a special blended moon with special emergent properties.

The mechanisms of blending that give us this special blended moon work generally throughout *Harold and the Purple Crayon.* When he needs to walk, he draws a path, and then sets off on his walk. When Harold wants to return home, he draws a window around the moon, positioning the moon where it would appear in his window if he were in his bedroom, and so he is automatically in fact in his bedroom and can go to sleep (Figure 10.1).

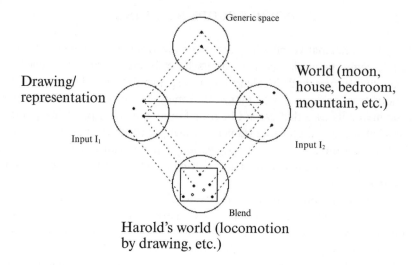

Generic space

Drawing/
representation

World (moon,
house, bedroom,
mountain, etc.)

Input I₁

Input I₂

Blend

Harold's world (locomotion
by drawing, etc.)

Figure 10.1.   Blending network for *Harold and the Purple Crayon.*

Child Harold's blended world has new kinds of causality and event shape
that are unavailable from either the domain of drawing or the domain of spatial living. Blends of this sort are found widely throughout art and literature.

DOUBLE-SCOPE BLENDING AND ATTRIBUTIONS OF MIND

Imaginative double-scope blending is equally the mainstay of everyday
thought and understanding. Consider, as an example of routine blending,
our perception of a seal. The eyes of a seal are remarkably like the eyes of a
human being. When we see a seal at the seashore, it is impossible to resist the
conclusion that we and the seal share a category. Compelling and evident
analogies leap out at us, between the seal's appearance and ours, between the
seal's motion and ours. Our human eyes align toward an object as our limbs
propel our bodies toward it, and it seems to be no different for the seal.

We immediately forge a mental blend of ourselves and the seal. The result
is a conception of a seal that has not only all of the seal's appearance and
motion but additionally a feature we know only of ourselves—the possession
of a mind (Figure 10.2).

In the mental blend, we conceive of a seal as having a mind something like
ours, lying behind its appearance and motion. In the mental blend, the seal's
eyes are not merely open, round, clear, and active, but also alert, intelligent,
inquisitive, and perceptive. It *inspects* us with wide-eyed, penetrating *attention*. It *intends* to *pursue* an object. It has perception, appetite, and memory.

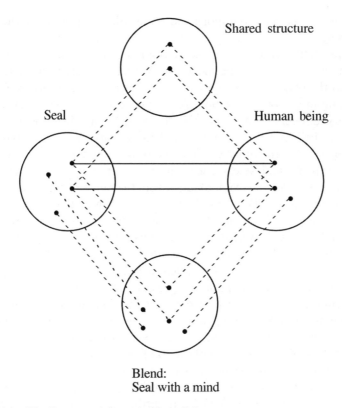

Figure 10.2. Blending network for seal with a mind.

We believe in this blend completely, long before we have any refined scientific evidence for it.

This is the sort of blend we assemble unconsciously, from early childhood, for any other human being. In the standard blend that we use for conceiving of another human being, the human being has not only all the organismic appearance and movement that we routinely perceive when we pay attention to the person, but also something we project to it of ourselves—the possession of a mind. It has perception, sensation, and intention behind its appearance and movements, just as we have perception, sensation, and intention behind ours. In the blend, the person whom we watch has mental states that accord with what we see.

We are adept at varying the conceptual structure that we project to the blend. When we perceive that someone is in a situation or condition that is not identical to ours, we can project their situation or condition to the blend, giving their perspective to the blend, with consequences for the thoughts we imagine them to have. When we see that someone's behaviour is unlike our own even in identical conditions, we adjust the projection to the blend accordingly.

The projection of mind to the seal automatically gives the seal some viewpoint, but we can vary the specific details. We can choose specific details that belong to the conditions of the seal. Alternatively, we can mix in elements that belong to our own condition. At the one extreme, the seal has a viewpoint very different from ours in both location and disposition, and we apprehend the blended seal-with-a-mind from a distance, as a strange and foreign species. At the other extreme, the blend can be given our own first-person viewpoint, and we can see, in the blend, through the seal's eyes. (Try it: in imagination, be the seal looking at you, the human being, watching the seal from the seashore. Do you suddenly feel a little wet? Do you feel yourself trying to keep yourself afloat?) The nature of the mind possessed by the seal in the blend can also be varied: we can imagine what it is like to be a seal with seal-like abilities and preferences, or we can imagine what it is like to be something like us clothed in seal form. Such blending apparently outstrips by a vast distance anything a non-human species can perform.

Children routinely perform such acts of blending in conceiving of other human beings, and perhaps equally routinely in conceiving of animals, with the result that talking animals are the mainstay of the human nursery. Other species show no disposition to make dolls of other species and then attribute to them their own vocalizations, but the creative projection done by the human child can easily produce a seal who talks, who makes friends with us, who invites us to come swimming for his birthday party, and who winks at us collusively as we engage in adventures.

These are again 'double scope' blending networks, with inputs to the blend that have different (and often clashing) organizing frames and an organizing frame for the blend that includes parts of each of those organizing frames and has emergent structure of its own. *The Way We Think* presents the details of double scope blending in examples drawn from mathematics, science, grammar, counterfactual reasoning, causal reasoning, humour, the construction of identity, category extension, artefacts, and so.

In all such cases, there is emergent structure in the blend. In the case of the talking seal, the creature in the blend has specific properties that belong to neither the human being nor the seal, that is, to neither of the two mental concepts that feed the blend. Consider the speech of the talking seal. It might have a sound system for its language that includes barks and growls, and a grammar bizarre for a human being. No human being has such speech, and of course no seal has speech at all, but the talking seal has just this emergent style of speech.

It is an open cognitive scientific question how the modern human being, from infant to adult, activates these conceptions of other minds, and how these blended conceptions differ. One of the most important variations is whether the blend has a counterpart in our conception of our reality. The seal that we see at the beach has an immediate counterpart in our notion of our reality, while Donald Duck does not. We are not deluded, and the difference is strong.

Similarly, there is the question of how the human mind evolved so as to be able to make immediate recognition of other minds. Consider a range of hypotheses:

- Possibility 1: Human beings have 'Swiss Army Knife' minds, whose different capacities are like different tools, unrelated in their mechanisms and evolution, and operating separately but with some coordination in the brain. On this view, a separate module evolved to recognize other human beings as having minds, and that module has no particular computational relation to any other.
- Possibility 2: Human beings have the operation of double-scope blending, and put the notion of another mind together from scratch through blending every time they encounter a person or invent an imaginary being.

These are surely straw-man possibilities. Possibility 1 seems implausible because human beings do double-scope blending across many different and perhaps all conceptual domains, and do it for non-human beings. Possibility 2 seems implausible because it offers no place for efficiency and entrenchment. But there are two plausible possibilities:

- Possibility 3: People have double-scope blending that can achieve attributions of mind for non-human beings, but extremely early in life put together blending templates that serve them thereafter for dealing with people. These templates are quickly entrenched, and people 'live in the blend', never aware of the work that went into the template, but able to open it back up actively and on-line when they want to do new work. We never need to construct these templates afresh again. Instead, we activate the blend directly, just like that. This possibility allows for adjustment, so that the newborn who regards the voice-activated mobile as an intentional agent could refine its reactions later.
- Possibility 4: Genetic assimilation has picked up some of the work of double-scope blending in the case of human beings, so that human beings now have a head start in achieving the blending templates for other minds.

Possibilities 3 and 4 could combine: double-scope blending is responsible for our evolution of concepts of robust other minds and accordingly for our outstanding abilities for social cognition. Indeed, the adaptiveness of social cognition contributes to the much greater overall adaptiveness of double-scope blending. Modern human beings continue to do active double-scope blending with robust on-line construction when we assemble imaginary beings such as intelligent robots or a river that rises up in a Japanese animated film to express, in exotic ways, its pain at being polluted. But the basic human reaction to another human being does not need to be assembled from scratch.

IMAGINATIVE BLENDS: THE SELKIE

Let us consider a remarkable blend that has no counterpart in our conception of reality: a blend of *seal* and *human being*. This is the concept of a *selkie*. Selkies have new properties. In the folklore of the Orkney Islands, they are shape-shifting beings. When in seal form, a selkie can shed its coat to become a human being, or rather, something deceptively like a human being. When in human form, it can converse and mate with a human being. Selkies shed their coats in the moonlight and dance on the level shore. A prudent selkie hides its coat carefully before cavorting. Here we see a case where the emergent meaning in the blend includes not new properties for a seal but in fact a new species that falls into the category of neither human being nor seal.

In the selective projection to the blend, the selkie when out of its coat has the anatomical parts and proportions of a human being but the sleek and lithe movements of the seal. Accordingly, when out of their coats, selkies are sexually irresistible to human beings. In the Orkney legends, a man sometimes steals the coat of a female selkie to compel her to agree to marry him if she ever wants to regain her coat.

But male selkies also shed their coats and slip into villages to mate with deliriously grateful women. Selkies have a relation to their coats that is a blend of a seal's relation to its skin and a human being's relation to clothes. Selkies take off their clothes to have fun, and are vulnerable when thus 'naked'.

BLENDS OF BLENDS

It is common in art to work with many blends, and to make blends of blends. A particularly elaborate development of the selkie legend is offered in a well-known modern tale for older children titled 'Aunt Charlotte and the NGA Portraits' (Turner 1995). NGA is the acronym for 'National Gallery of Art', the one in Washington, DC. It sits next to the Capitol Building on the National Mall.

'Aunt Charlotte and the NGA Portraits' presents a character named Olga Weathers. Halfway into the story, the reader discovers that Olga is a selkie lacking her coat. The word 'selkie' never occurs in the story, and no prior knowledge of selkies is required to understand the story.

Olga has the mental character of a woman but, understandably, no native taste for the human world. She would prefer a life of swimming in the water. Wearing her coat, she would have something like the body of a seal, naturally. But not quite, since her coat can be removed, and when it is, she becomes a woman. But not quite, since, when she is a woman, she retains her knowledge of the sea and retains, too, the remarkable instinctive capabilities of a marine mammal.

Olga Weathers has features possessed by no seal. Neither seal nor woman can lose its skin or assume the skin of another species. Neither seal nor woman can be transformed into a member of another species. And it is not only Olga who is different in the world of this story. A real man in our world cannot obtain a wife by stealing the skin of a seal, but in the story, a man can try to get a wife by stealing the coat of a female selkie.

These things are possible in Olga's world. She switches from species to species according to whether she is wearing her coat. She is never either woman or seal, but always something different, and this difference counts in the story as her 'magic'. A mean man, it turns out, did steal her coat. He hoped she would marry him in order to regain it but she refused to marry him, because she knew he would have kept her coat forever, and she would never have been free. He thought she was helpless and had no choice, but she was not powerless, and she had a few friends who helped her make a home on Ocracoke, a seaside town in North Carolina, where she earned her living by helping the fishermen. Olga can tell where the fish are, and she can foretell the weather, and she has a sense for the conditions of the sea. The fishermen therefore pay her for advice. In Olga's World, it seems, boats have an intentional nature, too, or at least, they can hear a selkie, and they are happy to comply with her requests. She can call the boats home when they are lost. As luck would have it, the man who stole her coat was injured while hunting narwhals. The wound turned septic and he died without telling her where he had hidden her coat. So there is Olga, beached on Ocracoke.

In the blending network that produces this selkie, the shape and movement that are projected from the human being input and from the seal input to Olga do not make her lithe and frisky. On the contrary, her body is massive, like a seal's, and she has relative difficulty moving on land, as a seal might. She is hefty. Her long hair combs out in perfect waves. She is herself a kind of undulation whenever she passes over the sand.

Olga's world, inhabited by selkies, is brushed to that extent by the magic of shape-shifting, the magic of moving from one category to another, of blending incompatible elements such as woman and seal to make not just a mental blend but elements in the world to which the blend refers.

PICTURE WORLDS

There is another magic pattern of blending in Olga's world, and this additional magic is also based on a very familiar pattern of blending, one that concerns our everyday, entirely pedestrian concept of representation. Human beings effortlessly understand the concept of 'representation'. As a matter of straightforward practice, we routinely put something and its representation into mental correspondence. The representational element is understood as 'representing' a world or a scene or an element in a scene (Figure 10.3).

It is extremely common for us to blend these two related spaces and in so doing to compress the 'outer-space' relation of *representation* between them into a unique object in the blend, as in Figure 10.4.

For example, a person and a photograph are two quite different things, but we can blend the photographic element and the person. In the blend, the person is fused with the photographic element. We point at the picture and say, 'This is John'. Of course, we are not deluded in the least: we know that, in the contributing space with the person, John is three-dimensional and moves. We know that the photograph is two-dimensional and does not move. But the conceptual blend in which the representation of John is fused with John is extremely useful. Most blends of this sort, but not all, have outer-space connections not only of representation but also of analogy between the representation and the element represented. That is, the visual image that is the representation of John is visually and topologically analogous to John himself: there are two images of eyes in the representation and two eyes in John's head; the two images of eyes in the representation are above the image of the nose in the representation just as the John's actual two eyes are above John's actual nose; and so on (Figure 10.5). This is, of course, just the kind of blending network we saw in *Harold and the Purple Crayon*.

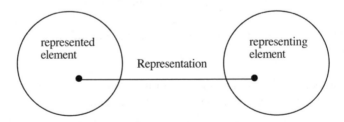

Figure 10.3.   A Representation vital relation connecting elements in different inputs.

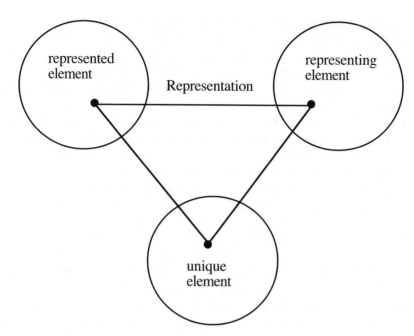

Figure 10.4. Blend of represented element and representing element.

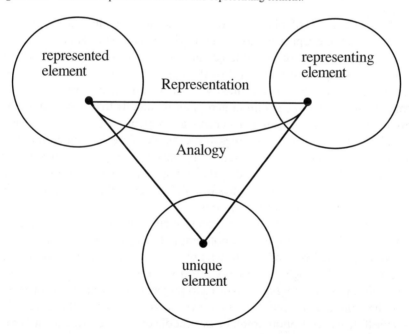

Figure 10.5. Blend of represented element and representing element, with an additional Analogy vital relation.

In addition to the contributing mental space that contains the representation and the other contributing mental space that contains what is represented, there is yet another contributing mental space that can be brought into this common 'compression of representation' network. A window, or a gap in the curtains or the fence, or a portal of any sort gives us a view. When we catch only a punctual view through a portal, we get a framed glimpse. Many vital conceptual relations create a connection between a framed representation and a framed glimpse. For example, a photograph of a person and a framed glimpse of the same person are strongly analogous not only in the content of what is viewed but also in the fact that there is a viewer of that content. It seems to be conventional to blend the photograph of a person with a framed glimpse of the person, so that, in the blend, the representation of the person is the person while the entire representation is a framed glimpse of the part of the visual field the photograph represents, including the person. (So if you show someone a mug shot against a wall, and ask 'what's to the left?', the answer is likely to be 'more of the wall', and if you ask, 'what's below?', the answer is likely to be 'the rest of the person', even though the picture does not contain these elements. They are projected instead from our conception of the image as a framed glimpse.) We often say not only that the photograph gives us a 'glimpse' but also that a true visual glimpse is a 'snapshot'.

We project much of what we know about a framed glimpse to the blended space in which the representation is fused with what it represents. Principally, we know that what we see in a framed glimpse is only part of a world that has spatial and temporal extent not directly represented in the framed glimpse. The ability to conceive of a framed glimpse as part of a larger spatial and temporal world may be common across all mammals that have vision, and this tendency to take a limited percept as implying a larger context may extend across all sensory modalities. For example, if we feel something small in the dark, we take it immediately to be part of a larger spatial and temporal world. Human beings, and perhaps dogs and dolphins, are very adept at conceiving of rich dynamic scenes with full spatial and temporal continuity on the basis of very partial perceptions.

When we blend a framed representation such as a photograph with our concept of a framed glimpse, the photograph thereby becomes a spatially and temporally limited part of a rich dynamic world with temporal and spatial continuities and changes that are not directly represented. Our conception of the conditions of photography leads us to project to the blend many elements from the represented scene that have no visible counterpart in the representation itself. If we see a photograph of the middle of a bridge, we routinely and naturally conceive of the bridge as extending beyond the frame. We conceive of the person on the bridge as obscuring elements behind her.

But of course we can do just the same thing with a painting or a sketch. We project to the blend elements that correspond to our understanding of the reality of a framed glimpse even though there is no visible counterpart of them in the representation itself, and we do this even when we know that the representation is fictitious. In the blend, the painted woman on the painted bridge is obscuring something from our view even if the painter invented both her and the bridge.

In the case of Olga, the blend that derives from all three contributing spaces—that is, the representation, what it represents, and a framed glimpse of what it represents—is reified: this blend is 'true' in her world, in the following way. Olga's world has paintings, in fact the same paintings that exist in our world. But in Olga's world, those paintings actually are rich dynamic worlds of their own, and the few elite viewers in the world who in fact see properly, that is, with intelligence and open-minded insight, can indeed see the dynamic painted worlds that the paintings present. When they look at paintings, the people move, the sea rolls, the wind blows, vehicles enter and depart from the scene.

This emergent structure in the blend—rich, dynamic worlds inside the paintings—comes in part from projection of what we know about a glimpse through a window or portal. We know that if we prolong the glimpse to a stare, we might, looking through the portal, see change, dynamism, movement. Just so, in Olga's world, if you are talented and trained and you stare at the painting, you might see change, dynamism, movement. Why do you see it? In Olga's world, the answer is straightforward: because it is *there*.

Olga, of course, is one of those who see properly. When she looks at a painting, or at least a certain painting, she can see the people in it move, breathe, and act, because in the blend they in fact do, and in Olga's world, the blend is real. In the reified mental array that blends the painting, what it represents, and a prolonged view of what it represents, the representation of a person is not merely a person but indeed a person who has received very full projections from our notion of staring through a window at a world: the blended painted person can move, converse, think, plan, become hungry, eat, and so on. Yet the projections from the space of the person are not complete: in this blend, these painted people do not age. With a few exceptions, they are unaware of anything outside the world of the particular painting they inhabit.

INTO AND OUT OF THE FRAME

We are all familiar with a basic 'Picture World' blending template. We use this template routinely. In it, there is a further set of correspondences between the representation and what it represents, as follows. Suppose that in our real world we have a bridge over a canal. Well, something can literally be part of that scene. If the physics works out right, that thing can literally be put into the scene or removed from the scene. For example, we can row a real gondola into the real scene. Over in the representation, that is, the picture, there can be individual representations that can be created there; they can be erased or otherwise made invisible. So, for example, the painter can do something with paint and a paintbrush that results in the existence of a representation of a gondola as part of the represented scene. There is an outer-space correspondence, that is, a correspondence between two of the contributing spaces, that connects two acts: putting something into a real scene, and taking some action that results in a new element in a representation. This correspondence connects two caused changes and their visible results. That outer-space correspondence can be compressed in our routine 'Picture World' blending template to yield, in the blend, a blended causality. The blend fuses these two caused changes, so that the performing of actions that result in a representational element in the representation is fused with 'putting' what it represents 'into' the 'scene'. We say, 'the painter put a gondola into the painting'. Of course, we are not at all deluded: while a gondola must exist before it can be rowed into the Grand Canal, the exact flat composition of paint that represents the boat in the representation does not in fact exist as such to be 'put' into the picture until the artist is quite finished taking the artistic action. We use such expressions all the time, as when we say that the artist 'put some flowers into the sketch' but then 'took them out', or 'Hey! You forgot to put Grandma into your sketch'. The blend that fuses the representation with what it represents gives a very natural way to think and speak about representations at human scale. It lets us recruit for the purpose of talking about representations and their creation the deeply understood logic of manipulating objects. So our notion of the creation of a representation already has some structure that can be projected to the blend to support the idea of 'putting' an element 'into' the representation. This blend has some remarkable emergent structure: we can for example 'put' a 'mountain' into the picture. Indeed, we can 'put' 'the moon' or 'the sun' into the picture, even though in the real world we cannot perform the corresponding action.

There is yet further useful structure in what we know of looking through a portal onto a scene. One of the things we know about a window or portal on a real scene is that we can throw things through it or go through it ourselves, and then be part of what we previously only saw. We can project to the blend this action of 'entrance', to give, in the blend, the possibility of moving something from our world into the picture world.

Olga's world reifies the 'Picture World' blend and additionally provides the possibility of moving an object from our world into the picture world.

The man who stole Olga's coat as a means of compelling her to marry him hid it not under a rock or up a tree or in any other normal locale in our world, but instead inside a painting, of Venice, by Canaletto. Within the logic of Olga's world, he literally 'hid' it 'in' Canaletto's painting. The coat is there, in the painting, in the exact sense that it was here, outside the picture, where any actual coat ought to be, but he moved it from here to there, and now it is there and not here. Olga's coat, in accordance with the physics of our world, can be in only one location. But in the hyper-blend that comes of blending Olga's Selkie World network and her Picture World network, this location can literally be inside a painting, and there is a means of moving things from locations outside the painting to locations inside the painting.

Olga's ignorance of the fact that her suitor hid her coat in the Canaletto painting presented her with a difficulty, but she overcame it, partly by studying art history to help her locate its hiding place. When she has located the painting, she faces a far greater challenge. As the suitor-thief had anticipated, it is not so easy for the land-bound selkie to take the coat out of the painting. To get to it, you must first physically enter the painting. But Olga cannot do that; she is too stout to squeeze through the frame. More daunting still, there is nothing but water across the bottom of the frame. Olga, massive and cumbersome, would fall into the water, and, unable to swim in her present unfortunate form, would drown. It is extremely witty to manipulate a selkie through fear of drowning.

Olga's world is a blend of two blending networks. One is the blend in which there are selkies, Selkie World. The other is a Picture World blend in which representation is compressed: in this Picture World network, the outer-space representation link between two separate mental inputs is compressed into uniqueness in the blend, so that the representation and what it represents are fused there into a single element. In this Picture World blend, the painting of the water really is water, for example, even as it is part of the painting. The Picture World blending network in Olga's World has, as mentioned, yet another input to the blend: the concept of a portal, such as a window, on a real scene. Projecting *portal* to the Picture World blend results in a Picture World that is much fuller than our view of it, a Picture World into which we can insert elements from the external world, such as a coat.

In the blend of blends that comes from blending these two blending networks, there is a selkie, and her coat can be hidden inside a painting (Figure 10.6). In Olga's world, although the separate Picture Worlds that correspond to individual pictures are rich, they do not possess anything like the completeness of our world. Someone who enters this world from the outside finds that the world inside the Picture World fades out. If you are in the Canaletto Picture World, and you walk through the marketplace to where the side streets lead deeper into the city, and you open yet one more door, you are then confronted with 'impenetrable grey mist'. There is not anything there, you see. As a character in the story says, 'It's a painting. It only goes so far.' There are other ways in which the Picture World in Olga's world is unlike our world, some of them influenced by projections from the representation input. For example, one can enter the Canaletto Picture World, and take a chicken away from its marketplace and dine on it. But when you go back, the chicken is still there. 'It's a painting', the story explains. 'When you go back, everything will be just exactly as it was before you came.'

Well, not exactly. Olga recruits a young girl to help her. This girl, Charlotte, is a talented but solitary child, adept at solving puzzles. She is visiting Ocracoke in November with her adequate but bored mother and adequate but distracted father. Through Olga's tacit coaching, Charlotte learns to see the people moving in the Canaletto painting. It is not clear to the reader that even a talented and motivated human child could perceive the Picture World of Canaletto's painting of Venice without both Olga's training and influence: Charlotte encounters the painting in Olga's home, which is perhaps a magical place itself. Olga sings, puts her arm around Charlotte, and unpins her own long hair so its smooth waves brush across Charlotte's bare arm. Charlotte sees, and a few minutes later goes through the frame to retrieve the coat. Charlotte is much smaller than Olga, and she can swim very well.

In general, 'Picture World' is a generic double-scope conceptual integration network which we have at our mental disposal to apply to any picture. It guides the mental act of blending and offers options. It does not dictate all

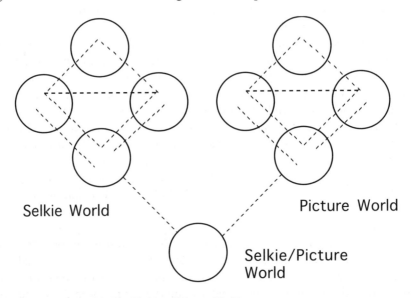

Figure 10.6. Blend of Selkie World and Picture World.

the details of the particular picture world. For example, some picture worlds can be entered by outsiders, others cannot. In some picture worlds, a visitor from outside the picture can be perceived by those who inhabit the picture, but in other cases, the visitor is invisible to the natives.

In Olga's world, the picture worlds can be entered, at least by those who have the knack to see that they are picture worlds. Insight brings new possibilities, a central theme of this story. In Olga's world, the usual blend of understanding and seeing that we all know and deploy ('I *see* what you are saying') undergoes remarkable conceptual development. Charlotte must work on her literal ability to see. She must strive to attain advanced vision. As she looks at the painting, its elements and their movement become clearer and clearer. Seeing better, she understands deeply. She already had, as Olga knew, talent in that direction: solitary and friendless Charlotte spent her time on jigsaw puzzles, looking at each piece, seeing its significance, perceiving its place. After their first meeting, Olga and Charlotte worked together on jigsaw puzzles, and Charlotte improved. The idea that Olga might have superior perceptual abilities is naturally projected to her from our knowledge of a seal: we are familiar with the idea that many animals have perceptual abilities we lack—the ability to hear sounds we cannot hear, to see patterns we cannot. Olga explains to Charlotte why she attends to people: 'I like to piece together their actions in order to understand their thoughts.' Charlotte has honed the identical knack through inspecting her mother and father. She turns it on Olga, too, and figures her out. She sees. She looks at the Canaletto painting, and she sees.

Charlotte hooks her foot on the frame, which turns out to be as solid as a rock banister (because it is a rock banister), and throws herself over the banister through the frame into the Grand Canal. Most of the rest of the story presents the adventures of the real girl, Charlotte, inside the Picture World that happens to contain the hidden coat of a selkie.

DOUBLE-SCOPE BLENDING AND EVERYDAY LANGUAGE

All of these networks rely on an important power of blending, to compress outer-space relations to inner-space elements in blends. It is a useful virtue of compression that it can result in human-scale elements in the blend that can then be expressed through existing basic human-scale grammatical constructions. While a full integration network, with its network of outer-space relations, might be quite difficult to express without using language that is extensive, discursive, or periphrastic, compression can save the day. The compressed human-scale mental array in the blend can often fit into available grammatical forms. For example, 'Mom could make us work' seems entirely prosaic. But the workaday grammar underlying that sentence is readily available for a wonderful blend that is compressed in the right way: 'Honey, you could make a blind man see'. Here is an example that involves a cascade of blending compressions, but that can be fit into everyday grammatical constructions because the blending compressions result in a conceptual array that suits the grammar:

> A halloween costume that limits sight or movement is an accident lurking in disguise.—National Public Radio warning a few days before Halloween, October 2000.

Let us consider one of these examples in some detail. It is an advertisement broadcast on the radio a few days before a three-day holiday weekend:

> At South Shore Lumber, get no sales tax Friday, Saturday, Sunday, and Monday!

In one mental space, there is a person buying something at South Shore Lumber during Friday, Saturday, Sunday, or Monday. The buyer pays a price. In another mental space that is highly analogous but somewhat disanalogous to the first, the buyer pays the price and an additional amount, namely, sales tax on the price. In the blend, the buyer pays the price. But the blend now contains an element that is available in neither of the inputs; it is a compression of the outer-space disanalogy between the two spaces. That new imaginative element in the blend is an event, a transitive event in which what is transferred to the buyer has a certain property, namely, the property of being the absence of something that is in one of the inputs. The buyer receives both what he buys and something extra, the absence of sales tax. This conceptual structure is very compressed and familiar, and can be expressed in an existing common grammatical construction, a transitive verb phrase whose noun phrase has a quantifier in the determiner sequence: 'get no sales tax'. One customer 'gets a screwdriver'; another 'gets a sheet of plywood'; and they both 'get no sales tax'. This last phrase prompts us to construct an entire blending network in order to understand the disanalogy between the two input spaces, and, motivated by that disanalogy, to go to South Shore Lumber (Figure 10.7).

Now consider a somewhat different example. I overheard someone ask in the Sangre de Cristo mountains, 'At what altitude do the deer turn into elk?' Here, we actually notice a compression pattern that is highly productive but usually unremarked. We notice that the analogy and disanalogy between the two mental spaces is compressed. In the blend, the outer-space analogy has been compressed to an inner-space category (the animals), and the outer-space disanalogy is compressed to a change for that category (the animals turn from deer to elk). Of course, no one is fooled or deluded. We know per-

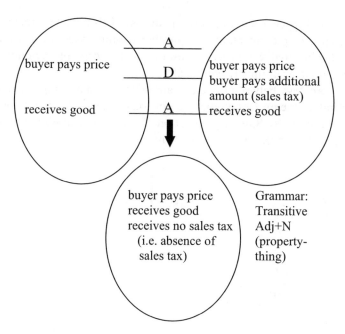

Figure 10.7.   Blending network for Get No Sales Tax.

fectly well that one species of animal does not change into a different species of animal. But the compressed blend has human-scale structure that can be expressed in an existing and relatively simple clausal construction. 'At what altitude do the deer turn into elk?' is striking, but the same conceptual and grammatical patterns sound perfectly straightforward in expressions like 'The new theory is that dinosaurs turned into birds'. In the outer-space, diffuse array of inputs, dinosaurs did not turn into birds. Instead, organisms were born and died over very long stretches of time. None of those organisms itself changed in any of the relevant ways. Instead, there were analogies and disanalogies across these organisms in a long line of descent, and cause–effect connections between ancestors and descendants. Those analogies and dis-analogies are compressed into change for a category in the blend: dinosaurs turned into birds. These compressions make it possible to use existing gram-matical forms to evoke the blend and hence the integration network. New ideas usually do not require new grammatical constructions. Instead, what they require for their expression is imaginative compression into a blend that fits existing grammatical.

Now consider a third phrase, heard on a National Public Radio broadcast:

We are eating the food off our children's plates. When we over-fish, we eat not only today's fish but tomorrow's fish, too.

In one mental space, we have a certain amount of fishing. This mental space has reference to present reality. In another mental space, we have a lower level of fishing that would lead causally to an acceptable amount of fish reproduction later in time (Figure 10.8).

The disanalogy between these two amounts of fish is compressed so that, in the blend for the present moment, a portion of present fishing is now 'over-fishing' (Figure 10.9). Similarly, a portion of present consumption of fish can be thought of as 'over-consumption' (Figure 10.10).

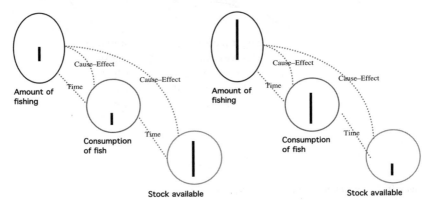

Figure 10.8. Mental space networks for fishing and stock, under two different initial conditions.

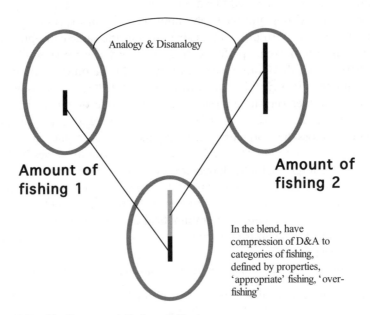

Figure 10.9. Blending network for 'over-fishing'.

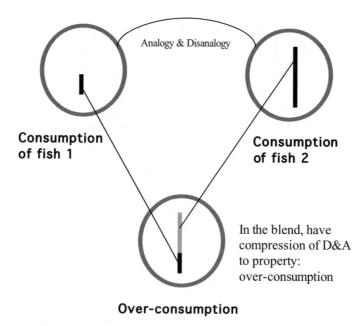

Consumption
of fish 1

Analogy & Disanalogy

Consumption
of fish 2

In the blend, have
compression of D&A
to property:
over-consumption

Over-consumption

Figure 10.10. Blending network for 'over-consumption'.

There are cause–effect vital relations between the over-fishing and the eating of the fish, and there is also a long-range Cause–Effect vital relation between the over-fishing and the smaller amount of fish reproduction and accordingly the smaller number of fish in the future. A blending network is created for a hypothetical future. In it, the disanalogy between the small number of fish that will be available in the future as a consequence of the over-fishing and the number of fish that would be there under appropriate fishing is compressed: from both of those future spaces we project the category *fish* to the hypothetical blend for the future, and the outer-space disanalogy between the inputs is compressed to a particular property: *missing*. Now we have *missing fish* in the blend for the hypothetical future (Figure 10.11)

The Time vital relation between now and the future is compressed by scaling it down to a day, so that, in the blend for the hypothetical future, the future is tomorrow. The *missing fish* in the blend for the future are now part of tomorrow's fish, the missing part. Then there is another compression: the cause–effect relations between eating fish now, fishing a lot now, and the missing part of tomorrow's fish are compressed into one scene in which the fish are missing tomorrow because we are eating them now (Figure 10.12).

This structure fits a standard frame of indulgence. We all know the normative stricture against raiding the icebox and eating up food reserved for

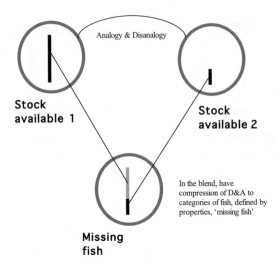

Figure 10.11. Blending network for 'missing' fish.

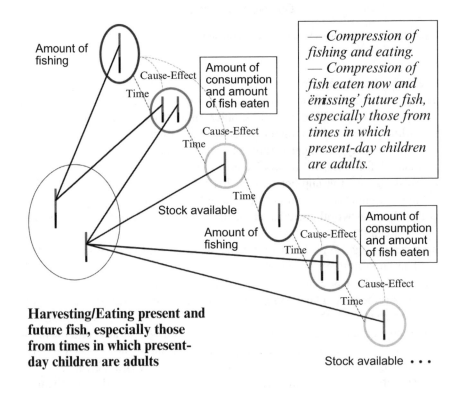

Figure 10.12. Blending network for Harvesting/Eating over time.

tomorrow. Dramatically, there is an additional compression that brings even the one-day lag down to the immediate moment. Those missing fish are not only in the space for tomorrow. Now the future fish are compressed with the food that is on our children's plates. But the food is 'missing'. Why? Because we are taking it from them and eating it ourselves. We are eating the food off our children's plates. This compression produces a highly human-scale scene, with a strong judgemental framing (Figure 10.13). (Note, incidentally, that we are taking the food off our children's plates, not the fish off their plates, because fish is not, for the relevant audience, the mainstay of child fare. It is also more exhaustive and serious to take their food than their fish.)

Again, no one is fooled by the blend. The fishing that is happening today out in the oceans is completely unlike taking away the food your children are eating today in order to eat it yourself. But the compressed blend, expressible in basic grammatical forms, evokes the entire and elaborate integration network, with the appropriate normative inferences.

Human beings, all of them, are geniuses at double-scope blending. They produce imaginative compressions inconceivable to other species. But they do it so routinely that we notice the performance only very rarely, such as when a writer places it explicitly on stage, as it were, drawing attention to it. Even

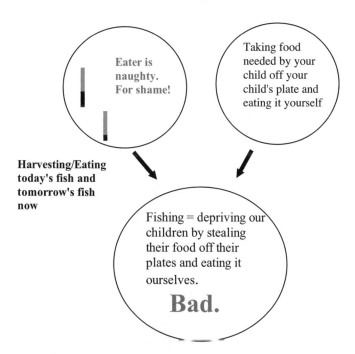

Figure 10.13. Blending network for Fishing/Eating food off our children's plates.

then we miss the extraordinary systematicity of the operation and sophistication of the operation. It is only now that cognitive science is beginning to
unearth the real powers of the imagination to show how different from their
ancestors human beings really are.

References

Fauconnier, G. 1997: *Mappings in Thought and Language.* Cambridge: Cambridge
    University Press.
Fauconnier, G. and Turner, M. 1998: Conceptual integration networks. *Cognitive
    Science,* 22(2) (April–June), 133–187.
Fauconnier, G. and Turner, M. 2002: *The Way We Think: Conceptual Blending and the
    Mind's Hidden Complexities.* New York: Basic.
Goguen, J. 1999: An introduction to algebraic semiotics, with application to user
    interface design. In Nehaniv, C. (ed.), *Computation for Metaphor, Analogy, and
    Agents.* Berlin: Springer-Verlag, 242–291.
Johnson, C. 1983: *Harold and the Purple Crayon.* New York: Harper & Row.
Turner, M. 2001: *Cognitive Dimensions of Social Science: The Way We Think About
    Politics, Economics, Law, and Society.* New York: Oxford University Press.
Turner, M. 2003: The Blending Website: http://blending.stanford.edu.
Turner, M. W. 1995: Aunt Charlotte and the NGA Portraits. *Instead of Three Wishes.*
    New York: Greenwillow Books. 45–71.

Part V

COGNITIVE ARCHITECTURE OF THE IMAGINATION

11

Specialized Inference Engines as Precursors of Creative Imagination?

PASCAL BOYER

Abstract. We usually consider imagination in terms of its high-end, creative products such as literature, religion, and the arts. To understand the evolution of imaginative capacities in humans, it makes more sense to focus on humble imaginations that are generally automatic and largely unconscious, and help us produce representations of, for example, what people will say next, that people exist when out of sight, or what aspects of our environment are potentially dangerous. These examples suggest that there may not be one faculty of imagination but many specialized 'what if' inferential systems in human minds.

INTRODUCTION

HOW DOES IMAGINATION WORK and how did it evolve? We have intuitive and seemingly plausible answers to these two questions. We tend to assume that imagination works mostly by suspending some principles that normally constrain inferential processes. We also assume that imagination evolved because it allowed organisms to transcend the limits of the here and now and to create entirely new objects and techniques.

Unfortunately, these two assumptions are not altogether compatible, at least not in this vague form. First, organisms evolve by small increments that provide efficiency gains in solving particular problems, not by hitting upon a grand new strategy for dealing with *any* odd problem (Williams 1966). Second, suspending inferential principles should result not in novel insight but in the proliferation of irrelevant associations, hardly an efficient strategy (Tooby *et al.* 2000).

Proceedings of the British Academy **147**, 239–258. © The British Academy 2007.

Part of the problem may be that we usually consider the hallmark of imagination as *creativity* or *originality*— and we then try to work downwards, as it were, from such grandiose and exceptional achievements to more common underlying cognitive processes (Boden 1991, 1994). But human imagination does not just produce high flights of creative fancy. It is also involved in the production of highly stable and fairly predictable representations of possible situations. In some domains of experience, human minds seem automatically to suggest 'what if' alternatives to current or past experience. For instance, faced with a negative outcome, we cannot help imagine what would have happened had the actual conditions been slightly different (Roese and Olson 1995). We cannot look at a tool without figuring out in what way and for what purpose it may be used (Grafton *et al.* 1997). We interpret certain aspects of the environment as signs of other agents' presence, natural or supernatural (Barrett 2000). We are often led to think of potential dangers in our environments for which there are only indirect cues (Fiddick 2004). In such situations, the production of 'what if' scenarios is largely outside conscious control and deliberation, although the results, in the form of possible outcomes, are consciously experienced. So, when we consider the evolution of imagination, it may make sense to start with this humble capacity, at the low end of the imagination spectrum, and then see to what extent it is involved in the creativity that we find characteristic of human imagination (Ward 1995).

Considering this partly tacit form of imagination may be of help in addressing two central questions about human imagination, concerning *domain-generality* and *premise-generation* respectively. The question of domain-generality is this: Can we describe imagination of this kind as the output of a particular *faculty*, a functionally distinct system that handles counterfactuals and their consequences? Or is it, alternatively, the output of several specialized 'what if' inference engines, each of which is dedicated to a particular domain of occurrences and possible scenarios? These two accounts of productive imagination rely on different assumptions about the neuro-cognitive processes involved and carry different implications for what could be expected from productive imagination.

The question of premise-generation is this: are there any constraints on the processes that create the first steps (the premises) of imaginary activities? A very attractive account of imagination depicts it as a random generation of thoughts, followed by the selective retention of those thoughts that support enough inferences to constitute 'viable' imaginary scenarios. Or is there an early selection of imagination premises? Again, these alternative accounts imply very different evolutionary and functional processes.

PREMISE GENERATION: A LATE SELECTION MODEL

We have a great number of studies about the way a mind handles imaginative productions, once it entertains some counterfactual assumption (e.g. *I am a kangaroo*). But we know little about the processes that make some such assumptions (*I am a giraffe*) much more likely than others (*prime numbers are mischievous*).

To illustrate how this issue of premise generation is both central and generally ignored in cognitive models of imagination, consider the closely related domain of pretence. Pretence starts in young children some time around 18 months. It involves typical behaviours such as behaving towards an object (a cardboard box) as if it was another one (a car), and in later developments the child behaving as though they were an animal or another person. There are at least three different computational accounts of pretence, in terms of simulation (Gordon and Olson 1998), propositional attitudes (Leslie 1987) or hypothetical reasoning (Nichols and Stich 1999). These models are accounts of *pretence management*, as it were, rather than *pretence creation*. Our cognitive models of pretence combined with relevant neuroimaging and neuropsychological evidence reveal some fundamental ways of processing counterfactual information.

This leaves aside the matter of how these pretence premises are generated. This is a difficult question, notably because it is difficult to formulate in a precise and tractable way. Perhaps the best way is to start with obvious observations about the occurrence of pretence in children. Pretence is an early development and is highly principled, as I stressed above, but it is interesting that it is also somewhat constrained in its themes and targets. Children generally start by pretending that one common, accessible object (a plastic box) is a more interesting but inaccessible one (like a truck), or that a person-like object (doll, toy animal) really is animate; they also develop animal pretence, behaving like their idea of a tiger or dog or elephant; later they also pretend with social roles, acting like doctors, shopkeepers, etc. We know very little about these limits, because our cognitive models operate downstream, as it were, from premise generation.

There is one very tempting way of solving this question—which I would call 'psychological selectionism'. The assumption would be that there are *no* principled processes that generate imaginative premises. That is, the generation of such initial premises is a random process of thought associations produced by the simple relaxation of constraints ordinarily imposed on trains of thought and inferences. Under this account, it would seem difficult to explain why human imagination tends to go back to the same themes, over and over again, and eschew some possible conceptual combinations. But the difficulty could be solved by the other half of a Darwinian model, the process of selective retention. Although there are random mutations of thoughts that produce many possible imagination premises, they are not equally 'fit' in the human mind (Campbell 1960). This is what I would call a *late-selection* model, in the sense that the selection of particular contents occurs, in functional terms, after a generation phase during which there is no constraint on what thoughts are entertained.

This is a very tempting hypothesis, not just because it is clearly parsimonious, but also because at least some phenomenology of imagination seems compatible with it. Hypgnagogic states for instance often include associations that are extraordinarily difficult to express once the mind is fully conscious again. One entertains associations such as *my sister really is a prime number, electricity is parallel to cheese* which lead to other thoughts of the same kind—unless, that is, one becomes sufficiently awake to consider them, at which point their very content seems to evaporate. The same occurs in various altered states of consciousness induced by either 'disciplines' (e.g. meditation, self-hypnosis) or the use of drugs. Importantly, even in such states, not all associations are that elusive. From dreams or hallucinations or semiconscious states we can also retrieve associations such as *my sister just turned into a huge lobster* or *it is raining needles* that are perfectly fine imagination premises. So we do sometimes experience both quasi-random generation of thoughts of different 'fitness' and a subsequent selection of those that are 'fit' for further processing.

RELEVANCE AND EARLY SELECTION

The mutation-selection account may be insufficient. First, imagination-premises are rarely as diverse as a random generation process would imply. Indeed, hypnagogic states and altered states of consciousness are remarkable precisely because they include thoughts that do not stand the test of processing, as it were. In most other contexts, the imagination-premises that become accessible to conscious inspection are all fit for processing. Second, it is difficult to explain how random generation and selective retention would result in the recurrent themes that we observe in such domains as religious imagination or literary fiction, and in fact in most domains of human imagination, as we will see below.

These limits on the range of recurrent human imagination would suggest that the selection of imagination premises operates, not in terms of formal processing capacity, but in terms of the connections between those premises and background knowledge. One may speculate that imagination premises survive cycles of processing and transmission to the extent that they generate novel inferences, relative to semantic memory; and that these novel inferences would be all the more likely to be retained as they require less processing effort. Understanding imagination-premises in this way, in terms of relevance (Sperber and Wilson 1995), would certainly begin to explain some of the differences mentioned above. Some possible imagination premises (e.g. the artefact without physical existence) support fewer inferences than other ones (e.g. the person without physical existence). For instance, an invisible person may have designs on you, may be watching you, may form moral judgements about you, may be an ally or enemy, etc.; an invisible object is hard to detect . . . and that's that. This difference may explain the different cultural distributions of these two types of concepts (Boyer 2000). So it would seem that a relevance-based model could in principle account for some recurrent themes of human imagination, in terms of a selective process that links them with non-imaginary assumptions.

But the relevance interpretation implies that the generation of imagination-premises (and not just their selection) is crucially dependent on prior representations in semantic memory. Relevance is not just a function of novel inferences generated but also of the processing effort required to activate assumptions that would support these inferences. This is where the organization of semantic memory has a direct effect. To remain in the domain of religious imagination, why is it that non-physical spirits are universal while punctuate spirits (e.g. that exist only on Wednesdays) are never considered? A simple answer would be that it takes great effort to represent the concept of a person (from which a spirit concept is derived) and remove the feature of temporal continuity from its representation. In other words, a feature of semantic memory (that persons are continuous, not punctuate) makes the *generation* of imagination premises with punctuate persons very unlikely.

In the following I will follow this strategy in the description of several domains of imagination, arguing that there may be an *early selection* process that makes certain conceptual combinations much more likely than others. This pre-selection process stems from the fact that in most domains of knowledge we routinely process 'what if' scenarios that produce counterfactual assumptions and inferences from these assumptions. These spontaneous, generally non-controlled imaginings, in my view, constitute templates on which more deliberate and creative imagination then builds more original scenarios that undergo creative selection. If this is the case, if most knowledge domains include some what-if inference engine, it would follow that these inference engines are independent and specialized—in other words that there is not one imagination but many specialized imaginations.

GODS, DEAD PEOPLE, AND IMAGINARY FRIENDS

Representations of supernatural agents are universal in human cultures, with very similar features (Boyer 1994a) and may have been present from the earliest stages of the cultural explosion in human evolution (Burkert 1996; Mithen 1996 and Chapter 1). In the past 15 years, various accounts of specific features of religion have converged to constitute what could be called a common or 'standard' model of religious thought and behaviour, based on the notion that religious concepts are a by-product of ordinary cognition (Lawson and McCauley 1990; Boyer 1994b, 2001; Barrett 1996; Pyysiainen 2001; Atran 2002). They 'parasitize' cognitive structures that evolved for other, non-religious reasons. This presupposes a 'selectionist' view of human cultural evolution, as presented in theories of meme-transmission and cultural epidemics (Boyd and Richerson 1985; Sperber 1996). Religious concepts and norms that we find widespread in human cultures are those that resist the eroding, distorting influence of individual transmission better than others.

The standard account stipulates that there is a limited catalogue of supernatural concepts, a subset of which is found in religious systems. Supernatural concepts (found in religion but also in fantasy, dreams, 'superstitions', etc.) are informed by very general assumptions from domain concepts such as PERSON, LIVING THING, MAN-MADE OBJECT. A spirit is a special kind of person, a magic wand a special kind of artefact, a talking tree a special kind of plant. Such notions are salient and inferentially productive because they combine (i) specific features that violate some default expectations for the domain with (ii) expectations held by default as true of the entire domain (Boyer 1994a; Barrett 1996). These combinations of explicit violation and tacit inferences are culturally widespread and may constitute a *memory optimum* (Barrett and Nyhof 2001; Boyer and Ramble 2001). That is, they are better recalled than conceptual combinations that are either more outlandish or more in conformity with expectations.

A subset of this supernatural repertoire consists of religious concepts proper, which are taken by many people as, firstly, quite plausibly real and secondly, of great social and personal importance. These concepts generally describe *intentional agents* so that all standard agency assumptions are projected onto them (Lawson and McCauley 1990). These agents are generally construed as combining (i) explicitly transmitted, counter-intuitive physical or biological features (going through walls, being eternal, born of a god's thigh, etc.), together with (ii) tacitly projected, standard mental features (having perception, memory, intentions and beliefs). In other words, concepts of gods and ancestors require minor but consequential 'tweaking' of standard theory of mind (Barrett and Keil 1996). In this sense, the anthropomorphism that is widespread in religious concepts (Guthrie 1993) is also extremely selective. The domain of human features that is invariably projected is *intentional agency*, more frequently and more consistently than any other type of human characteristics.

A similar and related projection is found in the familiar but under-studied phenomenon of interaction with dead people. As Jesse Bering and colleagues have shown, common intuitions about the dead, especially the recently dead, are independent from explicit statements of beliefs in the afterlife (Bering 2002). That is, people's judgements about whether, for example, a dead person can think, remember, etc., are only partly predicted by religious or metaphysical commitments. A strong intuition seems to be that mental states seem all the more likely to be projected onto the dead, the more 'purely mental' they are and the more distant from physiology. So the dead are described as *thinking* and *remembering* more often than *feeling*, which occurs more often than *being hungry* (Bering 2002). Indeed, a common feature of interaction with the recently dead is a discrepancy between biological intuitions, which have no problem representing the cessation of function associated with death (Barrett 2005), and our social intuitions which do not stop with biological death (Boyer 2001): thus the recurrent phenomenon of being angry with the dead or proud of them as if they were real social partners.

Another salient case of a common domain of productive imagination is the frequent creation of imaginary friends by young children. From an early age (between 3 and 10) many children (perhaps more than half of them) engage in durable and complex relationships with such agents (Taylor 1999 and Chapter 4). These imagined persons or personified animals, sometimes but not always derived from stories or cartoons or other cultural folklore, follow the child around, play with her, converse with her, etc. Taylor's studies show that having long-term relationships with non-existent characters is not a sign of confusion between fantasy and reality (Taylor and Hort 1990). Young children know perfectly well that their invisible companions are not 'there' in the same sense as real friends and other people.

SOCIAL INTELLIGENCE AND THE ABSENT AGENT

Why is it that a significant part of social interaction takes place with either imagined supernatural agents or actual but deceased agents? Perhaps this feature of spontaneous human imagination is less surprising given human capacities for 'mind-reading' or 'theory of mind', geared to interpreting other agents' (or one's own) behaviour in terms of goals, beliefs, memories, and inferences (Leslie 1987; Perner 1991; Whiten 1991). Experimental studies of mindreading, especially of its developmental aspects, have generally focused on actual interaction. Participants were required to infer unobservable mental states or future behaviour from observable phenomena such as objects, facial expressions, or previous utterances.

The capacity is of great evolutionary advantage, given the human dependence on social interaction. Humans live in a 'cognitive niche' (Tooby and DeVore 1987), in that they, more than any other species, depend on information, especially on information provided by other human beings, and on information about other human beings. This dependence means that mental dispositions that help maintain rich and flexible representations of others, of their goals and their mental states, is crucial.

Representations of agents *in absentia* are a constant feature of human thinking. Many, perhaps most, of our thoughts about other people are entertained when they are not around. Memories of what people did or said, as well as expectations, fears, and hopes of what they may do, are a constant theme of trains of thought and ruminations (and also the quintessential subject matter of social gossip). It may be a special feature of the human mind that we can create such representations and more importantly run social inferences about them. It is certainly a central capacity of human thinking, appears early, is universal and distinctive of normal human minds. This capacity to engage in social interaction *in absentia* is probably at the origin of all the other dispositions for simulated interaction described above.

But why should we have this capacity? From an evolutionary standpoint, it would seem that such thoughts take time and energy away from consideration of present people. An explanation may be that thoughts about absent agents are necessary and useful given the computational constraints of social interaction. Any such situation presents us with a whole gamut of possible actions from our partners as well as possible reactions to our own behaviour. Reactions on our part should be fast but also appropriate. The potential cost of mismanagement of social relations is huge for humans, given their dependence on cooperation for survival (Boyd and Richerson 1990; Gintis 2000). Now there is a trade-off between speed and appropriateness, given the complexity of inferences required for even the simplest social interaction (Cosmides and Tooby 1997). What each actor did or said may convey several intentions, to which there may be several possible responses, and so on.

One way to bypass this computational hurdle may be to have a prepared catalogue of possible interaction scenarios. These would be constructed when the other agent is not around, which would allow sluggish explicit inferences and the slow comparison of different scenarios in terms of plausibility. These scenarios would include appropriate responses. They could be tagged in memory in such a way that they can be quickly activated in actual interaction and provide an intuitive guide to apposite behaviour.

There is some preliminary evidence for the preparation and use of such scenarios in actual social behaviour (Malle *et al.* 2001; Saarni 2001). To focus on one of the domains mentioned above, Taylor notes that the relationship with an imagined companion is a stable one, so the child must compute the companion's reactions, taking into account not just the imagined friend's personality but also past events in their relationship. What the companion does or says is constrained by their personality and must remain consistent and plausible even in this fantastic domain. Also, companions are often used to provide an alternative viewpoint on a situation. They may find odd information unsurprising or frightening situations manageable (Taylor 1999). So imaginary companions may constitute a form of *training* for the social mind, helping build the social capacities required to maintain coherent social interaction (Taylor and Carlson 1997).

These examples illustrate the *early-selection* process I outlined above. That is, imagination premises seem to be constrained in their generation, even before they are entertained and found inferentially rich or poor. Explicit, and apparently quite diverse, religious concepts are rooted in ordinary and recurrent ways of thinking about absent agents, which are informed by largely tacit principles. This 'absent-agent' cognition, in the view proposed here, creates a whole domain of possible scenarios and inferences about non-physically present agents. Some of these scenarios are then taken up by explicit imagination to become religious thought. Note that only *some* of them will do. As I said above, not all concepts of non-present agents are 'good' for such purposes. Some are too distant from ordinary intuition to support inferences (e.g. gods that exist only on Wednesdays), and some are not attention-grabbing. In this view, then, religious and other supernatural thoughts are the outcome of a late-selection of representations pre-selected by everyday, largely tacit processes of productive imagination.

MIMESIS AS AN EVOLUTIONARY ISSUE

To proceed one step further in the possibilities of imaginative creation, why do people spend inordinate amounts of time and energy thinking about agents they know to be pure fiction? Why the obvious emotional investment in these imagined agents?

There are two puzzles about fiction. One is the classical conundrum about reference, that is, the extent to which we activate standard knowledge in order to make sense of fictional situations and processes. Like other forms of counterfactual thinking, fiction requires both a limited suspension and a massive preservation of default assumptions about the world—and different genres can be defined in terms of how these two operations are handled. Terms such as 'suspension of disbelief' do not adequately convey the complexities of this very special cognitive activity. Most philosophers and critics interested in the issue have traditionally focused on the logical aspects of fiction (Searle 1979).

Another puzzle concerns the motivation for literary fiction, that is, the evolutionary scenarios that could lead to our common need for and enjoyment of fiction. It would seem at first sight that these have little to do with evolution by natural selection. Attention to non-existent situations and people may be a diversion from actual ones; only the latter would seem to matter as far as survival and reproduction are concerned.

Progress in these two questions may require that we consider another striking phenomenon, the fact that literary fiction (either oral or written) tends to focus on a limited number of recurrent themes, despite massive cultural and historical differences. Despite the occasional opacity induced by different norms and practices, the literary productions of other cultures are generally extremely easy to understand and enjoy, in contrast to other domains of culture such as music or food or clothing. The main reason is that it is very easy to identify exotic themes, genres, and rhetorical devices as broadly similar to familiar ones. Why is it that literature is about a small catalogue of themes and situations? It is clear that literary themes are very close to evolutionary concerns, such as protection against predators (or pseudo-predators such as the Big Bad Wolf), parental investment, proper relations with kin and non-kin, the fitness cost of being orphaned and interacting with stepparents (Leoutsakas 2004), and of course cultural identity and mate-selection, as any reader of Henry James and Jane Austen will confirm.

It is only recently that evolutionary anthropologists and cognitive scientists have started to consider this question and thereby to address the issues of logical status and possible adaptive value (Carroll 1995; Storey 1996; Hogan 2003). A useful starting point to survey these models is to observe that for most people in most human cultures, fiction is of great interest by virtue of its *mimetic* properties. (In view of this cultural universal, it is of course rather unfortunate that the fashion in recent literary studies has been a dogmatic denial of the phenomenon. Literary theorists' vituperative refusal to consider that texts could ever refer to anything has led them to ignore the potential contribution of psychological and biological research to understanding the appeal of literary fiction. On the sorry state of current literary theory, see, e.g., Easterlin and Riebling, 1993; Storey, 1996; Turner, 1996; Carroll, 2004.) Also, literary fiction is not just general counterfactual thinking but, overwhelmingly, counterfactual thinking about *persons*. The first feature has been the object of recent cognitive research, aimed at showing that a narrative capacity was central to the development of the modern human mind about 100,000 years ago (Dautenhahn 2003), that it is pervasive in human cognition (Bruner 1991; Turner 1996; Hogan 2003), and that it appears very early in cognitive development (Ackerman 1988; Fivush *et al.* 1995). One of the universal features of fiction is the construction of *characters*, that is, imagined agents whose personalities are stable enough to provide a source of expectations and inferences along a narrative. This would suggest that creating and enjoying stories is, among many other things, an exercise in speculative intuitive psychology (Zunshine 2003). In a similar way as absent-agent cognition, it may be valuable mostly for the training it provides, for its pedagogical function (Steen and Owens 2001). What fiction provides is an extensive catalogue of persons and situations, in combinations that are varied enough and complex enough to provide putative scenarios for future interactions as well as the means to make sense of past interactions.

FICTION AND INTUITIVE PERSONOLOGY

This functional interpretation may be insufficient, at least if we construe 'theory of mind' in the narrow sense used in current developmental research. The term in principle denotes the capacities involved in ordinary 'mindreading'. But in practice most studies of theory of mind have focused on the fundamental concepts and processes involved in the capacity, e.g. the concepts of 'belief' and 'intention' and 'agent', and their absence or impairment in some pathologies (Leslie 1994; Baron-Cohen 1995).

Fiction certainly requires (and may help train) those basic parts of 'theory of mind', the detection of inferences, the differentiation between actual states of affairs and various persons' representations of those states of affairs. But it is difficult to see this as its main benefit, mainly because such basic capacities are developed very early and in a robust way in normal minds.

Actual social interaction does not just require the fundamental processes of theory of mind, but also a vast knowledge-base about the way persons behave, an intuitive human psychology in the broader sense (Astington 2003). Smooth social interaction generally requires intuitions that amount to adequate understandings of motivation, feeling, memory, emotion, and reasoning in other agents. Consider even the simplest operations of everyday mindreading. They require assumptions about mental functioning, the connections between intentions and actions, the way people estimate their own actions, the way they are motivated by greed or benevolence or spite, the way a disappointing experience can modify their behaviour, and so on. Each of these assumptions is also modulated, in the case of persons we know, by specific parameters that constitute that person's personality.

One might call this domain of knowledge an intuitive *personology*, a tacit set of principled intuitions on how behaviour is generated in human beings and how these agents differ from one another. This is the domain of intuitive principles that inform people's expectations about others' behaviours. These principles describe both what people are in general and along what dimensions they may differ as individuals. There are few accounts of this domain in psychology. For instance, the intuitive explanation of behaviour used to be described in social psychology in terms of attribution theory (Heider 1958) which is psychologically insufficient (Harvey *et al.* 1981) and is not entirely consistent with more recent findings on theory of mind (Malle *et al.* 2000). Even in personality psychology, what matters are real differences between people, not people's conceptions of these differences, although people routinely construct social psychological and personality-based explanations of others.

A central task in narrative comprehension is the attribution of causes to behaviours, in terms of intentions, stable dispositions, and contextual factors. Also, an essential tension in fiction is the interplay between pure-observer and pure-actor viewpoints (Todorov 1977). On these two fronts, it would seem that the enjoyment of fiction provides a rich training-ground by providing us with a rich and varied set of exercises in applied personology.

This is why I would suggest that literary imagination, like its religious counterpart, is in large part the outcome of an early selection of themes and templates, a set of implicit constraints on what premises can feed into imaginative consideration. True, literary fiction, especially with the use of literacy, explores fictional worlds often far removed from our common intuitions about persons. However, the genres most commonly enjoyed by most people in most cultures remain very close to these intuitions, while providing a refined set of central or extreme examples. Fiction about exceptional people in normal situations or normal people in exceptional situations may help fine-tune our knowledge-base about the fewer people we actually encounter in social interaction.

VARIOUS DOMAINS OF RITUALIZED BEHAVIOUR

One salient form of cultural and personal imagination is the creation of complicated rituals. Characteristics of ritualized behaviour include stereotypy, rigidity, repetition, and apparent lack of rational motivation. Behaviour of this kind is found in cultural rituals, religious or not; in many normal children's complicated routines; in the pathology of obsessive-compulsive disorders (OCDs); in normal adults around certain stages of the life-cycle. These various behaviours may be different manifestations of a specialized mental system with particular neural correlates (Boyer and Lienard 2006).

Standard criteria for OCD in the DSM-IV include (a) intrusive thoughts that (b) cause distress and (c) are accompanied by ritualistic behaviours that

(d) disturb normal activity and (e) are recognized as irrational by the patient (American Psychiatric Association 1995). Typical obsessions include contamination and contagion (fear of catching other people's germs, ingesting contaminated substances, passing on diseases to one's children or others), possible harm to others or to oneself (e.g. handling kitchen utensils and wounding people), as well as social ostracism following shameful or aggressive acts (thoughts about assaulting others, shouting obscenities, exhibitionism, etc.). Most patients are aware that their obsessions are unreasonable and their rituals pointless but report that neither is easily controlled. In most cases the obsessive thoughts are accompanied by rituals supposed to allay anxiety. Some patients engage in bouts of washing or cleaning tools or utensils. Others verify that they locked their door, rolled up the car window, or turned off the gas knobs. Still others are engaged in constant counting activities or need to group objects in sets of particular numbers.

Most normal children develop ritual-like behaviours at some point between the ages of 2 and 10. They report concerns about dirt and cleanliness, and demonstrate a preoccupation with just-right ordering of objects, preferred household routines, repeating action over and over or a specific number of times, strongly preferred food, rituals for eating, awareness of minute details of one's home, hoarding, bedtime rituals.

PRECAUTION SYSTEMS AND THEIR MIMICRY

Some clinical psychologists have suggested that OCD is a perturbation or exaggeration of functions to do with protection from fitness threats (Mataix-Cols *et al.* 2005). The major domains of obsessiveness correspond to particular dangers of evolutionary significance (contagion, harm to infants, social offence, hoarding of precious resources). Szechtman and Woody (2004) put forward a general neuropsychological model of OCD pathology centred on what they call the 'safety motivation system'. The system is present in all normal human beings and monitors external clues of danger. Note that the system deals only with clues of *potential,* not currently detectable, danger. Security-motivation is distinct from the various fear-mechanisms that handle *actual,* currently present danger.

This makes sense of the particular neural structures involved in the pathology. Like Tourette syndrome and some forms of attention-deficit disorders, OCD corresponds to a specific dysfunction of the basal ganglia and of their connectivity, especially of cortex–striatum–thalamus–cortex loops. These structures are involved in the construction of motor 'chunks' or action routines so that a failure of inhibitory connections from the striatum is probably involved in such behaviours. Cortical structures are also involved, in particular the anterior cingulate and orbitofrontal cortex (OFC). Given the anterior cingulate's role in the detection or prevention of errors and the OFC's role in inhibition, it would seem that OCD pathology combines a hyper-vigilance to possible cues for required motor action in the environment with a difficulty in inhibiting reactions to such cues, even when they prove to present a minimal threat.

If this model is valid, the kind of imagination deployed in the creation of individual rituals (by children and patients) or collective ceremonies seems largely constrained by the kinds of actions and action-sequences identified by a prior Precaution system. It is of course perfectly possible to create many other kinds of ceremonies that go beyond the themes of contagion, predation, and social offence. But it is also remarkable that most rituals in most places tend to revolve around these themes and to use action-patterns that are typical of this prior system.

SPECIALIZED INFERENCE ENGINES

In each of the domains surveyed here, high-end creative elaborations (fiction, religious belief, ritual) seem to be rooted in the more modest achievements of an everyday form of productive imagination. Supernatural agency is an extension of ordinary absent agency; religious and other social rituals are off-shoots of a Precaution system; fiction requires and enriches our everyday personology. In each of these domains, too, we find that ordinary productive imagination stems from the operation of 'what if' systems or rather a 'what if' component of diverse knowledge systems. Our ordinary agency systems can function in conditions where the usual stimulus that triggers them (the physical presence of an agent) is removed or replaced with a memory or a generated representation of the agent. In the same way, our personology can be applied to non-existent agents and still deliver constrained inferences about fictional situations. Our Precaution systems go beyond immediate danger to potential threats to fitness that are generally possible rather than actual. Our capacities for handling tools monitor properties of objects (such as affordances) that only exist relative to a particular range of possible goals.

The operation of 'what if' inferences seems constrained by different principles in the different domains we have surveyed. For instance, the Precaution system responds only to particular cues in the environment and delivers emotional responses (in the form of slightly or radically increased anxiety) as well as typical responses (disgust, avoidance, cleaning, ordering). Our intuitions about absent agents are couched in the mentalistic idiom of theory of mind, connecting behaviour to beliefs and goals and perceptions. Our intuitive personology takes these mentalistic descriptions of behaviour as an input and produces causal descriptions in terms of such processes as motivation and reasoning.

Obviously, this does not mean that all creative imagination is bound to follow these well-trodden paths. It only means that there is a strong likelihood, all else being equal, that themes preselected by intuitive inference mechanisms will be found at the basis of creative imagination. In terms of a relevance model, this would be because their processing cost is less than that of manufacturing entirely novel imagination premises (Sperber and Wilson 1995).

IS THERE A COUNTERFACTUAL FACULTY?

Our examples also suggest that the cognitive processes involved are *specific* to each domain. The way a precaution system generates descriptions of potential danger is not at all the way absent-agent cognition creates descriptions of mental states. Different circumstances trigger activation of these different forms of spontaneous productive imagination and the operating principles are different too. This stands in contrast to the traditional way of considering imagination and counterfactuals as the outcome of a central reasoning process, supposedly similar in its operating principles whatever the domain considered. The most precise cognitive accounts focus on counterfactuals, and specify general processes that should be briefly compared to the model outlined here.

In Kahneman's model of norms and comparisons (Kahneman and Miller 2002), each event triggers activation of memories for similar events, which together construct a 'norm' relative to which the current situation is evaluated. The different availability of alternatives is what drives the construction of counterfactuals. The fact that you *could* have avoided this fender-bender by braking a bit earlier is highly salient because the occurrences of braking early enough are highly accessible (Kahneman and Miller 2002). However, the theory does not account for the obvious connection between counterfactuals and current goals. For instance, 'upward' conditionals (in which imagined situations are better than the actual one) seem to be a default while 'downward' conditionals seem to require more effort (Roese and Olson 1997). This is the starting point of Roese and colleagues' 'two-stage' model of conditionals, in which goal-obstruction or failure creates a need for counterfactual production, and norms and categories support the content of the counterfactual (Roese *et al*. 2005). These different models predict the production of and reactions to counterfactuals *in general*, not in different domains. The same can be said of most developmental research in this domain, focusing on children's *general* ability to detach themselves from factual assumptions (Kavanaugh and Harris 2000; Robinson and Beck 2000).

In the current state of this research, it is not possible to say whether such domain-general models can be reconciled with (or can supersede) the domain-specific processes presented here. For one thing, domain-general models are not 'general' in the sense that they have been tested in a variety of cognitive domains and found to have the same explanatory power in all of them. They are general only in the sense that their authors *assume* that similar processes would operate across domains. As a consequence potential domain-differences are rarely explored. (There are of course exceptions. Consider for instance Tetlock (1998) in the domain of politics, showing how the interaction of world-view premises and outcomes shapes available counterfactuals. See also Fiske and Tetlock (1997) on the limits of moral imagination and moral counterfactuals.)

Classical domain-general models are probably insufficient. As Kahneman and colleagues point out, some counterfactuals are produced spontaneously while others are more deliberate and effortful (Kahneman and Miller 2002). This may be because part of the counterfactual production is operated by automatic processes, while the more creative part is under cognitive control (Roese *et al.* 2005). This description in terms of process-dissociation is very close to the model presented here, with both specialized inference systems and explicit, controlled creative imagination. However, once one admits that counterfactuals and imagination are elaborations on the basis of an automatic and constant production of relevant alternatives, it would seem that the latter must emanate from the various systems that produce efficient interpretations of current situations. And since these systems seem to be highly domain-specific, it is plausible to consider that creative imagination too is rooted in very diverse specialized imaginations.

References

Ackerman, B. P. 1988: Reason inferences in the story comprehension of children and adults. *Child Development*, 59, 1426–1442.

American Psychiatric Association 1995: *Diagnostic and Statistical Manual of Mental Disorders* (4th edn). Washington, DC: American Psychiatric Publishing, Inc.

Astington, J. W. 2003: Sometimes necessary, never sufficient: False-belief understanding and social competence. In Repacholi, B. and Slaughter, V. (eds), *Individual Differences in Theory of Mind: Implications for Typical and Atypical Development*. New York: Psychology Press, 13–38.

Atran, S. A. 2002: *In Gods We Trust. The Evolutionary Landscape of Religion*. Oxford: Oxford University Press.

Baron-Cohen, S. 1995: *Mindblindness: An Essay on Autism and Theory of Mind*. Cambridge, MA: MIT Press.

Barrett, H. C. 2005: Cognitive development and the understanding of animal behavior. In Ellis, B. J. (ed.), *Origins of the Social Mind: Evolutionary Psychology and Child Development*. New York: The Guilford Press, 438–467.

Barrett, J. L. 1996: Anthropomorphism, intentional agents, and conceptualizing god. Unpublished PhD dissertation, Cornell University.

Barrett, J. L. 2000: Exploring the natural foundations of religion. *Trends in Cognitive Sciences,* 4(1), 29–34.

Barrett, J. L. and Keil, F. C. 1996: Conceptualizing a non-natural entity: Anthropomorphism in god concepts. *Cognitive Psychology,* 31, 219–247.

Barrett, J. L. and Nyhof, M. 2001: Spreading non-natural concepts: The role of intuitive conceptual structures in memory and transmission of cultural materials. *Journal of Cognition and Culture,* 1(1), 69–100.

Bering, J. M. 2002: Intuitive conceptions of dead agents' minds: The natural foundations of afterlife beliefs as phenomenological boundary. *Journal of Cognition and Culture,* 2(4), 263–308.

Boden, M. A. 1991: *The Creative Mind: Myths and Mechanisms*. New York: Basic Books.

Boden, M. A. 1994: *Dimensions of Creativity*. Cambridge, MA: MIT Press.

Boyd, R. and Richerson, P. J. 1985: *Culture and the Evolutionary Process*. Chicago: University of Chicago Press, 111–132.

Boyd, R. and Richerson, P. J. 1990: Culture and cooperation. In Mansbridge, J. J. *et al.* (eds), *Beyond Self-interest*. Chicago, IL: University of Chicago Press, 111–132.

Boyer, P. 1994a: Cognitive constraints on cultural representations: Natural ontologies and religious ideas. In Hirschfeld, L. A. and Gelman, S. (eds), *Mapping the Mind: Domain-specificity in Culture and Cognition*. New York: Cambridge University Press, 391–411.

Boyer, P. 1994b: *The Naturalness of Religious Ideas: A Cognitive Theory of Religion*. Berkeley, CA: University of California Press.

Boyer, P. 2000: Functional origins of religious concepts: Conceptual and strategic selection in evolved minds [Malinowski Lecture 1999]. *Journal of the Royal Anthropological Institute,* 6, 195–214.

Boyer, P. 2001: *Religion Explained. Evolutionary Origins of Religious Thought*. New York: Basic Books.

Boyer, P. and Lienard, P. 2006: Why ritualized behaviour in humans? Precaution systems and action-parsing in developmental, pathological and cultural rituals. *Behavioral and Brain Sciences,* 29, 1–56.

Boyer, P. and Ramble, C. 2001: Cognitive templates for religious concepts: Cross-cultural evidence for recall of counter-intuitive representations. *Cognitive Science,* 25, 535–564.

Bruner, J. 1991: The narrative construction of reality. *Critical Inquiry,* 18(1), 1.

Burkert, W. 1996: *Creation of the Sacred: Tracks of Biology in Early Religions*. Cambridge, MA: Harvard University Press.

Campbell, D. T. 1960: Blind variation and selective retention in creative thought as in other knowledge processes. *Psychological Review,* 67, 380–400.

Carroll, J. 1995: *Evolution and Literary Theory*. Columbia: University of Missouri Press.

256 *Pascal Boyer*

Carroll, J. 2004: *Literary Darwinism: Evolution, Human Nature, and Literature*. New York: Routledge.

Cosmides, L. and Tooby, J. 1997: Dissecting the computational architecture of social inference mechanisms. *Ciba Foundation Symposium,* 208, 132–156; discussion 156–161.

Dautenhahn, K. 2003: Stories of lemurs and robots: The social origin of story-telling. In Mateas, M. and Sengers, P. (eds), *Narrative Intelligence*. Amsterdam: Netherlandsing Company, 63–90.

Easterlin, N. and Riebling, B. 1993: *After Poststructuralism: Interdisciplinarity and Literary Theory*. Evanston, IL: Northwestern University Press.

Fiddick, L. 2004: Domains of deontic reasoning: Resolving the discrepancy between the cognitive and moral reasoning literatures. *Quarterly Journal of Experimental Psychology: Human Experimental Psychology,* 57A(3), 447–474.

Fiske, A. P. and Tetlock, P. E. 1997: Taboo trade-offs: Reactions to transactions that transgress the spheres of justice. *Political Psychology,* 18(2), 255–297.

Fivush, R., Haden, C. and Adam, S. 1995: Structure and coherence of preschoolers' personal narratives over time: Implications for childhood amnesia. *Journal of Experimental Child Psychology,* 60(1), 32–56.

Gintis, H. 2000: Strong reciprocity and human sociality. *Journal of Theoretical Biology,* 206(2), 169–179.

Gordon, A. C. L. and Olson, D. R. 1998: The relation between acquisition of a theory of mind and the capacity to hold in mind. *Journal of Experimental Child Psychology,* 68(1), 70–83.

Grafton, S. T., Fadiga, L., Arbib, M. A. and Rizzzolati, G. 1997: Premotor cortex activation during observation and naming of familiar tools. *NeuroImage,* 6, 231–236.

Guthrie, S. E. 1993: *Faces in the Clouds. A New Theory of Religion*. New York: Oxford University Press.

Harvey, J. H., Town, J. P. and Yarkin, K. L. 1981: How fundamental is 'the fundamental attribution error'? *Journal of Personality and Social Psychology,* 40(2), 346–349.

Heider, F. 1958: *The Psychology of Interpersonal Relations*. New York: Wiley.

Hogan, P. C. 2003: *The Mind and its Stories: Narrative Universals and Human Emotion*. Cambridge; New York: Cambridge University Press.

Kahneman, D. and Miller, D. T. 2002: Norm theory: Comparing reality to its alternatives. In T. Gilovich, D. Griffin *et al.* (eds), *Heuristics and Biases: The Psychology of Intuitive Judgment*. New York: Cambridge University Press, 348–366.

Kavanaugh, R. D. and Harris, P. L. 2000: Pretense and counterfactual thought in young children. In L. Balter and C. S. Tamis-LeMonda (eds), *Child Psychology: A Handbook of Contemporary Issues*. New York: Psychology Press, 158–176.

Lawson, E. T. and McCauley, R. N. 1990: *Rethinking Religion: Connecting Cognition and Culture*. Cambridge: Cambridge University Press.

Leoutsakas, D. 2004: The orphan tales: Real and imagined stories of parental loss. *Dissertation Abstracts International Section A: Humanities and Social Sciences,* 64(7–A), 2605.

Leslie, A. M. 1987: Pretense and representation: The origins of 'theory of mind'. *Psychological Review,* 94, 412–426.

Leslie, A. M. 1994: Pretending and believing: Issues in the theory of TOMM. *Cognition,* 50(1–3), 211–238.

Malle, B. F., Knobe, J., O'Laughlin, M. J., Pearce, G. E. and Nelson, S. E. 2000: Conceptual structure and social functions of behavior explanations: Beyond person-situation attributions. *Journal of Personality and Social Psychology*, 79(3), 309–326.

Malle, B. F., Moses, L. J. and Baldwin, D. A. (eds) 2001: *Intentions and Intentionality: Foundations of Social Cognition*. Cambridge, MA: MIT Press.

Mataix-Cols, D., do Rosario-Campos, M. C. and Leckman, J. F. 2005: A multidimensional model of obsessive-compulsive disorder. *The American Journal of Psychiatry*, 162(2), 228–238.

Mithen, S. J. 1996: *The Prehistory of the Mind*. London: Thames and Hudson.

Nichols, S. and Stich, S. 1999: A cognitive theory of pretense. *Cognition*, 74, 115–147.

Perner, J. 1991: *Understanding the Representational Mind*. Cambridge, MA: MIT Press.

Pyysiainen, I. 2001: *How Religion Works. Towards a New Cognitive Science of Religion*. Leiden: Brill.

Robinson, E. J. and Beck, S. 2000: What is difficult about counterfactual reasoning? In P. Mitchell and K. J. Riggs (eds), *Children's Reasoning and the Mind*. Hove: Taylor and Francis, 101–119.

Roese, N. J. and Olson, J. M. (eds) 1995: *What Might Have Been: The Social Psychology of Counterfactual Thinking*. Hillsdale, NJ: Lawrence Erlbaum Associates.

Roese, N. J. and Olson, J. M. 1997: Counterfactual thinking: The intersection of affect and function. In Zanna, M. P. (ed.), *Advances in Experimental Social Psychology*, 29, 1–59).

Roese, N. J., Sanna, L. J. and Galinsky, A. D. 2005: The mechanics of imagination: Automaticity and control in counterfactual thinking. In Hassin, R. S., Uleman, J. S. and Bargh, J. A. (eds), *The New Unconscious*. New York: Oxford University Press, 138–170.

Saarni, C. 2001: Cognition, context, and goals: Significant components in social-emotional effectiveness. *Social Development*, 10(1), 125–129.

Searle, J. 1979: The logical status of fictional discourse. In French, P. A., Uehling, T. R. and Wettstein, H. K. (eds), *Contemporary Perspectives in the Philosophy of Language*. Minneapolis: University of Minnesota Press.

Sperber, D. 1996: *Explaining Culture: A Naturalistic Approach*. Oxford: Blackwell.

Sperber, D. and Wilson, D. 1995: *Relevance. Communication and Cognition* (2nd edn). Oxford: Blackwell.

Steen, F. and Owens, S. 2001: Evolution's pedagogy: An adaptationist model of pretense and entertainment. *Journal of Cognition and Culture*, 1(4), 289–321.

Storey, R. F. 1996: *Mimesis and the Human Animal: On the Biogenetic Foundations of Literary Representation*. Evanston, IL: Northwestern University Press.

Szechtman, H. and Woody, E. 2004: Obsessive-compulsive disorder as a disturbance of security motivation. *Psychological Review*, 111(1), 111–127.

Taylor, M. 1999: *Imaginary Companions and the Children Who Create Them*. New York: Oxford University Press.

Taylor, M. and Carlson, S. M. 1997: The relation between individual differences in fantasy and theory of mind. *Child Development*, 68(3), 436–455.

Taylor, M. and Hort, B. 1990: Can children be trained in making the distinction between appearance and reality? *Cognitive Development*, 5, 89–99.

258 *Pascal Boyer*

Tetlock, P. E. 1998: Close-call counterfactuals and belief-system defenses: I was not almost wrong but I was almost right. *Journal of Personality and Social Psychology,* 75(3), 639–652.

Todorov, T. 1977: *The Poetics of Prose.* Ithaca, NY: Cornell University Press.

Tooby, J. and DeVore, I. 1987: The reconstruction of hominid behavioral evolution through strategic modeling. In Kinzey, W. (ed.), *Primate Models of Hominid Behavior.* New York: SUNY Press, 183–237.

Tooby, J., Cosmides, L., Gallistel, C. R., Fernald, R. D., White, S. A., Sherry, D. F. *et al.* 2000: Evolution. In Gazzaniga, M. S. *et al.* (eds), *The New Cognitive Neurosciences* (2nd edn). Cambridge, MA: MIT Press, 1167–1270.

Turner, M. 1996: *The Literary Mind.* New York: Oxford University Press.

Ward, T. B. 1995: What's old about new ideas? In Smith, S. M., Ward, T. B. *et al.* (eds), *The Creative Cognition Approach.* Cambridge, MA: MIT Press, 157–178.

Whiten, A. (ed.) 1991: *Natural Theories of Mind: The Evolution, Development and Simulation of Everyday Mind-reading.* Oxford: Blackwell.

Williams, G. C. 1966: *Adaptation and Natural Selection. A Critique of Some Current Evolutionary Thought.* Princeton, NJ: Princeton University Press.

Zunshine, L. 2003: Theory of mind and experimental representations of fictional consciousness. *Narrative,* 11(3), 270–291.

12

A Module for Metaphor?
The Site of Imagination in the
Architecture of the Mind

DANIEL NETTLE

Abstract. An influential position in contemporary psychology is that the mind consists of a constellation of domain-specific, specialized computational mechanisms. Controversy remains about how global, integrative cognitive processes such as the imagination fit into such an architecture. I consider three possible conceptualizations of the imagination: as an operation of a domain-general central process in a Fodorian mind; as an operation of a specialized module in a massively modular mind; and finally as a product of low binding selectivity in Clark Barrett's 'cogzyme' mind. This final approach is much the most promising, as the key to the imagination seems to be the mapping of meaningful representations between dissimilar cognitive domains. I thus argue, partly through the link between imagination and schizotypy, that we should view imagination as a consequence of incomplete insulation between parallel specialized processes. Such de-insulation permits innovation and novelty, but also makes possible psychotic illness and delusional beliefs. Thus imagination, like any other evolutionary development, is likely to have costs as well as benefits.

THE IMAGINATION AND THE DOMAIN-SPECIFIC MIND

THE IMAGINATIVE CAPACITY OF *HOMO SAPIENS* has long been held to be one of that species' most notable features. For Darwin, imagination was 'one of the highest prerogatives of man' (cited in Roth 2003). Archaeologists and palaeoanthropologists have tended to judge the question of when there were people 'like us' less in terms of anatomical similarity, and more by the presence of clearly imaginative products such as figurines, decoration, and painted representation (Mithen 1996). As Roth points out, the centrality of imagination to what it is like to be human has not guaranteed its centrality within the models of mind developed by scientific psychology. The subject of this chapter is how we might conceptualize the place of the imagination within the overall architecture of the mind. The background to the ideas developed here is the rise of interest in the concept of the domain-specific, or modular, mind (Fodor 1983; Tooby and Cosmides 1992).

Fodor gave the first detailed elaboration of the thesis that much of human cognition is organized into a number of relatively autonomous subcircuits. The key features of these modules are that they are designed to solve a particular task, and act on a particular type of informational input, automatically, without their internal processes being available to other modules, and without drawing on any 'general' cognitive resources such as attention. Thus, the face perception module works fast and completely automatically whenever visual information fulfilling the criteria of being a face becomes available. It is impossible to look at a familiar face but decide not to recognize it until later on, when you have more time. Moreover, the question of how you recognized it (was it the curve of the chin?) is completely unavailable to, for example, the linguistic system. Face recognition is thus informationally encapsulated. It is unlikely that the circuitry that does the recognition is able to do anything that is not face recognition or some task closely modelled on it (recognizing a dog or a doll for example; Kanwisher 2000). Thus, face recognition is a good candidate for a modular process. In accordance with Fodor's criteria for modularity, this leads to a number of ancillary possibilities; chiefly, that it might be possible for brain damage to abolish face recognition capacities without impairing performance on anything much else, and that there might be brain circuits that are active in all and only face recognition tasks. Both of these predictions turn out to be the case, as reflected in acquired prosopagnosia, which is the selective impairment of face recognition capacity, and in the existence of neurons uniquely responsive to faces in the superior temporal sulcus of both monkey and man (Kanwisher 2000; Desimone 1991).

Fodor's model of the mind is a two-tiered one. Whereas a number of specialist tasks such as perception and language are handled by modules, there is also a general-purpose cognitive system that takes the output of the various modules and does characteristically human things with them such as planning, problem-solving, writing books, and so on (Figure 12.1). These processes have all the converse characteristics to modular cognition; slow, voluntary, effortful, and attentionally demanding. Processes within the general-purpose system are unencapsulated, which means in principle that you could write a book about how you deciphered Linear A (using general-purpose cognition) more easily than one about how you parse a sentence of ordinary spoken English (using a language module). Within the Fodorian mind, the imagination, ranging as it does across multiple domains and modalities, cannot itself be a module. The other possibility, then, is to locate it in the general-purpose system with all the other difficult-to-study, important and uniquely human characteristics such as reasoning.

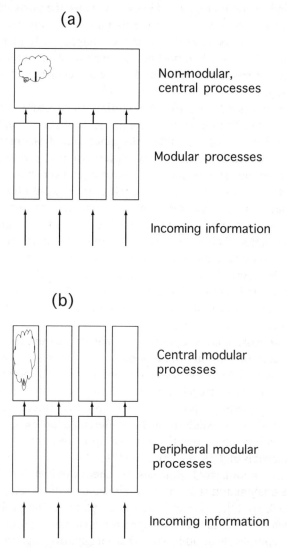

(a)

Non-modular,
central processes

Modular processes

Incoming information

(b)

Central modular
processes

Peripheral modular
processes

Incoming information

Figure 12.1. Two possible sites of the faculty of imagination in the architecture of the mind. (a) In a Fodorian mind, imagination is a property of domain-general central processes. (b) In a massively modular mind, imagination is a property of some domain-specific central module, designed for some function such as planning or problem-solving.

If this view is adopted, then imagination falls victim to what Fodor himself, with characteristic iconoclasm, calls the First Law of the Nonexistence of Cognitive Science (Fodor 1983). The thrust of this law is that cognitive science produces good, well-grounded models of basic processes that were not of much interest anyway, and shoves really key human processes such as imagination into the general-purpose system, the workings of which it is hard to get any kind of methodological handle on. Thus, the parts that are scientific are not very cognitive, and the parts that are really cognitive are in a box which might as well say 'And then a miracle happens'. If imagination is a general process, then there is almost nothing we can say about it beyond what it is not, namely localized, specialized, showing evidence of evolutionary design, and so on.

A more recent alternative to the Fodorian architecture is the so-called massive modularity hypothesis (Samuels 1998; Tooby and Cosmides 1992). According to Tooby and Cosmides, the whole mind is organized into a system of specialized processes. These cover not just low-level tasks like Fodor's modules, but all the major cognitive operations humans must perform in order to survive and reproduce. Thus, there would be a module for selecting a mate, one for tracking cooperative interactions with other people, one for thinking about plants and potential foods, one for thinking about the physical movements of objects, one for avoiding being murdered, and so on. The primary argumentation for such pervasive modularity is theoretical. Since the architecture of the mind has been shaped by Darwinian selection, it will end up optimized for solving the recurrent adaptive challenges human beings have faced. Each of those adaptive challenges—feeding, mating, avoiding predation, cooperation—has a different set of rules and constraints, and thus requires specialized cognitive machinery. The things you learn about feeding are really no help in finding a mate, and any system designed to be able to learn the two equally well would be inferior to two specialized systems in the same head, each triggered by the relevant scenarios. Thus, any mind consisting of a general-purpose computer whose resources and algorithms were equipotentially relevant to all the different adaptive domains would always be outcompeted by one that divided up its resources into specialized modules (Cosmides and Tooby 1992, p. 112).

The massive modularity hypothesis, as stated, would naturally lead to the view that the imagination is a module, designed by natural selection for some important task or other, perhaps advanced planning or problem-solving. However, such a view—in which imagination is domain-specific and specialized—seems completely at odds with what imaginative cognition is like, as I shall argue in the next section.

The massive modularity hypothesis, though influential, has raised scepticism, in particular about whether the globality, flexibility, and context-sensitivity of (at least some) human thought could originate from a mind entirely composed of autonomous and specialized devices (Over 2003; Stanovich and West 2003). Clark Barrett has recently outlined a model that satisfies Tooby and Cosmides' stipulation that natural selection produces specialized mechanisms, and yet preserves the fluidity and context-sensitivity of Fodor's central processes (Figure 12.2; Barrett 2005). He proposes that specialized cognitive mechanisms should not be seen as separate channels in the mind, but instead are more like enzymes in the chemical soup of the human cell. That is, they have affinities to particular kinds of information, which they bind to and transform in certain ways, just as enzymes have affinities for particular chemical substrates which they catalyse. Thus, for example, there may be a mate selection mechanism that has an affinity for cues of attractiveness in a member of the opposite sex, and turns these into a representation of a mating opportunity. However, crucially, information within the system is not partitioned into separate containers, as in a modular mind, but instead resides in a common mental pool of representations. Individual 'cogzymes' (i.e. specialized mental processes) take representations and transform them in ways specified by their design, but then return them to the common pool, where they are available to other cogzymes. Moreover, one cogzyme may uprate or inhibit another, just as happens with enzymes in complex chemical reactions. What previously appeared to be 'domain-general' processes such as reasoning may instead be complex central processes in the pool of representations that drawn on many different, interacting cogzymes. Barrett's model appears persuasive, and also offers a more satisfying conceptualization of the imagination than either Fodor's ill-defined central processes, or a modular account, as I shall outline below.

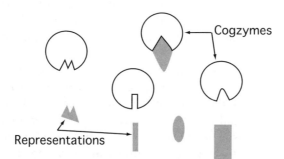

Figure 12.2. A Barrettian mind. Representations of information are in a common mental pool, where they interact with specialist cognitive processes or 'cogzymes', which have affinities for particular types of information. Imagination emerges as a consequence of incomplete binding selectivity between representation types and cogzymes.

THE BASIS OF THE IMAGINATION

As the Introduction to this volume notes, imagination is clearly a multi-faceted, family resemblance term. One ordinary-language meaning of the imagination is essentially visual imagery ('seeing in the mind's eye'), while another is counter-factual thinking ('in my imagination, I can see what will happen if the bridge collapses'). Both of these kinds of imagination could easily turn out to be capacities of particular domain-specific processes. For example, cognition about objects in the physical world could usefully make use of both visual imagery and counterfactual reasoning. Indeed, each of these two topics has proved relatively amenable to experimental investigation, suggesting, in accordance with the first law of the non-existence of cognitive science, that they are probably not the phenomena of greatest interest. However, there is another sense of imagination, which seems closer to the sense in which imagination is a true hallmark of modern human cognition. This is the sense in which a poem, a scientific theory, or a mathematical proof could be said to have required a leap of the imagination.

The key to imagination in this sense seems to be the production of a novel representation from an input by bringing to bear information from another domain. Let me illustrate this point with two brief examples that would by common consensus be considered highly imaginative. First, consider Sylvia Plath's poem *Old Ladies' Home*. Plath describes the residents of an elderly persons' home as, 'Frail as antique earthenware/One breath might shiver to bits'. We have an intuitive, evolved, specialized way of thinking about persons (social intelligence), and the natural currency of that intuitive process is things like beliefs, desires, and intentions. For physical objects, there is a different intuitive processing (physical intelligence) centred around spatial position, physical integrity, and object permanence. Plath here uses the language of the latter to talk about the former, drawing out the isomorphism that the death of an agent is in the domain of social cognition what the loss of object integrity is in cognition about physical objects.

Describing the activity of the ladies, the poet writes, 'Needles knit in a bird-beaked/Counterpoint to their voices'. One can almost hear the click-click of the needles in the sound of the first of these two lines, through the repeated initial *n* sound followed by repeated *b*. However, we are normally unaware of the acoustic resemblances of language to non-linguistic sounds, since an automatic domain-specific process intervenes to turn speech into meaning. Writing and reading poetry generally, as here, requires taking the line and treating it not just as language, but also as a non-linguistic stream of sound. In other words, the signal must be allocated *both* to linguistic processing, and to non-linguistic sound processing, yielding in both cases some representation of the knitting process, namely the linguistic semantics of knitting and something like its actual sound.

Plath finishes the poem 'And Death, that bald-headed buzzard/Stalls in halls where the lamp wick/Shortens with each breath drawn.' Once again, the meaning of this sequence involves taking a subject that would normally be allocated to social cognition (the ladies), and using schemas to do with predation or scavenging (the buzzard), and combustion, which is part of intuitive physics, to reframe their impending mortality.

As a second example, consider the development of game theory by Nobel prize winner John Nash (Nasar 1998). Game theory is a framework for considering the likely evolution of behaviours, in scenarios where the payoff to an actor depends not only on his or her own behaviour but on that of others with whom he or she interacts. A classic game-theoretic scenario would be the decision how long fishermen should wait before re-fishing a depleted salmon river. The individually rational decision might be to wait until the salmon are completely grown and fish them then. However, a rational person, realizing that the others will realize that it is rational to wait until the salmon are full-grown, will wait until a month *before* this, and fish without competition. However, a rational person, realizing that the others will work this out and start fishing one month before the salmon are full-grown, will only wait until *two* months before. And so on.

Modelling the outcome of these types of interaction turns out to be quite simply done using some basic mathematics. You simply treat the actors as a physical system governed by a matrix of payoffs and a maximization function. Nash's work is imaginative because this is not the usual way of thinking about people. Game theory fundamentally concerns human social interactions. Again, we would normally think about these with an intuitive belief/desire psychology—what the fishermen *want*, when they *intend* to fish and so on. Thinking about the salmon problem, folk psychology just tells us that the fishermen *want* and *intend* to wait, but game theory tells us that the salmon will get fished early despite everyone's intentions to the contrary. (Natural selection, of course, 'knows' this, which is why it has given us such emotions as moralistic outrage, anger, and guilt.) Thus, Nash's imaginative leap lies in applying mathematics, an outgrowth presumably of specialized cognition for thinking about objects in the physical world, to the social domain, where normally another, quite different, specialized process would be in force.

The common thread in poetry and game theory is metaphor, in the broad sense of 'a mapping or transfer of meaning between dissimilar domains' (Modell 2003). The imaginative creations involve seeing that a problem within one domain (of language or social interaction) can actually be processed, perhaps simultaneously, in another (sound or physical systems).

This results in a novel representation that would not have been available by following the normal algorithms internal to the domain in which the problem was first conceived (Chiappe 2000).

It is unclear that insights such as Plath's or Nash's can be produced by the application of deliberate cognitive effort. Indeed, it is unclear that the imaginative leap, as distinct from the solving of the details, need be slow or voluntary. It seems more likely that this kind of cognition arises where cognitive operations from one domain spontaneously interact with the information that properly belongs to another. In Barrett's (2005) terms, the cogzymes designed to take information relating to, say, naive physics, interact with representations of the social world, or vice versa. This 'non-selectivity' in the cogzyme pool could well reduce average efficiency in carrying out everyday cognitive tasks, but it produces occasional moments of arresting creativity. The appropriate metaphor for capturing the basis of the imagination using the cogzyme model would be that of 'binding selectivity'. In biochemical systems, enzymes with high binding selectivity only interact with a very narrow range of substrate molecules. Enzymes with lower binding selectivity would react to some degree with a much wider range of molecules. Lowering average binding selectivity in a system would increase the number and complexity of different reactions in response to different chemical inputs, though it might also render more chaotic and inefficient the production of key reactions.

Steven Mithen has been a champion of the view that truly modern cognition, with its symbolic and artistic capacities, arises not from the development of additional domain-specific capacities, but from the partial breakdown of inter-domain cognitive barriers (Mithen 1996). Within the Barrett model, we might rephrase this by saying that in the modern mind, binding selectivity of cogzymes to different information types has become lower, producing creative imagination of the type we have discussed. This hypothesis seems compelling, but has scarcely been studied in the experimental psychology laboratory, in part due to the difficulty of getting an experimental handle on the types of cognitive processes required. One fruitful source of evidence for the informational fluidity model is to be found in studies of psychopathology, particularly schizophrenia. This requires, first of all, an explanation of the link between psychopathology and creative imagination.

IMAGINATION AND PSYCHOPATHOLOGY

It may seem a leap to move from imagination to cognitive functioning in schizophrenia, but there are reasons for doing so. A full review is beyond the scope of this chapter (see Nettle 2001). Suffice it here to say that there is

evidence of increased rates of psychopathology, including psychosis, in individuals judged by society to be highly creative (Ludwig 1988; Richards *et al.*
1988), and in their first degree relatives (Heston 1966; Karlson 1970;
Richards *et al.* 1988). Moreover, the contents of psychotic states can only be
described as imaginative. Patients often have elaborate systems of delusional
beliefs, in which real events and facts will be minutely and consistently interwoven with non-veridical constructions, often fantastical or paranormal in
nature. Paranoid thinking contrives to discover ingenious connections
between apparently disparate domains, and the characteristic 'crooked logic'
of thought disorder involves generating novel connections in much the way
that the imaginative examples given in the previous section do. (On the
connection between positive symptoms of psychosis and the imagination, see
also Currie 2000.) Nash himself was of course affected by psychosis for
many years.

Perhaps most importantly, there is evidence of a shared cognitive style in
what we would recognize as imaginative cognition and in psychosis. People
diagnosed with schizophrenia show relative impairments on a wide variety of
psychological tasks. One exception is those tasks that have been proposed as
measures of creativity. An example is the alternate uses test, in which the participant has to come up with as many different uses for an everyday object as
possible. As the banal uses are soon exhausted, much of the variation on this
task arises from the person's ability to draw possible uses from completely
different domains than that for which the object is designed. Schizophrenia
patients show a large advantage on this task compared with controls, and
indeed, when a group of 'highly creative' normals were tested, their performance was essentially indistinguishable from that of the patients (Keefe and
Magaro 1980). A similar pattern is found on a task where non-standard,
novel criteria for sorting objects must be devised by the subject (Dykes and
McGhie 1976). The performance of schizophrenia patients is enhanced. This
is in sharp contrast to tasks where more obvious sorting criteria set by the
experimenter must be discovered and adhered to, such as the Wisconsin card
sorting task, where patients are impaired relative to controls.

Researchers studying schizophrenia distinguish between the condition
itself, and the cognitive or personality style that underlies it. For the former
to develop requires the presence of the latter, but the latter may also be found
in subclinical or even benign form, and only in some cases is converted into
frank psychotic illness. The underlying personality configuration is known as
schizotypy (Claridge 1997). Schizotypy is conceptualized as a continuous
trait. It can thus be measured within the general population using standard
personality scale designs (Mason *et al.* 1995). Psychotic (bipolar as well as
schizophrenic) patients are reliably high scorers on these scales, but there are
also high scorers with no history of treated mental illness (Nettle 2006).

Factor analysis of schizotypy scales reveals several independent subdimensions (Claridge *et al*. 1996). In particular, a factor relating to unusual ideas, beliefs and experiences (which are the positive symptoms of schizophrenia) can be reliably separated from a factor characterized by anhedonia (the inability to gain pleasure from normally pleasurable experiences) and social withdrawal. This latter factor corresponds to the negative symptoms of schizophrenia. It is the positive, unusual ideas factor that has generally been related to creativity or imagination (Schuldberg 2000). For example, poets and visual artists score higher than controls, and as highly as schizophrenia patients, on the Unusual Experiences schizotypy scale (Nettle 2006).

Schizotypes (by which it is meant high scorers on schizotypy scales who are psychiatrically normal) have often been used in research as models for schizophrenia (Claridge 1997). This is because they are presumed to show many of the cognitive hallmarks of schizophrenia without the medication, negative symptoms, institutionalization, stigma, and frank psychosis that make cognition in schizophrenia hard to study. However, schizotypes can also be used as a model of highly active imagination. There are several justifications for so using them. First, there are the conceptual similarities and epidemiological links between serious mental illness and imaginative creativity, as noted above, and schizotypy is the linking construct. Second, schizotypy scores are elevated among arts students (O'Reilly *et al*. 2001), and among poets and visual artists (Nettle 2006), relative to the general population. Third, scores on the positive dimensions of schizotypy scales (those which measure unusual beliefs and experiences) correlate with performance on tasks that have been proposed as measures of creativity (Green and Williams 1999; Weinstein and Graves 2002). One such task is the Remote Associates Test (Mednick 1962). Here, participants have to find a word that links three others presented to them, such as Manners–Round–Tennis, where the link word is Table. The solution requires accessing simultaneously a number of competing meanings in disparate semantic domains. Other tasks correlated with positive schizotypy include generating as many words as possible beginning with a given letter, completing a partial diagram in as many ways as possible, or generating as many different or original instances or uses for a stimulus as possible. Thus schizotypes seem, from multiple perspectives, to represent the workings of an active imagination.

COGNITIVE MECHANISMS IN SCHIZOTYPY

It has long been known that schizophrenia patients show a marked impairment on tasks where one source of information has to be ignored and another attended to. They show more intrusions and interference from the ignored channel in dichotic listening experiments than controls (Wishner and Wahl 1974). This has been interpreted as a defect in the mechanism that limits the flow of information into conscious awareness to that which is the current object of attention. However, the account could just as easily be framed in terms of an inherently low binding selectivity of specialized processing mechanisms.

Support for this view also comes from various types of priming experiment. In normal volunteers, pre-exposure to a word such as DOG decreases reaction time to recognize a word such as CAT. There is some evidence that in schizophrenia patients and in schizotypes, this priming is abnormally quick and potent (Spitzer *et al.* 1993; Evans 1997). Of particular interest here is the suggestion that the performance of some patients is particularly enhanced compared with controls when the semantic relationship between prime and target is indirect, as in LION-STRIPES (Spitzer *et al.* 1993). The priming seen here is best explained by the prime activating the representation of TIGER, which activates the representation of STRIPES. One is tempted to say that this is a rather imaginative association, and the schizotypal enhancement presumably arises from their semantic representations interacting rather more freely than in controls. Schizotypes judge two loosely associated words to be more closely related in meaning than controls do (Mohr *et al.* 2001), though their associations do not become completely indiscriminate.

Priming can also be negative. In general, subjects show a reaction time *increase* to name a word when, in the previous phase of the experiment, they have had to ignore the same word. This is presumed to occur because in the 'ignoring' phase, the representation of the stimulus is inhibited, and this inhibition has then to be overcome when, in the next phase, the same representation needs to be accessed. High schizotypes, however, show reduced inhibition (Beech and Claridge 1987; Beech *et al.* 1989). If anything they show some facilitation from having seen the word before. When the ignored word in the priming phase is semantically related to (rather than identical to) the word they then have to name (e.g. CAT–DOG), high schizotypes are clearly facilitated, whereas low schizotypes are inhibited (Beech *et al.* 1991). The best interpretation of these effects is that streams of processing that should be inhibited by attentional set are not inhibited in high schizotypes; instead, multiple processing streams remain active and can affect each other.

The core feature of schizotypal cognition thus has been described as 'an inability to exclude from intrusion into consciousness material from either external stimuli or internally stored associations . . . [which would be] normally excluded because of their irrelevance to ongoing activity' (Maher 1983). The positive symptoms of psychosis, delusions, and hallucinations are of course the examples *par excellence* of this leaky filter (Frith 1979). The view can be rephrased in the terms of Barrett's cogzyme model. Schizotypal cognition, then, involves a broader range of interactions between mental representations and cogzymes than would otherwise be observed, and consequently there is a broader set of cogzyme–representation pairings, both above and below the level of consciousness.

Priming effects related to schizotypy occur at very fast presentation speeds, when the participant may not even be consciously aware of the prime (Beech *et al.* 1989). In the indirect priming example, the semantic circuit for LION should not, in a sense, activate the meaning of STRIPES. Semantic activation should spread laterally only a small distance, and be subject to sharp inhibition beyond this. The alternative is a world of chaotic and numinous associations. However, in schizotypy, the leakage or facilitation of part-connected semantic representations is super-normal. The negative priming and dichotic listening examples can be interpreted in the following way. Attention should inhibit certain specialized and automatic processing streams (for reading or monitoring a sound source, for example) when they are not useful to the current task demand (which is to ignore them). However, in schizotypes, these inhibitory processes are reduced in effectiveness.

This formulation explains perfectly the double dissociation with schizophrenia patients in convergent versus divergent tasks. They are relatively impaired when they have to follow an experimenter's criteria for sorting items/cards into groups or categories, and relatively enhanced when they have to come up with their own idiosyncratic ones. They are impaired on IQ tests, but have an advantage on the novel uses task. Increasing the number of cogzyme–representation interactions is bound to reduce the efficiency of a convergent task in which only one interaction is actually needed. On the other hand, it will increase the fecundity of precisely that set of tasks where it is the number or richness of different interactions that is measured — namely, tasks of divergent thinking. It also explains some of the brain imaging findings with respect to schizophrenia. Imaging studies have reliably found differences in activity in the schizophrenic and non-schizophrenic brain. However, the nature of the difference depends very much upon the task. No single area reveals itself as consistently hyper-active or hypo-active. Instead, there is a marked tendency for multiple areas to remain active in the patients, even in tasks which in normal subjects would shift the locus of activation to one particular (specialized) brain region. Thus, the underlying abnormality may be one of how a whole circuit of brain regions allocate their activity appropriately for a given situation (Andreasen *et al.* 1998).

Given that we have defined the essence of imagination as a mapping of meaning between dissimilar domains, and taking schizotypy as a model of the imagination at its most productive, we can thus define imagination as the often simultaneous interaction of multiple cogzyme–representation pairings.

CONCLUSIONS: IMAGINATION AS LOW BINDING SELECTIVITY

We have examined some evidence for a tentative hypothesis that the cognitive basis of the imagination is enhanced cross-talk between different specialized processing types. The psychological effect of this cross-talk is an enhanced ability to process one type of thing as if it were another, or to make semantic links between apparently unrelated entities. Some caveats are in order, though. Many of the experimental examples reviewed, such as semantic priming or dichotic listening, have concerned lateral activation and inhibition *within* the same processing domain (word meaning or hearing). The examples of imaginative thought we have reviewed concern making a mapping *between* quite different domains, for example, seeing people as physical systems, or language as non-linguistic sound. It would be illuminating to investigate whether high schizotypes are enhanced on a task where a problem normally allocated to one domain has to be processed using another. If schizotypy is related to some general systemic property of the brain, then within-domain fluidity may correlate with between-domain fluidity, but this has not yet been demonstrated.

To return to the overall picture of cognitive architecture presented at the outset, it is clear from this view that imagination is neither a domain-specific process itself, nor a domain-general capacity that operates on the output of domain-specific processes. Instead, it is a product of incomplete informational encapsulation between processes that themselves show evidence of specialized design. In other words, specialized mechanisms show lowered or incomplete selectivity for particular types of information.

Steven Mithen may well be right (Mithen 1996; Chapter 1) to argue that the key to the truly modern human mind was not the addition of new specialized abilities but the partial breakdown of the barriers between the existing ones. This is generally viewed as a highly adaptive change, permitting a flowering of new creative behaviours and innovations. However, it is worth remembering that all evolutionary changes have costs as well as benefits. The effective insulation of different cognitive processes from each other has functional advantages in terms of the convergent efficiency of those processes within their proper domain. The breakdown of separation between them may reduce their efficiency, and lead to some other non-adaptive results. For one thing, around 1 per cent of the human population, those individuals, perhaps in which the binding selectivity is lowest, is afflicted by socially and practically impairing psychotic illness. More generally, the breakdown of processing separation between natural history, intuitive physics, and social cognition has some odd and not necessarily functional consequences. Most human beings believe in supernatural agents whose desires and intentions affect natural forces; many believe in astrological systems whereby natural cycles affect human motives; many believe in telepathy, animism, shamanic possession, or Cabbalistic speculation. These strange cross-modal beliefs—in which implausible associations between events in one domain and consequences in another are considered as real—may reflect a real cost of the low binding selectivity mind. What the compensatory benefit may be is beyond the scope of this paper, but whatever it is, it has been sufficient to allow *Homo sapiens,* the imaginative ape, to dominate the globe in a manner achieved by no other primate.

References

Andreasen, N. C., Paradiso, S. and O'Leary, D. 1998: Cognitive dysmetria as an integrative theory of schizophrenia: A dysfunction in cortical-subcortical-cerebellar circuitry? *Schizophrenia Bulletin,* 24, 203–218.

Barrett, H. C. 2005: Enzymatic computation and cognitive modularity. *Mind and Language,* 20, 259–287.

Beech, A. R. and Claridge, G. 1987: Individual differences in negative priming: relations with schizotypal personality traits. *British Journal of Psychology,* 78, 349–356.

Beech, A. R., Baylis, G. C., Smithson, P. and Claridge, G. 1989: Individual differences in schizotypy as reflected in measures of cognitive inhibition. *British Journal of Clinical Psychology,* 28, 117–129.

Beech, A. R., McManus, D., Baylis, G. C., Tipper, S. and Agar, K. 1991: Individual differences in cognitive processes: Towards an explanation of schizophrenic symptomatology. *British Journal of Psychology,* 82, 417–426.

Chiappe, D. L. 2000: Metaphor, modularity and the evolution of conceptual integration. *Metaphor and Symbol,* 15, 137–158.

Claridge, G. (ed.) 1997: *Schizotypy: Implications for Illness and Health.* Oxford: Oxford University Press.

Claridge, G., McCreery, C., Mason, O., Bentall, R., Boyle, G. and Slade, P. 1996: The factor structure of 'schizotypal' traits: A large replication study. *British Journal of Clinical Psychology,* 35, 103–115.

Currie, G. 2000: Imagination, delusion and hallucinations. *Mind and Language,* 15, 168–183.

Desimone, R. 1991: Face-selective cells in the temporal cortex of monkeys. *Journal of Cognitive Neuroscience,* 3, 51–67.

Dykes, M. and McGhie, A. 1976: A comparative study of the attentional strategies of schizophrenic and highly creative normal subjects. *British Journal of Psychiatry,* 128, 50–56.

Evans, J. L. 1997: Semantic activation and preconscious processing in schizophrenia and schizotypy. In Claridge, G. (ed.), *Schizotypy: Implications for Illness and Health.* Oxford: Oxford University Press, 80–97.

Fodor, J. A. 1983: *Modularity of Mind.* Cambridge, MA: MIT Press.

Frith, C. D. 1979: Consciousness, information processing and schizophrenia. *British Journal of Psychiatry,* 134, 225–235.

Green, M. J. and Williams, L. M. 1999: Schizotypy and creativity as effects of reduced cognitive inhibition. *Personality and Individual Differences,* 27(2), 263–276.

Heston, J. J. 1966: Psychiatric disorders in foster home reared children of schizophrenic mothers. *British Journal of Psychiatry,* 112, 819–825.

Kanwisher, N. 2000: Domain specificity in face perception. *Nature Neuroscience,* 3, 759–763.

Karlson, J. L. 1970: Genetic association of giftedness and creativity with schizophrenia. *Hereditas,* 66, 177–181.

Keefe, J. A. and Magaro, P. A. 1980: Creativity and schizophrenia: An equivalence of cognitive processes. *Journal of Abnormal Psychology,* 89, 390–398.

Ludwig, A. M. 1988: *The Price of Greatness: Resolving the Creativity and Madness Controversy.* New York: Guilford Press.

Maher, B. A. 1983: A tentative theory of schizophrenic utterance. In Maher, W. B. (ed.), *Progress in Experimental Personality Research,* Volume 12. New York: Academic Press, 1–52.

Mason, O., Claridge, G. and Jackson, M. 1995: New scales for the assessment of schizotypy. *Personality and Individual Differences,* 1, 7–13.

Mednick, S. A. 1962: The associative basis of the creative process. *Psychological Review,* 69, 220–232.

Mithen, S. 1996: *The Prehistory of the Mind.* London: Thames and Hudson.

Modell, A. 2003: *Imagination and the Meaningful Brain.* Cambridge, MA: MIT Press.

Mohr, C., Graves, R. E., Gianotti, L. R. R., Pizzagalli, D. and Brugger, P. 2001: Loose but normal: A semantic association study. *Journal of Psycholinguistic Research,* 30(5), 475–483.

Nasar, S. 1998: *A Beautiful Mind.* London: Faber and Faber.

Nettle, D. 2001: *Strong Imagination: Madness, Creativity and Human Nature.* Oxford: Oxford University Press.

Nettle, D. 2006: Schizotypy and mental health amongst poets, artists and mathematicians. *Journal of Research in Personality,* 40, 876–890.

O'Reilly, T., Dunbar, R. and Bentall, R. 2001: Schizotypy and creativity: An evolutionary connection? *Personality and Individual Differences,* 31(7), 1067–1078.

Over, D. E. 2003: From massive modularity to metarepresentation: The evolution of higher cognition. In Over, D. E. (ed.), *Evolution and the Psychology of Thinking.* Hove: Psychology Press, 121–144.

Richards, R., Kinney, D. K. and Lunde, I. 1988: Creativity in manic-depressives, cyclothymes, their normal relatives, and controls. *Journal of Abnormal Psychology,* 97, 281–288.

Roth, I. 2003: Just imagine. . .. *Trends in Cognitive Sciences,* 7, 475–477.

Samuels, R. 1998: Evolutionary psychology and the massive modularity hypothesis. *British Journal for the Philosophy of Science,* 49, 575–602.

Schuldberg, D. 2000: Six subclinical spectrum traits in normal creativity. *Creativity Research Journal,* 13(1), 5–16.

Spitzer, M., Braun, U., Hermle, L. and Maier, S. 1993: Associative semantic dysfunction in schizophrenia: Direct evidence from indirect semantic priming. *Biological Psychiatry,* 34, 864–877.

Stanovich, K. E. and West, R. F. 2003: Evolutionary versus instrumental goals: How evolutionary psychology misconceives human rationality. In Over, D. E. (ed.), *Evolution and the Psychology of Thinking.* Hove: Psychology Press, 171–230.

Tooby, J. and Cosmides, L. 1992: The psychological foundations of culture. In Tooby, J. (ed.), *The Adapted Mind: Evolutionary Psychology and the Generation of Culture.* New York: Oxford University Press, 19–136.

Weinstein, S. and Graves, R. E. 2002: Are creativity and schizotypy products of a right hemisphere bias? *Brain and Cognition,* 49(1), 138–151.

Wishner, J. and Wahl, B. 1974: Dichotic listening in schizophrenia. *Journal of Consulting and Clinical Psychology,* 4, 538–546.

Part VI

ATYPICAL IMAGINATION
AND BRAIN MECHANISMS

13

Autism and the Imaginative Mind

ILONA ROTH

Abstract. Current accounts of the characteristic features of autistic conditions embody a curious paradox. Autism is usually assumed to entail impairments of the imagination. Symptoms consistent with this view are prominent throughout the clinical and research profile of Autism Spectrum Disorders (ASD). Yet some individuals with an autism spectrum diagnosis display remarkable gifts in fields typically associated with creative imagination, such as music, art, and poetry. While the essential creativity of their work has been questioned, it has also become popular to suggest that some individuals of outstanding and well-recognized creative talent—Samuel Beckett, Andy Warhol, Ludwig Wittgenstein, and Albert Einstein for instance—suffered from autistic spectrum conditions. This claim seems to imply that autism not only is compatible with creative imagination, but in some sense promotes or facilitates it.

In this chapter I outline the evidence for impairments of the imagination in ASD, and show how these problems align with key psychological models of autism. I evaluate the evidence for elements of preserved imagination, considering autistic visual art and insights from my research into autistic spectrum poetry. I conclude by highlighting broader implications of the complex relationship between autism and the imagination.

Terminology

I generally use 'autism' and 'ASD' in this chapter as shorthands for the spectrum of related conditions known as Autism Spectrum Difficulties or Disorders. Occasionally 'autism' refers to the classical diagnostic sub-group within the wider autism spectrum. Asperger syndrome denotes a more able sub-group. I use either 'non-autistic' or 'neurotypical' to refer to the typically functioning individuals with whom autistic groups are compared in research.

Proceedings of the British Academy **147**, 277–306. © The British Academy 2007.

AUTISM: A DISORDER OF THE IMAGINATION?

AUTISM SPECTRUM DISORDERS ARE DIAGNOSED on the basis of a three-part profile of symptom clusters known as the 'diagnostic triad'. One of these symptom groups—rigid adherence to routine, repetitive activity, and narrowly focused interests—represents a set of behavioural and cognitive biases that is clearly consistent with a lack of imaginative cognition. The other two clusters—impairments in communication and in social interaction—also embrace difficulties in imaginative thinking processes. These clinically derived diagnostic criteria are complemented by observational and experimental evidence suggesting difficulties in several kinds of imaginative thought.

Impaired pretend play is one such problem. At 18 months of age most typically developing children will employ a toy brick as a cake or 'drink' from an empty tea-cup. Children with an incipient autistic condition typically fail to show pretence at this age (Baron-Cohen *et al.* 2000). Moreover, while pretence becomes increasingly complex and social in the later development of neurotypical children, involving role-playing games such as 'doctors' or 'families', children with an autistic spectrum diagnosis develop little pretence of any kind.

Difficulties in imagining what other people are thinking and feeling, the capacity known as theory of mind or ToM, have been widely documented over the past twenty years, constituting one of the most influential psychological accounts of autistic disorders (see Baron-Cohen 2001 for a review). People with ASD have particular difficulties with false belief, considered the litmus test for theory of mind, since it involves understanding that someone else's belief about an aspect of reality might be different from their own, and erroneous. In a simple experimental test of false belief understanding, the child being tested watches while two dolls are used to enact a scenario. One character, Sally, hides her marble in one of two boxes and then leaves the scene. While she is away the other character, Ann, moves the marble to the other box. When Sally returns, the child is asked to indicate in which box she will look for her marble. The majority of typically developing children pass this test at around 4 years, indicating that Sally will look where the marble was first hidden. Some 80% of children with autism fail this task—they are able to indicate the original and new position of the marble, but fail to understand where Sally will actually look for it (Baron-Cohen *et al.* 1985).

Of the able autistic spectrum participants who pass this test, a majority fail more difficult tests tapping understanding of 'double bluff' thinking; for instance, an elaborated scenario in which Sally secretly spots Ann relocating her marble. Moreover, theory of mind difficulty is not confined to these rather contrived situations. For instance, Happé (1994) found that autistic participants fail to understand scenarios in which one character's utterance to another is ironic, a white lie, a deliberate lie, or an attempt to persuade. A common factor linking failure in these different contexts is a difficulty in intuitively conceiving or imagining the intentions that are behind what people do and say.

Language skills vary considerably among autistic individuals and among clinical sub-groups on the spectrum: for instance, individuals with Asperger syndrome usually speak fluently and have few difficulties with grammar or syntax. Yet throughout the spectrum individuals may have difficulty in understanding non-literal or metaphorical language (Happé 1993), in other words, with the dimension of language most closely associated with imaginative thinking. Thus phrases such as 'keeping the wolf from the door' may be interpreted literally by an autistic child, and even evoke an anxious checking of the garden. The failure of autistic adults to appreciate irony or sarcasm (Happé 1994) may render them easy targets for teasing or bullying.

A difficulty in understanding and generating narratives has obvious implications for literary imagination and potentially for a much wider domain. Belmonte (2007) proposes that narrative, broadly considered, is fundamental to both the operations of the human mind and the workings of the brain. Bruner and Feldman (2000) studied the ability of high-functioning autistic 15-year-olds to follow stories and to re-tell them in their own words. Though the children could recount main story events in the correct sequence, their omission of key details, such as deceptions perpetrated on the characters, suggested that the stories did not evoke the understanding of their true significance that most neurotypical readers would share. Bruner and Feldman argue that children become socialized through interpersonal transactions with an intrinsically narrative form. Hence a lack of narrative understanding will profoundly affect the capacity of people with autism to engage with social groups and wider culture. Other studies (e.g. Baron-Cohen and Frith 1986) have suggested that autistic children's difficulties might not be with the narrative form per se, but with the human intentions that provide the thread of so much narrative. Autistic children were able to arrange sets of pictures to form a story, provided that the basis for the narrative was a causal or mechanical sequence of events. In contrast, when the correct sequence depended on understanding the intentions and behaviour of human characters in the pictures, their performance was impaired.

Besides its human content, narrative is frequently fictitious or fantastical, a medium that adult autistic individuals are known to find difficult. A study by Craig *et al.* (2000) compared the abilities of autistic and control children to suggest either realistic or fantasy endings to stories. The autistic children's difficulty in generating fantasy stories was interpreted as showing a deficit in creative imagination. Extending this exploration of creative imagination to other tasks, Craig and colleagues found that autistic children had difficulty in drawing a fantastical creature (Craig *et al.* 2001), in generating ideas for imaginative adaptations of a toy, and in suggesting imaginative uses for a piece of foam (Craig and Baron-Cohen 1999).

The autistic capacity for mental imagery (see Pearson in Chapter 9), presents a more mixed pattern. Craig *et al.* (2001) interpreted autistic difficulties in drawing fantastical figures as reflecting a difficulty in forming mental images of 'unreal' entities but not of veridical ones. However, there is anecdotal evidence that some autistic individuals have intact or even enhanced capacity for both forms of imagery. Temple Grandin, an author and academic with 'high-functioning' autism, describes how her predominantly pictorial thinking has enabled her to 'build entire systems in her imagination', helping her to design enhanced equipment for humane cattle handling during veterinary procedures and slaughter (Grandin 1995).

In general, the picture of imagination deficits is not all-or-none, with people at the 'high-functioning' end of the spectrum experiencing fewer difficulties. Some aspects of these deficits have also been challenged. For instance, Lewis and Boucher (1988) demonstrated that children with ASD may be encouraged to engage in pretend play given certain task conditions. Leevers and Harris (1998) failed to replicate the finding, by Craig and colleagues, that autistic children had difficulty drawing imaginary creatures.

Nonetheless, the indications are that many people with ASD have difficulties with aspects of imaginative thought. This is especially intriguing because the pattern embraces forms of imagination which have often been treated as unrelated (see Roth in the Introduction to this volume). A parsimonious interpretation—that a common process, or causal chain of processes, underpins this pattern—would also suggest a relationship between certain forms of imagination in neurotypical individuals. In practice, there may be more than one substrate for the deficits, but the idea of a unifying 'core deficit' has played an important role in some key models which are summarized next.

IMAGINATIVE DEFICITS AND
THEORETICAL MODELS OF AUTISM

Empirical theory of mind findings have engendered a family of *Theory of Mind* (ToM) models in which faults in a mentalizing process or mechanism also undermine a wide range of other cognitive activities and behaviours. The central assumption is that humans intuitively adopt an 'intentional stance' (Dennett 1987) that enables them to attribute a wide range of mental states — beliefs, desires, intentions, goals, thoughts, memories, emotions, and so on — to themselves and others. One consequence is to give a special status to propositions such as 'the marble is in the first box' when preceded by phrases such as 'Sally thinks that. . .'. If Ann has moved the marble, the proposition about the position of the marble is false, yet the statement '*Sally thinks* that the marble is in the first box' need not be so. Leslie (1987) proposed that understanding both pretence and false belief depends on this ability to 'decouple' propositions that are embedded in an intentional context from their relationship with reality. Specific features of Leslie's account — the bracketing of pretence and false belief, and the idea that an innate cognitive module serves as the 'decoupling' mechanism — have been challenged. However, it is clear that some means for people to intuitively understand other people's mental states is important. Without it, the 'social' imagination involved in understanding and predicting behaviour would clearly be affected, as when autistic individuals fail to understand another person's false belief or deceit. By extension this intentional deficit could affect other forms of imagining. In relation to figurative language such as metaphor the inability to process a speaker's (or writer's) intentions would prevent the autistic person moving beyond the literal mapping of words and phrases to their referents. Similarly, difficulties with understanding narrative could arise because the thread or 'plot' of so much narrative depends upon the ability to attribute intentionality to the characters.

One problem with this approach is how far it can be plausibly extended to those phenomena, including repetitive behaviour and narrowly focused interests, that do not have an obviously social character. An autistic child may spend all day obsessively arranging toys by colour or shape, while an autistic adult may pore for hours over the telephone directory. Baron-Cohen (1989) has argued that a person whose capacity for intentional attributions is compromised will be effectively blind to the social forces that give everyday events and activities most of their meaning and coherence, and will therefore resort to repetitive activity and narrowly focused interests as a form of substitute stimulation.

This type of behaviour, however, lends itself readily to an alternative explanation in terms of *executive function* problems (see Hill 2004 for an overview). Executive function embraces cognitive capacities such as planning activities to achieve a goal, shifting one's mental 'set' or focus to undertake new tasks, and inhibiting irrelevant responses. Significantly, executive function promotes the fluency, flexibility, and capacity for innovation that are some of the hallmarks of creative imagination. Most people with autism have difficulties with executive function tasks, analogous to those of neurological patients with damage to the frontal lobes of the brain, known to be crucial for executive function. Conversely, people with autism may excel at carrying out routine activities that require a sustained focus in a narrow field.

A wide range of imagination-related difficulties in autism have been attributed to executive dysfunction (Russell 1997). For instance, when an autistic child is asked to complete a story, draw a fantastical figure, or suggest new uses for a toy (see Craig *et al.* 2001), his main difficulty could be in disengaging sufficiently from the stimuli he can see in order to generate new or different ideas. Yet this approach poses the opposite problem to ToM models, in not readily accounting for difficulties in 'social imagination'.

A third class of model invokes generic principles to transcend these difficulties of ToM and executive function approaches. For instance, Currie and Ravenscroft (2002) propose *recreative imagination* as a general capacity to see, think, and respond to the world *as if* from an alternative perspective, whether the perspective of another individual, or the self's own hypothetical perspective at a time or place other than the here and now. Arguably an impaired capacity for such imaginative projection would affect both 'social' and 'non-social' forms of imagining. Thus understanding another person's thoughts and feelings may involve the ability, essentially, to think or feel what that person is feeling. Pretending may depend on projecting oneself into playful imaginary scenarios such as 'being' a pirate. Finally, executive-type capacities such as planning and innovating may require the capacity to project oneself into hypothetical situations in order to evaluate the outcomes of actions before carrying them out.

While full evaluation of this complex field is beyond the scope of this chapter, there is a clear rationale for suggesting that, in autism, one or a small number of underlying processes imposes constraints in many situations where imaginative behaviour is called for.

Yet this conclusion begs questions about the talent of some autistic individuals in creative fields. One view might be that creative imagination is preserved in autism because it operates relatively independently of mentalizing, executive function, or projective forms of imagination, and is less cognitively demanding. In keeping with this suggestion, Whiten and Suddendorf (in Chapter 2) argue that inventiveness is a comparatively simple skill compared with the secondary representation involved in mindreading. Currie and Ravenscroft argue that a person may be creative without recourse to the complex forms of perspective taking implied by recreative imagination. Though such distinctions dispose of the paradox, they do so through restrictive definitions of creative imagination, which may underplay its complexities. An alternative resolution would be to argue that the scope for true creativity in autistic art is highly constrained—that it is more skilled and accomplished than imaginative. This is the broad implication of recent models that represent autistic thought as a way of processing information that generates both skills and deficits for the individual. In the ensuing sections of this chapter autistic work in two creative fields—art and poetry—is shown to highlight some difficult issues for these recent accounts.

AUTISM, IMAGINATION, AND THE CREATIVE ARTS

Many autistic individuals have special skills that do not attract widespread interest—for instance, in completing complex jigsaw puzzles. A smaller minority have more notable and surprising skills. Many of these so-called 'savant' skills such as numerical calculation, popularized in the film *Rainman*, probably do afford limited scope for creativity. Skills in prototypically imaginative fields include visual art and music.

Savant skills or talents have usually been defined as isolated, narrow areas of ability in the context of profound disability (Treffert 1989). However, it appears that many 'savants' have more than one area of special ability. For instance, Stephen Wiltshire, the creator of many beautiful architectural drawings, and Tito Mukhopadhyay, a writer and poet, are both musical too. The notion that special talents invariably mismatch with the general level of functioning is also misleading in the case of some 'high-functioning' individuals. For instance, the writers Donna Williams and Wendy Lawson are both academically able individuals, leading fulfilled and independent lives. Donna is a university graduate with special skills including autobiography, poetry, and visual art. Wendy Lawson is pursuing a PhD, alongside her career as a poet, writer, and public speaker. Individuals such as these do not conform to the traditional definition of a 'savant'.

Notwithstanding these somewhat different profiles of autistic talent, the issue is the same. If the outputs that enable some autistic individuals to pursue professional careers as artists, musicians, or writers are not in some sense creative, this begs the question of how they are produced, and how they achieve their impact.

Characteristics of Autistic Visual Art

In the past thirty years, a number of savant visual artists have achieved considerable public prominence through both the exhibition and sale of their works, and published studies of how they achieve their artistic skill. Undoubtedly such artists existed in previous eras, but the recent group has benefited from the growing public interest in autism, and opportunities for dissemination, including the specialist publishing house Jessica Kingsley, live art shows focusing on disabled artists, and Internet sites.

Lorna Selfe's important studies of a profoundly autistic child artist called Nadia (Selfe 1977, 1983) highlighted key characteristics which provide a point of comparison for work by more recent artists. Despite being socially withdrawn, clumsy, and lacking all but a few words of spoken language or forms of gesture, in her third year Nadia spontaneously developed an outstanding capacity to draw animals. By the age of 4 she was drawing exquisite pictures of horses, soon followed by cockerels and cavalrymen. These drawings were derived from Nadia's observations of images in books but, as Selfe shows, they were not copies. Her pictures also had realistic detail and accurate proportions and perspective (Figure 13.1). Drawings by typically developing children of this age are wobbly, schematic images, with sticks for arms and legs, circles for heads, and no depth. Their drawing ability develops slowly through a series of recognizable stages (Figure 13.2). Formal principles such as how to represent perspective may appear only as a result of later instruction.

The early, spontaneous onset of a fully fledged drawing skill is characteristic of other autistic artists such as Stephen Wiltshire. At the age of 4, he was totally unresponsive to surrounding activities but would sketch compulsively for hours on end, scribbling on scraps of paper when he was not provided with materials. Stephen's preferred topic has always been buildings, often within visually complex urban settings, such as the London Docklands, Manhattan, and Venice. These scenes, typically drawn after he has briefly glanced at the subject matter, are executed with meticulously accurate attention to detail, proportion, and perspective (see Figure 13.3), to the extent that in the foreword of an early book about Stephen's work, the architect Sir Hugh Casson wrote: 'Happily, every now and then, a rocket of young talent explodes and continues to shower us with its sparks. Stephen Wiltshire . . . is one of these rockets' (Casson in Wiltshire 1987). As a teenager attending art school, Stephen was encouraged to experiment with new techniques, and to deal with more diverse subject matter, including the human figure. These attempts had only moderate success, since Stephen's motivation to extend his artistic language was limited (Pring *et al.* 1997). Human figures, when they do appear in his drawings, are typically inciden-

PLATE 1

Wash Day in Pakistan by Richard Wawro.

PLATE 2

St. Paul's and St. Andrew's Methodist Church and the Migraine Type Lightning and the Elves by Jessica Park.

Figure 13.1. A drawing of a horse, by Nadia, aged about 4 years. From Selfe, L. (1977) *Nadia: A Case of Extraordinary Drawing Ability in an Autistic Child.* © Academic Press, London.

tal to the main scene, and less skilfully executed than his outstanding drawings of buildings (Figure 13.4).

Such characteristics have helped establish an influential general account of autistic visual art. Autistic artists are represented as highly atypical in that their sophisticated drawing skills emerge early, apparently spontaneously, and completely by-passing the usual stages in the development of neurotypical children's art. They appear impelled to draw, devoting hours to producing copious sketches or paintings, yet they are said to lack the desire, characteristic of non-autistic artists, to shape, refine, and improve their work.

Figure 13.2. Drawings of a man and dog by typically developing children: top right, 3 years 10 months; top left, 4 years 1 month; second and third rows, 4 years 8 months and 5 years 1 month; bottom right, 5 years 8 months; bottom left, 6 years. From Silk, A. M. J., and Thomas, G. V. (1986) Development and differentiation in children's figure drawings. *British Journal of Psychology* 399–410.

The work itself is characterized as highly detailed and realistic, impoverished in human content or emotional valence, and so memory-dependent that it is often thought of as eidetic or photographic.

Selfe suggested that Nadia was able to draw as she did *because of* her lack of language. Correspondingly, it has been argued that language temporarily impairs the early drawing efforts of typically developing children because they do not draw what they see, but rather access attributes of the subject matter, which they have conceptualized, memorized, and verbally labelled as 'horse', 'bird', and so on, in order to draw 'what they know' (see Costall 1995 for a critical overview). Building on these observations, Humphrey (1998) has proposed that, lacking the symbolic capacity furnished by language, Nadia was merely engaged in faithfully representing what she had seen on a two-dimensional surface. He goes on to point out that Nadia's work bears a striking resemblance to prehistoric cave paintings of animals such as those at Lascaux and Altamira. Rather than convincing him that cave paintings represent the emergence, 30,000 plus years ago, of the cognitive capacity for artistic creativity (see Mithen in Chapter 1 for instance), he concludes quite the opposite: that the prehistoric art, like its modern autistic counterparts, was achieved via an essentially mechanical exercise, unmediated by the

Figure 13.3. *View from San Giorgio Maggiore* by Stephen Wiltshire. The drawing was made in 1991 when Stephen was 15. © Stephen Wiltshire.

Figure 13.4. *Central Park* by Stephen Wiltshire (2005). One of very few architectural scenes including human figures. © Stephen Wiltshire.

symbolic processes that are the hallmark of the typical modern human mind. This notion of drawing produced by 'read-out' from a hypothetical 'sensory core' (Costall 1995) offers no scope for imaginative transformation of the subject matter, because representation is tied closely and inextricably to the spatial characteristics of the original model. It may well be that autistic artists benefit from the preserved or enhanced capacity for visual imagery described by Temple Grandin (1995). But as Pearson (in Chapter 9) and Geake and Kringelbach (in Chapter 14) emphasize, imagery lends itself not only to reproduction of reality, but to creative transformations.

A wider review of autistic art highlights such transformations. For instance, the late Richard Wawro, though he often based his paintings on images viewed once, transformed what he remembered into bold, impressionistic works, displaying a vibrant and original use of colour. The human figures in Richard's works were portrayed with sensitivity (see Plate 1).

Jessica Park's work frequently features faithful representations of everyday objects and buildings (Plate 2). Yet she executes her works in an arresting 'pop-art' palette of colours, with some highly imaginative additions. In Jessica's account of this painting (Park 2001), the 'glowing doughnuts all over the sky are elves', while the 'zigzagging objects are lightning. They look white but they are three different pastels. . ..I see them when I have migraine'. The transformation of everyday objects, rendered quasi-photographically, by the use of 'non-real' colour is reminiscent of the work of Andy Warhol, hailed by many as a creative genius. Ironically, Warhol is also considered by some to have shown strongly autistic features (Paradiž 2002). Even Stephen Wiltshire's works, though they often appear as faithful renditions of real world scenes, are transformative in their lively, dynamic use of line (Hermelin 2001). It is worth noting that the painter Canaletto, who also specialized in highly accurate, realistic paintings of contemporary Venetian scenes, was not, presumably, considered lacking in creative talent.

The most interesting test case for this discussion is that of Gilles Tréhin, a young man on the autism spectrum with many talents, of which art is his most outstanding. Like Stephen Wiltshire, Tréhin's work focuses on precise line drawings of buildings and complex urban scenes, and, like Wiltshire, Tréhin drew spontaneously from an early age, depicting buildings in proper perspective, a skill that had to be painstakingly 'discovered' by the artists of the Renaissance. But though Tréhin's work resembles Wiltshire's at a superficial glance, there is one critical difference: it is drawn from his imagination. Over a period of 20 years, Tréhin has executed dozens of complex, meticulous drawings, depicting the districts, buildings, streets, and monuments of an entirely imaginary city called 'Urville'. In the recent book of his work (Tréhin 2006), each drawing is accompanied by a description of the buildings, their economic and cultural history, and the people who made their mark there.

These fictitious vignettes include some references to real historical periods and architectural genres, rendering the fantasy even more convincing. Figure 13.5 shows Tréhin's drawing of Place de la Catalogne, while his caption demonstrates the facility and considerable wit with which he mixes real names and dates with fictitious characters and events.

This brief survey indicates that while different savant artists have some common characteristics, their art is by no means stylistically uniform. Theoretical approaches that reduce it simply to a form of 'memory read-out' are contentious, though enhanced visual imagery may well facilitate their skill. While there may be imaginative constraints in this body of work, these are difficult to characterize in terms that both embrace the artists considered, and differentiate them reliably from non-autistic artists. The evaluation continues with models of autistic thought as a 'processing style'.

AUTISTIC DEFICITS AND ARTISTIC SKILLS: TWO SIDES OF A COIN?

Francesca Happé and Uta Frith have developed the concept of *weak central coherence* to explain how people with ASD process information. (See Happé and Frith 2006 for a recent overview.) The core idea is that the processing style of neurotypical individuals is 'centrally coherent': that is, at levels from perceptual processing, to the extraction of meaning from language and other complex cognitive stimuli, they process information holistically, and in context, so as to elide irrelevant detail and extract meaning. In contrast the autistic information processing style is characterized by 'weak central coherence', in which attention to local detail takes precedence over the processing of global configuration and meaning.

Depending on the task, this weak central coherence may be either beneficial or detrimental to the individual's performance. It appears beneficial in the so-called embedded figures test in which a small element, such as a triangle must be located within a complex geometric pattern. Neurotypical individuals find it very difficult to pick out the individual shape from the surrounding context of shapes. In contrast, people on the autism spectrum find this easy to do, apparently because their search for the embedded shape is unencumbered by attention to the overall configuration (Joliffe and Baron-Cohen 1997). A task in which weak central coherence is detrimental is one where the same item of information must be interpreted differently according to the context. For instance, Happé (1997) asked participants to read aloud a word such as 'tear' in the context of sentences evoking either a 'tear' in the eye or a piece of fabric. Autistic participants made many errors, suggesting

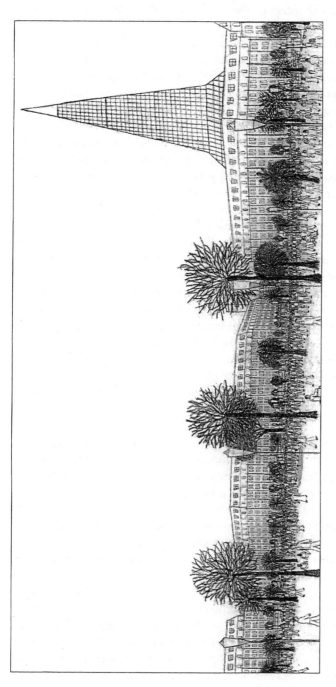

Place de la Catalogne (3rd, 4th, 6th and 7th arr.) and page 108. 1867—Architect: Hugues Pizerotto (1831–1907). The square comprises a wide open space, and marks the boundary between Urville before and after Laballière. It is now affected by heavy traffic twenty-four hours a day. The film *Le labyrinthe carré* in 1974 by director Josiane Destillesc (born 1939) was set here. Since 1982, every June, the Catalmusics festival has showcased established and new artists, with Urvillians gathering to hear local bands such as Donne de la Voix, Lou Grapau, Sine Qua Non, Thé au Riz, Shoobap, Contrôle Dynamite, Huile à Volonté, El Djezair Blues, Cache-Moi C'la and Chat Perché, and more widely known artists such as Les Rita Mitsuko, Touré Kounda, Noir Désir, Les Négresses Vertes, Mano Negra, Zebda, the Pixies, Nirvana and Radiohead. The festival lasts for three days and attracts almost 50,000 people to the square.

Figure 13.5. *Place de la Catalogne (3rd, 4th, 6th and 17th arr.)* and explanatory caption by Gilles Tréhin (2006). From Tréhin, G. (2006) *Urville.* © Jessica Kingsley Publishers, London.

that they were unable to integrate the specific stimulus with context in order to interpret it appropriately.

The late Beate Hermelin and her colleagues explored the relevance of this model to understanding autistic savant talents in studies summarized in *Bright Splinters of the Mind* (Hermelin 2001). Hermelin suggests that autistic talents ranging from expertise in calculating, to music and the visual arts are both characterized and constrained by this processing style. In relation to autistic visual art, weak central coherence actually involves two somewhat distinct assumptions—firstly that the work will display an obsessive attention to visual detail at the expense of configurational properties, and secondly that the subject matter will be executed without reference to its meaning or context. Considering the first assumption, the work of certain autistic artists, including Wiltshire, Tréhin, and Park, displays great attention to detail (see Figures 13.3, 13.5, and Plate 1). Yet these works also suggest a masterly grasp of how parts fit together to form coherent wholes. Wiltshire and Tréhin do not just draw isolated buildings—their outstanding talent is to produce complex architectural scenes, in which the parts are superbly articulated within the overall configuration. It may be that an examination of the stages by which these artists execute their drawings would reveal a detail-oriented strategy. That is, on the weak central coherence account, we would expect Wiltshire and Tréhin to work 'down-up', adding elements of the scene one-by-one, while non-autistic artists should rough out the overall form of the scene before filling in the detail. Descriptions of Wiltshire's working methods are consistent with this proposal. But since his finished works do not lack unity or coherence, the model applies only with this considerable qualification.

The fit of the model to Nadia's sketches is even less satisfactory. At a purely visual level, her work gives the impression of detail sacrificed in favour of the overall configuration. The drawings have a pared down, almost insouciant quality reminiscent of the casual preparatory sketches in the notebooks of celebrated artists. Attention to detail is evident only in the sense that aspects such as anatomical proportions and perspective are flawlessly delivered. Moreover, Selfe noted that when Nadia was given a tracing of one of her own drawings with the head missing, she would immediately complete it, indicating her concern that the object should be whole.

The second assumption, that autistic visual art is executed in isolation from meaningful context, is also problematic, especially in the case of Tréhin's work. The whole purpose of his drawings and their captions is to explicate the historical, geographical, architectural, and cultural attributes that form the concept of Urville. The drawings clearly signify a meaningful imaginary world for Tréhin, which transcends their physical representation on the page. Nadia seems closer to fitting this assumption, and Humphrey considers her work paradigmatic of art as a visual transcription, unmediated by meaning or symbolism. Yet though Nadia could not name the animals she was drawing, her subject matter was far from indiscriminate. She had different favourites across time, starting at 3 years with horses, then moving to horses and riders, birds, dogs, other animals, and human figures. Moreover, Selfe found no evidence that Nadia was transcribing individual exemplars from memory onto paper—on the contrary, her drawings were apparently composites based on different images she had seen, in which details such as orientation were inevitably transformed. In this sense, Nadia appeared to have formulated overall concepts of the living kinds she was drawing, even though she could not express them in words. Further work is needed to establish what meanings artists such as Stephen Wiltshire attach to their pictures. In general, while the weak central coherence model evokes the attention to detail found in much autistic art, it is difficult to frame this idea in a way that captures the stylistic variability between artists, the unity and coherence of individual works, and the personal significance that they clearly have for the artists.

An alternative model of autistic skills and deficits (Baron-Cohen 2003, p. 63) portrays the autistic cognitive style as high on 'systemizing', the drive to understand and build systems, where a system is defined as: 'anything which is governed by rules specifying input–operation–output relationships'. Correspondingly, the person with ASD is portrayed as low on empathy. Emotional empathy impairment, consistently highlighted in Peter Hobson's important work (2002) is here reflected in Baron-Cohen's reformulation of theory of mind as the combined ability to imagine or understand others' thoughts and feelings and take their perspective, *and* to respond appropriately to their emotional states. This high-systemizing, low-empathizing profile evokes the prototypical representation of autistic thinking as highly structured and orderly, but essentially unimaginative and lacking in human insights. Baron-Cohen suggests that people with this profile will gravitate towards rule-bound or 'systemic' activities and interests, including maths, physics, chemistry, logic, rather than to more 'human', creative and less systemic domains such as the caring professions, arts, and humanities. A large-scale study relating Cambridge University undergraduates' chosen degree courses to their scores on an autism questionnaire that tapped some features of empathizing and systemizing broadly supported this claim. There were a disproportionate number of students with an autistic-like profile among students in engineering and other systems-oriented disciplines (Baron-Cohen *et al.* 2001).

This *low empathizing–high systemizing* model implies that people on the autism spectrum should not be drawn to activities such as art at all, and it is probably true that the proportion of autistic people in the arts and humanities

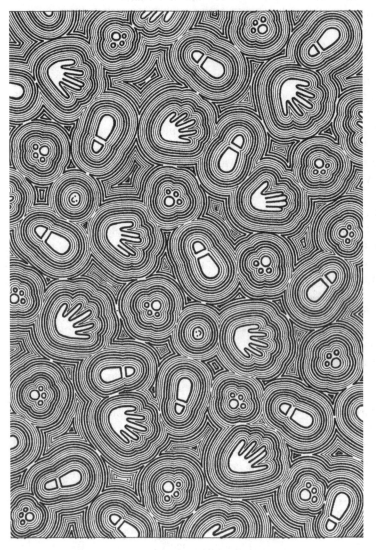

Figure 13.6. *Symbolic Impressions MK-81* by Peter Myers (2001). The first 80 versions of this drawing were in colour. From Myers, P., Baron-Cohen, S. and Wheelwright S. (2004) *An Exact Mind: An Artist with Asperger Syndrome.* London: Jessica Kingsley Publishers. © Peter Myers.

is small. But where art *is* the preferred activity, Baron-Cohen suggests that its stylistic features conform to the model. His view is informed by the drawings of Peter Myers (Myers *et al.* 2004)—see Figure 13.6. In this typical example of Myers' work, every millimetre of space is painstakingly filled, replicating the patterning used throughout the picture. The claim that this design is governed by a set of rules for filling the space does seem convincing.

Similar claims could be made about Wiltshire's and Tréhin's work, both of which appear highly systematic in their deployment of architectural elements. Nadia's work is not so easily interpreted as exceptional systemizing. While her work may well be driven by an implicit set of rules for drawing animals, all competent artists could be said to have internalized drawing conventions specifically relevant to their chosen domain. Richard Wawro's work may be seen as adopting some impressionistic principles, but then so too does the work of key impressionist artists. To summarize, Baron-Cohen's model captures some features of some autistic art, notably the systematic repetition of particular artistic devices, the relative dearth of human content, and the lack of emotional valence. However, systemizing is defined at a level of generality that does not reliably discriminate attributes of autistic art from those of other artists.

In conclusion, the two models outlined here interpret autistic art as the outcome of a processing strategy—weak central coherence or systemizing—which leaves little scope for creative imagination. While both approaches capture key features of some autistic visual art, they do not encompass its stylistic variety and are not adequately informed by systematic evaluation of its imaginative features. I now turn to my research on poetry by autistic writers, considering predictions from the empathizing–systemizing model within a broader evaluation of imagination and self-expression in this work.

IMAGINATIVE SELF-EXPRESSION IN POETS ON THE AUTISM SPECTRUM?

> When you are trying to think blue
> And end up thinking black
> You can be sure to be frustrated
> Time and again it happens to me
> And I get quite helpless
> Otherwise why should I get up and spin myself
> Spinning my body
> Brings some sort of harmony to my thoughts
> So that I can centrifuge away all the black thoughts
> I realise that the faster I spin
> The faster I drive away the black

From Poem 4 by Tito Mukhopadhyay (at age 11 years), a poem from
his book *Beyond the Silence: My Life, the World and Autism*,
published by the National Autistic Society.

Tito Mukhopadhyay is one of several recently published poets with an
autism spectrum diagnosis. On a more speculative note, an autistic disorder
has been ascribed to Samuel Beckett (Glastonbury 1997), W.B. Yeats, and
Lewis Carroll (Fitzgerald 2004).

Of all the media in which autistic talent might manifest itself, poetry is the
most surprising. Though sometimes descriptive, it embodies no ready counterpart for the asymbolic, memory-based transcription of reality, which,
though erroneously, has minimized the perceived creativity of autistic visual
art. Poetry appears, *par excellence*, an intensely abstract, symbolic, and free-
flowing form of linguistic expression. To write poetry without creative imagination or the capacity to express insight into the human condition would
seem something of an oxymoron—both appear quintessential tools of the
poet's trade. Yet, considering Baron-Cohen's systemizing–empathizing profile
for autism, it might be argued that poetry writing can be approached purely
as a language system, governed by systematic rules acquired in much the same
way as the rules for solving quadratic equations. Would it be in principle
possible to write poetry in this way, and what would it be like?

Ricks (2005) has suggested that the key defining feature that sets poetry
apart from prose, is the way the lines are set out on the page:

> ... in poetry, the line endings are significant, and they effect their signifi-
> cance—not necessarily of rhythm, and whether of force or of nuance—by
> using their ensuing space, by using a pause which is not necessarily a pause of
> punctuation and so may be only equivocally a pause at all. Lines of prose end
> with a soft return; lines of poetry end with a hard return. (Ricks 2005, p. 14)

If Ricks is correct, a person who is good at systemizing should be able to
acquire rules for the spatial disposition of words, and produce writing that
has at least the physical appearance of poetry. Similarly, traditional stylistic
devices such as rhyme and rhythm lend themselves to rules that should be
accessible to a good systemizer. In short, people who score highly on systemizing should be capable of writing that meets formal and stylistic criteria for
poetry, such as the spatial arrangement and auditory patterning of words.
With low scores on empathizing, we would also expect their poetry to lack
expressed awareness of human thoughts and feelings, whether their own or
other people's. But poems produced in this way, devoid of the figurative and
expressive qualities that we normally associate with poetry, would most likely
appear as minimal, mechanical, and unaccomplished works—examples of
the craft without the art. C. John Holcombe's definition of the distinctive
qualities of poetry contrasts sharply with Ricks' minimalist definition in

emphasizing the rich texturing and complex juxtaposing of words we associate with poetry in its fullest sense:

> Words for poets have meanings, appropriate uses, associations, connotations, etymologies, histories of use and misuse. They conjure up images, feelings, shadowy depths and glinting surfaces. Their properties are marvellous, endless, not to be guessed at from casual inspection. And each property—meaning, association, weight, colour, duration, shape, texture—changes as words are combined in phrases, rhythms, lines stanzas and completed poems. (C. J. Holcombe, at www.poetrymagic.co.uk)

A key aim of the research was to explore whether autistic poetry transcends the minimal level, whether it captures Holcombe's 'images, feelings, shadowy depths and glinting surfaces' to the same extent as neurotypical poetry, and whether it has distinctive qualities of its own. An earlier study (Dowker *et al.* 1996) contributed relevant findings concerning a single poet with Asperger syndrome. However, the comparison of one poet with a single 'control' poet who, while physically disabled, had very different intellectual and social competencies, make these findings difficult to interpret. The research summarized here employed the technique of linguistic content analysis in a much wider evaluation of autistic poetry and comparison with the works of a range of neurotypical poets. The poets also completed a questionnaire exploring their reflections about formative influences, and the motivations for and goals of their work. This research is discussed further in Roth (2007).

Autistic and Neurotypical Poetry Compared

To date, work by five published autistic spectrum poets has been analysed, each sample being compared with a selection of work by several neurotypical poets, suitably matched in terms of gender, age, and educational level. The autism spectrum poets whose work we have studied include two males, aged 11 and 20, and females, aged 24, 41, and 53 with diagnoses of autism or Asperger syndrome.

The basis for the analysis was a set of coding categories and definitions, which were refined until they could be reliably and consistently employed by coders working independently of one another. Some 190 autistic poems (4008 lines) and 190 non-autistic poems (3904 lines) were randomly sampled and coded for both 'whole poem' and 'line-by-line' features. Table 13.1 shows a summary of the poetic features coded using this system. The frequency counts for each coded feature were statistically analysed.

Overall, the autistic poetry shared many of the characteristics of non-autistic poetry, and appeared not as a minimal interpretation of the craft, but as an exploration of its stylistic, imaginative, and expressive possibilities.

Table 13.1. Examples of features coded by content analysis.

Coding category	Examples of features coded
Global features	Theme of poem
	Poet's 'voice'—autobiographical, biographical
	Literary devices—rhyme, rhythm, refrain
Literary devices	Alliteration/assonance
Imaginative devices	Complex figurative language; metaphor; simile
'Self-aware' language	Reflections on own mental states and self-concept
'Other-aware' language	Reflections on another's thoughts, concept of other
Non-specific mentalist language	Mental state references not specifically attributed

While each poet had different stylistic emphases, there was flexibility in their deployment of styles across poems, and variation among poets. Much of the poetry was in free verse form; relatively little consisted of the equal-length stanzas or rhyming couplets predicted by a rule-following or systemizing approach to poetry.

Linguistic Devices

The autistic poetry was in no way dominated by formal literary features to the exclusion of imaginative features such as metaphor, and content expressing thoughts and feelings. The usage of rhyme, rhythm, and refrain was modest and very similar to that of the non-autistic poets. One literary device—alliteration and assonance—was employed significantly less, in statistical terms, by autistic poets than neurotypical poets. The autistic poet who used this device least of the five does not use speech as a principal medium of communication, and may not therefore use implicit speech to 'hear' how his poetic phrases sound. However, this poet's capacity for rhyme, which would also require the words to be sounded, seems inconsistent with this proposal. And while the overall frequency of alliteration and assonance was lower, there was some accomplished use of these devices, as in this poem extract by Craig Romkema:

> Ghana caught my attention first,
> Panama, Zambia, Corsica,
> Then Kayla, Jessica, Erica, Elena,
> Iowa, South Dakota,
> And best of all,
> Mozzarella,
> Lovely sibilance of sounds.

From 'The Search', by Craig Romkema (1996) in his book
Embracing the Sky, published by Jessica Kingsley,
© Craig Romkema.

Imaginative Devices

This analysis treats figurative words and phrases as an index of imagination. Themes of the poetry were also considered. The present results were arresting in two respects. Firstly, as a group the autistic poets made substantial use of metaphor—as much overall as the non-autistic poets—although the five varied in how much they employed, in keeping with their individual stylistic preferences. Secondly, all used simile to a much lesser extent than metaphor, though simile was also relatively rare in the neurotypical poetry. Previous findings (Happé 1994) suggest that simile is more accessible than metaphor to people with ASD, while understanding irony is especially difficult. The possibility that somewhat different skills are involved in understanding figurative language (the task in Happé's study) and in spontaneously generating it within poetry requires further research.

In terms of imaginative characteristics and scope, the autistic poetry had some distinctive features. Fantasy was infrequent among the themes of this poetry, though it also included works with a surreal quality:

> Standing on the edge of black inspiration night,
> Lure of Strawberry Fields for ever,
> Backed up in a duel,
> Against a knight of the night in shining armour

> Life behind glass, a living death made tolerable
> Pure fear of the one touching touch which could shatter the glass forever
> And send the tightrope walker plummeting from her tightrope,
> Into the knowing of the unknown

> From 'Becoming Three-dimensional' by Donna Williams (2004) in her book *Not Just Anything: A Collection of Thoughts on Paper*, published by Jessica Kingsley, © Donna Williams.

A statistical analysis of metaphor sub-types showed that the autistic poets provided fewer 'exceptionally creative' metaphors, defined for the purposes of coding as images related in a way that was both original and penetrable. More of their metaphors were either moderately creative or idiomatic figures of speech, such as 'bright new worlds' or 'pompous talking heads'. However, one of these poets also produced more 'idiosyncratic metaphors', in which the relationship between the metaphorical expression and that which it represents was not entirely clear. Such metaphors are difficult to understand, but are also highly original.

Humour was not formally coded in this study, because of the difficulty of agreeing an operational definition for use in objective coding. A different evaluation is underway to explore humorous qualities. Neither the autistic nor the non-autistic poetry gave a markedly humorous impression, though lines such as Donna Williams' 'Some people are stormy weather' surely have an ironic humorous appeal.

If figurative language use is a legitimate index, these results do demonstrate the capacity for creative imagination among autistic poets. The differential use of metaphor sub-types by the autistic and non-autistic poets suggests some qualitative or quantitative contrasts which merit further investigation. Of course, the creative impact of a poem is not purely, or even principally, a function of its use of metaphor: a poem may be replete with metaphors that do not evoke an imaginative response. The systematic methodology used here to analyse metaphors and their sub-types also took into account the meaningful context of each individual poem. However, the method is necessarily limited in the scope it offers to embrace the poet's metaphorical intentions. Further studies addressing these complex questions are in progress.

These findings once again seem at odds with the predictions of the systemizing approach. While the ability to use literary devices such as rhyme and rhythm lends itself to a systemizing strategy informed by a set of rules, it is hard to see how a grasp of subtle ambiguities of language required to write metaphorically could be acquired or implemented in this way. Given the explanatory value of the systemizing approach in explaining other aspects of autism, this merits further investigation.

Poetic Perspectives

The most strikingly distinctive feature of the autistic work was the pronounced focus on the self. The themes chosen by autistic poets mostly concerned the self or relationships between the self and others, while the non-autistic poets also wrote often about philosophical, political, or fantastical topics, as well as about nature, places, or events. The autistic spectrum poets also wrote predominantly from their own 'voice'—that is, speaking about themselves, from their own perspective. When not writing in this way, they preferred the descriptive, non-perspectival voice appropriate to commenting on places or events. They rarely wrote from the perspective of another. In contrast, while the non-autistic poets also wrote often from their own 'voice', they quite frequently took another's perspective as well as adopting the non-perspectival voice.

The Language of 'Self' and 'Other'

This analysis yielded results echoing those for perspectives. Overall, the autistic poets referred substantially more often to their own thoughts, sensations, emotions, and desires than to the corresponding mental states of others. This self-referential language was significantly more frequent than for non-autistic poets, who showed a more even balance between self- and other-related language.

This finding is of particular interest. Recent accounts suggest that 'self' and 'other' are co-constituted in autism (Iacoboni 2006), such that autistic individuals who lack theory of other minds will also lack self-awareness. Assuming that the poets' use of mental state language serves as one index of their mental state awareness, the present pattern suggests, by contrast, that their capacity for self-reflection may be selectively preserved or enhanced.

The wider rationale for exploring mental state language in this study was that a capacity to express ideas about the 'the human condition' is one of the attributes to be expected of poetry that transcends the minimal level. The autistic poetry in this study meets this requirement, but does so predominantly through the poet's inward-directed reflections on the self.

Poets' Reflections on Their Work

Although the questionnaire data gathered alongside this analysis present a mixed picture, some of the poets' reflections do echo the rather solipsistic character of the autistic poetry described here. Two adult autistic poets who reflected most eloquently upon the questions posed, described the formative influences upon their work as intensely personal. While neurotypical poets emphasized the role of a parent, teacher, or school in engendering their interest, these two described their poetic skill as arising unconsciously and instinctively from their interest in words. Similarly, while the source of inspiration for many neurotypical poets included childhood experiences, observations on the world, and so on, one autistic poet described her inspiration as 'From ME. My thoughts. My experiences'. There were differences, too, in the extent of acknowledged interest in the works of other poets.

Here perhaps in this personal focus is a clue to the particular character, constraints, and potential of autistic creativity. There is relatively less poetry in which the poet projects into an alternative perspective, or into a world outside his or her own experience, yet a particularly powerful evocation of the private world(s) of the poet. The projective or perspectival character of the poetic work therefore permeates and shapes its creative character such that these two major forms of imagination seem integral, not independent as some researchers have proposed.

CONCLUSION

Popular views about the mental world of the person with autism may range from thinking that he or she does not really have an inner life, but lives entirely in the 'here and now', to the assumption that individuals with autism are all eccentric geniuses. The present chapter has addressed the elusive dimension of thought at the heart of these contrasting views—the imagination—and has aimed to dispel some myths and contribute some insights through a wide-ranging appraisal of autistic skills and capabilities in this area. The outcome is far from a definitive conclusion about imagination in autism, but rather a demonstration of the complex questions that must be addressed, concerning both autism and the imagination itself.

As the Introduction to this volume made clear, imagination has numerous facets. Different views of its primary forms, and how or whether they interrelate, have surfaced throughout this volume. Autism Spectrum Disorders provide a useful test case for considering these relationships. The evidence reviewed early in this chapter does suggest that many people on the spectrum have difficulties in activities calling for social and more individual forms of imagination. Interpretations that link these difficulties to generic substrates are appealing. However such explanations need to be flexible to exceptions— not all autistic people have the same impairments.

While exceptional accomplishments are comparatively rare, this is not a rationale for excluding them from theory, since problems with the imagination are integral to the definition of the disorders regardless of ability level. An adequate description and evaluation of the imaginative character of these skills proves to be complex and puzzling, calling for careful analysis of the artistic output in comparison with non-autistic works, and in relation to the predictions of relevant models. Such an exploration of autistic visual art yields partial and inconsistent conclusions. Much of it is accurate, systematic, and attentive to detail, and some of it is reality-bound. But, as became clear, no one theoretical template fits all this work, and the implicit or explicit dismissal of its imaginative qualities may involve criteria that are not consistently applied in other contexts. Moreover, these criteria are inevitably grounded within a neurotypical framework of thought: a picture drawn from accurate memory of a scene may, in many circumstances, seem less imaginative than one that is the product of our fantasies. Yet, to the person on the autistic spectrum, this may not be so (Mills 2007).

The capricious quality of such standards is yet further exposed by the work of Andy Warhol, perhaps himself autistic. The creativity attributed to his realistic and repetitive images of soup cans and films icons indicate that such judgements are shaped not only by 'substantive' features of the work but also, or even especially, by its audience impact. Hermelin believed that autistic artists lack the motivation to impress. Whether Warhol profited accidentally from the prevailing zeitgeist, or set out to do so is therefore a matter of some interest!

While the creative bases of poetry and visual art cannot be directly compared, poetry in some ways furnishes a more robust test of imaginative qualities than visual art. The systematic analyses revealed indisputably imaginative qualities, particularly in the poets' use of figurative language. The poets' imagination had a distinctively self-reflective emphasis, though they also explored other themes, adopted other voices and considered the mental worlds of others. Some interesting questions are under further investigation, for instance, concerning the precise emotional impact and appeal of these works. This analysis again recognizes that the subtle interplay between the artist's intentions and the audience's expectations and responses must be evaluated alongside the work's more 'substantive' features.

The extent to which specificity is characteristic of autistic talents merits further consideration. Hermelin considers these talents as highly focused, confined to a narrow area within a particular cognitive domain. While some savant visual artists fit this picture, the role of parents or mentors in channelling creative activity in this particular direction needs to be evaluated. Several of the poets studied here have multiple talents, including visual art in at least one case.

Finally, I turn briefly to claims that a wide range of exceptionally creative people are on the autistic spectrum (Fitzgerald 2004; James 2005). Fitzgerald's interesting claims for luminaries such as W.B. Yeats and Lewis Carroll necessarily rely upon retrospective analyses of documentary accounts produced with other motives than clinical diagnoses. As such, they must be treated with considerable caution. Fitzgerald is at his most convincing in highlighting indicative personality traits of talented individuals, such as aloofness, sustained and energetic focus on a specific topic, and an imperviousness to social conventions. Such autistic-like personality traits would no doubt serve the creative genius well both in diverging from the norm, and getting things done. But the character of their creative output also needs to be considered. The research reported in this chapter shows that the autistic writing has personal and even solipsistic qualities. A question for further consideration is whether a work as fantastical and as universally appealing as *Alice in Wonderland* might come from a similar stable.

Note. I would like to thank Alison Sillence for her research assistance with the poetry studies described in this chapter; The British Academy for funding the poetry project; all the poets who participated, and also those poets and their publishers who have permitted the reproduction of extracts from their poetry; similarly all the artists and their publishers and families who have permitted reproduction of their works.

References

Baron-Cohen, S. 1989: Do autistic children have obsessions and compulsions? *British Journal of Clinical Psychology*, 28, 193–200.

Baron-Cohen, S. 2001: Theory of mind and autism: a review, in Special Issue of the *International Review of Mental Retardation*, 23, 169.

Baron-Cohen, S. 2003: *The Essential Difference*. London: Allen Lane.

Baron-Cohen, S. and Frith, U. 1986: Mechanical, behavioural and intentional understanding of picture stories in autistic children. *British Journal of Developmental Psychology*, 4, 113–125.

Baron-Cohen, S., Leslie, A. and Frith, U. 1985: Does the autistic child have a 'theory of mind'? *Cognition*, 21, 37–46.

Baron-Cohen, S., Wheelwright, S., Cox, A., Baird, G., Charman, T., Swettenham, J., Drew, A. and Doehring, P. 2000: The early identification of autism: the Checklist for Autism in Toddlers (CHAT) (2000). *Journal of the Royal Society of Medicine*, 93, 521–525.

Baron-Cohen, S., Wheelwright, S, Skinner, R., Martin, J. and Clubley, E. 2001: The Autism Quotient (AQ): Evidence from Asperger syndrome/high functioning autism, males and females, scientists and mathematicians. *Journal of Autism and Developmental Disorders*, 31, 5–17.

Belmonte, M. 2007: Human but more so: What the autistic brain tells us about the process of narrative. In Osteen, M. (ed.), *Autism and Representation*. New York: Routledge.

Bruner, J. and Feldman, C. 2000: Theories of mind and the problem of autism. In Baron-Cohen, S, Tager-Flusberg, H. and Cohen, D. J. (eds), *Understanding Other Minds: Perspectives from Developmental Cognitive Neuroscience*. Oxford: Oxford University Press, 267–291.

Costall, A. 1995: The myth of the sensory core: the traditional versus the ecological approach to children's drawings. In Lange-Küttner, C. and Thomas, G. V., *Drawing and Looking*. Hemel Hempstead: Harvester Wheatsheaf, 16–26.

Craig, J. and Baron-Cohen, S. 1999: Creativity and imagination in autism and Asperger syndrome. *Journal of Autism and Developmental Disorders*, 29, 319–326.

Craig, J., Baron-Cohen, S. and Scott, F. 2000: Story-telling ability in autism: A window into the imagination. *Israel Journal of Psychiatry*, 37, 64–70.

Craig, J., Baron-Cohen, S. and Scott, F. 2001: Drawing ability in autism: A window into the imagination. *Israel Journal of Psychiatry*, 38, 242–253.

Currie, G. and Ravenscroft, I. 2002: *Recreative Minds: Imagination in Philosophy and Science*. Oxford: Oxford University Press.

Dennett, D. 1987: *The Intentional Stance*. Harvard, MA: MIT Press.

Dowker, A., Hermelin, B. and Pring, L. 1996: A savant poet. *Psychological Medicine*, 26, 913–924.

Fitzgerald, M. 2004: *Autism and Creativity: Is there a Link between Autism in Men and Exceptional Ability?* Hove: Brunner-Routledge.

Glastonbury, M. 1997: 'I'll teach you differences': On the cultural presence of autistic lives. *Changing English*, 4, 51–65.

Grandin, T. 1995: *Thinking in Pictures: And Other Reports from My Life with Autism*. New York: Doubleday.

Happé, F. G. E. 1993: Communicative competence and theory of mind in autism: A test of relevance theory. *Cognition*, 48, 101–119.

Happé, F. G. E. 1994: An advanced test of theory of mind: Understanding of story characters' thoughts and feelings by able autistic, mentally handicapped and normal children and adults. *Journal of Autism and Developmental Disorders*, 24, 129–154.

Happé, F. G. E. 1997: Central coherence and theory of mind in autism: Reading homographs in context. *British Journal of Developmental Psychology*, 15, 1–12.

Happé, F. and Frith, U. 2006: The weak central coherence account: Detail-focused cognitive style in autism spectrum disorders. *Journal of Autism and Developmental Disorders*, 36, 5–25.

Hermelin, B. 2001: *Bright Splinters of the Mind: A Personal Story of Research with Autistic Savants*. London: Jessica Kingsley.

Hill, E. L. 2004: Evaluating the theory of executive dysfunction in autism. *Developmental Review*, 24, 189–233.

Hobson, P. 2002: *The Cradle of Thought*. London: Macmillan.

Humphrey, N. 1998: Cave art, autism and the evolution of the human mind. *Cambridge Archaeological Journal*, 8(2), 165–191.

Iacoboni, M. 2006: Failure to de-activate in autism: The co-constitution of self and other. *Trends in Cognitive Science*, 10, 431–433.

James, I. 2005: *Asperger's Syndrome and Exceptional Achievement: Some Very Remarkable People*. London: Jessica Kingsley.

Joliffe, T. and Baron-Cohen, S. 1997: A test of central coherence theory: Can adults with high-functioning autism or Asperger's syndrome integrate fragments of an object? *Cognitive Neuropsychiatry*, 6, 193–216.

Leslie, A. 1987: Pretence and representation: The origins of 'theory of mind'. *Psychological Review*, 94, 412–426.

Leevers, H. and Harris, P. 1998: Drawing impossible entities: A measure of the imagination of children with autism, children with learning disabilities and normal 4-year-olds. *Journal of Child Psychology and Psychiatry*, 39, 339–410.

Lewis, V. and Boucher, J. 1988: Spontaneous, instructed and elicited play in relatively able autistic children. *British Journal of Developmental Psychology*, 6, 325–339.

Mills, B. 2007: Autism and the imagination. In Osteen, M. (ed.), *Autism and Representation*. New York: Routledge.

Myers, P., Baron-Cohen, S. and Wheelwright, S. 2004: *An Exact Mind: An Artist with Asperger Syndrome*. New York: Jessica Kingsley.

Paradiž, V. 2002: *Elijah's Cup: a Family's Journey into the Community and Culture of High-Functioning Autism and Asperger's Syndrome*. New York: The Free Press.

Park, C. C. 2001: *Exiting Nirvana: A Daughter's Life with Autism*. London: Aurum Press.

Pring, L., Hermelin, B., Buhler, M. and Walker, I. 1997: Native savant talent and acquired skill. *Autism*, 1(2), 199–214.

Ricks, C. 2005: All praise to proper words. *The Times Literary Supplement*, 25 February, 12–15.

Roth, I. 2007: Imagination and the awareness of self in autistic spectrum poets. In Osteen, M. (ed.), *Autism and Representation*. New York: Routledge.

Russell, J. (ed.) 1997: *Autism as an Executive Disorder*. Oxford: Oxford University Press.

Selfe, L. 1977: *Nadia: A Case of Extraordinary Drawing Ability in an Autistic Girl*. London: Academic Press.

Selfe, L. 1983: *Normal and Anomalous Representational Drawing Ability in Children*. London: Academic Press.

Tréhin, G. 2006: *Urville*. London: Jessica Kingsley.

Treffert, D. A. 1989: *Extraordinary People*. London: Bantam.

Wiltshire, S. 1987: *Drawings*. London: Dent.

14

Imaging Imagination: Brain Scanning of the Imagined Future

JOHN G. GEAKE AND MORTEN L. KRINGELBACH

'IMAGINATION, n. A warehouse of facts, with poet and liar in joint ownership.'

The Devil's Dictionary, Ambrose Bierce

Abstract. In this chapter we review an emerging literature concerning the neuroimaging of various subcomponents of imagination. The preliminary conclusions of this review are two-fold. First, acts of imagination recruit similar networks in the brain to those used for the sensory and motor processing during corresponding actions in, or interactions with the real world (with the important exception that imagined movements do not activate the primary motor cortex). That the majority of studies reviewed have been concerned with visual imagery was inevitable since this is the form of imagination for which most neuroimaging experiments have been conducted. It should be noted that this first conclusion is relevant to all forms of imagination, and not just those of veridical imagery, where there is a 'real world' referent for the imaginary content. Second, the selection processes used in subcomponents of imagination such as anticipation, mindedness, and counterfactual thinking rely on widely distributed subcortical and cortical networks within the brain, consisting of important components such as the cingulate cortex, the dorsolateral prefrontal cortex, the cerebellum, and the orbitofrontal cortex. These neural structures play quite different functional roles in the complex interactions of real and imagined acts that constitute human thought and behaviour. Further knowledge of the precise functional roles of the interacting networks can be expected from neuroimaging in the coming years, perhaps through the technical breakthroughs which we imagine in a Coda and which could potentially facilitate and enhance our understanding of imagination in the future.

Proceedings of the British Academy **147**, 307–326. © The British Academy 2007.

THE NEUROSCIENTIFIC APPROACH TO THE IMAGINATION

IT HAS TO BE SAID that few neuroimaging studies have deliberately sought evidence for the neural correlates of imagination as such, mainly because of the challenge in constructing unambiguously falsifiable hypotheses about such a broad mental phenomenon. This neglect of imagination might also be a result of its long banishment by behavioural psychology. In fact, many neuroimaging studies have regarded subjects' imagination as experimental noise, i.e. off-task thinking. Nevertheless, over the past decade, imagination, along with consciousness, has emerged as one of the exciting cutting-edge areas of study within neuroscience. Progress, as with all neuroscientific experiments, has relied on the deconstruction of the broad concept, imagination, into investigable components. This, in turn, is not without its conceptual and pragmatic challenges.

Neuroscientific evidence for the brain substrates of imaginative thought has been sought by recording the neural correlates of the six overlapping subcomponents of imagination that Roth identifies in the Introduction to this volume: prediction through anticipation; perceptual, sensory and motor imagery, including pain; pretence; mindedness and empathy (theory of mind); counterfactual thinking including delusion; and creativity (see Figure 14.1). The results of these various experimental approaches therefore offer neuroscientific perspectives on the phenomena discussed by other authors in this volume: prediction (Boyer in Chapter 11, Whiten and Suddendorf in Chapter 2); perceptual imagery (Pearson in Chapter 9); pretence (Taylor *et al.* in Chapter 4, Whiten and Suddendorf in Chapter 2); mindedness (Currie in Chapter 8, Mithen in Chapter 1, Roth in Chapter 13); counterfactual thinking (Blackmore in Chapter 3, Boyer in Chapter 11, Taylor *et al.* in Chapter 4); and creativity (Cook in Chapter 6, Cross in Chapter 7, Mithen in Chapter 1, Nettle in Chapter 12, Roth in Chapter 13, Turner in Chapter 10, Whiten and Suddendorf in Chapter 2).

The main neuroimaging methods at the basis of this chapter are positron emission tomography (PET), functional magnetic resonance imaging (fMRI), event related potential (ERP), electroencephalography (EEG), electromyography (EMG), magnetoencephalography (MEG) and transcranial magnetic stimulation (TMS). We recommend readers not familiar with these approaches to the relevant sections of either the *Oxford Companion to the Mind* (Gregory 2004), the *Handbook of Functional Neuroimaging of Cognition* (Cabeza and Kingstone 2001), or Van Horn's chapter on cognitive neuroimaging in *The Cognitive Neurosciences III* (Van Horn 2004).

There are important caveats to the claims of any neuroimaging research that depends on the strengths and limitations of the method employed. These include: the validity of the various surrogate variables (e.g. haemodynamic

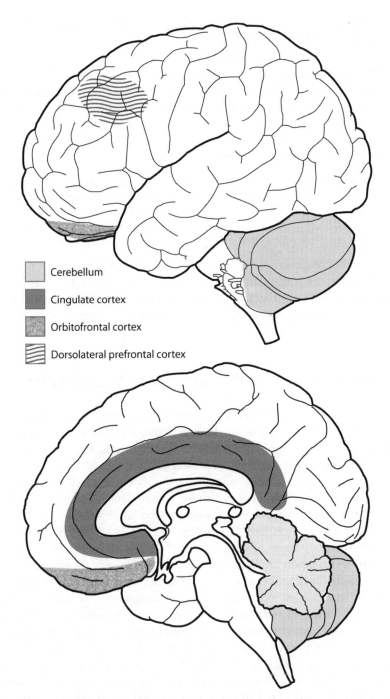

Figure 14.1. Some areas of the human brain that have been shown with neuroimaging to be involved in imagination.

fluctuation, relative electric dipole strength) for measuring neural activity; limits to spatial and temporal resolution; the statistical nature of activation data; constraints on the type and extent of tasks that subjects can undertake while being imaged; subject selection and limits on generalizability; and, the subjective experience of being imaged, and its possible effects on imagination.

A more fundamental constraint on interpretation is that, owing to the correlational nature of most neuroimaging data, the mapping between structure and function is not one-to-one, or simple. As Nobel Laureate Sir Charles Sherrington, warned nearly 70 years ago:

> To suppose the roof-brain [cerebral cortex] consists of point to point centres identified each with a particular item of intelligent concrete behaviour is a scheme over simplified and to be abandoned. Rather, the contributions which the roof-brain ... makes toward integrated behaviour will ... resolve into components for which we at present have no names. (Sherrington 1938, p. 181)

Sherrington's prescience, we suggest, still holds. Understanding just how our brain, through the contributions of its myriad functional centres, enables us to be imaginative is still largely an act of imagination. However, thanks to modern neuroimaging technologies, a convergence of evidence is informing such imaginative endeavour.

CONCEPTUAL AND THEORETICAL CONSIDERATIONS

A broad distinction may be drawn between imagination as a mental product and as a mental process. In the first sense, imagination is a cognitive state stimulated by other cognitive states whether these arise 'internally' or consist of responses to percepts. But, imagination can also be the mental process which creates such 'products', or moreover, mentally manipulates them as required for planning, scheming, or any act of creative thinking. Further, the mental processes required for the latter are likely to extend beyond mental resourcefulness, involving what are often described as 'imaginative insights' or 'leaps of imagination'. To a neuroscientist, these various aspects of imagination are likely to have dissociable neural correlates.

That said, functional and even neuroanatomical dissociation does not necessarily mean that more general hypotheses about imagination must remain uninformed. The most parsimonious general hypothesis is that the brain exploits similar structures and processes in dealing with internally generated mental activity, such as images, as it does in dealing with externally generated activation, such as percepts. At first pass, this seems to beg the question of which areas are involved in those forms of imagination which arise 'purely internally': if I dream up a new story in my mind, or mentally conjure up a fantastical creature, there is not usually or necessarily an external event or activity which corresponds to this. Interestingly, the (albeit limited) evidence indicates that the brain conjures up such images as if they had external referents. In other words, the *Parsimony Hypothesis* can be applied to such cases as well.

Evidence for the Parsimony Hypothesis is found in studies of neural activations in visual cortex arising from seeing a particular object and then visualizing that same object with eyes closed. For example, Kosslyn *et al.* (1999) used PET to show that Area 17 in early visual cortex (V1) was activated when subjects visualized a recently perceived display with their eyes shut. To address the acknowledged limitation to such neuroimaging studies, viz. that the results are correlational and not causal, Kosslyn *et al.* (1999) then employed repetitive TMS on Area 17 to demonstrate the predicted performance impairment indicative of the necessary involvement of Area 17 in all visual information processing, imagined or otherwise. Similarly, Ganis *et al.* used fMRI to map the neural correlates accompanying the act of perceiving or imagining drawings of familiar objects. They concluded that:

> visual imagery and visual perception draw on most of the same neural machinery ... the spatial overlap was neither complete nor uniform; the overlap was much more pronounced in frontal and parietal regions than in temporal and occipital regions. This finding may indicate that cognitive control processes function comparably in both imagery and perception, whereas at least some sensory processes may be engaged differently by visual imagery and perception (Ganis *et al.* 2004, p. 226).

Support for this view comes from Grossman and Blake (2001) who found similar activation patterns in superior temporal sulcus for perceived and imagined motion, although the fMRI (BOLD)[1] activation was weaker for the imagined motion.

Nevertheless, such results, interesting as they are, have little to say about the creative aspects of imagination, in which imaginative mental products may have no 'real-world' correlates. There are several putative global accounts of how the brain is creatively imaginative. One popular cognitive approach is captured by the suggestion that imagination is the outcome of a neural Darwinism—that the brain generates thousands of mental images every second, but only the most salient come to mind or consciousness. However, it is not clear how one could employ neuroimaging to test this directly, although studies of the neural correlates of consciousness might be

---

[1] Neural activity changes the proportion of oxygenated blood in the brain. By measuring the oxygenated blood using functional magnetic resonance imaging (fMRI), the location and size of the neural activity can be assessed. This technique is called the blood oxygen level dependent (BOLD) signal, or haemodynamic response.

informative. A more recent and neurally specific model of brain function is the Dynamic Workspace Hypothesis (DWH) which is inspired by the research of a number of researchers (most recently Baars 1989; Dehaene *et al.* 1998; Mesulam 1998) (see Figure 14.2). The DWH offers a neural mechanism for the Parsimony Hypothesis, in that once perceptual information has been processed, the modules for which it is efferent regard it as the same as imagined information with similar efferents. In most normal cognition, we can distinguish between percepts and mental images by their associated contexts. However, experiments with inattentional blindness (Simons 2000) and spontaneous confabulation (Schnider and Ptak 1999) reveal how easily the brain can be deceived in this regard. Moreover, pathologies such as schizophrenia are characterized by symptoms involving an inability to distinguish between

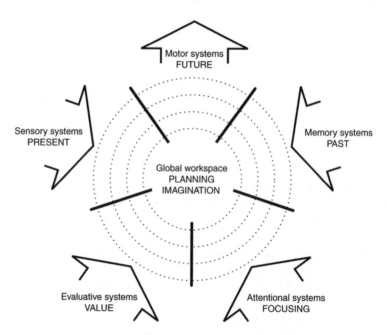

Figure 14.2. Tentative model of the global workspace. The figure represents the five main types of processors connected to the global workspace: sensory, memory, attentional, evaluative, and motor systems. Each concentric ring represents a different synaptic level and the connections from one zone to another are reciprocal. The binding of the various processors is accomplished through effortful processing and long-range workspace connectivity which establishes coherence between two or more informationally distributed workspace regions. The activation of the global workspace may lead to activation of motor systems but may also lead to the projecting, imagining, of such possible futures without a direct motor component. Inspired by Baars (1989), Mesulam (1998), and Dehaene *et al.* (1998).

internally and externally generated auditory and visual imagery. Importantly in this model, certain parts of the brain have privileged global access to information and these *global workspace* neurons are central to consciousness, and thus also to the subset of consciousness that is imagination.

Some direct evidence for the DWH which is consistent with the predictions of neural Darwinism, has been provided by two related studies of the 'Aha' experience, the sensation of a sudden flash of insight which accompanies successful solution in problem-solving tasks (Jung-Beeman *et al.* 2004). First, fMRI revealed increased activity in the right hemisphere anterior superior temporal gyrus for insight relative to non-insight solutions, i.e. solutions which emerge gradually and without an 'aha' moment. Second, EEG recordings revealed a sudden burst of high-frequency (gamma-band) neural activity in the same area beginning 0.3 seconds prior to insight solutions. The researchers noted that this right anterior temporal area is associated with making connections across distantly related information during comprehension, so 'although all problem solving relies on a largely shared cortical network, the sudden flash of insight occurs when solvers engage distinct neural and cognitive processes that allow them to see connections that previously eluded them' (Jung-Beeman *et al.* 2004, p. 500).

IMAGINATION AS PREDICTION

Perhaps the simplest form of imagination is prediction—the mental representation of possible future events or experiences. There is a considerable literature on predicting or anticipating the next stimulus in a particular sequence of, say, movements or rewards. Sophisticated predictions are performed by the cerebellum which has been proposed to function like a Smith-predictor (Miall *et al.* 1993). A number of recent neuroimaging papers have investigated the role of cerebellum in predicting not only motor sequences but also in the prediction of other higher cognitive and emotional functions (Dreher and Grafman, 2002; Nitschke *et al.* 2003; Tanaka *et al.* 2004). Behaviourist studies of prediction of rewards and punishments have classically concentrated on the role of various structures within the basal ganglia. Recently, it has been proposed that dopaminergic neurons and the orbitofrontal cortex are involved in a network for reward prediction (Schultz *et al.* 1997) and this proposal has received support from human neuroimaging experiments (Ploghaus *et al.* 2000; Berns *et al.* 2001; Pappata *et al.* 2002; Tanaka *et al.* 2004; Tricomi *et al.* 2004). It should be noted, however, that real-life prediction and anticipation processes are anything but simple and it is unlikely that simple-minded behaviourism will elucidate the richness of neural mechanisms involved in prediction (Kringelbach 2004a).

Some of these studies suggest that prediction is largely subliminal or non-conscious rather than conscious. Consistent evidence for such a claim has been provided by several studies into the placebo effect, where the effect of the placebo is based on a *false belief*. In a PET study, Petrovic *et al.* (2002) found that not only was activity in rostral anterior cingulate cortex (ACC) and lateral orbitofrontal cortex correlated with pain relief through analgesia, but that similar activations were found in placebo responders (and not, crucially, in placebo non-responders). The authors conclude that there are related neural mechanisms for real and placebo analgesia, a finding in support of the Parsimony Hypothesis. Other evidence that real and imagined percepts are supported by common neural structures comes from two fMRI studies into the anticipation of pain (Wager *et al.* 2004). Here, the administration of placebos was related to decreases in activation in various parts of the pain network, including the thalamus and insula, and increases in activation of prefrontal areas including the ACC, associated with pain anticipation.

That anticipation or prediction is usually unconscious should not be surprising. Unconscious processing is attributed to the ventral information processing stream in the brain, which is temporally privileged over the dorsal information stream required for conscious processing (e.g. Goebel *et al.* 1998). In other words, unconscious processing happens faster than conscious thought. If this were not so, it could be noted, then musical improvisation within a group, as in jazz or rock music, would not be possible. Nor, for that matter, would most conversation or spontaneous speech.

This is not to say that all imaginative experience is unconscious. We now consider the case of imagination as the generation of mental imagery—a process that is often conscious.

IMAGINATION AS IMAGERY

Mental imagery, as defined by Pearson (Chapter 9) is a quasi-perceptual state of consciousness involving simulation or re-creation of sensory-like experience—colloquially seeing things in the mind's eye. We can imagine in all sensory modalities, and within (at least) visual, auditory, and motor domains, images can be novel, creative, or even fanciful, as well as remembered. However, it is the latter imagery that has been the main focus of neuroimaging studies as it is hoped that the associated neural correlates might be informative of the elusive structures and functions involved in memory storage and recall. To this end, visual imagery for remembered stimuli is both psychologically privileged and the easiest to facilitate in a brain scanning environment. Ishai *et al.* (2002) employed fMRI to study the neural correlates of short- and long-term memory for perceived and imagined complex visual images (famous faces). The imagined faces (long-term memory) activated a subset of the network of regions activated by the perceived images (short-term memory), which included the areas known to be involved in facial recognition such as the lateral fusiform gyri. However, the imagined faces activated additional areas including the hippocampus (the subcortical organ that have been implicated in laying down spatial memories), and the inferior frontal gyrus, an area implicated in studies of selection for action and working memory. This finding, consistent with the more recent fMRI study of real and imagined drawings reviewed above (Ganis *et al.* 2004), suggests that the Parsimony Hypothesis might be rather too parsimonious.

Nevertheless, convergent evidence for the coincidence of neural structures involved in imagery and perception comes from several studies into imagined motion. Goebel *et al.* (1998), in an fMRI study comparing perceived and imagined motion, found that the Area MT/MST in V1, known to be involved in motion detection, was also activated during motion imagery, along with areas in lateral prefrontal cortex. Consistent with the DWH they concluded that 'a complex cortical network of motion-sensitive areas driven by bottom-up and top-down neural processes' (Goebel *et al.* 1998, p. 1563) is necessary for both objective and imagined motion detection. Lamm *et al.* (2001) used fMRI and ERPs to show that imagined dynamic imagery activated a network of cortical regions, importantly the premotor areas, but also including the occipital and parietal cortices, and dorsolateral prefrontal cortex, and that the activations persisted until the imagined task was completed.

Mental rehearsal of motor sequences has become a central feature of sports psychology: athletes, notably gymnasts and high-divers, now spend a lengthy period of inwardly focused attention immediately pre-performance. Kuhtz-Buschbeck *et al.* (2003) combined fMRI and TMS to examine the relationships between imagined mental rehearsal and execution of simple and complex motor tasks. Premotor, posterior parietal, and cerebellar regions, a network involved in motor performance, were more active during mental rehearsal of the complex task. A similar network was delineated by Binkofski *et al.* (2000) with fMRI in subjects while they executed a series of motor instructions, with imagery of the task-activating inferior prefrontal areas. The precise location of these frontal activations was found to lie in Broca's area, a region known to be involved in speech production. This finding is interpreted as evidence for a human analogue of the mirror-neurons found in non-human primates (e.g. Rizzolatti *et al.* 1996). In turn, this could suggest that imagination is not exclusive to human cognition, i.e. that the higher mammals, including monkeys and apes, dogs and cats, all enjoy an imaginative life. More recent studies have suggested that mirror neurons in many other areas of the brain support sympathetic imagination in humans, i.e. our capacity for putting ourselves in other people's shoes (for a review see Adolphs 2002).

An extreme form of involuntary mental rehearsal of motor execution is apparent with the experience of phantom limbs. To investigate the neural correlates of phantom limb movement and associated pain, Lotze and co-workers (2001) used fMRI to compare the real and imagined movements of upper limbs of healthy controls and upper-limb amputees. While imagining movement of their phantom hand, amputees showed higher activations in contralateral primary motor and sensory-motor areas than controls when imagining their own hand movements. This difference was not apparent when amputees imagined movements of their intact hands. Evidence for a greater degree of cerebral reorganization, contra the Parsimony Hypothesis, was seen with phantom limb pain which activated neighbouring areas in motor cortex for facial musculature.

A more common form of mental rehearsal is observed in professional musicians whose performances, particularly solo roles such as playing concerti, are often from memory. Lotze *et al.* (2003) compared EMG activation maps of professional and amateur violinists during actual and imagined performance of the first 16 bars of Mozart's violin concerto in G major (KV216). Compared with the amateur violinists the professional musicians showed higher activity in auditory cortex and sensorimotor cortex, among a suite of areas, but only during execution, not during imagination. The researchers interpreted these findings as evidence that in professional musicians, 'a higher economy of motor areas frees resources for increased connectivity between the finger sequences and auditory as well as somatosensory loops, which may account for the superior musical performance' (Lotze *et al.* 2003, p. 1817). However, motor and auditory systems only became co-activated in real performance situations. That is, in this case the neural processes underpinning imagined and real performances are dissociable.

Whereas relatively few of us are professional musicians, we all must, from time to time, have to navigate around complex urban or rural environments from memory. Perceived but unremembered features of the landscape can be surprising, as can be the efficacy of the feeling that, despite incomplete certainty, one is heading in the right direction. To investigate the neural correlates of such remembered visuo-spatial imagery, Rosenbaum *et al.* (2004) used fMRI to scan subjects while they undertook a series of mental navigation tasks in their familiar urban environment (downtown Toronto). A suite of areas was activated, including medial and posterior parietal cortex, and regions of prefrontal cortex associated with working memory load. Again, these findings are supportive of the DWH account of complex neural processing. Interestingly, activity in the right medial temporal lobe did not include the hippocampus, the subcortical organ involved in laying down memories, suggesting that imagined spatial layouts might be dependent on a network of other regions involved in topographic information processing.

A common experience for all of us is how remembered imagery can often be invoked cross-modally, e.g. the recall of a visual image triggered by associated percepts in other domains, such as sounds or smells. Lundstrom et al. (2003) used fMRI to study the retrieval of imagined visual images through word associations. Significant activations in both the posterior precuneus and left lateral prefrontal cortex suggested that explicit retrieval of item–context associations requires a functional network, similarly to Goebel et al. (1998), and much as the DWH predicts. Consistently, Bensafi et al. (2003) measured nasal airflow in human subjects while they imagined sights, sounds, and smells. Only during olfactory imagery did subjects spontaneously sniff, with imagery of pleasant odours involving larger sniffs than imagery of unpleasant odours. Bensafi et al. (2003) argued that the motor activity of sniffing assists in the creation of imaginary olfactory percepts.

Although such intra-domain associations might not be unexpected, for those who experience the phenomenon of synaesthesia, *perception* in one modality can be invoked by stimulation in another (Ramachandran and Hubbard 2003). For example, common words, numbers, or letters are often reliably associated with experiences of particular colours. The study of synaesthete subjects offers an opportunity to gain evidence for the neural substrates of some aspects of imagination, in a parallel way to the investigation of other modes of cognition where concomitant evidence for neural causality has been traditionally sought in cognitive dysfunction, particularly with clinical subjects suffering brain lesions (Ramachandran and Hubbard 2001). In an earlier study, Paulesu et al. (1995) used PET to study the neurophysiology of colour-word synaesthesia. In addition to the expected 'language areas', synaesthetes showed activations in the visual association areas of the inferior temporal and parietal cortices, and in the right prefrontal cortex, but not in the early visual areas. This suggests that in synaesthetes, colour-word visual experience occurs without activation of the visual cortex, but rather in areas associated with language. This finding, while supportive of the DWH, is evidence against the Parsimony Hypothesis. However, more recent and extensive neuroimaging research *has* shown activation of colour areas of visual cortex with synaesthetic experience, in direct support of the Parsimony Hypothesis (Hubbard et al. 2005). Interpretation of these data of synaesthetes might be interestingly informative of the neurotypical case where the perceptual experience of early infants is typically synaesthetic, and normal development is regarded as a growth away from synaesthesia, but which is incomplete in some people for reasons not completely understood (Ramachandran and Hubbard 2003).

Another comparison subpopulation is composed of those who have suffered from some post-natal sensory deprivation, such as blindness onset in childhood. What differences in imagination might these people have? To begin to address this question, Morris *et al.* (2001) studied the responses to fearful faces by a partially blindsighted patient, i.e. someone whose conscious experience is that of being blind in one hemifield. Co-activated responses in a subcortical network including the amygdala, thalamus, and superior colliculus demonstrated that fear-related stimuli can be processed independently of conscious visual awareness. By way of follow-up, researchers at Oxford have studied late-blind individuals who have retained synaesthetic colour perception (Steven and Blakemore 2004; Steven *et al.* 2005). Most had been without any form of colour vision for more than a decade. All perceived colours when they heard or thought about letters, numbers, and time-related words (days of the week and months of the year). One saw Braille characters as coloured dots when he touched them. These results suggest that: 'the neural activity underlying synaesthesia occurs after the establishment of a visual representation. . . . Synaesthesia can persist for very long periods with little or no natural experience in the referred modality and therefore does not depend solely on continuing associative learning' (Steven and Blakemore 2004, p. 855).

Sadly, until the objective evidence for the synaesthetic experience was secured, many self-reports by synaesthetes were not believed. Similar scepticism is aroused by those other forms of imagination which feature conscious or unconscious pretence: imbuing entities or events with imaginary properties, or even fantastical phenomena, e.g. a childhood belief in fairies. Religious experience falls into this category of imagination, and several neuroimaging studies have sought associated neural correlates. One investigation employed PET to measure the relationship between serotonin receptor density and self-ratings on a personality scale measuring religious behaviour and attitudes (Borg *et al.* 2003). The authors concluded that: 'the serotonin system may serve as a biological basis for spiritual experiences [and] . . . that the several-fold variability in [serotonin] receptor density may explain why people vary greatly in spiritual zeal' (Borg *et al.* 2003, p. 1965). Excessive religious zeal, of course, can be disabling. Puri *et al.* (2001) also used PET to study the neural correlates of religious delusions in psychiatric patients. Religious delusions were associated with high levels of activation in the left temporal cortex, and reduced activation in the left occipital cortex. Interestingly, similar activations in the temporal cortex have been associated with false memories of alien abduction (Holden and French 2002).

IMAGINING OTHER MINDS

Informative as the preceding studies might be for understanding how our brains are imaginative, their relevance pales when compared with the importance of using our imagination for conceiving the thoughts and feelings of others. In navigating around our social environment, prediction, anticipation, pretence, and sometimes delusion are all aspects of our imaginative repertoire. Not surprisingly, then, the majority of neuroimaging studies about imagination have been concerned with understanding the neural functioning of mindedness or theory of minds (ToM). For example, both Fletcher *et al.* (1995) and Gallagher *et al.* (2000) found ToM correlates in the left medial prefrontal cortex when comparing fMRI activations induced by stories involving mental attributions as compared with stories involving physical attributions. In contrast, Saxe and Kanwisher (2003) showed that similar reasoning about the mental states of other people produced higher fMRI (BOLD) activations in the temporo-parietal junction. Moreover, Ferstl and von Cramon (2002) showed with fMRI that the role that the medial prefrontal cortex plays in coherent language processing is independent of concomitant ToM processes. Some resolution between these different findings has been provided by studies into the neural correlates of the distinctive roles of self and other as the basis of human self-consciousness by Vogeley *et al.* (2001) and Ruby and Decety (2003). Using fMRI and PET respectively, these investigations supported the predicted neural dissociations between perceptions of self, with activations in the temporo-parietal junction, and perceptions of other, with activations in the left temporal cortex. Both perceptions activated the frontal region of the anterior cingulate cortex.

In a follow-up fMRI study, Vogeley *et al.* (2004) investigated the neural dissociations between taking a first-person perspective centred upon one's own body as opposed to a third-person perspective taking the viewpoint of someone else. Common activations were seen in a network of occipital, parietal, and prefrontal areas. Differences in activations induced by third-person perspective over first, and first-person perspective over third, were found in distinct subregions of the temporal, parietal and pre-motor cortices, laterally and sometimes bilaterally. Vogeley *et al.* concluded that: 'the data suggest that in addition to joint neural mechanisms, for example, due to visuospatial processing and decision making, third-person and first-person perspectives rely on differential neural processes' (2004, p. 817). Such a conclusion builds on earlier work by Zacks *et al.* (1999) which used fMRI to reveal distinct functional areas near the parietal–temporal–occipital junction for egocentric and object-based spatial transformations.

This not unexpected functional modularity of personal perspective raises the interesting question of what neural correlates might be associated with various social interactions between self and other. Is it simply a matter of interaction between the separate neural associates of self and other, or do other neural functions and structures become additionally involved to enable the interaction? One experimental approach (across fMRI, PET, and MEG) has been to investigate the simpler but crucial non-linguistic interactions involved in responding appropriately to various facial expressions (Kringelbach 2004b; Kringelbach and Rolls 2003). Interestingly, the neural correlates of changing behaviour in response to changes in another's facial expression were not found in the fusiform gyrus facial recognition area, but in the frontal areas involved in decision making: the orbitofrontal and anterior cingulate/paracingulate cortices (Kringelbach and Rolls 2004). Emotional attribution was further investigated by Decety and Chaminade (2003) by comparing subjects' responses to sad stories told by actors with either congruent or incongruent emotional expressions. PET activations of emotional mismatch were seen in the ventromedial prefrontal cortex and the superior frontal gyrus, suggesting that feelings of sympathy rely on separate networks for shared experience and affect. The explanatory efficacy of these findings to predict the aetiology of various neuro-psychiatric disorders was reviewed by Blair. He argued that:

> in autism ... the basic response to emotional expressions remains intact but that there is impaired ability to represent the referent of the individual displaying the emotion. In psychopathy, the response to fearful and sad expressions is attenuated and this interferes with socialization resulting in an individual who fails to learn to avoid actions that result in harm to others. In acquired sociopathy, the response to angry expressions in particular is attenuated resulting in reduced regulation of social behaviour (Blair 2003, p. 561).

Appropriate reciprocation as the behavioural indicator that one has correctly inferred another's mental states is important for mutually beneficial cooperation. In antagonistic situations, such as when playing games, counter-factual thinking—imagining what might have been or what if—clearly becomes important. To this end, SciFi buffs who yearn for a robot-mediated future will be interested in three fMRI studies which all showed that prefrontal regions, but no other brain regions, were more active when subjects interacted (played games) with other human subjects than when they interacted with a computer (McCabe *et al.* 2001; Rilling *et al.* 2004; Gallagher *et al.* 2002). From these findings, it could be concluded that in these interactional situations, the perceived capacity for intentionality is critical for the activation of those brain regions involved in imagining of other minds.

CREATIVE IMAGINATION

Whereas we may prefer not to attribute mental states to computers, what about the imagined mental states of characters in fiction, especially those of our own creation? As a 'higher' process of imagination, creativity involves the generation of 'highly novel original ideas and cultural products' (Roth, Introduction to this volume). Perhaps not surprisingly, the difficulties in framing controlled measures of creativity in experimental environments have restricted neuroscientific progress in this area until very recently. Nevertheless, neural correlates of creative thinking have been sought and found. Jung-Beeman *et al.*'s (2004) fMRI and EEG study of the 'Aha' experience showed right temporal involvement in insight, a component of creative thinking. Investigating a separate component of creativity, Bechtereva *et al.* (2004) found PET activations in the left parieto-temporal cortex of subjects engaged in verbal creation tasks. In an fMRI study to investigate the neural correlates of creative intelligence operationalized as fluid analogy making, Geake and Hansen (2005) found a network of activations in prefrontal and parietal areas for deep compared with shallow fluid analogies, consistent with the DWH (Figure 14.3). A further ROI analysis showed a linear correlation between subjects' intelligence measures and fMRI (BOLD) activation in prefrontal areas involved with working memory.

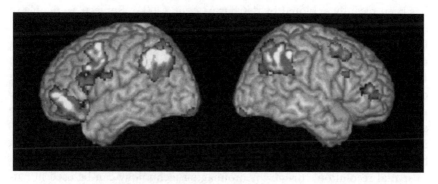

Anterior ◄—— LH ——► Posterior   Posterior ◄—— RH ——► Anterior

Figure 14.3. Significant clusters of neural activation, as determined by fMRI, associated with fluid analogizing tasks (Geake and Hansen 2005). These active clusters, associated with creative thinking, form a network of frontal and other cortical regions.

SUMMARY

Imaging and other neuroscientific techniques offer a potential handle on the architecture of the imaginative mind, helping to show how the neural bases of imaginative activities are organized. There is no one 'module' for imagination; nor even a series of modules for the different forms of imagination discussed. Rather, imaginative processes are highly distributed activities which recruit many different brain areas and networks. The complex relationships within and between these various networks are captured by the Dynamic Workspace Hypothesis (Dehaene *et al.* 1998). In any event, some common operating principles underlie different forms of imagination. These include parsimony, obviously relevant to cases where imaginative activity has corresponding referents in the 'outside world', but interestingly applicable to wholly imagined mental phenomena.

IMAGINING IMAGING

We conclude with a Coda featuring an indulgence of our own imagination, *Imagining Imaging*. In the future, could neuroimaging becoming an everyday diagnostic and even recreational tool for expanding human imagination and consciousness, as Roth (2004) conjectured? Geake and Cooper (2003) imagined an educational future in which imaging technology becomes more powerful yet miniaturized and cheap, in a parallel manner to the development of computer technology, so that schools acquire class sets of personal neuro-imagers for the diagnosis of learning difficulties. Remediation is then effected through biofeedback provided by real-time neuroimaging. Such a scenario has been recently explored by deCharms *et al.* (2004). Subjects were able to learn to voluntarily control neural activations in their somatomotor cortices from feedback provided by real-time fMRI. Similar EEG-based feedback research has been undertaken with musicians (Egner and Gruzelier 2003). Importantly, this learning effect was shown to be additional to improvement due to practice-based neural plasticity. In other words, neuroimaging can be used, not just to measure imagination, but also to influence it. As for Geake and Cooper's conjectured future developments of miniaturized imaging technologies, the first releases of near infrared encephalography (NIEG) wireless headsets are now commercially available. Despite its considerable limitations to spatial resolution, this new neuroimaging technology can be used in natural settings, making it more user-friendly than current laboratory-based equipment. Furthermore, the DWH predicts that the most important neural correlates are network connectivities rather than spatial modularizations. To this end, diffusion tensor imaging (DTI) and its concomitant analysis are now allowing researchers to begin to construct neural connectivity maps. Perhaps the future of imaging our imagination is closer than we imagine?

References

Adolphs, R. 2002: Trust in the brain. *Nature Neuroscience*, 5, 192–193.

Baars, B. J. 1989: *A Cognitive Theory of Consciousness*. Cambridge University Press: Cambridge, MA.

Bechtereva, N. P., Korotkov, A. D., Pakhomov, S. V., Roudas, M. S., Starchenko, M. G. and Medvedev, S. V. 2004: PET study of brain maintenance of verbal creative activity. *International Journal of Psychophysiology*, 53, 11–20.

Bensafi, M., Porter, J., Pouliot, S., Mainland, J., Johnson, B., Zelano, C., Young, N., Bremner, E., Aframian, D., Khan, R. and Sobel, N. 2003: Olfactomotor activity during imagery mimics that during perception. *Nature Neuroscience*, 6, 1142–1144.

Berns, G. S., McClure, S. M., Pagnoni, G. and Montague, P. R. 2001: Predictability modulates human brain response to reward. *Journal of Neuroscience*, 21, 2793–2798.

Binkofski, F., Amunts, K., Stephan, K. M., Posse, S., Schormann, T., Freund, H. J., Zilles, K. and Seitz, R. J. 2000: Broca's region subserves imagery of motion: a combined cytoarchitectonic and fMRI study. *Human Brain Mapping*, 11, 273–285.

Blair, R. J. 2003: Facial expressions, their communicatory functions and neuro-cognitive substrates. *Philosophical Transactions of the Royal Society of London B Biological Science*, 358, 561–572.

Borg, J., Andree, B., Soderstrom, H. and Farde, L. 2003: The serotonin system and spiritual experiences. *American Journal of Psychiatry*, 160, 1965–1969.

Cabeza, R. and Kingstone, A. 2001: *Handbook of Functional Neuroimaging of Cognition*. Cambridge, MA: MIT Press.

Decety, J. and Chaminade, T. 2003: Neural correlates of feeling sympathy. *Neuropsychologia*, 41, 127–138.

deCharms, R. C., Christoff, K., Glover, G. H., Pauly, J. M., Whitfield, S. and Gabrieli, J. D. 2004: Learned regulation of spatially localized brain activation using real-time fMRI. *Neuroimage*, 21, 436–443.

Dehaene, S., Kerszberg, M. and Changeux, J. P. 1998: A neuronal model of a global workspace in effortful cognitive tasks. *Proceedings of the. National Academy of Sciences USA*, 95, 14529–14534.

Dreher, J. C. and Grafman, J. 2002: The roles of the cerebellum and basal ganglia in timing and error prediction. *European Journal of Neuroscience*, 16, 1609–1619.

Egner, T. and Gruzelier, J. H. 2003: Ecological validity of neurofeedback: modulation of slow wave EEG enhances musical performance. *Neuroreport*, 14, 1221–1224.

Ferstl, E. C. and von Cramon, D. Y. 2002: What does the frontomedial cortex contribute to language processing: coherence or theory of mind? *Neuroimage*, 17, 1599–1612.

Fletcher, P. C., Happe, F., Frith, U., Baker, S. C., Dolan, R. J., Frackowiak, R. S. and Frith, C. D. 1995: Other minds in the brain: a functional imaging study of 'theory of mind' in story comprehension. *Cognition*, 57, 109–128.

Gallagher, H. L., Happe, F., Brunswick, N., Fletcher, P. C., Frith, U. and Frith, C. D. 2000: Reading the mind in cartoons and stories: An fMRI study of 'theory of mind' in verbal and nonverbal tasks. *Neuropsychologia*, 38, 11–21.

Gallagher, H. L., Jack, A. I., Roepstorff, A. and Frith, C. D. 2002: Imaging the intentional stance in a competitive game. *Neuroimage*, 16, 814–821.

Ganis, G., Thompson, W. L. and Kosslyn, S. M. 2004: Brain areas underlying visual mental imagery and visual perception: an fMRI study. *Brain Research: Cognitive Brain Research.*, 20, 226–241.

Geake, J. G. and Cooper, P. W. 2003: Implications of cognitive neuroscience for education. *Westminster Studies in Education*, 26, 7–20.

Geake, J. G. and Hansen, P. C. 2005: Neural correlates of intelligence as revealed by fMRI of fluid analogies. *NeuroImage*, 26(2), 555–564.

Goebel, R., Khorram-Sefat, D., Muckli, L., Hacker, H. and Singer, W. 1998: The constructive nature of vision: Direct evidence from functional magnetic resonance imaging studies of apparent motion and motion imagery. *European Journal of Neuroscience*, 10, 1563–1573.

Gregory, R. L. 2004: *The Oxford Companion to the Mind* (2nd edn). Oxford: Oxford University Press.

Grossman, E. D. and Blake, R. 2001: Brain activity evoked by inverted and imagined biological motion. *Vision Research*, 41, 1475–1482.

Holden, K. J. and French, C. C. 2002: Alien abduction experiences: Some clues from neuropsychology and neuropsychiatry. *Cognitive Neuropsychiatry*, 7, 163–178.

Hubbard, E. M., Arman, A. C., Ramachandran, V. S. and Boynton, G. M. 2005: Individual differences among grapheme-color synesthetes: Brain–behavior correlations. *Neuron*, 45(6), 975–985.

Ishai, A., Haxby, J. V. and Ungerleider, L. G. 2002: Visual imagery of famous faces: effects of memory and attention revealed by fMRI. *Neuroimage*, 17, 1729–1741.

Jung-Beeman, M., Bowden, E. M., Haberman, J., Frymiare, J. L., Arambel-Liu, S., Greenblatt, R., Reber, P. J. and Kounios, J. 2004: Neural activity when people solve verbal problems with insight. *PLoS Biology*, 2, E97, 500–510.

Kosslyn, S. M., Pascual-Leone, A., Felician, O., Camposano, S., Keenan, J. P., Thompson, W. L., Ganis, G., Sukel, K. E. and Alpert, N. M. 1999: The role of area 17 in visual imagery: Convergent evidence from PET and rTMS. *Science*, 284, 167–170.

Kringelbach, M. L. 2004a: Food for thought: hedonic experience beyond homeostasis in the human brain. *Neuroscience*, 126, 807–819.

Kringelbach, M. L. 2004b: Learning to change. *PLoS Biology*, 2, 577–579.

Kringelbach, M. L. and Rolls, E. T. 2003: Neural correlates of rapid context-dependent reversal learning in a simple model of human social interaction. *Neuroimage*, 20, 1371–1383.

Kringelbach, M. L. and Rolls, E. T. 2004: The functional neuroanatomy of the human orbitofrontal cortex: evidence from neuroimaging and neuropsychology. *Progress in Neurobiology*, 72, 341–372.

Kuhtz-Buschbeck, J. P., Mahnkopf, C., Holzknecht, C., Siebner, H., Ulmer, S. and Jansen, O. 2003: Effector-independent representations of simple and complex imagined finger movements: a combined fMRI and TMS study. *European Journal of Neuroscience*, 18, 3375–3387.

Lamm, C., Windischberger, C., Leodolter, U., Moser, E. and Bauer, H. 2001: Evidence for premotor cortex activity during dynamic visuospatial imagery from single-trial functional magnetic resonance imaging and event-related slow cortical potentials. *Neuroimage*, 14, 268–283.

Lotze, M., Flor, H., Grodd, W., Larbig, W. and Birbaumer, N. 2001: Phantom movements and pain. An fMRI study in upper limb amputees. *Brain*, 124, 2268–2277.

Lotze, M., Scheler, G., Tan, H. R., Braun, C. and Birbaumer, N. 2003: The musician's brain: functional imaging of amateurs and professionals during performance and imagery. *Neuroimage*, 20, 1817–1829.

Lundstrom, B. N., Petersson, K. M., Andersson, J., Johansson, M., Fransson, P. and Ingvar, M. 2003: Isolating the retrieval of imagined pictures during episodic memory: activation of the left precuneus and left prefrontal cortex. *Neuroimage*, 20, 1934–1943.

McCabe, K., Houser, D., Ryan, L., Smith, V. and Trouard, T. 2001: A functional imaging study of cooperation in two-person reciprocal exchange. *Proceedings of the National Academy of Sciences of the USA*, 98, 11832–11835.

Mesulam, M. M. 1998: From sensation to cognition. *Brain*, 121, 1013–1052.

Miall, R. C., Weir, D. J., Wolpert, D. M. and Stein, J. F. 1993: Is the cerebellum a Smith predictor? *Journal of Motor Behavior*, 25, 203–216.

Morris, J. S., DeGelder, B., Weiskrantz, L. and Dolan, R. J. 2001: Differential extra-geniculostriate and amygdala responses to presentation of emotional faces in a cortically blind field. *Brain*, 124, 1241–1252.

Nitschke, M. F., Stavrou, G., Melchert, U. H., Erdmann, C., Petersen, D., Wessel, K. and Heide, W. 2003: Modulation of cerebellar activation by predictive and non-predictive sequential finger movements. *Cerebellum*, 2, 233–240.

Pappata, S., Dehaene, S., Poline, J. B., Gregoire, M. C., Jobert, A., Delforge, J., Frouin, V., Bottlaender, M., Dolle, F., Di Giamberardino, L. and Syrota, A. 2002: *In vivo* detection of striatal dopamine release during reward: A PET study with [(11)C]raclopride and a single dynamic scan approach. *Neuroimage*, 16, 1015–1027.

Paulesu, E., Harrison, J., Baron-Cohen, S., Watson, J. D., Goldstein, L., Heather, J., Frackowiak, R. S. and Frith, C. D. 1995: The physiology of coloured hearing. A PET activation study of colour-word synaesthesia. *Brain*, 118 (Pt 3), 661–676.

Petrovic, P., Kalso, E., Petersson, K. M. and Ingvar, M. 2002: Placebo and opioid analgesia—imaging a shared neuronal network. *Science*, 295, 1737–1740.

Ploghaus, A., Tracey, I., Clare, S., Gati, J. S., Rawlins, J. N. and Matthews, P. M. 2000: Learning about pain: The neural substrate of the prediction error for aversive events. *Proceedings of the National Academy of Sciences of the USA*, 97, 9281–9286.

Puri, B. K., Lekh, S. K., Nijran, K. S., Bagary, M. S. and Richardson, A. J. 2001: SPECT neuroimaging in schizophrenia with religious delusions. *International Journal of Psychophysiology*, 40, 143–148.

Ramachandran, V. S. and Hubbard, E. M. 2001: Synaesthesia: A window into perception, thought and language. *Journal of Consciousness Studies*, 8(12), 3–34.

Ramachandran, V. S. and Hubbard, E. M. 2003: The phenomenology of synaesthesia. *Journal of Consciousness Studies*, 10(8), 49–57.

Rilling, J. K., Sanfey, A. G., Aronson, J. A., Nystrom, L. E. and Cohen, J. D. 2004: The neural correlates of theory of mind within interpersonal interactions. *Neuroimage*, 22, 1694–1703.

Rizzolatti, G., Fadiga, L., Gallese, V. and Fogassi, L. 1996: Premotor cortex and the recognition of motor actions. *Brain Research: Cognitive Brain Research*, 3, 131–141.

Rosenbaum, R. S., Ziegler, M., Winocur, G., Grady, C. L. and Moscovitch, M. 2004: 'I have often walked down this street before': fMRI Studies on the hippocampus and other structures during mental navigation of an old environment. *Hippocampus*, 14, 826.

Roth, I. 2004: Imagination. In Gregory, R. L. (ed.), *The Oxford Companion to the Mind* (2nd edn). Oxford: Oxford University Press, 443–447.

Ruby, P. and Decety, J. 2003: What you believe versus what you think they believe: a neuroimaging study of conceptual perspective-taking. *European Journal of Neuroscience*, 17, 2475–2480.

Saxe, R. and Kanwisher, N. 2003: People thinking about thinking people. The role of the temporo-parietal junction in 'theory of mind'. *Neuroimage*, 19, 1835–1842.

Schnider, A. and Ptak, R. 1999: Spontaneous confabulators fail to suppress currently irrelevant memory traces. *Nature Neuroscience*, 2, 677–681.

Schultz, W., Dayan, P. and Montague, P. R. 1997: A neural substrate of prediction and reward. *Science*, 275, 1593–1599.

Sherrington, C. 1938: *Man On His Nature*. Cambridge: Cambridge University Press.

Simons, D. J. 2000: Attentional capture and inattentional blindness. *Trends in Cognitive Science*, 4(4), 147–155.

Steven, M. S. and Blakemore, C. 2004: Visual synaesthesia in the blind. *Perception*, 33, 855–868.

Steven, M. S., Hansen, P. C. and Blakemore, C. 2005: Activation of colour-selective areas of visual cortex in a blind synaesthete. *Cortex*, 42(2), 304–308.

Tanaka, S. C., Doya, K., Okada, G., Ueda, K., Okamoto, Y. and Yamawaki, S. 2004: Prediction of immediate and future rewards differentially recruits cortico-basal ganglia loops. *Nature Neuroscience*, 7, 887–893.

Tricomi, E. M., Delgado, M. R. and Fiez, J. A. 2004: Modulation of caudate activity by action contingency. *Neuron*, 41, 281–292.

Van Horn, J. D. 2004: Cognitive neuroimaging: History, developments, and directions. In Gazzaniga, M. S. (ed.), *The Cognitive Neurosciences III* (3rd edn). Cambridge, MA: MIT Press, 1281–1294.

Vogeley, K., Bussfeld, P., Newen, A., Herrmann, S., Happe, F., Falkai, P., Maier, W., Shah, N. J., Fink, G. R. and Zilles, K. 2001: Mind reading: neural mechanisms of theory of mind and self-perspective. *Neuroimage*, 14, 170–181.

Vogeley, K., May, M., Ritzl, A., Falkai, P., Zilles, K. and Fink, G. R. 2004: Neural correlates of first-person perspective as one constituent of human self-consciousness. *Journal of Cognitive Neuroscience*, 16, 817–827.

Wager, T. D., Rilling, J. K., Smith, E. E., Sokolik, A., Casey, K. L., Davidson, R. J., Kosslyn, S. M., Rose, R. M. and Cohen, J. D. 2004: Placebo-induced changes in FMRI in the anticipation and experience of pain. *Science*, 303, 1162–1167.

Zacks, J., Rypma, B., Gabrieli, J. D., Tversky, B. and Glover, G. H. 1999: Imagined transformations of bodies: an fMRI investigation. *Neuropsychologia*, 37, 1029–1040.

Index

338

Index

inventiveness (*cont.*)
  definition, 36
  great ape case study, 31, 37–45
  imagination as, 34, 51–2
  in infants, 37
  and perspectival imagining distinguished,
    xxviii
  pretence vs., xxvi, 34–7
IQ, correlation with musical ability, 159
IQ tests, schizophrenia and, 270
irony, 174, 279, 299, 300
Ishai, A., 314
Isturitz bone pipes, 160

James, Henry, 170, 171, 173–4
Jamison, Kay Redfield, xxxiv
Japanese rock formation, 131–9 Figs. 6.1–7
Jastrow ambiguous duck–rabbit figure, 202,
  203 Fig. 9.8
Java, 12
Jericho, 23
Jerison, H.J., 53
Jessica Kingsley, 284
jigsaw puzzles, 283
Joffe, T.H., 161
Johanson, F.D., 8
Johns, Jasper, 140
Johnson, Crockett, *Harold and the Purple
  Crayon*, 215–16 Fig. 10.1; 222
Jomon of Japan, 23
Jung-Beeman, M., 313, 321

Kahneman, D., 253, 254
Kaluli peoples of Papua New Guinea, 152
Kant, Immanuel, xxii–xxiii
Kanwisher, N., 319
Karmiloff-Smith, A., 12
Kawai, N., 49
Kekulé, Friedrich August von, 189
Kerman, Joseph, 124, 125, 126
Key, C.A., 10
Kingstone, A., *Handbook of Functional
  Neuroimaging of Cognition*, 308
Kirby, S., 15, 17
knowledge
  bases, 249, 250
  children's assimilation of conceptual, xxxii,
    101–18
  conceptual, 183–184
  and creativity, 4, 11
  domain, 12, 14, 243, 252
  domains and fluidity, xxxiii, xxxiv, 18–21
    Fig 1.6
  and imagination, Einstein's view, xix
  'folk', xxx, 265
  see also domain specificity; modularity

Koenig, Melissa, xii–xiii, xxxii, 101–18, 308
Köhler, W., 49
koine aesthesis, xxi
Kosslyn, Stephen M., 205–6, 207, 311
Kramer, Lawrence, 126, 127
Kringelbach, Morten L., xiii, xxx, xxxv, 289,
  307–23
Krumhansl, Carol, 149, 151
Kuhtz-Buschbeck, J.P., 315

LaBarre, W., 155
labelling, verbal influence on perception,
  203–4 Fig. 9.9
laboratory studies, of imagery and creative
  thought, 187–208
Lahr, M.M., 17
Lamm, C., 315
Langer, S., 155
language, 260
  in autistic poets, 297–301
  and children's drawing skills, 286
  and development of domain-general
    intelligence, 158–9
  as a distinct mental module, 12
  double-scope blending and everyday,
    229–36
  as enabling distributed cognition, 17, 24
  and evolution of theory of mind, 7
  human use of, 62
  as a memetic parasite, 68
  motor component of, 156
  music and meaning, 155–7
  open-endedness in, 36
  origin of, 15–18
  possible limitation on creative imagery,
    204–5
  relationship with communication, 169–85
  segmentation, 17
  separate evolution from music, 69
  see also communication; linguistic devices;
    verbal representations
language processing, medial prefrontal cortex
  in, 319
Lascaux cave paintings, 286
Lawson, B., 190
Lawson, Wendy, 283
Leakey, R., 11
Learned, J., 83
learning
  capacity for, 62
  from other people's testimony vs. first-hand
    experience, 104–5
  difficulties, personal neuroimagers and, 322
  trial-and-error, 37
learning effect, and neural plasticity, 322
Leevers, H., 280
Leslie, A.M., xxvii, 34–5, 36, 47, 281